Discussions in Dispute Resolution

Discussions in Dispute Resolution

The Foundational Articles

Edited by
ART HINSHAW, ANDREA KUPFER SCHNEIDER, AND
SARAH RUDOLPH COLE

OXFORD
UNIVERSITY PRESS

OXFORD
UNIVERSITY PRESS

Oxford University Press is a department of the University of Oxford. It furthers the University's objective of excellence in research, scholarship, and education by publishing worldwide. Oxford is a registered trade mark of Oxford University Press in the UK and certain other countries.

Published in the United States of America by Oxford University Press
198 Madison Avenue, New York, NY 10016, United States of America.

Library of Congress Cataloging-in-Publication Data
Names: Hinshaw, Art, author. | Schneider, Andrea Kupfer, author. | Cole, Sarah R., author.
Title: Discussions in dispute resolution : the foundational articles / Hinshaw, Schneider, and Cole.
Description: New York, NY : Oxford University Press, 2021 | Includes bibliographical references.
Identifiers: LCCN 2020042846 | ISBN 9780197513248 (hardback) |
ISBN 9780197513255 (UPDF) | ISBN 9780197513262 (EPUB) | ISBN 9780197513279 (Digital-Online)
Subjects: LCSH: Dispute resolution (Law)—United States. | Mediation—United States. | Arbitration and award—United States. | Negotiation—United States. | Dispute resolution (Law)
Classification: LCC KF9084 .H56 2021 | DDC 347.73/9—dc23
LC record available at https://lccn.loc.gov/2020042846

DOI: 10.1093/oso/9780197513248.001.0001

3 5 7 9 8 6 4 2

Printed by Integrated Books International, United States of America

Note to Readers

This publication is designed to provide accurate and authoritative information in regard to the subject matter covered. It is based upon sources believed to be accurate and reliable and is intended to be current as of the time it was written. It is sold with the understanding that the publisher is not engaged in rendering legal, accounting, or other professional services. If legal advice or other expert assistance is required, the services of a competent professional person should be sought. Also, to confirm that the information has not been affected or changed by recent developments, traditional legal research techniques should be used, including checking primary sources where appropriate.

(Based on the Declaration of Principles jointly adopted by a Committee of the American Bar Association and a Committee of Publishers and Associations.)

Contents

Acknowledgments

A book like this could not be created without the contribution of many people. First and foremost, we would like to thank our contributors for their belief in us and this project. Their contributions form the backbone of the book and are what makes this project compelling. They generously devoted their time and energy to this project before we had a landing place, trusting that we would make it happen. Moreover, we placed restraints on them they weren't used to having—a tight word count and limited references—which caused us to engage in vigorous rounds of editing. Despite these constraints, they produced top-notch work within relatively short time frames in spite of other demands on their time.

We appreciate all of the work our publisher, Oxford University Press, has done as we've moved through the publication process. Specifically, we thank Jamie Berezin for serving as our editor-in-chief and Mark Longaker for guiding us through the process and keeping us on task.

As law school faculty members, there are many institutional players we should thank, including: Beverly Kosik, Carrie Kratochvil, Allyson Hennelly, Jay Jenkins, and Lindsay Stephens for excellent administrative work. Thanks also to the Southeast Association of Law Schools for allowing us to convene four conference panels, one for each section of the book, at the 2017 SEALS Conference, as much of what was discussed there provided the seeds for our commenters to cultivate for their commentary. Finally, we want to give a hearty thank you to research assistants who helped with the project in a variety of ways: Taylor Chase, April Kutz, Dominic Rosso, and Will Ruffing from Marquette; and Kate Pokorski from Arizona State.

We would also like to thank those who inspired us throughout the three years of this project: our families. Art would like to thank his wife, Sarah, for patiently listening and providing support during the ebbs and flows of this project and to their children, Hannah and Eli, for consistently demonstrating the use of curiosity to engage with the world. Andrea thanks her three boys for continuing to point out the difference between teaching negotiation and successfully implementing it (they themselves are wonderful instructors) and to Rodd, for providing humor and patience throughout it all. We both miss the stage of daily negotiations with our children. Sarah would like to thank Douglas Cole for supporting her during this project, as he does for all of her work, and to her sons, Sam and Josh, for providing her the frequent opportunity to utilize her skills as an arbitrator.

We also are thankful for the opportunity to work with each other. Working with good friends can be tricky at times, but that has not been our experience here as we've worked well together from the very beginning. As a result, our friendship is stronger and our respect and admiration for each other has only deepened. In fact, we look forward to our next project together!

Special mention goes to Mary E. Sigler, a former faculty member at the Sandra Day O'Connor College of Law at Arizona State University. One day in casual conversation, she mentioned a book project she was a part of, *Conversations in Criminal Law*. In that volume, which gives an overview of contemporary issues in criminal law, leading criminal law scholars nominated pieces for inclusion. The more she discussed the book's content and the energy the project created, the more it seemed like a similar project in dispute resolution would produce similar results. When asked directly about that idea she said, "Of course it could, and ADR sounds like an ideal place to do it." We are forever indebted.

Finally, we would like to explicitly thank the journals that allowed us to reprint the original works that inspired both the dispute resolution field and this book.

The New Federal Arbitration Law by Julius Henry Cohen and Kenneth Dayton, reprinted with permission and originally published at 12 VA. L. REV. 265 (1926).

Commercial Arbitration by Soia Mentschikoff, reprinted with permission and originally published at 61 COLUM. L. REV. 846 (1961).

Mediation: Its Forms and Functions by Lon L. Fuller, reprinted with permission and originally published at 44 S. CAL. L. REV. 305 (1971).

Why the "Haves" Come Out Ahead: Speculations on the Limits of Legal Change by Marc Galanter, reprinted with permission and originally published at 9 LAW & SOC'Y REV. 95 (1974).

Varieties of Dispute Processing by Frank E.A. Sander, speech originally published at 70 F.R.D. 111 (1976).

Bargaining in the Shadow of the Law: The Case of Divorce by Robert H. Mnookin and Lewis Kornhauser, reprinted with permission and originally published at 88 YALE L.J. 950 (1979).

Machiavelli and the Bar: Ethical Limitations on Lying in Negotiation by James J. White, reprinted with permission and originally published at 1980 AM. BAR FOUND. RES. J. 926.

The Theory and Practice of Mediation: A Reply to Professor Susskind by Joseph B. Stulberg, reprinted with permission and originally published at 6 VT. L. REV. 85 (1981).

Toward Another View of Legal Negotiation: The Structure of Problem Solving by Carrie Menkel-Meadow, reprinted with permission and originally published at 31 UCLA L. REV. 754 (1984).

Against Settlement by Owen M. Fiss, reprinted with permission and originally published at 93 YALE L.J. 1073 (1984).

Pursuing Settlement in an Adversary Culture: A Tale of Innovation Co-Opted or "The Law of ADR" by Carrie Menkel-Meadow, reprinted with permission and originally published at 19 FLA. ST. L. REV. 1 (1991).

The Mediation Alternative: Process Dangers for Women by Trina Grillo, reprinted with permission and originally published at 100 YALE L.J. 1545 (1991).

Panacea or Corporate Tool?: Debunking the Supreme Court's Preference for Binding Arbitration by Jean R. Sternlight, reprinted with permission and originally published at 74 WASH. U. L.Q. 637 (1996).

The Limits of Integrative Bargaining by Gerald B. Wetlaufer, reprinted with permission and originally published at 85 GEO. L.J. 369 (1996).

Understanding Mediators' Orientations, Strategies, and Techniques: A Grid for the Perplexed by Leonard L. Riskin, reprinted with permission and originally published at 1 HARV. NEGOT. L. REV. 7 (1996).

Employment Arbitration: The Repeat Player Effect by Lisa B. Bingham (now Lisa Blomgren Amsler), reprinted with permission and originally published at 1 EMP. RTS. & EMP. POL'Y J. 189 (1997).

Table of Contributors

References are to page numbers of comments.

Introduction

Imagine if settlement were not the default mode of resolving disputes in American court systems. How many years would it take from filing a civil claim until the trial would begin? How many judges would need to be hired to maintain a semblance of timeliness as claims worked their way through the system? Would the political realities of the day allow for such hiring? We already know that it currently takes years to reach trial. And this is when more than 99 percent of filed civil claims never make it to trial in the federal courts—and the numbers in state courts are not far behind. It is time to acknowledge the inescapable conclusion. Our judicial system is not a system of trials but a system of alternative means of resolution.

The settlement of civil claims has been a part of human history for a long time—approximately four thousand years ago in ancient China, mediation was a common method of settling disputes between fishermen, and in ancient Athens civil claims were subject to nonbinding arbitration before trial. Even during the darkness of the Middle Ages, English and French courts proclaimed Lovedays where litigants would meet to resolve their differences.

While arbitration was robust in colonial and early America, dispute resolution lost its footing to the court system as the United States grew into a bustling and burgeoning country. And while dispute resolution processes emerged briefly from time to time, they were dormant until the enactment of the Federal Arbitration Act and collective bargaining grew out of the labor movement. But it wasn't until 1976, when Frank Sander delivered his famous remarks at the Pound Conference, that the modern dispute resolution movement was born. By the year 2000, alternative dispute resolution (ADR) transformed from a populist rebellion against the judicial system to mainstream legal practice. Today, lawyers and retiring judges look to arbitration and mediation for a career pivot, and law schools train law students in the finer arts of dispute resolution practice as both providers and advocates.

With this backdrop, we thought it fitting to honor both the field and its intellectual leaders by revisiting the works that provided the theoretical bases for the revolution. Documenting the academic underpinnings of the modern dispute resolution movement is not a task to be taken lightly. And, as process scholars, we recognize that structure often determines process, so we focused on the book's structure first.

Structure

This project was inspired by a book entitled *Criminal Law Conversations*. In that book, editors solicited criminal law scholars to nominate pieces for inclusion and then asked

Discussions in Dispute Resolution. Art Hinshaw, Andrea Kupfer Schneider, and Sarah Rudolph Cole, Oxford University Press (2021).
 DOI: 10.1093/oso/9780197513248.001.0001

other scholars to comment on them. We focused on articles rather than books, in part because we thought doing so would make this endeavor more interesting and more helpful for the academy. Most scholars in the field have read the critical books—such as *Getting to Yes*—more than once and refer back to them regularly. Thus, their familiarity with those volumes has remained relatively constant. Articles, on the other hand, are typically digested and set aside to be remembered for one or two ideas, or used for the excerpt that a casebook author may think is important. For this reason, we thought academics who may have taught these articles would be engaged with these pieces in ways that both delighted and surprised them. And many of them told us that was the case.

Our book's basic organizational structure is based on the field's basic structure. It has three major subsets—negotiation, mediation, and arbitration—but we knew that wouldn't be enough. Many of the early works we planned to consider for inclusion are about disputing and dispute resolution more generally and therefore would not easily fall into those three categories. To make room for those pieces, we included a fourth category, public policy. And while some may quibble with that terminology, it best captures the ideas related to settlement and how dispute resolution is most profitably employed.

Our most difficult issue was timing—how old would a piece need to be to be considered foundational? The 1990s were the decade of dispute resolution's exponential growth, so there are strong arguments that our cutoff should have been 1989 or the mid-1990s. Ultimately, that felt too early, in part because several major response and reflection pieces came out during that period of dramatic expansion. Yet the 2000s seemed a little late for a piece to be foundational. The year 2000 seemed to be a place where we could most easily delineate the works of founding generation and second-generation ADR academics, so only pieces published before the year 2000 were considered for this volume.

Methodology

Determining which articles to include in this volume was the most important aspect of this project. Difficult choices needed to be made, and subjective calls on our part were not appropriate for this project. We thought, if we are honoring the field, the best way to do so would be to engage the field in the determination of what should make the cut.

To do this, we assigned various sections of the book to each of us based on our respective areas of expertise. Then we came up with a list of articles for each section that we thought should be in the running for foundational status, and made sure that the three of us were comfortable with each list. Then we circulated that list to our peers, experts whose opinions we trusted, and asked them to vote on the four pieces that should be considered foundational in each category and let us know if there was an article that should have been on the list that was not. Not surprisingly, several of our colleagues commented on the difficulty of the task. The top four vote-getters in each category appear in this book. And, again, we want to note how challenging this particular stage was. We have no doubt that there are legitimate arguments with the articles chosen—and those left out—through this process.

At this point, one selection—Frank Sander's *Varieties of Dispute Processing*—deserves special mention. Not simply because of its impact, which was enormous, but because some may argue that it is not deserving of inclusion because it did not appear in an academic journal like the rest. In fact, it is not an article but rather a speech that was reprinted in the Federal Rules Decisions reporter. We included it here because the speech was an academic paper that Professor Sander presented to a nonacademic audience. It very easily could have appeared in an academic journal after the speech, even though it did not.

Commentary Guidelines

The guidelines to our commentators were as follows: discuss why this article is foundational. Nothing more. We expected the commentators to take that directive in different directions, and they did not disappoint. Additionally, due to space limitations, we planned on having no reference section for each comment, requiring each citation to be a part of the text like in legal briefs. Our commenters pushed back on this, so we agreed to a total of five references at the end of each comment in order to keep these comments succinct, readable, and useful. Even five was difficult for many commenters as it conflicts with their academic training that requires citations for everything. We thank our commenters for their flexibility with this requirement.

Conclusion

Our goal of re-engaging dispute resolution academics with the field's foundations has exceeded our expectations in several ways. The commenters have expressed their enthusiasm for the project from its inception, long before a book contract was in the offing. Several have told us that going back to these pieces reminded them of what originally drew them to the field and gave them deeper understanding of the nuances in those pieces. Others expressed surprise by what they read, not remembering areas in some of the articles that appear contrary to basic ADR values. In reviewing the commentary, we witnessed and cheered the creativity resulting from reviewing the classics with fresh eyes. We are grateful to the commenters for sharing their thoughts and for the variety and richness of their discussions, which we expect to be widely excerpted and cited in future ADR books, articles, and lectures.

PART 1
NEGOTIATION

Article 1.1

Bargaining in the Shadow of the Law: The Case of Divorce

Robert H. Mnookin and Lewis Kornhauser

88 Yale Law Journal 950 (1979)

This article suggests an alternative way of thinking about the role of law at the time of divorce. It is concerned primarily with the impact of the legal system on negotiations and bargaining that occur outside the courtroom. We see the primary function of contemporary divorce law not as imposing order from above, but rather as providing a framework within which divorcing couples can themselves determine their postdissolution rights and responsibilities. This process by which parties to a marriage are empowered to create their own legally enforceable commitments is a form of "private ordering." . . .

II. The Elements of a Bargaining Model

Whether or not one accepts the desirability of private ordering, it is clear that most divorcing couples do not require adjudication of their disputes. It is therefore appropriate to analyze how the legal system affects the bargaining behavior of divorcing couples. . . .

3. The Relationship of Custody and Money

***

Economic analysis suggests that a parent may, over some range, trade custodial rights for money. Although this notion may offend some, a contrary assertion would mean that a parent with full custody would accept no sum of money in exchange for slightly less custody, even if the parent were extremely poor. Faced with such alternatives, most parents would prefer to see the child a bit less and be able to give the child better housing, more food, more education, better health care, and some luxuries. Suggesting the possibility of such trade-offs does not mean that the parent would be willing to relinquish all time with the child for a sufficiently large sum of money. Indeed, with a minimum level of resources, a parent may have a parallel minimum of custodial rights for the reduction of which no additional payment, however large, could be adequate compensation. . . .

Robert H. Mnookin and Lewis Kornhauser, *Bargaining in the Shadow of the Law: The Case of Divorce* In: *Discussions in Dispute Resolution*. Edited by: Art Hinshaw, Andrea Kupfer Schneider, and Sarah Rudolph Cole, Oxford University Press (2021).
 DOI: 10.1093/oso/9780197513248.003.0001

B. Toward a Theory of Divorce Bargaining

Ideally, a bargaining theory would allow us to predict how alternative legal rules would affect negotiations between particular spouses and the deal, if any, they would strike.... Unfortunately, no existing theory of bargaining allows confident prediction of how different legal rules and procedures would influence outcomes; nor is there much information about current patterns and outcomes of the bargaining process.

What follows is not a complete theory. Instead, we identify five factors that seem to be important influences or determinants of the outcomes of bargaining, and then offer some observations on the bargaining process.

1. Parental Preferences

* * *

Informed bargaining requires a parent to assess accurately his or her own preferences concerning custodial alternatives. Yet the assessments are difficult and complicated. The information each parent has relates to the actual division of child-rearing tasks in an ongoing family. Dissolution or divorce inevitably alters this division, and the parent may discover new advantages or disadvantages to child-rearing responsibilities. Moreover, the parents' own needs may alter drastically after divorce. A parent interested in dating may find the child an intrusion in a way that the child never was during marriage. Additionally, a parent's interest in children may vary according to their age....

Parental preferences, of course, will not generally be determined solely by self-interested judgments; a bargaining theory must take note of possible altruism or spite. One hopes that parental preferences reflect a desire for their children's happiness and well-being, quite apart from any parental advantage....

2. How Legal Rules Create Bargaining Endowments

Divorcing parents do not bargain over the division of family wealth and custodial prerogatives in a vacuum; they bargain in the shadow of the law. The legal rules governing alimony, child support, marital property, and custody give each parent certain claims based on what each would get if the case went to trial. In other words, the outcome that the law will impose if no agreement is reached gives each parent certain bargaining chips-an endowment of sorts.

***

If private ordering were allowed, we would not necessarily expect parents to split custody and money the way a judge would if they failed to agree. The father might well negotiate for more child-time and the mother for less. This result might occur either because the father made the mother better off by giving her additional money to compensate her for accepting less child-time, or because the mother found custody burdensome and considered herself better off with less custody. Indeed, she might agree to accept less money, or even to pay the father, if he agreed to relieve her of some child-rearing responsibilities. In all events, because the parents' tastes with regard to the trade-offs between money and child-time may differ, it will often be possible for the parties to negotiate some outcome that makes both better off than they would be if they simply accepted the result a court would impose.

3. Private Ordering Against a Backdrop of Uncertainty

Often, the outcome in court is far from certain, with any number of outcomes possible. Indeed, existing legal standards governing custody, alimony, child support, and marital property are all striking for their lack of precision and thus provide a bargaining backdrop clouded by uncertainty. The almost universal judicial standard for resolving custody disputes is the "best interests of the child." Except in situations when one parent poses a substantial threat to the child's well-being, predicting who will get custody under this standard is difficult indeed, especially given the increasing pressure to reject any presumption in favor of maternal custody. Similarly, standards governing alimony and child support are also extraordinarily vague and allow courts broad discretion in disputed cases....

4. Transaction Costs

The transaction costs that the parties must bear may take many forms, some financial and some emotional. The most obvious and tangible involve the expenditure of money. Professional fees-particularly for lawyers-must be paid by one or both parties. In addition, there are filing fees and court costs. More difficult to measure, but also important, are the emotional and psychological costs involved in the dispute-settlement process. Lawsuits generally are emotionally burdensome; the psychological costs imposed by bargaining (and still more by litigation) are particularly acute in divorce.

The magnitude of these transaction costs, both actual and expected, can influence negotiations and the outcome of bargaining. In the dissolution process, one spouse, and that spouse's attorney, can substantially affect the magnitude of the transaction costs that must be borne by the other spouse. As is generally the case, the party better able to bear the transaction costs, whether financial or emotional, will have an advantage in divorce bargaining....

5. Strategic Behavior

The actual bargain that is struck through negotiations-indeed, whether a bargain is struck at all-depends on the negotiation process. During this process, each party transmits information about his or her own preferences to the other. This information may be accurate or intentionally inaccurate; each party may promise, threaten, or bluff. Parties may intentionally exaggerate their chances of winning in court in the hope of persuading the other side to accept less. Or they may threaten to impose substantial transaction costs-economic or psychological-on the other side. In short, there are a variety of ways in which the parties may engage in strategic behavior during the bargaining process.

Opportunities for strategic behavior exist because the parties often will not know with certainty (1) the other side's true preferences with regard to the allocational outcomes; (2) the other spouse's preferences or attitudes towards risk; and (3) what the outcome in court will be, or even what the actual odds in court are. Although parents may know a great deal about each other's preferences for money and children, complete knowledge of the other spouse's attitudes is unlikely....

C. Lawyers in the Dispute Settlement Process

Private ordering suggests new perspectives on the role of lawyers in divorce....

1. The Roles of Lawyers

Lawyers perform a number of functions in the divorce process:

a. *Source of information*. Lawyers can provide the basic information about each spouse's bargaining endowment-the applicable legal norms and the probable outcome in court if the case is litigated. Indeed, as noted earlier, imprecision in the applicable legal standards increases one's need for legal advice. A rational client will want an accurate assessment of the possible costs of alternative modes of dispute settlement. Lawyers are also an important source of information about transaction costs, a major element of which will be legal fees.

b. *Counselor*. The lawyer may help the parties determine what their real interests are. Divorcing spouses may not have carefully examined the financial questions or their own preferences for child-rearing responsibilities.

c. *Clerk*. To secure a divorce, even when there is no dispute, it is typically necessary for certain legal procedures to be followed and for various forms to be completed. To the extent the forms and the procedures are intricate, divorcing couples may require legal assistance even though there is no dispute whatsoever.

d. *Negotiator*. Lawyers can serve as negotiators with the other spouse or the other spouse's lawyer. Some parties may find negotiation extremely difficult, particularly given the anger and sense of guilt that often accompany divorce. Negotiators can be hired in the marketplace for legal services.

e. *Litigator*. When there is a dispute that must go to court, the lawyer has responsibility for marshaling and presenting relevant evidence and making the necessary legal arguments....

E. The Role of Courts

Because divorce has become so widespread in this country, it is probably the most common occasion for ordinary citizens to interact with courts and the legal system. These contacts, to the extent they seem superfluous and unduly unpleasant, may contribute to public cynicism about law and its processes. Consideration of the issue from our perspective of private ordering highlights the need for general reform and gives specific support to the oft-asserted desirability of removing undisputed divorce cases from court dockets....

Conclusion

Viewing the process of divorce from the perspective of private ordering does not make previously intractable family law problems disappear. If anything, the world seems even more complex, since the analysis requires us to examine the effects of alternative rules and procedures on informal and formal bargaining about which we have little understanding. There now exists no bargaining theory that can yield accurate predictions of the expected outcomes with different legal rules, even when rational, self-interested parties are only negotiating over money issues. Divorce bargaining is often considerably more complex.

Given the absence of powerful theory or systematic data, this essay makes no claims to being definitive. It instead suggests a theoretical perspective that permits a broader analysis of the probable consequences of family law rules and procedures. It also more sharply exposes a set of questions of enormous social importance. If one accepts the proposition that the role of the legal system in determining the consequences of divorce should reflect an emphasis on dispute settlement, then the inadequacies of our current system are readily apparent. The analysis does not imply that the state should simply withdraw all resources from the process and leave it to the divorcing spouses to work things out on their own, unassisted by any professional help or legal protection. Instead, this inquiry should emphasize the desirability of learning more about how alternative procedural mechanisms might facilitate dispute resolution during a typically difficult and painful time in the lives of parents and children alike.

The perspective certainly has implications far broader than family law.... [W]e hope this article will stimulate and encourage further work by others in a variety of contexts. Theoretical and empirical research concerning how people bargain in the shadow of law should provide us with a richer understanding of how the legal system affects behavior, and should allow a more realistic appraisal of the consequences of reform proposals.

Comments

Bargaining in the Shadow of the Law: The Case for ADR as a Field of Study

Elizabeth C. Tippett

I. Introduction

Mnookin and Kornhauser's *Bargaining in the Shadow of the Law* is a critically important work for the alternative dispute resolution (ADR) field because it legitimized the study of negotiation within the legal academy. It did so by tethering bargaining to jurisprudence. Without Mnookin and Kornhauser's insight that bargaining is a function of legal rules, the law remains confined to its portrayal in a standard first-year curriculum.

Second, the article challenged a hierarchical command and control view of the law, where legal rules prescribe how parties can and should behave. Mnookin and Kornhauser turned this view on its head, arguing that the law serves primarily as a constraint and influence on private ordering. From this vantage point, bargaining becomes a worthy—or even superior—counterpart to litigation.

Third, the article presents both a descriptive and normative view of lawyering that places bargaining front and center. It's not just that negotiation is critical to a lawyer's role. Good negotiating depends on legal skills and knowledge. Bargaining is not a collection of distributive tactics reminiscent of a used car dealer, but an elegant combination of the lawyer's knowledge and of the client's needs and preferences. In this view, legal bargaining demands the same level of knowledge and sophistication as the best closing argument.

Above all, Mnookin and Kornhauser proved that this complex interplay of rules, process, preference, and gamesmanship is worthy of serious scholarly attention.

A. Negotiation as Inextricably Linked to Legal Rules

In *Bargaining in the Shadow of the Law*, Mnookin and Kornhauser argued that bargaining was a function of legal rules. Like all great insights, it seems intuitive in retrospect. But without this theory, legal settlement is mostly posturing, bluffing, puffing, and strategy, perhaps with the occasional appeal to relationship building. When unmoored from the law, it is all too easy to dismiss negotiation as unworthy of serious study at a law school. Perhaps a case might be made that negotiation is important

Elizabeth C. Tippett, Bargaining in the Shadow of the Law: *The Case for ADR as a Field of Study* In: *Discussions in Dispute Resolution*. Edited by: Art Hinshaw, Andrea Kupfer Schneider, and Sarah Rudolph Cole, Oxford University Press (2021).
 DOI: 10.1093/oso/9780197513248.003.0002

because it's part of what lawyers do. But it's an unregulated side dish—a "frolic and detour" from weightier matters.

Mnookin and Kornhauser managed to fit negotiation within the framework of what lawyers already know: legal rules, fees, and client expectations. Their background in law and economics lends an almost mathematical character to their approach. Their theory lends itself to the kind of predictive analytics, where outcomes are a function of substantive rules and the bargaining endowments they produced, as well as parties' aversion to risk, relative priorities, and tolerance for transaction costs. They nevertheless acknowledged that strategic behavior can skew parties' behavior, and that bargaining is complex and somewhat unpredictable. Near the end of the article, they caution, "[t]here now exists no bargaining theory that can yield accurate predictions of the expected outcomes with different legal rules, even when rational, self-interested parties are only negotiating over money issues" (Mnookin & Kornhauser, p. 996).

Later scholars would point out the missing variables from Mnookin and Kornhauser's theoretical model. For example, John Coffee examined "entrepreneurial litigation"—also known as strike suits—with dubious legal merit, whose primary purpose is to extract a small settlement by exploiting the threat of large litigation costs (Coffee). In those cases, the bargaining reflected less the client's legal entitlements and more the lawyer's entrepreneurial self-interest. Others noted that structural inequities and power gaps placed some parties at particular disadvantage in bargaining, in ways that might systematically disadvantage them relative to judicial outcomes. Still others noted that parties behaved in ways that seemed irrational, which paved the way to apply insights from behavioral economics to the bargaining context. Nevertheless, to identify and fill gaps in a model is to acknowledge its usefulness, and ultimately enhance its power. Mnookin would likewise devote substantial scholarly attention to these gaps in later works, especially the respects in which lawyers' interests can diverge from their clients.

B. Substantive Law as Subservient to Bargaining

Bargaining in the Shadow of the Law made stronger claims about the importance of bargaining to the legal process than the word "shadow" suggests. The article challenged a hierarchical command and control view of the law, where legal rules prescribe how parties can and should behave. Mnookin and Kornhauser disagreed, arguing that the law serves primarily as a constraint and influence on private ordering.

In the words of Michael Saks, "settlement is where the action is" (Saks). In this view, the law serves a primarily rhetorical function—a credible threat of what will transpire in the absence of the bargain. The true value of the legal system lies in bargaining; litigation is a mere sideshow. Thus, Mnookin and Kornhauser analogize a trial as a "carefully rehearsed and jointly produced play for the court" (Mnookin & Kornhauser, p. 953).

In support of this narrative, Mnookin and Kornhauser remind us that—in the context of the divorce—the parties own the dispute, know their needs best, and have to live with the outcome. The issue-by-issue constraints of legal rules generally do not align with the dependent nature of parties' interests relating to custody and money. In this context, negotiated outcomes are preferred, and litigation represents a value-destroying alternative for those who overplay their hand or call the other's bluff.

Mnookin and Kornhauser's work was firmly embedded in the context of divorce law. They largely avoided generalizing beyond it, except to note in the conclusion that legal entitlements may shape negotiated outcomes in other contexts as well. Nevertheless, their implicit argument about the role of courts and the value of bargaining has served as a counterpoint, and often convenient foil, in countless later works. Owen Fiss's provocative argument in *Against Settlement*, published five years later, does not cite Mnookin and Kornhauser, yet is primarily directed at undermining the idea that settlement might be a worthy rival to litigation.

C. Bargaining as an Essential Form of Lawyering

Mnookin and Kornhauser also sought to broaden academic definitions of lawyering that previously placed a premium on legal writing and oral advocacy. Although lawyers indisputably negotiated as part of their job, it was not necessarily presumed to be a legal skill. Instead, negotiation could be portrayed as a series of distributive tactics recognizable at a used car dealership.

Mnookin and Kornhauser challenged that assumption by explaining that legal negotiations are informed by the likely result should a court ultimately decide the case. Their argument was both descriptive and normative. While they acknowledged that lawyers use strategic tactics in their negotiations, they also described a "norm-centered model"—in which parties "invoke rules, cite precedents, and engage in reasoned elaboration." Mnookin and Kornhauser argued that the invocation of rules was not simply a form of posturing but a joint "elaboration" of the parties' likely alternatives that would inform their decision-making.

Their argument also had a prescriptive component. An unprepared lawyer who has not researched the case law prior to the negotiation disserves her client in equal measure to one who has not prepared for an oral argument. The law informs each party's bargaining endowment. Ignorance of that endowment might lead a lawyer to squander his client's rights in favor of a bad deal, or sacrifice a good deal to preserve a shoddy case.

In some respects, Mnookin and Kornhauser placed lawyer-negotiators above judges as the preferred resolver of legal disputes. Judges don't know the parties' needs nearly as well as the lawyer, who can craft a deal in consultation with clients. Lawyers, unlike judges, have the power to bundle issues and make trade-offs to maximum benefit. Lawyers have the potential to be efficient in the Pareto-optimal sense. Informed, but unconstrained by legal rules, they can identify the package that best meets their client's needs. Although strategy may get in the way, negotiation has a potentially large upside over judicial rulings that is largely beyond even the most skillful judge's reach.

Bargaining in the Shadow of the Law also claims exclusive jurisdiction for lawyers over the settlement of lawsuits. Without knowledge of relevant precedent, nonlawyers are poorly situated to assess the quality of deals available to their client. This issue remains relevant to ongoing debates as jurisdictions experiment with allowing nonlawyers to serve in roles previously limited to lawyers and scholars assess the costs of a justice system where parties often cannot afford a lawyer and negotiate a settlement pro se.

II. Conclusion

In the conclusion to their article, Mnookin and Kornhauser acknowledged that their analysis was limited to the divorce context, but noted that it might be applicable in others. They expressed "hope [that] this article will stimulate and encourage further work by others in a variety of contexts." They could not have imagined how influential their work ultimately would become, not only in how we think about negotiation, but how we structure law school curriculums, and define the role of lawyering itself.

References

John Coffee Jr., *The Regulation of Entrepreneurial Litigation: Balancing Fairness and Efficiency in the Large Class Action*, 54 U. Chi. L. Rev. 877 (1987).

Owen Fiss, *Against Settlement*, 93 Yale L.J. 1073 (1984).

Michael J. Saks, *Do We Really Know Anything about the Behavior of the Tort Litigation System—And Why Not?*, 140 U. Pa. L. Rev. 1147 (1992).

Taking Human Behavior Seriously

Rebecca Hollander-Blumoff

Robert Mnookin and Lewis Kornhauser's 1979 article, *Bargaining in the Shadow of the Law: The Case of Divorce*, marked a critical watershed moment for the dispute resolution field on many levels. First, the article was at the vanguard of a now decades-old movement to take negotiation seriously as an academic field. Second, the article modeled and encouraged context-specific negotiation analysis as it delved deeply into the context-specific nature of dispute resolution, first developing a careful analytical framework for analysis and then applying it to a particular field of bargaining—namely, the area of divorce. Third, and most significantly, the article grappled with the interstitial space between the human behavior of "bargaining" and legal endowments, and it was ultimately instrumental in bringing that interstitial space into the purview of legal scholarship. I address each of these contributions in turn.

Mnookin and Kornhauser eloquently linked the legal framework around divorce to the ways in which parties negotiated "on the ground." In their article, they began by examining the idea of private ordering in divorce, considering the limits and advantages of such a system as compared to one of adjudication. They then created a bargaining model for divorcing parties by first examining the potentially relevant doctrinal elements of such a model, highlighting three relevant areas of law: monetary elements (alimony and child support, timing and structure of payments); child custody; and the interplay between custody and money. They then developed a theory of divorce bargaining that considered parental preferences, the endowments created by legal rules, the nature of private ordering against a backdrop of uncertainty, the role of transaction costs, and strategic behavior. Synthesizing all of the factors facing divorcing spouses, the authors concluded that a negotiated agreement is typically advantageous to parties. Having developed a complex bargaining framework with structural legal elements, situational elements, and interpersonal and intrapersonal elements, the authors then applied this framework to pose several key questions about custody standards, visitation reform proposals, the role played by lawyers in such disputes, the idea of counsel for a child, and the role of the courts, including ceremonial functions, fairness, oversight for out of court agreements, and child protection. As the authors noted in their conclusion, after this exhaustive exploration of the factors affecting private ordering, "[i]f anything, the world seems even more complex."

In their examination of private ordering around the dissolution of marriage, Mnookin and Kornhauser broke ground, first, by making an effort to carefully and systematically examine all of the relevant factors that one would need to consider in order to understand private ordering in the divorce negotiation context. Mnookin and Kornhauser broke down a complex web of human behavior, interaction, and situational roles, not to mention emotional, financial, strategic, and tactical considerations.

Rebecca Hollander-Blumoff, *Taking Human Behavior Seriously* In: *Discussions in Dispute Resolution.* Edited by: Art Hinshaw, Andrea Kupfer Schneider, and Sarah Rudolph Cole, Oxford University Press (2021).
DOI: 10.1093/oso/9780197513248.003.0003

The murky and potentially overwhelming tapestry of human drama unfolding in the case of divorce negotiation behavior—perhaps, among areas of the law, a high-water mark for emotional entanglement and strong feelings—was subject to, of all things, cool and level-headed analysis and consideration. Even if it was multifaceted and included many moving parts, Mnookin and Kornhauser's exploration showed that such an effort to catalog relevant features of a particular negotiation process was feasible. Along with other roughly contemporary approaches to analyzing negotiation critically, such as Fisher and Ury's *Getting to Yes* framework, Mnookin and Kornhauser helped to usher in an era in which the study of negotiation was envisioned not as the domain of a schmoozy cult of personality, underhanded tricks, or facile manipulations but, instead, as a respected and robust field of interdisciplinary academic study.

Second, and quite tangibly, the article provided a template for a cottage industry of other explorations of bargaining in the shadow of the law. Other scholars took up the Mnookin and Kornhauser model of a critical analysis of the interplay between legal endowments and human negotiating behavior. A host of authors followed up on Mnookin and Kornhauser's expressed hope that "this article will stimulate and encourage further work by others in a variety of contexts." Indeed, the paradigm of dispute resolution "in the shadow" of legal endowments has been explored in scores of articles that explicitly acknowledge their intellectual debt to Mnookin and Kornhauser. Scholars have considered the role of bargaining in the shadow of copyright law, international law, trade agreements, criminal law, and religious rather than civil law, just to name a few. And Mnookin and Kornhauser have been vindicated in their belief that "[t]heoretical and empirical research concerning how people bargain in the shadow of law should provide us with a richer understanding of how the legal system affects behavior, and should allow a more realistic appraisal of the consequences of reform proposals."

The bargaining in the shadow of the law paradigm can extend beyond the relationship between substantive legal rules and negotiation behavior in a particular context. For example, I have used the bargaining in the shadow of the law framework to think about how legal process endowments rather than substantive endowments may cast a shadow over negotiation. Specifically, I have argued that legal rules around due process influence psychological norms for fair process treatment by decision makers in the legal system. These procedural justice norms, in turn, influence expectations around negotiation behavior in more informal dispute resolution contexts. In negotiation, where there is no third-party decision maker, procedural justice norms nonetheless create a backdrop of entitlement against which individuals may measure the process of their "extra-legal" negotiations. In my empirical research, I have found that individuals are more enthusiastic about and consider positively as a basis for long-term resolution agreements that are reached when parties treat one another fairly. Thus, I argue, people bargain not just in the shadow of their substantive legal entitlements but in the shadow of due process as well.

Mnookin and Kornhauser noted that the contacts that individuals have with the legal system "may contribute to public cynicism about law and its processes." In an effort to improve legitimacy of the legal system, the authors stated that thinking about the interplay between private ordering and the law "highlights the need for general reform and gives specific support to the oft-asserted desirability of removing undisputed divorce cases from court dockets." Understanding that private ordering may increase the legal system's legitimacy was also a novel contribution, suggesting that neither process can be considered entirely separately from the other. The legal system itself may gain legitimacy when we take seriously, even in its shadows, not just the substantive but also the process endowments that it gives. Mnookin and Kornhauser's insight that private ordering is done within a set of expectations about the rights and privileges given by the legal system has proved capacious, adaptable, and enduring, well beyond a mere invitation to look more closely at the interplay of legal endowments in any one specific field and its related bargaining behaviors.

But in terms of its broadest influence, Mnookin and Kornhauser's groundbreaking article does its most remarkable work simply by taking human behavior seriously. Although they referred to rational behavior on the part of divorce participants, nowhere in the article did the authors glorify a "rational actor" with perfectly predictable preferences and behaviors, or suggest that any set of preferences are erroneous. Instead, they took seriously individual and differential preferences, acknowledged disparities in knowledge and negotiation skill, and even frankly remarked on the variegated landscape of lawyer behavior. And they did all of this without in any way privileging one set of preferences, behavior, or skill set. Their interest in explaining how human behavior may be shaped by legal endowments was not derailed by any preconceived vision of what human behavior "should be."

Bargaining in the Shadow of the Law conceptualized the role of human behavior as fundamentally influenced by legal endowments, and suggested that a variety of pieces of human behavior were worth taking seriously. In the years since the publication of the article, legal scholarship has seen the rise of influence of law and economics, and then, subsequently, law and psychology and law and behavioral economics. In the following decades, psychology research on cognitive biases and heuristics has helped change and push forward our thinking about the specific ways in which legal endowments are perceived by different parties, as well as how those perceptions may affect legal negotiation. In particular, the work of Daniel Kahneman and Amos Tversky has led a revolution in our understanding of the world beyond the rational actor model, pushing forward the insights of Mnookin and Kornhauser to help understand not just *that* endowments matter but exactly *how* these endowments specifically are perceived and how they affect parties, potentially differentially based on their starting positions. For example, Mnookin and Kornhauser considered the distinction between strategic behavior from the perspective of an individual who has a right endowed to her versus an individual who does not have that same endowment. Subsequent research in the area of psychology on the endowment effect has suggested that behavior will be different around status quo entitlements. Mnookin and Kornhauser similarly explored the effect of risk preferences on bargaining, something that has also been extensively studied using empirical research in the intervening decades. But unlike so much of the early legal scholarship focused on the cognitive biases and heuristics literature, which conceptualized empirical findings on human behavior as evidence that rational actors had gone astray, Mnookin and Kornhauser took a more expansive and less judgmental view, merely engaging with human behavior as the authors found it.

The Mnookin and Kornhauser landscape of human behavior also, notably, distinguished the role of lawyers' behavior from that of the principals. They note that "it is startling how little we know about how lawyers actually behave," and add, in characteristically understated fashion, that "[o]bviously, lawyers are not all the same." Again, this blunt and nonjudgmental perspective on the heterogeneity of attorney behavior exemplifies the authors' approach—human behavior is something to be studied and understood *as it is*, not predicted from a set of prior assumptions. Future work valuably took up the work of grappling with the role of lawyers, the role of differences among lawyers, and the potential disparities between lawyer and client behavior, preferences, and incentives.

In sum, the contributions to the field of negotiation of this multifaceted article on "the case of divorce" are manifold. The article provided a rigorous exploration of a messy human process, bringing some conceptual order to the chaos of private divorce bargaining, and signaling that the field of negotiation was worth taking seriously. And it suggested the unique contextual dependency of negotiation processes, issuing an invitation to further examinations in other areas of bargaining which legal scholars eagerly took up. It provided a core, fundamental insight that legal endowments make a critical difference to parties even outside of court. But perhaps most importantly, it homed in on the role that real individuals played in crafting negotiated outcomes, and suggested that their skills and preferences also mattered. From their academic perch, Mnookin and Kornhauser treated the human beings engaged in divorce negotiation with respect and dignity by taking them seriously, without judgment. And in doing so, they provided one unique and multifaceted perspective on the dynamic interplay between the law and this very real human behavior, leading the way for so many more.

Bargaining in the Shadow of the Law: A Classic Article with a Contemporary Challenge

Rishi Batra

Bargaining in the Shadow of the Law: The Case of Divorce remains a classic of the dispute resolution literature because it stands for and crystallizes an idea that for us in in the dispute resolution field today now seems like a fundamentally obvious truth: that the outcome of private bargaining is impacted by the endowments granted to parties by legal rules. In this way, the article—aided by its excellent title—serves as a shorthand for those looking to communicate this idea.

Yet this shorthand obscures the other important parts of the framework that the authors lay out to analyze bargaining, including party preferences, transaction costs, uncertainty, and strategic behavior. In addition, the bargaining framework that has become the focus of the article overshadows some of the other now fundamental assumptions in the dispute resolution literature that are so cogently laid out in the article, such as the advantages of private ordering over legal decree, and the role of the lawyer as counselor and negotiator rather than solely advocate or litigator. For all its contributions, however, the article ultimately recognizes its own identity as a theoretical piece and serves up a challenge to contemporary scholars—a call for more research to better understand the theoretical and empirical aspects of negotiation.

I. An Excellent Title for an Excellent Concept

Mark Twain is credited as defining "classic" as "[a] book which people praise and don't read." One of the reasons for the enduring power of *Bargaining*, and a reason that it remains a classic, is that with a short, snappy title, it gives you a sense of the whole piece without having to read a single word. The most recognized contribution that Mnookin and Kornhauser make in this article is to coin the pithy turn of phrase "bargaining in the shadow of the law" and place it in the title. Even for those who merely see a citation to the article, it instantly invokes the concept that the authors want to convey—that is, that negotiation is always impacted, but not fully determined, by the entitlements provided by law. In this way, the article title joins a few rarified phrases in the dispute resolution field as a shorthand for a deep concept, such as *Against Settlement* (Fiss) or "the multidoor courthouse" (Sander). The enduring power of the phrase can be seen in the *many* imitations since the publication of their original article. While a cursory search shows the phrase "shadow of the law" shows up only once in a title of a law

Rishi Batra, Bargaining in the Shadow of the Law: *A Classic Article with a Contemporary Challenge* In: *Discussions in Dispute Resolution*. Edited by: Art Hinshaw, Andrea Kupfer Schneider, and Sarah Rudolph Cole, Oxford University Press (2021).
 DOI: 10.1093/oso/9780197513248.003.0004

journal article before 1979, in the last thirty years dozens of titular entities have ended up in the law's "shadow," including "contracting," "victims," and "slutwalking," among many others.

Yet even though the title encapsulates and crystallizes the concept of legal entitlements' impact on private bargaining, the focus in the title on the "shadow of the law" actually ends up eclipsing many other important aspects of the thesis that the authors espouse. This is evidenced by the fact that the phrase itself—"shadow of the law"—surprisingly appears only *once* outside the title and conclusion, under the heading of legal rules creating bargaining endowments (p. 968). Mnookin and Kornhauser, however, attempted a much broader project of explicating the structure of divorce bargaining and correctly pointed out that there are many other elements of a bargaining model other than legal entitlements that need to be considered to fully understand bargaining outcomes: the preferences of the parties, uncertainty and parties' tolerance for risk, transaction costs, and strategic behavior. By not highlighting these aspects in the title, these other aspects of their fully fleshed-out bargaining model are often ignored when considering the framework as a whole.

II. Many Other Fundamental Concepts

One of the most striking aspects to reading *Bargaining* today is how much of the rest of the article's contribution is spent on concepts, in addition to the "shadow of the law," that we regard as fundamental in current dispute resolution literature. The article was written at a time when divorce law was changing significantly, from fault grounds to the "no fault revolution" mentioned in its text (p. 953). This change greatly increased the amount of autonomy granted to parties in creating their own arrangements for divorce and minimized the role of the courts in this process. Today, we take for granted that this increased autonomy in settlement is generally good for parties, as "private ordering" has advantages over the use of courts to settle disputes. It is noteworthy that the authors of *Bargaining* felt the need to extensively justify the use of private ordering in divorce settlements, and the early part of their paper lays considerable grounds for why they believe divorcing spouses should have "broad powers to make their own deals" (p. 955).

The reasons given seem obvious to students of dispute resolution (and legal scholars more generally) today: reducing the financial cost of litigation, avoiding litigation uncertainty, time savings, the increased durability of a settlement to which parties consent, and the fact that parties are more knowledgeable about the dispute than the court, and have the ability to best evaluate the financial arrangements for themselves and custodial arrangements for their children. Especially in divorce, where there is a reduced need for precedent between these two parties who are not repeat players, private ordering would seem to be the obvious solution to maximize the preferences of the parties. However, the fact that these are now fundamental assumptions about why disputes should resolve privately was not canonical at the time, and to the extent we think of private ordering as the superior method of resolution in divorce as well as other domains today we owe to the contribution of these authors.

Another fundamental assumption of modern dispute resolution literature is the role of the lawyer as counselor and negotiator. Much of *Bargaining* is spent considering the role of the lawyer in the case of divorce, and the article goes through great lengths to emphasize that a lawyer is not solely an advocate for his client or solely a litigator in court, but has a role to play in ensuring that clients are informed about their bargaining options, and then in conducting the negotiation on their behalf (pp. 985–88). This would not come as a surprise to today's law students, who have the option and sometimes requirement of taking courses in legal negotiation, settlement, and client counseling, and whose first-year textbooks make efforts to discuss how most cases are resolved through settlement procedures. The authors also suggest that the lawyer's role in uncontested divorces, primarily the filling out of forms, could be simplified and better accomplished through nonlawyers, anticipating the online legal services for divorces today (p. 988).

III. The Shadow's Edge—What the Article Does Not Say

Despite the authors' efforts to create a bargaining framework for divorce negotiation, Mnookin and Kornhauser recognize the limits of the framework they are adopting and explicitly do not use the framework to make concrete predictions on how the "shadow of the law" will impact bargaining outcomes, in divorce or otherwise. The article is modest in the claims it makes, with qualifiers which suggest even if the bargaining framework is applied, outcomes "may" be impacted and "might" change the behavior of the parties. And the authors admit that "no bargaining theory … can yield accurate predictions of expected outcomes with different legal rules" even in the simple case of monetary negotiations, and they note that divorce bargaining is "considerably more complex" than a monetary bargain given the child custody and child support issues involved (p. 996).

Yet it is surprising that even in the most empirical part of the paper, that is, "The Bargaining Framework Applied" (p. 977), where Mnookin and Kornhauser use their bargaining framework to analyze three common custody standards, they come to few conclusions (pp. 977–80). They consider how a change in the legal standard—from "maternal preference" to "best interests of the child" or a "joint-custody rule" would reduce the certainty involved in the outcome, thereby disadvantaging the more risk-averse spouse, "probably" increasing the transaction costs and "seem[ing]" to help the more able negotiator. However, they are not definite in these conclusions, nor do they suggest if these are positive changes, and make no attempt to use the framework to try to define what the right custody standard should then *be.*

Similarly, the authors consider a proposal from a book called *Beyond the Best Interests of the Child* (Goldstein et al. 1973), which suggests that the custodial parent should completely control visitation by the noncustodial parent with no opportunity for the parents to agree to any other arrangement, an apparently controversial proposal that was the subject of much criticism at the time (pp. 980–85). The authors rightly point out that, considering the preferences of the parties for custody and visitation, this proposal could lead to increased disputes as well as impact support outcomes, and that generally limiting the parties' power to make legally enforceable agreements "may" make settlement more difficult. But Mnookin and Kornhauser do not then take a strong position on what limits *should* be placed on parties' power to reopen child custody and support agreements, suggesting that a middle position between extremes may be appropriate, and the framework they propose does not seem to guide them in a given direction. While the framework may give us a good sense of the contours of a dispute, the authors leave the analysis of what changes should be made to others.

And of course, the authors could not have anticipated all future elements of a bargaining model that have subsequently been explored in other literature. They make few allowances for the impact of irrational behavior or emotions on the bargaining space, which are obviously tied up with divorce negotiations. While they do mention barriers to negotiated agreement, such as spite, or a distaste for negotiation, it would be years before scholars of behavioral economics or other legal scholars shed more light on these factors. The issue of gender power imbalance, which other authors would dive deeply into in the future, is not mentioned. Despite these omissions, the authors do a remarkable job laying out fundamental contributions to the dispute resolution canon.

IV. A Call for Future Research

For all its fundamental contributions, perhaps the least appreciated part of the article is the call for future research contained all throughout the article. Mnookin and Kornhauser, as mentioned previously, recognize the limits of the framework they are adopting and note that this is a theoretical perspective which allows us to think broadly about the consequences of different rules and procedures (p. 996). They readily say more research is needed on all aspects of negotiation behavior. Specifically, they challenge others to learn more about how different procedural mechanisms may help resolve disputes, a challenge that scholars are just starting to meet with the empirical work on mediation in court settings. The authors point out that at the time there was little good information on how lawyers actually behave in negotiations, which is a difficulty that remains true today and will require more work from scholars to deepen our understanding of the practice of negotiation.

More generally, Mnookin and Kornhauser use their conclusion to ask scholars to apply their perspective of a bargaining model and its implications to other domains, such as automobile accidents and plea bargains (p. 997). Newer scholars like myself and others have taken up this mantle and continue to do so today. In doing so, we build on what are now fundamental truths in dispute resolution—the shadow of the law, the superiority of private ordering, and the negotiation role of lawyers—which *Bargaining in the Shadow of the Law* had given to us right from the first words of the title.

References

Address by Frank E.A. Sander at the National Conference on the Causes of Dissatisfaction with the Administration of Justice (Apr. 7–9, 1976), reprinted in Sander, *Varieties of Dispute Processing*, 70 F.R.D. 111 (1976).

Owen M. Fiss, *Against Settlement*, 93 Yale L.J. 1073 (1984).

J. Goldstein, A. Freud, & A. Solnit, Beyond the Best Interests of the Child (1973).

Bargaining in the Shadow of the Law Reassessed

Robert H. Mnookin

I'm delighted the editor decided to include an extract from *Bargaining in the Shadow of the Law: The Case of Divorce* in this volume, and I appreciate the generous comments of Professors Batra, Hollander-Blumoff, and Tippett concerning the article's importance to the development of dispute resolution scholarship. At least if measured by citations, the article turned out to be seminal to a degree I would never have anticipated in 1979. A 2012 empirical study determined that it is among the one hundred most cited law review articles of all time. Indeed, it ranked nineteenth. A good title obviously helps. In the future, I fear its ranking may be at risk—the phrase "bargaining in the shadow" has become so well known that the metaphor is increasingly invoked without a citation to our article as the scholarly source. So be it; we've had a good run. I am comforted by Rebecca Hollander-Blumoff's observation that the "article provided a template for a cottage industry of other explorations of bargaining in the shadow of the law" outside the divorce context.

In what follows, I want to focus on the article's relevance beyond family law. I will first summarize what I see as the article's most important *general* insights that are broadly relevant today to our understanding of law and the legal system. Next, I will briefly explore the idea that some conflicts—that might result in legal claims—are nonetheless typically resolved by bargaining outside the law's shadow.

Let me begin by identifying four key insights, developed in the context of divorce bargaining, that have more general applicability.

First, the overwhelming majority of legal conflicts are resolved not by judges through adjudication but instead through negotiations. This was the starting point for my analysis of divorce proceedings because the evidence showed the distributional questions arising out of dissolution rarely required adjudication. The same is also true of disputes in many other legal contexts. Few accident or tort claims are ever tried; most are settled. Contractual disputes are typically worked out through negotiation. Administrative proceedings typically result in consent agreements rather than agency actions after formal contested hearings. And criminal prosecutions typically end with a plea bargain, not a criminal trial.

Second, in these negotiations, law and the legal system are relevant but not in any simple, outcome determinative way. A party to a conflict may have the capacity to resort to court and have a judge resolve the dispute by imposing an outcome if negotiations fail. For this reason, the possibility of litigation may loom in the background. If it does, a disputant's perception of the opportunities and risks of litigation may influence bargaining behavior and may affect the outcome. Why? Because in deciding

Robert H. Mnookin, *Bargaining in the Shadow of the Law Reassessed* In: *Discussions in Dispute Resolution.* Edited by: Art Hinshaw, Andrea Kupfer Schneider, and Sarah Rudolph Cole, Oxford University Press (2021). © Oxford University Press.
DOI: 10.1093/oso/9780197513248.003.0005

whether the accept some negotiated deal rather than pursue litigation, a party can assess how well the deal serves her own interests and preferences in comparison to fighting it out in court.

Third, the article identified five factors the interplay of which would influence bargaining behavior and outcomes. These are (1) the preferences of the parties; (2) the bargaining endowments created by the both the substantive and procedural legal rules that would apply in adjudication; (3) the degree of uncertainty concerning the legal outcome if the parties go to court, which we pointed out was linked to the parties' attitudes toward risks; (4) transaction costs and the parties' respective abilities to bear them; and (5) strategic behavior.

Fourth, viewing law and the legal system from a bargaining perspective can reveal new insights into the impact of substantive law and various procedural requirements. Moreover, we demonstrated why assessing the wisdom of possible law reform proposals required a careful assessment of a reform's possible impact on out-of-court negotiations as well as its effects on judicial behavior in disputed cases. We illustrated how these factors might shed light on the divorce bargaining process and several family law reform proposals.

Lewis Kornhauser and I never claimed the framework created by these five factors represented a "complete theory," much less a formal model. Professor Tippett is surely correct that other variables might well be added. Indeed, we noted with regret at that time that "no existing theory of bargaining allows confident predictions of how different legal rules and procedures would influence outcomes." Some forty years later I think this is still the case. But I remain persuaded the five factors provide a helpful framework.

I. Disputes Outside the Law's Shadow

Since our article was published, several scholars have suggested that some legal disputes are resolved by negotiations entirely "outside" the law's shadow. I want to exclude from consideration disputes where as a practical matter no access to court is feasible, or where a party knows nothing about the possibility of judicially imposed remedy. In such circumstances there is no reason to assume law and the legal system will cast a shadow. So to be more precise: Are there contexts in which an adjudicated legal remedy is feasible and yet it appears as a general proposition that out-of-court negotiations are not in any way influenced by what might happen in court?

Robert Ellickson's book, *Order Without Law: How Neighbors Settle Disputes* (Harvard University Press, 1991), provides a fascinating example of a context where a legal remedy is available but negotiated deals appear to be uninfluenced by law. Indeed, Ellickson states he sought "to demonstrate that people frequently resolve their disputes in cooperative fashion without paying any attention to the laws that apply to those disputes" (p. VII).

Ellickson's book explores how adjacent landowners in Shasta County resolved conflicts arising when cattle strayed from one property to another. What made Shasta County especially interesting is that it contained areas which had two different sets of legal rules: "open range" areas where "an owner of cattle is not legally liable for damages stemming from his cattle's accidental trespass upon unfenced land" and "closed-range ordinances" that made cattleman strictly liable.

Ellickson discovered that "[m]ost cattlemen believe that a rancher should keep his animals from eating a neighbor's grass, *regardless of whether the range is open or closed*" (pp. 52–53) (emphasis supplied). As a result, even when the expected adjudicated outcome in "open range" areas would absolve the cattle owner of responsibility, disputants nonetheless settled their conflicts on the basis of a norm that imposed responsibility. Deviants who violated the shared norm were typically controlled through self-help or reputational sanctions.

Ellickson's research is an important reminder that in some contexts disputants may choose to resolve their disputes using shared community norms that are not reflected in the formal legal system. And that self-help remedies may be used to enforce such norms against deviants without resort to court.

Ellickson's findings pose some fascinating questions that I would hope scholars might explore: Under what circumstances are communal norms that are inconsistent with the formal legal norms likely to persist? When will reputational sanctions and self-help be sufficiently effective to constrain resort to the formal legal system?

There is a second context, far afield from cattle grazing, in which several scholars have claimed—incorrectly in my view—that bargaining is outside the law's shadow even though litigation is an available alternative: the world of plea bargaining. In *Plea Bargaining Outside the Shadow of Trial*, Professor Stefanos Bibas challenges the notion that "the likelihood of convictions at trial" and the "likelihood of post-trial sentence" largely determine plea bargains. He rejects the idea that plea bargaining is "just another case of bargaining in the shadow of expected trial outcomes."

Bibas points to evidence that plea deals often involve sentences that deviate substantially from the sentences typically imposed after criminal trials. He argues that "many plea bargains diverge from 'the shadows of trials' because bargaining is distorted both by (a) "many structural impediments," and (b) various psychological biases.

In my view, Bibas has set up a straw man. Our *Bargaining in the Shadow* framework does not assume disputants' decision-making can be captured by models of rational self-interested actors. I agree there are a variety of structural and psychological features that affect negotiated outcomes. No simple model of bargaining premised on economic rationality is adequate.

I also want to underscore an important point that I think our article made clear but which I fear Bibas (and perhaps others) may not have sufficiently appreciated. We never claimed that the "endowments" created by legal rules alone determine bargaining outcomes. Our framework identified five factors. Indeed, our article exposed the variety of reasons parties might negotiate deals far different from that a judge might have imposed. Evidence that plea bargained sentences typically differ from those imposed after trial for similar offenses in no way demonstrates that an assessment of the legal opportunities and risks of going to trial had no effect on a defendant's decision-making in pleading guilty.

In *Plea Bargaining and Criminal Law's Disappearing Shadow*, William Stuntz identifies what he characterizes as "deeper problem with plea bargains, one that goes squarely to the relationship between those bargains and bodies of law that define crimes and punishment."

Stuntz's argument is that the legal system gives the prosecutor too much power and discretion. The legislature has created substantive criminal law where the defendant's alleged behavior can be typically characterized as violating a large number of different and often overlapping offenses. These offenses often carry widely disparate sentences. By choosing from a broad "menu" of possible charges, the prosecutor can expose the defendant to wildly disparate punishments arising out a single set of actions.

According to Stuntz, the irony is that the prosecutor can credibly threaten a defendant with a punishment that no one in the system would think appropriate but which nevertheless could result because of mandatory minimum sentences or risks created under sentencing guidelines. Indeed, Stuntz argued that the legislature has created this system intentionally—in order to make sure most criminal defendants will plead guilty.

The parties bargain in the shadow of this broad prosecutorial discretion. This discretion means that a prosecutor's threat to overcharge is credible. In other words, the opportunities and risks the defendant would face at trial do influence the defendant's decision-making. Therefore, from my point of view, plea bargaining in Stuntz's world is very much in the law's shadow for two reasons. First, the opportunities and risks presented by a trial are taken into account by defendants in decision-making. Second, because the institutional framework giving prosecutors such broad discretion is itself created by the existing *legal* system.

Bargaining in the Shadow had an extended discussion of the extent to which "private ordering"—the disputants' power to make their own deal—was appropriate in the context of divorce. We underscored that "[t]he implicit policy questions are ones of emphasis and degree: to what extent should the law permit and encourage divorcing in couples to work out their own arrangements? Within what limits should parties be empowered to make their own law by private agreement? What procedural or substantive safeguards are necessary to protect various social interests?"

To state the obvious, plea bargaining involves negotiations in a radically different context than divorce bargaining. When there's a criminal charge, the state is the moving party. Moreover, the defendant has his or her liberty at stake. Unlike a divorce case, in the criminal law context, there is much less justification in terms of underlying social interests to defer to a negotiated deal, at least without substantial third-party review.

I am persuaded our existing criminal law system requires fundamental reform of the plea bargaining process. On normative grounds, the results produced by our current system of laws through plea bargaining seems appalling. I suspect Bibas is correct that "legally irrelevant factors sometimes skew the fair allocation of punishment" and that the operation of the plea bargaining process may not adequately calibrate sentences to proof of guilt. Stuntz's criticisms suggest an urgent need to constrain prosecutorial discretion. For me, the problems these scholars identify do not suggest plea bargaining is somehow beyond the law's shadow. To the contrary, their criticisms suggest the critical importance of taking into account the impact of law and the legal system on out-of-court negotiations.

References

Stephanos Bibas, *Plea Bargaining Outside the Shadow of Trial*, 117 HARV. L. REV. 2463 (2004).
ROBERT ELLICKSON, ORDER WITHOUT LAW: HOW NEIGHBORS SETTLE DISPUTES (1991).
William Stuntz, *Plea Bargaining and Criminal Law's Disappearing Shadow*, 117 HARV. L. REV. 2548 (2004).

Article 1.2

Machiavelli and the Bar: Ethical Limitations on Lying in Negotiation

James J. White

1980 American Bar Foundation Research Journal No. 4, 926

Upon the enactment of the Model Rules of Professional Conduct, published ethical norms will for the first time give explicit consideration to the lawyer's behavior in the process of negotiation.... The mere recognition of negotiation as a separate process worthy of unique rules is a large step. The purpose of this paper is to address the general question of truthfulness as that question is faced in Rule 4.2.

The difficulty of proposing acceptable rules concerning truthfulness in negotiation is presented by several circumstances. First, negotiation is nonpublic behavior. If one negotiator lies to another, only by happenstance will the other discover the lie. If the settlement is concluded by negotiation, there will be no trial, no public testimony by conflicting witnesses, and thus no opportunity to examine the truthfulness of assertions made during the negotiation...

The drafters appreciated, but perhaps not fully, a second difficulty in drafting ethical norms for negotiators. That is the almost galactic scope of disputes that are subject to resolution by negotiation.... More than almost any other form of lawyer behavior, the process of negotiation is varied; it differs from place to place and from subject matter to subject matter. It calls, therefore, either for quite different rules in different contexts or for rules stated only at a very high level of generality.

A final complication in drafting rules about truthfulness arises out of the paradoxical nature of the negotiator's responsibility. On the one hand the negotiator must be fair and truthful; on the other he must mislead his opponent.... I submit that a careful examination of the behavior of even the most forthright, honest, and trustworthy negotiators will show them actively engaged in misleading their opponents about their true positions. That is true of both the plaintiff and the defendant in a lawsuit. It is true of both labor and management in a collective bargaining agreement. It is true as well of both the buyer and the seller in a wide variety of sales transactions. To conceal one's true position, to mislead an opponent about one's true settling point, is the essence of negotiation.

Of course there are limits on acceptable deceptive behavior in negotiation, but there is the paradox. How can one be "fair" but also mislead? Can we ask the negotiator to mislead, but fairly, like the soldier who must kill, but humanely?

James J. White, *Machiavelli and the Bar: Ethical Limitations on Lying in Negotiation* In: *Discussions in Dispute Resolution.* Edited by: Art Hinshaw, Andrea Kupfer Schneider, and Sarah Rudolph Cole, Oxford University Press (2021).
DOI: 10.1093/oso/9780197513248.003.0006

Truthtelling in General

The obligation to behave truthfully in negotiation is embodied in the requirement of Rule 4.2(a) that directs the lawyer to "be fair in dealing with other participants." Presumably the direction to be fair speaks to a variety of acts in addition to truthfulness and also different from it. At a minimum it has something to say about the threats a negotiator may use, about the favors he may offer, and possibly about the extraneous factors other than threats and favors which can appropriately be used in negotiating. As I have suggested elsewhere, each of these issues has important ramifications, and each merits independent consideration by the drafters of the Model Rules and by lawyers. In this paper I ignore those questions and limit my consideration to the question of truth telling. * * *

Five Cases

Although it is not necessary to draft such a set of rules, it is probably important to give more than the simple disclaimer about the impossibility of defining the appropriate limits of puffing that the drafters have given in the current Comments. To test these limits, consider five cases. Easiest is the question that arises when one misrepresents his true opinion about the meaning of a case or a statute. Presumably such a misrepresentation is accepted lawyer behavior both in and out of court and is not intended to be precluded by the requirement that the lawyer be "truthful." In writing his briefs, arguing his case, and attempting to persuade the opposing party in negotiation, it is the lawyer's right and probably his responsibility to argue for plausible interpretations of cases and statutes which favor his client's interest, even in circumstances where privately he has advised his client that those are not his true interpretations of the cases and statutes.

A second form of distortion that the Comments plainly envision as permissible is distortion concerning the value of one's case or of the other subject matter involved in the negotiation. Thus the Comments make explicit reference to "puffery...."

A third case is related to puffing but different from it. This is the use of the so-called false demand. It is a standard negotiating technique in collective bargaining negotiation and in some other multiple-issue negotiations for one side to include a series of demands about which it cares little or not at all.... Such behavior is untruthful in the broadest sense; yet at least in collective bargaining negotiation its use is a standard part of the process and is not thought to be inappropriate by any experienced bargainer.

Two final examples may be more troublesome. The first involves the response of a lawyer to a question from the other side. Assume that the defendant has instructed his lawyer to accept any settlement offer under $100,000. Having received that instruction, how does the defendant's lawyer respond to the plaintiff's question, "I think $90,000 will settle this case. Will your client give $90,000?" Do you see the dilemma that question poses for the defense lawyer? It calls for information that would not have to be disclosed. A truthful answer to it concludes the negotiation and dashes any possibility of negotiating a lower settlement even in circumstances in which the plaintiff might be willing to accept half of $90,000. Even a moment's hesitation in response to the question may be a nonverbal communication to a clever plaintiff's lawyer that the defendant has given such authority. Yet a negative response is a lie.

It is no answer that a clever lawyer will answer all such questions about authority by refusing to answer them, nor is it an answer that some lawyers will be clever enough to tell their clients not to grant them authority to accept a given sum until the final stages in negotiation. Most of us are not that careful or that clever.... Thus despite the fact that a clever negotiator can avoid having to lie or to reveal his settling point, many lawyers, perhaps most, will sometime be forced by such a question either to lie or to reveal that they have been granted such authority by saying so or by their silence in response to a direct question. Is it fair to lie in such a case?

Before one examines the possible justifications for a lie in that circumstance, consider a final example recently suggested to me by a lawyer in practice. There the lawyer represented three persons who had been charged with shoplifting. Having satisfied himself that there was no significant conflict of interest, the defense lawyer told the prosecutor that two of the three would plead guilty only if the case was dismissed against the third. Previously those two had told the defense counsel that they would plead guilty irrespective of what the third did, and the third had said that he wished to go to trial unless the charges were dropped. Thus the defense lawyer lied to the prosecutor by stating that the two would plead only if the third were allowed to go free. Can the lie be justified in this case?

How does one distinguish the cases where truthfulness is not required and those where it is required? Why do the first three cases seem easy? I suggest they are easy cases because the rules of the game are explicit and well developed in those areas. Everyone expects a lawyer to distort the value of his own case, of his own facts and arguments, and to deprecate those of his opponent. No one is surprised by that, and the system accepts and expects that behavior....

The last two cases are more difficult. In one the lawyer lies about his authority; in the other he lies about the intention of his clients. It would be more difficult to justify the lies in those cases by arguing that the rules of the game explicitly permit that sort of behavior. Some might say that the rules of the game provide for such distortion, but I suspect that many lawyers would say that such lies are out of bounds and are not part of the rules of the game. Can the lie about authority be justified on the ground that the question itself was improper? Put another way, if I have a right to keep certain information to myself, and if any behavior but a lie will reveal that information to the other side, am I justified in lying? I think not. Particularly in the case in which there are other avenues open to the respondent, should we not ask him to take those avenues? That is, the careful negotiator here can turn aside all such questions and by doing so avoid any inference from his failure to answer such questions.

What makes the last case a close one? Conceivably it is the idea that one accused by the state is entitled to greater leeway in making his case. Possibly one can argue that there is no injury to the state when such a person, particularly an innocent person, goes free. Is it conceivable that the act can be justified on the ground that it is part of the game in this context, that prosecutors as well as defense lawyers routinely misstate what they, their witnesses, and their clients can and will do? None of these arguments seems persuasive. Justice is not served by freeing a guilty person. The system does not necessarily achieve better results by trading two guilty pleas for a dismissal. Perhaps its justification has its roots in the same idea that formerly held that a misrepresentation of one's state of mind was not actionable for it was not a misrepresentation of fact.

In a sense rules governing these cases may simply arise from a recognition by the law of its limited power to shape human behavior. By tolerating exaggeration and puffing in the sales transaction, by refusing to make misstatement of one's intention actionable, the law may simply have recognized the bounds of its control over human behavior. Having said that, one is still left with the question, Are the lies permissible in the last two cases? My general conclusion is that they are not, but I am not nearly as comfortable with that conclusion as I am with the conclusion about the first three cases.

Taken together, the five foregoing cases show me that we do not and cannot intend that a negotiator be "truthful" in the broadest sense of that term. At the minimum we allow him some deviation from truthfulness in asserting his true opinion about cases, statutes, or the value of the subject of the negotiation in other respects. In addition some of us are likely to allow him to lie in response to certain questions that are regarded as out of bounds, and possibly to lie in circumstances where his interest is great and the injury seems small. It would be unfortunate, therefore, for the rule that requires "fairness" to be interpreted to require that a negotiator be truthful in every respect and in all of his dealings. It should be read to allow at least those kinds of untruthfulness that are implicitly and explicitly recognized as acceptable in his forum, a forum defined both by the subject matter and by the participants.

Comments

Machiavelli and the Bar and Ethical Ratcheting

Michael Moffitt

At the time of its publication, J.J. White's essay, *Machiavelli and the Bar*, contributed a timely perspective on the challenges of drafting ethical constraints on negotiators' behaviors. With this brief response, I first situate the essay historically, suggesting that *Machiavelli and the Bar* could not have been written two decades earlier, nor would it have had much impact had it been written two decades later. Second, I highlight some of the ambivalence apparent in Professor White's analysis. Finally, I raise a concern about where White's logic would take (has taken?) the legal profession with respect to the important question of ethical norm-setting in the context of negotiations.

I. Situating *Machiavelli and the Bar*

Although some of White's observations in *Machiavelli and the Bar* can be (and often are) excerpted into stand-alone commentaries on the challenges associated with regulating private behavior between professionals, his essay as a whole is best understood as arising out of the confluence of two different arcs in the practice of law in the United States and in the development of the American legal academy.

The first historical context from which this essay emerges relates to the bar's efforts to self-regulate. At the time of the publication of *Machiavelli and the Bar*, the American Bar Association was engaged in internal debate about whether, and if so how, to revise the standards governing the practice of law. The debates about the potential shift from the Model Codes to the Model Rules included considerable hand-wringing and fretting about the consequences of different draft ethical provisions.

With the benefit of hindsight, we know several things with respect to this first arc. The Model Rules were adopted several years after this essay was written, and we have seen few conspicuous examples of the kinds of nightmares its detractors feared more than thirty years ago. At the time White penned *Machiavelli and the Bar*, however, this was not a foregone conclusion, and parts of the essay plainly reflect his concern both that the new Rules pass and that they not produce governance disasters.

The second important historical context from which this essay emerged is that at the time of its publication, the legitimacy of negotiation and alternative dispute resolution (ADR)—both within the profession and within the academy—was still in question. White was a pioneer of negotiation teaching in law schools (White 1967;

Michael Moffitt, Machiavelli and the Bar *and Ethical Ratcheting* In: *Discussions in Dispute Resolution*. Edited by: Art Hinshaw, Andrea Kupfer Schneider, and Sarah Rudolph Cole, Oxford University Press (2021). © Oxford University Press. DOI: 10.1093/oso/9780197513248.003.0007

Edwards & White 1977; Moffitt 2004). The American Bar Association had no "Section of Dispute Resolution." There were no specialty journals dedicated to the field. The dominant view of lawyering was one in which adversarial, courtroom advocacy was central—even though as a descriptive matter, settlement's statistical prominence had long been established. In *Machiavelli and the Bar*, one can hear White's gratitude (relief?) that the draft Rules even acknowledge negotiation as being a sufficiently important part of lawyering to justify regulation.

What we know now, with the benefit of more than thirty years since *Machiavelli and the Bar*, is that the legitimacy question was answered, definitively and in the affirmative. No longer are courses in negotiation indefinitely labeled as "experimental" (White 1967). Indeed, every accredited law school in the United States offers permanent courses on negotiation and ADR in its various flavors (Moffitt 2010). Six specialty law journals and more than a dozen law school research centers focus on these topics. The profession as a whole recognizes the importance of education and skill in this area. The only outlier data point suggesting serious debate in this area is the fact that most bar exams do not focus on negotiation questions, but I suspect that is more a function of test-design challenges than it is suggestive that bar boards of governors think negotiation does not matter to the competent practice of law.

I suggest, therefore, that *Machiavelli and the Bar* should be read in context, as though two questions were looming simultaneously in the background:

1. Shall we as a profession adopt an entirely new set of articulated ethical norms about all aspects of lawyering—one small piece of which addresses the question of candor in negotiation?
2. Shall we as a profession and as members of the academy view negotiation as a part of a lawyer's job—distinct and important enough even to merit separate treatment from other aspects of a lawyer's job?

I believe that holding these two questions simultaneously in mind as one (re)reads *Machiavelli and the Bar* may help to illuminate aspects that risk otherwise being unappreciated.

II. Recognizing the Ambivalence in *Machiavelli and the Bar*

An unfair oversimplification of *Machiavelli and the Bar*—particularly one written without the perspective(s) I have suggested above—might read like this:

Negotiation is really important, so you have to include it in an accounting of lawyers' duties. But negotiation is too complex and takes place in too many different contexts to make it the subject of a single set of ethical rules. Moreover, it takes place in private, so some might violate those ethical rules and get away with it. High ethical standards would risk punishing those who are trying to do the right thing. So really, I'm not sure one can articulate any ethical standards beyond a minimal level—so minimal in fact that it's not really distinguishable from the standards to which everyone in society is already held anyway. But still, thanks for including negotiation in this draft. I support the proposed Rule and hope the whole set gets adopted.

A more charitable (and perhaps more appropriate) reading of the essay would note at least two things: first, *Machiavelli and the Bar* is commendable for its candor. Yes, some parts of the essay appear to conflict—or at least be in serious and unacknowledged tension—with other parts of the essay. But such is the nature of any short and honest treatment of a nuanced policy addressing multiple, challenging dynamics and trade-offs.

Second, *Machiavelli and the Bar* is quotable. This I believe also to be among its most troubling aspects. But White employs turns of phrase in his essay that make it all but impossible for those of us teaching negotiation to avoid quoting him. His assertion, for example, "[t]o conceal one's true position, to mislead an opponent about one's true settling point, is the essence of negotiation," is laden with multiple easily challenged assumptions. Indeed, I think White is simply wrong about this assertion, at least as it is written. But linguistic parsimony makes several parts of his essay the delight of negotiation professors everywhere.

As to the critique that *Machiavelli and the Bar* is an essay that cannot make up its mind, what we are mostly seeing is authorial ambivalence. White does not want negotiation to be left out—not out of the academy, not out of the practice, not out of the rules governing the practice. White does not want a caricature of negotiation to be included, much less codified, into the profession's ethics. White does not want to see the importance of context disappear from negotiation, but he recognizes that the nature of the Model Rules demands universal application. White does not want to punish those who aim to follow ethical precepts, nor does he want to create conditions in which the overall fate of the Model Rules themselves is threatened because of slippery slope challenges in this one area of practice.

Some authors might try to assume away one or more of the challenges mentioned here. The task of Goldilocks Ethics Drafting (not too broad, not too specific) is daunting, after all. White's essay is helpful precisely because it is honest—even ambivalent.

III. "Ethical Ratcheting" and the Potentially Self-Fulfilling Nature of Minimalist Descriptive Normative Standards

My principal concern with *Machiavelli and the Bar* is that the consequence of one piece of White's logic, taken to its natural end, produces ethical ratcheting—a system in which ethical rules invariably can only loosen.

A ratchet (picture the kind of wrench one uses to remove tightened bolts, or if you prefer, turnstiles in the subway or at a stadium) operates using a fairly simple mechanism. Turned one way, it blocks or engages and cannot be moved without considerable force. Turned the other way, it freely spins without causing any real change.

Assume for the moment that White is correct when he asserts that ethical rules matter—that many attorneys will alter their behavior based on what the ethics rules say. White and the Model Rules themselves suggest that we cannot (or at least ought not) to prohibit certain behaviors among attorneys because many already engage in those behaviors. This appears to be the logic, for example, behind the explicit exclusion of "puffery" from the list of prohibited behaviors.

I am not picking an empirical fight here. Neither White nor I know the prevalence of behavior constituting puffery in negotiations in any particular context, much less across the broad spectrum of negotiation contexts to which the Model Rules are applied.

My concern is about where this logic leads.

Assume for the moment that White and the drafters of the Model Rules were correct that puffery happened regularly already among lawyers in 1980. Once the new Rules make the pronouncement that puffery is both permitted and commonplace, would we not expect to see lawyers engage in it routinely? Indeed, might it even be malpractice not to adopt a practice that is perceived as providing advantage and is explicitly permitted by the Rules? Given the Rules' pronouncement, one would expect soon to find that behavior to be commonplace—regardless of whether it was originally so.

What, then, about whatever the next level of deception beyond puffery—however that negotiation shenanigan might be described? If the definitional slope is slippery, as White suggests, then will we really be able to distinguish a piece of puffery from a shenanigan? If no, then surely some will begin to engage in shenanigans, because after all, everyone is already engaging in puffery. Once some lawyers engage in negotiation shenanigans, and once the line-drawing is shown to be hard between puffery and shenanigans, then what? If the logic behind permitting puffery was essentially, "lots of people do it already," should we expect the Rules then to be amended to permit shenanigans explicitly? If yes, then wouldn't shenanigans quickly become the ethical baseline, even the expected practice? And what would follow on after shenanigans?

What conditions would have to exists for the bar to draw a line tighter than that suggested by current practice? Could the bar ever draw a line such that attorneys would be held to a higher ethical standard than the one imposed upon their mentors and predecessors? We have seen regulatory conditions shift rapidly in some other regulatory contexts. But such conditions did not exist in 1980 as the Model Rules were under contemplation. One of the results is that the Model Rule codified acquiescence, even approval, of "puffery" and presumably other negotiation behaviors constituting less than perfect candor.

White quotes Judge Rubin as saying, "Another lawyer, or a layman, who deals with a lawyer should not need to exercise the same degree of caution that he would if trading for reputedly antique copper jugs in an oriental bazaar" (Rubin 1975). White criticizes Rubin largely on line-drawing grounds, namely, that no articulated rule for one kind of negotiations would fit well in all negotiations.

That in the context of the adoption of Model Rule 4.1 we were collectively unable to find a way to draw an acceptable line, however, does not mean that no such line is possible. Moreover, capitulating to the lowest common denominator of current presumed behavior among members of the profession abandons the aspirational aspects of ethics, abandons the prospective regulatory aspect of ethics, and creates real risk of self-fulfilling articulations of what behaviors are commonly accepted.

I worry that with respect to negotiation, therefore, the legal profession has put in place an ethical ratchet—one that exerts force only in the direction of fewer ethics.

References

Harry T. Edwards & James J. White, Problems, Readings and Materials on the Lawyer as Negotiator (1977).

Michael Moffitt, *Lights, Camera, Begin Final Exam: Testing What We Teach in Negotiation Courses*, 54 J. Legal Educ. 91 (2004).

Michael Moffitt, *Islands, Vitamins, Salt, Germs: Four Visions of the Future of ADR in Law Schools*, 25 Ohio St. J. on Disp. Resol. 25 (2010).

Alvin B. Rubin, *A Causerie on Lawyers' Ethics in Negotiation*, 35 La. L. Rev. 577 (1975).

James J. White, *The Lawyer as a Negotiator: An Adventure in Understanding and Teaching the Art of Negotiation*, 19 J. Legal Educ. 337 (1967).

Machiavelli and the Bar: J.J. White as Negotiation Ethics Architect

Peter R. Reilly

Professor White's seminal piece inspired my first law review article: *Was Machiavelli Right? Lying in Negotiation and the Art of Defensive Self-Help*. I continue to use White's article in the classroom for teaching about negotiation ethics because the piece sketches out core issues in a manner that is interesting, insightful, and, perhaps most important of all to my students: brief.

In choosing his title, Professor White reminds the reader there will always be some negotiators, whatever the percentage might be, who embrace the art of deception. As Niccoló Machiavelli wrote in *The Prince* nearly five hundred years ago, "[Y]ou must be a great liar . . . a deceitful man will always find plenty who are ready to be deceived" (Machiavelli, p. 50). There are many issues one might lie about in a negotiation, including: (1) the value of something (goods, services, etc.); (2) one's short-term or long-term goals; (3) the interests that underlie one's position in the negotiation; (4) one's bottom line; (5) one's willingness or ability to follow through on various threats or promises, for example, "I will see you in court!"; (6) one's alternatives to making a deal; (7) one's authority to bind his or her principal to particular deal terms; (8) the existence of other offers (or their terms) (Reilly, pp. 12–13).

On the first day of teaching my negotiation course, I tell the classic "orange" story from *Getting to Yes*, in which two fruit-loving siblings, both desiring the last available orange, resolve their dispute by cutting it down the middle, each taking half. The authors suggest that if the siblings had considered underlying interests—wherein one sibling was cooking and wanted only the peel, and the other sibling was hungry and wanted only the fleshy fruit—then both siblings could have achieved their entire goal rather than just half (Fisher, Patton, & Ury, p. 57). The story suggests that cooperation through information-sharing can lead to increased gains for both sides. As Robert Axelrod puts it, "[t]he key to doing well lies not in overcoming others, but in eliciting their cooperation" (Axelrod, p. 190).

But there's an important caveat to this line of thinking (and one that is sometimes undersold in the negotiation literature): engaging in cooperative and trusting behavior with other parties can potentially make one vulnerable to liars, even in simple and straightforward scenarios. Consider the situation, I tell my students, where my sister and I both want the last orange. I'm hungry, so my only true underlying interest is acquiring the fleshy fruit. My sister is cooking and wants only the peel. But even a small lie on my part can help me secure a superior deal:

ME: I want the orange.
MY SISTER: I want the orange, too.

Peter R. Reilly, Machiavelli and the Bar: *J.J. White as Negotiation Ethics Architect* In: *Discussions in Dispute Resolution*. Edited by: Art Hinshaw, Andrea Kupfer Schneider, and Sarah Rudolph Cole, Oxford University Press (2021). © Oxford University Press. DOI: 10.1093/oso/9780197513248.003.0008

ME: Why do you want the orange?
MY SISTER: I'm cooking, so I want the peel.
ME: I'm cooking, too, so it appears we both want the peel. If you leave me the fleshy fruit and also give me fifty cents, I'll postpone my cooking project and give you the entire peel.
MY SISTER: Deal!

By lying, I'm able to acquire the fleshy fruit—which is all I really wanted—as well as fifty cents, allowing me to buy more fruit. I ask my students if there is anything wrong, morally or ethically, with my lie. "After all," I argue, "the lie helped me surpass my goal, and, besides, what harm is there in making my sister think we both wanted to start a cooking project?" I then present to the class Professor White's proposition that "[t]o conceal one's true position, to mislead an opponent about one's true settling point, is the essence of negotiation" (p. 928). Some students enthusiastically agree with the proposition, saying something like, "I'm taking this course to learn whatever it takes to win." Others disagree and say something like, "Negotiation is not about deceit or dishonesty—it's about compromise and meeting in the middle."

I drill down deeper by again quoting Professor White's article: "On the one hand the negotiator must be fair and truthful; on the other he must mislead his opponent.... The critical difference between those who are successful negotiators and those who are not lies in this capacity both to mislead and not to be misled" (p. 927). For good measure, I emphasize White's warning that "[s]ome experienced negotiators will deny the accuracy of this assertion, but they will be wrong" (p. 927). To challenge Professor White's statement, I tell students the following (paraphrased) viewpoint espoused by a senior judge attending a negotiation training I once conducted for state court judges:

I never lie or mislead when I negotiate. I immediately tell the other side my bottom line. I tell them exactly what I need, and they can decide whether or not to give it to me. I consider any other approach to be engaging in a deceitful game.

I tell my students that I believe the essence of negotiation is information. Specifically, to what extent can one influence or persuade the other side to disclose, in a timely manner, complete and accurate information? A subset of that broader question involves untruth, dishonesty, or deceit. In other words, although anyone who gives testimony in a court of law is exhorted, and bound by law, to provide "the truth, the whole truth, and nothing but the truth," that is not the case in negotiation. Although trials take place in public, with transcribers, witnesses, and sometimes even recordings of the proceedings, negotiations usually occur in private, with the only record being the occasional set of notes scribbled by participants. A major part of the dance of negotiation, then, is figuring out what can be done to get the other side to disclose information that is comprehensive and truthful rather than incomplete, shaded, or simply untrue.

More than anything else, Professor White's article persuaded me that it is nearly impossible to draft a single norm or standard for ethical negotiations. As White puts it, "truth and truthful behavior at one time in one set of circumstances with one set of negotiators may be untruthful in another circumstance with other negotiators" (p. 929). White effectively sets forth many of the differences among negotiators—regional, ethnic, professional, and so forth—that can, in turn, result in differences with respect to negotiation truthfulness and candor. I concur with White's conclusion that "unless [the Model Rule drafters] wish to rely on the norms in the various subcultures in the bar to flesh out the rules, they will have to draft an extensive and complex body of rules" (p. 931).

In the end, Professor White suggests that the strict rule on truthfulness that was proposed in the January 30, 1980, discussion draft of the Model Rules might not be effective because (1) the words of the rule are subject to many different interpretations, (2) the rule conflicts with the idea that lawyers are zealously committed to their client's case; and (3) the rule might interfere with lawyers prevailing at trial or achieving optimal settlement results. These shortcomings, suggests White, might lead the rule to be "so widely violated as to be a continuing hypocrisy that may poison the application of the remaining rules" (p. 937). Ultimately the drafters did in fact water down the rule, replacing it with the less-restrictive Rule 4.1 as set forth in the May 30, 1981, proposed final draft of the Model Rules. I would guess (although it might be impossible to prove) that it was concerns set forth in *Machiavelli and the Bar* that helped convince the drafters to soften the rule.

There is another train of thought from *Machiavelli and the Bar* that appears to have influenced those writing the subsequent version of the Model Rules (i.e., the May 30, 1981, proposed final draft). Professor White argued in his piece that negotiators must be allowed "some deviation from truthfulness" in the following three situations: (1) "in asserting [one's] true opinion about cases, statutes, or the value of the subject of the negotiation in other respects"; (2) "in response to certain questions that are regarded as out of bounds"; and (3) "in circumstances where [one's] interest is great and the injury seems small" (pp. 934–35). In carving out these limited situations for less-than-complete truth-telling, Professor White appears to be suggesting that negotiation is in a sense a game that everyone knows and plays from early childhood onward and, given the dynamics of that game, there will be certain matters one should almost expect the other side to lie about. Given the similarities in form and content, it appears that Professor White's carveout idea might be the genesis for the following important caveat in the Comment section to Rule 4.1 (as set forth in the proposed final draft issued on May 30, 1981):

> Under generally accepted conventions in negotiation certain types of statements ordinarily are not taken as statements of fact. Estimates of price or value placed on the subject of a transaction and a party's intentions as to an acceptable settlement of a claim are in this category, and so is the existence of an undisclosed principal except where nondisclosure of the principal would constitute fraud.

Professor White concludes his article by pointing out that "[t]here are other, more formidable obstacles" to bringing about effective ethics rules for negotiation: such rules must ultimately be adopted and enforced—no small feat within America's fiercely independent and decentralized judicial system composed of a dizzyingly expansive assortment of courts, bar committees, and agencies at the local, state, and federal levels. As White puts it, "[t]o enact stern and righteous rules in Chicago will not fool the people in Keokuk. The public will not believe them, and the bar will not follow them" (p. 938). In the sixteen years since I started teaching negotiation in law schools,

I have observed what seems to be waning student support for negotiation ethics rules. Specifically, there have been more comments in class supporting a caveat emptor ethic of negotiation, along with a scrapping of all attorney-mandated rules and directives concerning negotiation behaviors and ethics.

Indeed, a small number of students from my business negotiation classes have even suggested, while discussing *Machiavelli and the Bar*, that the rules might have the unintended consequence of placing lawyers at a competitive disadvantage vis-à-vis their nonlawyer counterparts. To paraphrase these students, "why would businesses hire lawyers to negotiate on their behalf when those lawyers are bound by ethics rules that others sitting at the negotiation table are not forced to follow?" Other students have suggested it is simply too difficult to tell when a statement actually crosses (versus merely tiptoeing up to) the lines drawn by negotiation ethics rules—a conclusion very much in line with Professor White's declaration that "anyone who says he can consistently tell a 'puff' from a warranty is a fool or a liar" (White, Uniform Commercial Code § 9.4).

To me, *Machiavelli and the Bar* is seminal because it quickly orients students to some of the most central and important issues we'll be addressing the entire semester. The examples and hypotheticals used by Professor White engage students at both a theoretical and practical level, and the article effectively says to students, "This material will not be easy, but it will nevertheless be fun and interesting." Who could ask for more from a work of scholarship?

References

Robert Axelrod, The Evolution of Cooperation (1984).

Roger Fisher, William Ury, & Bruce Patton, Getting to Yes: Negotiating Agreement without Giving In (1991).

Niccolò Machiavelli, The Prince (Robert M. Adams trans., 1977) (1532).

Peter R. Reilly, *Was Machiavelli Right? Lying in Negotiation and the Art of Defensive Self Help*, 24 Ohio St. J. on Disp. Resol. 481 (2009).

James J. White & Robert S. Summers, Uniform Commercial Code (4th ed. 1995).

Machiavelli and the Bar: Prescient in Part

Lauren A. Newell

In *Machiavelli and the Bar*, Professor James J. White favors adoption of Model Rule 4.1, governing truthfulness in statements to others, but cautions that the Rule may be ineffective in practice. In doing so, White lays the groundwork for later empirical studies examining attorneys' compliance with the enacted Rule. This response compares White's predictions with those studies' findings. I conclude that White was right to be concerned about the Rule's efficacy, but not necessarily for the reasons he imagined.

I. The Language Compared

White's essay analyzes Rule 4.2(b)(2) of the January 30, 1980, Model Rules of Professional Conduct Discussion Draft. The proposed language required a lawyer not to

> make a knowing misrepresentation of fact or law, or fail to disclose a material fact known to the lawyer, even if adverse, when disclosure is ... necessary to correct a manifest misapprehension of fact or law resulting from a previous representation made by the lawyer or known by the lawyer to have been made by the client....

A modified version of Rule 4.2(b) was formally adopted in 1983 as Rule 4.1 of the Model Rules of Professional Conduct, which has remained essentially unchanged since its adoption:

> In the course of representing a client a lawyer shall not knowingly:
> (a) make a false statement of material fact or law to a third person; or
> (b) fail to disclose a material fact to a third person when disclosure is necessary to avoid assisting a criminal or fraudulent act by a client, unless disclosure is prohibited by Rule 1.6.

Rule 1.6 prohibits disclosure of client confidences without the client's informed consent, unless disclosure falls within one of the enumerated exceptions.

The proposed and adopted Rules are similar in concept, though not identical in phrasing. Both require disclosure of "material" facts. The adopted language is somewhat more straightforward, mandating disclosure to avoid assisting in "a criminal or fraudulent act," rather than "to correct a manifest misapprehension of fact or law." Also, the adopted Rule is expressly limited by the Rule protecting client confidences; the proposed Rule has no similar limitation.

Lauren A. Newell, Machiavelli and the Bar*: Prescient in Part* In: *Discussions in Dispute Resolution*. Edited by: Art Hinshaw, Andrea Kupfer Schneider, and Sarah Rudolph Cole, Oxford University Press (2021).
DOI: 10.1093/oso/9780197513248.003.0009

II. White's Predictions

White foresaw two significant difficulties in implementing Rule 4.1. The lesser of the two was the Rule's imprecision. White acknowledged that the Rule's language might be ambiguous in practice, leaving the Rule subject to varying interpretations and susceptible to a number of "line-drawing problems" (p. 936). Notably, lawyers would have to judge whether a fact was "material," whether a "manifest misapprehension" of fact or law had occurred, and whether that manifest misapprehension "resulted" from the lawyers' or clients' previous representations, thereby making the Rule's application less uniform (p. 936). White largely dismissed the imprecision concern as a problem inherent in this type of ethical rule, which must simply be tolerated.

The more important concern for White was that the Rule created tension between lawyers' disclosure obligations and their duty to be zealous advocates for their clients. Requiring a lawyer to disclose information even when detrimental to the client's case "asks the lawyer not only to act contrary to his selfish interests but also to violate the important psychological association with his client and his client's case" (p. 938). This tension is problematic because it sets lawyers up to fail: either they must choose to violate the Rule, or they must choose to sacrifice their own and their clients' interests. White posited that many lawyers would choose violation over sacrifice. That is, lawyers would consciously choose to disregard the Rule because it asked them to do something they were unwilling to do, whether for self-interested or client-focused reasons.

Thus, White's predictions were twofold: first, the Rule's interpretation would be part art and part science, making its application somewhat inconsistent. Second, lawyers might privilege successful client representation over ethical compliance, thereby undermining Rule 4.1 in particular and the Model Rules generally.

III. Empirical Work

Since White's essay was written, attorney negotiating ethics have been a frequent topic of academic discussion but seldom the subject of rigorous empirical work. The primary exception is a 2011 study of 734 practicing lawyers by Professors Art Hinshaw and Jess K. Alberts, which asked the lawyers how they would act in a hypothetical negotiation featuring a client who threatens to sue his ex-girlfriend for infecting him with a fatal sexually transmitted disease called DONS. Before the lawyers meet to negotiate a settlement, the client reveals to his lawyer that he is immune to DONS. He instructs his lawyer to proceed with the negotiation as though he were infected and not to disclose his immunity to opposing counsel (i.e., not to disclose a material fact where nondisclosure would constitute fraud). Hinshaw and Alberts asked the respondents what they would do in the negotiation.

Overall, approximately 30 percent of all respondents would agree not to disclose the information under at least some circumstances, 50 percent would comply with Rule 4.1 and disclose the information, and 20 percent were unsure how they would respond (Hinshaw & Alberts, p. 120). For my purposes, the important inquiry is not *how many* respondents would choose to violate Rule 4.1, but rather *why* they would do so. Hinshaw and Alberts's findings concerning the reasons for Rule 4.1 violations fall broadly into two buckets: problems comprehending the Rule, and problems reconciling the Rule with competing legal principles.

Regarding comprehension, 16 percent of respondents failed to recognize that the client's immunity was a material fact in this negotiation (Hinshaw & Alberts, p. 122). Moreover, only 61 percent of respondents correctly indicated that failing to disclose the client's DONS-negative status was a misrepresentation; the remaining 39 percent either believed it was not (26 percent) or were not sure (13 percent) (Hinshaw & Alberts, p. 123). Hinshaw and Alberts attribute their findings to "the considerable confusion among some attorneys regarding the elements of Rule 4.1" (Hinshaw & Alberts, p. 148). Similarly, in three other (though much smaller and less rigorous) surveys of lawyers in 1988, 2008, and 2009, a "large minority" of respondents reported they would handle hypothetical negotiation scenarios in ways that violated Rule 4.1, due partly to confusion regarding the ethical standards governing negotiation truthfulness (Hinshaw, Reilly, & Kupfer Schneider, pp. 284–85). The surveys' findings revealed a "disconcerting" "degree of confusion or misunderstanding" among practicing lawyers in applying the Rules (Hinshaw, Reilly, & Kupfer Schneider, p. 278).

Regarding reconciliation, the three most important rationales given by Hinshaw and Alberts's respondents for agreeing not to disclose the DONS-negative status were (1) their belief that Rule 1.6's protection of client confidences trumped their disclosure obligations; (2) their belief that attorney-client privilege protected the information; and (3) the fact that the client had requested that the information not be disclosed. Concern that disclosure would compromise their role as zealous advocates was rated as much less important. Taking the stated rationales at face value, Hinshaw and Alberts concluded that these lawyers understood Rule 4.1 but misunderstood its interrelation with competing ethical rules (Hinshaw & Alberts, p. 149). Similarly, Hinshaw et al. pointed to difficulties reconciling "the legal profession's two most cherished values: a commitment to the client and a commitment to justice" as a reason for the responding lawyers' willingness to engage in unethical negotiation behavior (Hinshaw, Reilly, & Kupfer Schneider, p. 278).

IV. Partial Prescience

Comparing White's predictions to the empirical evidence gathered thirty years later, we see that White's essay was prescient—in part. White was right that a substantial portion of lawyers might violate Rule 4.1 in the course of their negotiations. Yet he may have been right for the wrong reasons. In suggesting this, I am relying heavily on these few studies' findings because of the present dearth of empirical work, but more research is certainly necessary before drawing any firm conclusions.

White described the proposed Rule as "clear and explicit," though still predicted deviations in lawyers' application of the Rule (p. 935). White's prediction thus implies that lawyers would understand the Rule but would make conscious choices to reach different outcomes. Contrary to this prediction, the empirical evidence suggests that lawyers do not comprehend the Rule's elements and reach different conclusions because of their miscomprehension. Professor Charles B. Craver supports this interpretation, asserting that many lawyers' understanding of Rule 4.1 is partly inaccurate, while Professor Peter Reilly calls the Rule and related standards "far from crystal clear" (Craver, p. 726; Reilly, p. 533). In sum, White's prediction that lawyers' application of the Rule would vary seems to be correct, but the reason appears to be more confusion and misunderstanding on the lawyers' part than the deliberate choice and opportunistic line-drawing White foresaw.

White also predicted a scenario in which competitive, client-focused, yet highly self-interested lawyers understood the regulatory scheme but chose to violate the Rule to further their negotiation success. Again, White's prediction implies a degree of conscious choice in the lawyers' noncompliance. The previously referenced studies' findings suggest something different: a negotiating landscape in which lawyers want to follow the ethical rules but are confused about how to weigh conflicting parts of the regulatory scheme. Taking the lawyers' stated rationales for nondisclosure at face value, their noncompliance stems from misunderstanding the interplay between the disclosure and client confidence rules, not a deliberate, self-interested choice to disregard the disclosure rule when it is disadvantageous. Their confusion is likely attributable to the language in the adopted Rule 4.1 subjecting it to Rule 1.6, which was not present in the proposed language. While the proposed Rule "unequivocally resolves conflict between client confidentiality and disclosure," with disclosure trumping confidentiality, the adopted Rule calls upon lawyers to reconcile the two duties (p. 935). The end result is violation of Rule 4.1, as White predicted, but because of misapplication of the Rules, not overzealousness.

V. Knaves or Fools?

After comparing the predictions and the aftermath, I am left wondering which is better: lawyers who know the rules but ignore them to gain a negotiating advantage, or lawyers who do not understand the rules and who gain a negotiating advantage through their ignorance. Neither group is blameless, one having opted to do wrong (even if for a somewhat noble, client-centered purpose) and the other having failed to learn to do right. There is some vague comfort in the (perhaps naïve) notion that lawyers would comply with Rule 4.1 if they understood how to do so. This suggests legal negotiators would act more ethically if the Rule were further clarified, or if they were better educated about its workings, whereas White's essay suggests that Rule 4.1 will inevitably be violated because of something inherent in negotiation and in lawyers themselves.

White cautioned that "to draft effective ethical rules is close to impossible," and he urged the drafters "to make the appropriate trade-off between what is 'right' and what can be done" (p. 921). To know what can be done, we need to understand better how, when, and why Rule 4.1 violations occur. White's work is seminal because it predicts answers to these questions. Our field needs more empirical work to test those predictions.

References

Charles B. Craver, *Negotiation Ethics: How to Be Deceptive Without Being Dishonest/How to Be Assertive Without Being Offensive*, 38 S. Tex. L. Rev. 713–34 (1997).

Art Hinshaw & Jess K. Alberts, *Doing the Right Thing: An Empirical Study of Attorney Negotiation Ethics*, 16 Harv. Negot. L. Rev. 95–163 (2011).

Art Hinshaw, Peter Reilly, & Andrea Kupfer Schneider, *Attorneys and Negotiation Ethics: A Material Misunderstanding?*, Negot. J. 265–87 (July 2013).

Peter Reilly, *Was Machiavelli Right? Lying in Negotiation and the Art of Defensive Self-Help*, 24 Ohio St. J. on Disp. Resol. 481–534 (2008).

Confronting Lying in Negotiation

James J. White

Negotiation is not only the way lawyers determine what one will pay another in a traditional sale of an asset; it is also the method by which the great share of lawsuits are resolved. Because lying is private activity and because it is often richly rewarded, negotiation is a welcoming environment for a liar. This welcome is enhanced by the fact that deception, short of lying, is permissible and, indeed, at the heart of much negotiation. Worse, because the line between permissible deception and impermissible lying about material matters is indistinct, a liar can readily rationalize his behavior as permissible even when an objective person would find otherwise.

Some academics, a sprinkling of practicing lawyers and the American Bar Association (ABA) have bemoaned this state of affairs. Most would like to change lawyer behavior; a few may be more interested in changing the public's perception of sleaziness than in change of the actual practice. But what can be done?

I. The Model Rules

In the 1970s the ABA published model rules of Ethical Conduct. Among these rules in the early drafts was Section 4.2, "Fairness to Other Participants." This rule barred "knowing misrepresentation of fact or law, or fail[ure]l to disclose a material fact known to the lawyer . . ." The drafters bolstered and expanded the reach of Section 4.2 by adding two pages of comments on "Fairness, Disclosure, and Tactics." These comments even endorsed the maintenance of a "fair and courteous tenor."

This first draft of the new rules went beyond ethical rules: What does "courtesy" have to do with ethics? The rules also appeared to wander into the realm of permissible deceit by barring all "knowing misrepresentations of fact and law." For example, one might read those rules to bar dissembling about one's reservation price, yet most regard such dissembling as a perfectly permissible tactic.

In its final version, Section 4.1, the ABA wisely, bars only "false statements of material fact or law." The comments make clear that "certain statements ordinarily are not taken as statements of material fact." The same comment recognizes that "[e]stimates of price or value placed on the subject of a transaction and a party's intentions as to an acceptable settlement of a claim are ordinarily in this category . . ."

In my opinion the current version of 4.1 is about as good as one can do. It explicitly recognizes that parties may mislead and even make conscious misstatements of nonmaterial facts without violating the ethical standards. Having only twelve words, Section 4.1(a) is appropriately spare and has no needless words to court unintended interpretation.

James J. White, *Confronting Lying in Negotiation* In: *Discussions in Dispute Resolution.* Edited by: Art Hinshaw, Andrea Kupfer Schneider, and Sarah Rudolph Cole, Oxford University Press (2021). © Oxford University Press.
DOI: 10.1093/oso/9780197513248.003.0010

But what does 4.1 do on the battlefield of legal negotiation? Surely Rule 4.1 does not deter a determined liar even if the liar knows the rule. It might lead a negotiator in the way of righteousness if that person were not determined to lie. But how large is the cult of determined liars compared with the others? And how many negotiators understand the rule or ever consider it?

The empirical research gives some hints, but because of the impossibility of directly observing actual negotiations, the research is based on lawyers' answers to hypothetical cases. Of course, we assume that subjects, who freely admit to violation of 4.1 in such hypothetical cases where they have no skin in the game, will find it even easier to violate the rule where they do. The studies show an apparent willingness to deviate from the behavior dictated by 4.1 (Hinshaw et al. 2013; Hinshaw & Alberts 2009). The authors give the subjects the benefit of the doubt by attributing some of the deviation to ignorance of the rules. One study showed that the subjects, whether honest or not, were skeptical of the honesty of other lawyers. It is a fair summary of these studies to say that they do nothing to dispel the belief that lawyers frequently violate 4.1 in their professional negotiations.

II. What to Do?

If we conclude that rules such as 4.1 will have only a limited effect on lying, how should we train our students? Can we turn all of them into sour skeptics? And if we can, should we? My experience in teaching negotiation, where the outcomes in mock negotiations between students determined the students' grades, tells me that we can influence student expectations. At bottom, my class negotiations were not mock negotiations over a hypothetical lawsuit or sale of land; they were real negotiations for something valuable, namely, a good grade. I believe that the post-negotiation class discussion was sufficiently painful for some that it changed their behavior not only in later negotiations in the class but also in life.

We can also teach some of the protective practices used by good negotiators. First, one should collect whatever information is available about one's opposite number. Even in a large community of lawyers, each practitioner will leave a trail and often that trail can be dug up. Second, one should always have skepticism of assertions of the value of the item at hand, whether it is the price of grain in Moscow or the likely final position of a prosecutor in a plea bargain. Where comparable values can be found, one should not be too quick to pass them by. Third, one should protect his own reputation; a plaintiff's lawyer who never goes to trial will pay for that lack of exposure. Finally, a good negotiator should be slightly paranoid; that is, she should look backward, however uncomfortable that might be, to see if she achieved a good settlement in cases that never went to trial and in commercial deals that were made.

III. Conclusion

I concede first that my suggestions about negotiation rise barely to the level of platitudes, and second that these platitudes may be quickly forgotten and easily put aside in the busy practice of law. But to protect against another's dissembling requires more than a facile mind. Forget that at your risk.

References

Art Hinshaw & Jess K. Alberts, *Doing the Right Thing: An Empirical Study of Attorney Negotiation Ethics*, 16 Harv. Negot. L. Rev. 90 (2011).

Art Hinshaw, Peter Reilly, & Andrea Kupfer Schneider, *Attorneys and Negotiation Ethics: A Material Misunderstanding?*, 29 Negot. J. 265 (2013).

Article 1.3

Toward Another View of Legal Negotiation: The Structure of Problem Solving

Carrie Menkel-Meadow

31 UCLA Law Review 754 (1984)

Introduction

When people negotiate they engage in a particular kind of social behavior; they seek to do together what they cannot do alone. Those who negotiate are sometimes principals attempting to solve their own problems, or, more likely in legal negotiation, they are agents acting for clients, within the bounds of the law. . . .

In order to contrast the adversarial model with the problem-solving model several key concepts must be defined and criteria for evaluation of the models made explicit. . . . The models described here are based on orientations to negotiation, that is, how we approach our purpose in negotiation, rather than on the particular strategies or tactics we choose. . . . A general model demonstrates the relationship of negotiation orientations to negotiation results:

Orientation → Mind-set → Behavior → Results.

The orientation (adversarial or problem solving) leads to a mindset about what can be achieved (maximizing individual gain or solving the parties' problem by satisfying their underlying needs) which in turn affects the behavior chosen (competitive or solution searching) which in turn affects the solutions arrived at (narrow compromises or creative solutions).

* * *

C. Consequences of the Adversarial Assumptions. The Limits of Linearity

When negotiators adopt zero-sum conceptions of the problems or transactions they seek to resolve or plan, they unnecessarily limit themselves in a number of ways. First, by assuming single-issue negotiations in which parties value the single item

Carrie Menkel-Meadow, *Toward Another View of Legal Negotiation: The Structure of Problem Solving* In: *Discussions in Dispute Resolution*. Edited by: Art Hinshaw, Andrea Kupfer Schneider, and Sarah Rudolph Cole, Oxford University Press (2021).
 DOI: 10.1093/oso/9780197513248.003.0011

equivalently, they may fail to consider whether the parties have other needs or issues that consequently may go unresolved. Second, by focusing on maximizing immediate, individual gain, negotiators may fail to appreciate the long-term consequences of a particular solution.... Third, zero-sum, single-issue conceptions of negotiation problems often fail to consider transaction costs, both in terms of process costs to the client in the use of an adversarial approach and the costs of a less than optimal solution. The adversarial negotiation conception narrowly limits potential solutions by encouraging negotiators to develop mind-sets about possible solutions which include only court solutions or commonly used solutions that may not meet the parties' needs....

A. The Underlying Principles of Problem Solving. Meeting Varied and Complementary Needs

Parties to a negotiation typically have underlying needs or objectives-what they hope to achieve, accomplish, and/or be compensated for as a result of the dispute or transaction. Although litigants typically ask for relief in the form of damages, this relief is actually a proxy for more basic needs or objectives. By attempting to uncover those underlying needs, the problem-solving model presents opportunities for discovering greater numbers of and better quality solutions. It offers the possibility of meeting a greater variety of needs both directly and by trading off different needs, rather than forcing a zero-sum battle over a single item.

The principle underlying such an approach is that unearthing a greater number of the actual needs of the parties will create more possible solutions because not all needs will be mutually exclusive. As a corollary, because not all individuals value the same things in the same way, the exploitation of differential or complementary needs will produce a wider variety of solutions which more closely meet the parties' needs....

B. The Structure of Problem Solving

1. Identifying the Parties' Underlying Needs and Objectives

... [P]roblem solving begins by attempting to determine the actual needs of particular clients....

Ascertaining the client's needs will, of course, begin with the initial interview.... [I]n thinking ahead to the negotiation which might occur, a lawyer might begin by asking the client such general questions as "how would you like to see this all turn out?" or "what would you like to accomplish here?" before channeling the client's objectives in directions the lawyer knows are legally possible. The client may be the best source of ideas that go beyond what the court or the legal system might commonly permit. Once the client's ideas are brought to the surface, the lawyer can explore the needs they are meant to satisfy, and the legal and nonlegal consequences of these and other solutions.

Since so many legal problems are reduced to monetary solutions, consideration of the economic needs and objectives of the client faced with a dispute or transaction is a good place to begin. What are the monetary requirements now-compensation, return on investment, liquidity for payment? What might be the future monetary needs? What is the money needed for? Are any cheaper means available? Are there cash substitutes that are available and acceptable? What are the tax consequences of payment/receipt now? Later? What payment structure is desirable—lump sum, installments? Why? What are the transaction costs or solution costs of negotiation as opposed to litigation?

Next the lawyer might consider that with which she is most familiar—the legal issues....

The negotiator might consider how any solution affects the client's relationship to others.... The negotiator might also ask the client to consider the personal feelings generated by the dispute or transaction....

Finally, the negotiator might also consider the ethical concerns of the parties. How fair do they desire to be with each other? What are the consequences of acting altruistically or dishonestly now? In the future? Will there be feelings of guilt later for "taking advantage" of the other side? ...

Ideally, this framework for determining the parties' needs must be considered from both parties' perspectives. At the very least, it should encourage lawyers and clients to consider whether all the potential needs presented by a negotiation have been canvassed....

2. Creating solutions

a. Meeting the Parties' Needs Having identified the parties' needs one can begin the search for solutions with those that are suggested by the parties or that otherwise directly meet the parties' needs.

For example, in a personal injury case the injured plaintiff may have economic needs for compensation and rehabilitation costs that extend into the future. In such cases, structured settlements, paid over time, and according to a variety of formulas, may more closely meet the needs of the parties than a single lump sum payment....

b. Expanding the Resources Available Of course, the parties' needs will not be sufficiently complementary in all cases to permit direct solutions. Needs may conflict or there may be conflict over the materiel required to satisfy the needs. In addition to focusing on the parties' needs as a source of solutions, negotiators can attempt to expand the resources that the parties may eventually have to divide. In essence, this aspect of problem-solving negotiation seeks wherever possible to convert zero-sum games into non-zero-sum or positive-sum games. By expanding resources or the materiel available for division, more of the parties' total set of needs may be satisfied. Indeed, as the literature on legal transactions and the economic efficiency of such transactions makes clear, the parties come together to transact business precisely because their joint action is likely to increase the wealth available to both. To the extent that principles of wealth creation and resource expansion from transactional negotiation can be assimilated to dispute negotiation, the parties to a negotiation have the opportunity to help each other by looking for ways to expand what is available to them.

Various substantive strategies may increase the materiel available for distribution. Resources can be expanded by exploring what could be distributed, when it could be distributed, by whom it would be distributed, how it could be distributed and how much of it could be distributed....

C. The Process of Problem-Solving Negotiation

The process of problem-solving negotiation is likely to be very different from the linear, reciprocal concession patterns leading to compromise in adversarial negotiation. This section reviews how problem-solving negotiation processes are likely to differ from adversarial negotiation.

1. Planning

As the discussion thus far should indicate, the crux of the problem-solving approach is the conceptualization and planning which precede any execution of the negotiation. A problem-solving conception of negotiation should be distinguished from cooperative or collaborative negotiation. The latter refers to particular behaviors engaged in during the negotiation, such as "being flexible, disclosing information and establishing good relationships with the other negotiator." These behaviors may be useful in problem-solving negotiations, but they can also be used as tactics in adversarial negotiations where their purpose is to achieve greater individual gain. The conceptualization used in planning problem-solving negotiation is useful in all negotiation, regardless of the particular behaviors chosen in the executory stages. Planning may indicate that needs are truly incompatible and call for the use of adversarial strategies to maximize individual gain, or that resort to adjudication is necessary....

2. Execution

To the extent that both parties engage in a problem-solving negotiation structure, the negotiation is likely to resemble a fluid brainstorming session. Even if only one party has engaged in a problem-solving planning process, the negotiation need not be reduced to an adversarial exercise. First, the parties may begin with a greater number of possible solutions simply because two heads are better than one. In addition, as empirical research has demonstrated, when both parties approach negotiation with the objective of working collaboratively, more of the information reflecting the parties' needs may be revealed, facilitating the search for solutions.... On the other hand, even a single problem solver can propose alternative ways of measuring liability that may eventually be successful, if she has accurately determined the other party's needs....

Conclusion

This Article has outlined a systematic approach to legal negotiation premised on the notion that agreements will be more effective when the parties conceive of their purposes as solving the problem or planning the transaction, rather than winning or gaining unilateral advantage. The creative problem-solving approach outlined here depends on two structural components: (1) identifying the parties' underlying needs and objectives, and (2) crafting solutions, first by attempting to meet those needs directly, and second, by attempting to meet more of those needs through expanding the resources available. By utilizing such a framework for negotiations, the parties should recognize the synergistic advantage of such an approach over the adversarial and manipulative strategies of zero-sum negotiations. Parties should be able to achieve solutions to disputes that would not have been possible in court-ordered resolutions.

The argument for problem-solving negotiation depends on two major propositions. The first is that in a court system which is authorized primarily to award only polarized decisions and limited remedies, the parties will be able to better craft solutions outside of the official legal arena where greater variability can be achieved. Second, by seeking to expand resources before dividing them, the parties may accomplish better results for themselves individually and increase the joint gain to both.

***

The attraction of the problem-solving approach to negotiations is that it returns the solution of the problem to the client and forces the lawyer to perform her essential role in the legal system-that of solving problems. By using her professional expertise to canvas possible solutions to the problems and by constantly referring back to the client's real needs and objectives, the lawyer can make the negotiation process more responsive, while at the same time reducing the client's desire for potentially destructive unilateral victory. . . .

In focusing on problem solving for mutual gain, the lawyer will execute one of her obligations to the society that charters her profession. By decreasing the pressure on the official dispute resolution machinery in situations where mandatory, authoritative, and dichotomous results are not required, the lawyer increases the efficiency of the total dispute resolution system. And, perhaps by helping the parties articulate their real needs and objectives, legal negotiators will increase participation in the decision-making process with less destructive conflict between all those involved than currently exists within our assumptions of adversarial bargaining. By viewing legal negotiation as an opportunity to solve both the individual needs and problems of their clients, and the broader social needs and problems of the legal system, negotiators have an opportunity to transform an intimidating, mystifying process into one which will better serve the needs of those who require it. Whether or not this will work, we don't yet know. But what can we lose by trying?

Comments

We Are All Problem Solvers Now

Russell Korobkin

I. A Paradigm Shift

Time was, negotiation—at least in the professional sphere—was understood as a zero-sum process in which buyers and sellers, or plaintiffs and defendants, would stake out extreme opening positions, haggle relentlessly, and compromise somewhere in the middle in order to reach a grudging agreement. Howard Raiffa famously labeled this the "negotiation dance."

Over the past generation, the academic community has come to understand this view of negotiation as entirely "distributive" in nature, as being descriptively incomplete and, more importantly, prescriptively suboptimal. Carrie Menkel-Meadow's *Toward Another View of Legal Negotiation: The Structure of Problem Solving* was one of a handful a works in the early 1980s—and the singular work aimed specifically at lawyers and legal scholars—that changed this paradigm, redirecting the field of negotiation theory from what Menkel-Meadow calls the "adversarial" approach to what she labels "problem solving." The lasting importance of an academic article can often be identified, in hindsight, by just how obvious the thesis seems today. We are all problem solvers now. Of course. How could we ever have thought any differently? In the twenty-first century, there really is no competing paradigm at all. I can think of no higher praise than this.

It would be hard to overstate not only the extent to which this shift has been accepted by the academic community but also the importance of this paradigm shift. Zero-sum haggling remains common in the work-a-day practice of law, with plaintiffs' lawyers demanding a king's ransom to sign away their claims, defendants' lawyers offering minuscule "nuisance value" in response, and hours then spent with both sides locked in mortal combat over a single issue—usually money. But nearly every lawyer who studies negotiation in law school, either in a stand-alone course devoted to the subject or an aspect of more general clinical course in legal practice, is now taught that this is not a normatively desirable approach to dealmaking or dispute resolution. Instead of focusing all of their energy on dividing the gains-of-trade (or "cooperative surplus") that can be generated if parties reach a negotiated agreement, negotiators should try to increase that cooperative surplus by designing agreements in ways that permit both parties to obtain *most* of the value that they seek. Or, to use the popular metaphor, good negotiators focus at least as much attention (and probably more) on expanding the size of the pie rather than dividing the pie. The bigger the pie, the more likely both parties can be satisfied.

Russell Korobkin, *We Are All Problem Solvers Now* In: *Discussions in Dispute Resolution*. Edited by: Art Hinshaw, Andrea Kupfer Schneider, and Sarah Rudolph Cole, Oxford University Press (2021).
DOI: 10.1093/oso/9780197513248.003.0012

Toward Another View pushes beyond this fundamental normative point by explaining just how this goal is achieved: specifically, by seeing negotiation as an opportunity to address the parties' core needs that are often buried below stated demands that they receive more money, or pay less money, or otherwise get more of a divisible asset that is of equal value to both sides.

II. Deeper Insights

Toward Another View is primarily an article about a big idea, and that idea is its principle legacy. But it also packs a tremendous amount of texture and nuance. Each time I return to it, as I have regularly over the two decades in which I have taught and written about negotiation, I find new insights to appreciate. I will mention just three of these here.

First, Menkel-Meadow explains that problem-solving is not just a different way of conducting negotiations, but a different way of understanding the fundamental task of negotiation. The adversarial approach leads to competitive, agent-focused mindset, in which the negotiator strategizes how she can conduct the negotiation dance to maximize her benefit alone. The problem-solving approach, in comparison, requires the negotiator to think deeply, and be concerned with satisfying, both parties' needs (pp. 775–78, 794).

This fundamental difference in mindset means that problem solvers are not only more likely to imagine creative solutions when they prepare to negotiate, they are more likely to avoid competitive, reactive dynamics at the bargaining table that can stifle cooperation and harm relationships. To take one example, when neighbors experience a conflict because one prefers to play his stereo loudly while the other craves quiet, a problem-solver might suggest the former wear headphones or the latter use earplugs (pp. 807–9). But even if these solutions don't work in a particular case (he likes to dance while listening to music; her ear canals are sensitive to the earplugs), the problem-solving orientation can provide a platform for them to search for other mutually agreeable solutions rather than turning to lawsuits.

Second, Menkel-Meadow's broad range of examples demonstrates that problem-solving is a productive approach in dispute settlement negotiations as well as in transactional settings. In my experience, it is far easier to convince negotiation students of the value of a problem-solving orientation when they are negotiating a deal, where it is easier to spot a range of needs and differences in preference intensities, than in dispute settings, in which one party has filed a claim demanding money and the other wants to pay as little as possible.

Menkel-Meadow makes two important and distinct, although related, points here. The first point is that money is only a means to satisfy other material ends, which can often be satisfied in different ways, and at greater or lesser cost. When negotiators look beyond dollars to underlying needs, what appears on its face to be a single-issue, zero-sum dispute over money often yields to a multilayered analysis (pp. 795, 798). To use one of Menkel-Meadow's examples, a personal injury plaintiff might demand money, but he wants money to buy a new car, and the defendant might have a cost advantage in providing such a car (pp. 787–88).

The second point is that monetary demands often cloak nonmaterial, psychological, and social needs, which a problem-solving approach has the potential to satisfy for the mutual benefit of the parties. While a plaintiff might request money to pay for physical rehabilitation, a job that provides both rehabilitation and "psychological self-worth which accompanies employment" might satisfy the plaintiff's full panoply of needs far better than a cash payment (p. 798).

Third, Menkel-Meadow explains that while an adversarial negotiator uses the same type of agent-focused, assertive skills as a courtroom lawyer, the problem-solving paradigm to negotiation calls for a different set of professional skills and worldview (pp. 789–92). This calls into question, and perhaps uncomfortably for the bar, whether trial lawyers should be the agents negotiating out-of-court settlement agreements. "[I]t may be unwise," Menkel-Meadow writes, for "the ten percent of cases which are tried [to] control the types of solutions which are achieved in the other ninety percent of cases" (p. 792). While the transaction costs of having to bring a second (litigation) agent up to speed on the details of a dispute if settlement negotiations fail might be sufficient to justify the dominant litigator-as-negotiator-and-trial-attorney model of dispute resolution, Menkel-Meadow's observations suggest this issue is due a more serious debate than it has yet to receive in the legal profession.

III. Refinements and Limitations

As is true for many, if not most, paradigm-shifting innovations, *Toward Another View*, in succeeding beyond what I expect were Menkel-Meadow's wildest hopes at the time it was published, might have pushed the pendulum slightly too far away from what was the conventional wisdom at the time. This is no slight to the article, much less to its author: excessive qualifications to its bold claim would have likely reduced the article's impact. But here I propose a few modest modifications—which I consider friendly amendments—to the scope of what is now the (uncontested) dominant paradigm.

First, bilateral negotiations between principal parties or their lawyers take place within a complex web of economic relationships that make up a market economy, and where there are many alternatives, the problem-solving approach is sometimes neither necessary or even desirable. Although it is generally correct that parties would be better off seeking an agreement that will directly satisfy underlying needs rather than haggling over money, they will, in some circumstances, be best served by dividing the pie and using their resulting share to transact with third parties to satisfy their individual interests, rather than looking to their counterpart in the focal negotiation to satisfy those interests.

For example, Menkel-Meadow points out that a plaintiff buyer who purchased a car with mechanical problems but badly needs transportation and a defendant car dealer might both be better off if the plaintiff sacrifices on her uncertain fraud claim and the dealer provides a loaner car from his inventory to help her get to work (pp. 773–74). In a world made up of just these two actors, this is undoubtedly true. But the parties' total welfare might actually be maximized if they settle the claim for 50 cents on the dollar and the plaintiff rents a car from a third party (who perhaps has a car more desirable to the plaintiff and can transact with her without the relationship baggage) while the defendant sells the car it has in stock to a different potential buyer who covets that particular model. This will not be the case when the negotiators' relationship is better described as a bilateral monopoly: plaintiffs cannot agree to confidentiality clauses with parties other than the defendant; divorcing spouses cannot sell weekend days with their children to a third party and use the proceeds to buy weekday visitation with other children. But my point is that the relative value of the problem-solving paradigm depends on the existence (or lack thereof) of potential third-party negotiation partners.

Second, commercial customs often evolve to automatically provide Pareto-efficient solutions to common problems, thus obviating the need for negotiators to identify problem-solving solutions in individual negotiations. Menkel-Meadow correctly points out that standard-form contract terms and the ubiquitous "industry custom" can hinder creative problem-solving by channeling transactions in ways that fail to take advantage of mutually advantageous trade-offs (p. 792), but these institutions also often routinize efficient trade-offs and reduce the need for (and value of) individual negotiators demonstrating good problem-solving skills.

For example, defendants who are repeat litigants will usually value the secrecy of settlements more than plaintiffs will value the ability to brag about their success. This means that adding a confidentiality clause to a settlement agreement can satisfy an important need of the defendant at relatively low cost to the plaintiff and thus increase the deal's joint value. But the fact that confidentiality is usually important to defendants has led to confidentiality clauses becoming a customary and often expected features of many types of civil settlements, such that confidentiality clauses are written into "off the shelf" settlement agreements. The upshot is that neither side has to conduct an assessment of the parties' needs and then suggest adding such a term—it is already there (a fact that leads to some consternation when such a clause in a case of public interest is reported in the media).

Third, the value created by a problem-solving orientation to negotiation can, ironically, increase the need for distributive bargaining rather than eliminate it, especially where side-payments are possible (which they usually are). If the plaintiff asks for $20,000 because she needs a new car, the problem-solving model suggests the defendant should provide a car if he can do so at a lower cost. Fair enough, but the plaintiff might reasonably ask why the defendant should keep all of the cost savings rather than sharing it with the plaintiff, probably through a cash transfer, and they will probably have to haggle over that cooperative surplus. In some types of negotiations, there are social norms against cash side-payments (for example, in Menkel-Meadow's wonderful hypothetical of a husband who prefers to vacation in the mountains and a wife who prefers the seashore selecting a mountain resort on a lake where hiking and swimming are both available (p. 799)), but even in those cases there is usually the possibility of in-kind side-payments that are primarily distributive in nature (who should get to choose the restaurant at which to dine at the mountain resort when the spouses prefer different types of cuisine?).

***

The problem-solving paradigm described in *Toward Another View* cannot eliminate adversarialism, a certain amount of which is unavoidable as long as people use negotiation as a means of obtaining the support of others for the achievement of their goals. But it continues, thirty-five years later, to provide the most useful analytical structure that we have for charting a course for navigating this most fundamental of human interactions.

It's Not the Lawyers We Need to Convince: Commentary on *Legal Negotiation* by Carrie Menkel-Meadow

Erin R. Archerd

Legal Negotiation may be a magnum opus, but it was only the opening salvo in career now spanning four decades. So many of the ideas and themes that came to mark Carrie Menkel-Meadow's career are here, reflected largely in the meticulously researched literature review that plays out in the footnotes: women and the law, social science and human behavior, and the importance of ethics. And that's just the footnotes.

The main text provides a comprehensive overview of negotiation theory, in which Menkel-Meadow illustrates the distributive/integrative divide, the dangers of competitive negotiation strategies, and the limitations of negotiating based on perceived legal outcomes. Alas, for this contracts professor, her proposed turn of phrase "bargaining in the shadow of the form contract" never caught on like "bargaining in the shadow of the law," but her key linguistic contribution in this article certainly did—the lawyer as problem solver (p. 766).

A major limitation with the old models of negotiation, Menkel-Meadow explains, is that they inhibit creativity. They force negotiators to be competitive and reactive rather than creative and proactive. She argues that adversarial models narrow the range of possible solutions because they fail to exploit differences in values between the parties that can lead to additional solutions. Problem-solving negotiation becomes a creative exercise of uncovering the underlying needs of the parties to come up with more and better solutions to the problem.

Yet even thirty-five years after Menkel-Meadow wrote this article, many lawyers still treat a problem-solving, interest-based approach as the exception rather than the rule. While most law schools now have courses in alternative dispute resolution (ADR) or negotiation, in which students are exposed to interest-based negotiation concepts, few law schools require students to take these courses or include much exposure to negotiation in their first-year curriculums. When I ask my ADR students why they are taking my course, many respond along the lines of "Because I'm more interested in being a problem solver than a fighter." The lawyer as problem solver, at least, is a practice model that students have available to them, but even a generation after Menkel-Meadow's article, lawyers are still not comfortable fully employing the interest-based approach she suggests.

Some of this may be the result of the difficulty in changing long-standing practices in legal education, but much of it may come from the continuing discomfort of lawyers to fully embrace interest-based, problem-solving negotiation. *Legal Negotiation*—and much of the dispute resolution literature—is aimed at educating lawyers about the

Erin R. Archerd, *It's Not the Lawyers We Need to Convince: Commentary on* Legal Negotiation *by Carrie Menkel-Meadow*
In: *Discussions in Dispute Resolution.* Edited by: Art Hinshaw, Andrea Kupfer Schneider, and Sarah Rudolph Cole, Oxford University Press (2021). © Oxford University Press. DOI: 10.1093/oso/9780197513248.003.0013

power of problem-solving, but what is largely missing is a realistic plan for educating clients about why they should want their lawyers to use this approach.

After four decades of promoting the role of lawyer-as-problem-solver, shouldn't the type of in-depth client interviewing and counseling that Menkel-Meadow proposes have permeated more deeply into our legal culture? What is it about the problem-solving approach that is still so difficult or counterintuitive for lawyers? Even lawyers who embrace problem-solving negotiation rarely dig into their clients' interests to the extent Menkel-Meadow advocates for in *Legal Negotiation*.

Legal Negotiation does not present an easy approach, in which a few maxims and handy strategies allow lawyers to swiftly tap the potential of interest-based negotiation. Menkel-Meadow's problem-solving model requires that lawyers acquire a deep understanding of their clients' needs. She begins by offering simple, open-ended questions for clients, like, "How would you like to see this all turn out?" Then, she suggests lawyers discuss economic needs, transition to legal issues, and consider the client's relationships, personal feelings, and ethical considerations.[1]

These first few categories—economics, legal claims, and continuing relationships—will strike today's legal negotiators as obvious, but the latter categories—feelings and ethics—are ones that lawyers shy away from in their discussions with clients. In examining feelings, she asks things like, "What are [clients'] motivations for pursuing their aims in the negotiation?" and in questioning ethics she asks, "What are the consequences of acting altruistically or dishonestly now.... Will there be feelings of guilt later for 'taking advantage' of the other side?"[2]

Her discussion of understanding client needs is not the focus of her article, but without gaining a comfort with this step, how are lawyers supposed to build a foundation for their legal negotiations?

Topics like feelings and personal ethics are hard to picture many lawyers raising with clients. If a lawyer needs to understand these to problem-solve with clients, then we need to do more as a profession to prepare clients to expect these kinds of questions from lawyers and encourage lawyers to ask these questions. Instead, lawyers outsource these questions to other professionals, and many lawyers continue to avoid using interest-based negotiation models.

Rather than harnessing the power of an interest-based approach, lawyers still worry that they or their clients will look soft if they appear to be considering more than economic interests, and so they either do not consider them, or refrain from discussing them, during settlement negotiations, and even during discussions with their clients.

As a mediator as well as an attorney by training, I wonder if lawyers have ceded some of the power of an interest-based negotiation approach to mediators. In situations where lawyers could, or should, use an interest-based approach, they choose not to, thinking they can save the "win-win" touchy-feely talk for when they are called upon to mediate their case.

Attorneys' continued lack of consideration of the full spectrum of client concerns in negotiations has allowed other ADR processes to thrive in areas where emotional and ethical concerns are common. One area that might best illustrate this ceding of control to mediators—as well as a move by attorneys to regain their place in field—is family law. Mediation has become a common way of resolving family law disputes like divorce, and spouses frequently use this process without attorneys present. As the use of mediators in divorce disputes grew, attorneys began to develop the process of collaborative lawyering, in which divorcing spouses' attorneys agree to work together using an interest-based model to negotiate a divorce settlement.

Yet collaborative lawyers create the space for their discussions by agreeing they won't litigate on behalf of their clients if a collaborative settlement fails. Isn't the point of *Legal Negotiation* and the lawyer as problem solver that lawyers should be finding ways to incorporate interest-based approaches in their day-to-day legal negotiations without removing litigation as an alternative? Does the lawyer as problem solver require a level of inquiry into and candor about parties' core concerns that lawyers will simply never be comfortable providing? A level of inquiry that essentially requires taking litigation off the table before attorneys are able to fully embrace it?

Today, the greatest barrier to problem-solving negotiation may come from clients, many of whom still carry the image of lawyer as hired gun. Clients hire lawyers to fight for them against another party who has wronged them in some way. They want the "shot across the bow" that will alert the other side that they are serious about their dispute, or they want a fighter to protect them from the aggression of the other side, or they hire lawyers to make sure that advantageous deals are struck.

Even though law schools have begun to educate lawyers about their role as problem solvers, they have not effectively educated the public to change its expectations of lawyers' role. Lawyers must please their clients, and when the client is paying for a fighter, it can be frustrating to have the conversation turn to seemingly soft factors like relational interests and alternatives to a litigated outcome. Menkel-Meadow suggests that incorporating notions of morality and justness are what separate a problem-solving model from an adversarial model, but *Legal Negotiation* never seems to fully confront how hard it will be for lawyers to talk about these topics with their clients.[3]

The most difficult conversations are not with the other side, but with the client. In order to have the conversation about the client's interests and concerns, the lawyer must broach the delicate subject of not litigating the case; in essence, the lawyer has to explain to the client that she is not going to do what clients think they are paying her to do. Rather than sue, she is likely going to settle, and in order to settle most effectively, she is going to have to take the client's time and money getting to know the client rather than (or in addition to) drafting motions to badger the other side. The client may well see this process as unnecessary, a waste of time, or even as a form of unethical bill-padding—after all, she doesn't need to pay a lawyer to explore her feelings and interests; she has hired a lawyer to file a lawsuit (or defend against one). And even if the lawyer does convince her client that it is worth the client's time to explore feelings and ethics, the lawyer needs to have a counterpart representing the other side who *also* has a client who approves of a more collaborative negotiation posture. How to signal this is one of the fundamental problems of interest-based negotiation.

This seeming ceding of interest-based negotiation techniques from lawyers to mediators or other neutrals, then, is eminently sensible. To maintain the role of zealous advocate in the eyes of the client who still expects his lawyer to be aggressive and adversarial, the lawyer needs to have the procedural cover to change roles to the problem solver. When a judge or a mediator says to a client something like, "This could go either way; you need to consider the emotional costs of litigation," it creates the opening to have conversations about feelings and ethical concerns. The answer to why the lawyer as problem solver has not been more widely adopted, then, is much broader than the training or temperament of lawyers. It is the education of the general public about how lawyers ought to behave.

Legal Negotiation requires both greater patience and greater self-confidence than many lawyers may possess, not so much with respect to other lawyers, but with respect to clients. It requires that lawyers push back against their own clients, to convince them to see beyond their anger and explore their own interests. It calls on that lawyer to spend the time to get to know his client's interests beyond the information seemingly needed to file and litigate a claim or to complete the transaction at hand, even though clients might view these discussions as a waste of time. And when lawyers get to the negotiation table, it requires a level of psychological sensitivity and verbal fluency in interactions with both clients and the opposing side that many lawyers may fear they do not possess.

So why is it in a *lawyer's own interest* to have the difficult conversation with her client about settlement using a problem-solving approach that embraces topics like feelings and personal morality? The best decisions are rarely made in anger. If, after having taken the time to seriously explore settlement, the client still wants to litigate, then an attorney can feel confident that the client is prepared for the hardships of litigation—the time, money, and stress that a lawsuit can bring. Clients need to understand that these questions are critical and necessary preparation to resolve any dispute. Law schools and the practicing bar need to do more to educate the public about lawyers' role in resolving disputes outside of the courtroom.

It's not the lawyers we need to convince of the value of problem-solving. It's the public.

Counseling about More Than the Law

Andrea Kupfer Schneider

At the end of Professor Menkel-Meadow's landmark article, she notes "the attraction of the problem-solving approach to negotiations is that it returns the solution of the problem to the client and forces the lawyer to perform her essential role in the legal system—that of solving problems" (p. 841). While most view this article as a call to change the mindset of lawyers to engage in the problem-solving method of negotiation, I want to focus on its underlying message—a lawyer's essential role includes counseling about more than the law. In fact, as this article was being written in the early 1980s, the Kutak Commission added Model Rule 2.1, authorizing attorneys to counsel clients about the consequences of their actions beyond the law. Professor Menkel-Meadow gives us the road map to do that. Moreover, Professor Menkel-Meadow's explanation is even more compelling, because it is based on a shift in mindset and is the first to utilize interdisciplinary literature.

I. Assumptions of an Adversarial Model and the Narrowing of Disputes

Professor Menkel-Meadow argues that the paucity of empirical studies led to an assumption of an adversarial model of legal negotiation that, like Hobbes might say, was nasty, brutish, and short—or, as she puts it, "manipulative, competitive and adversarial" (p. 781). While recognizing "the difficulty with this zero-sum approach to negotiation is not that it is necessarily wrong in all cases," she asserts that this assumption "has become the tail that wags the dog" (p. 784). Adversarialism itself had become the focus of negotiation rather than the purposes of the negotiation itself.

Menkel-Meadow's own characterization of her article (and *Getting to Yes*) is that these works both correct that assumption and notes that lawyers have the potential to transform disputes "back into what they were before the legal system narrowed them" (Menkel-Meadow 1985, p. 34). In her 1985 article, Menkel-Meadow explains that lawyers can either narrow or expand a dispute's scope in stages—and, in fact, the lawyer's role in defining, channeling, and labeling may happen in the client interview, when the lawyer starts negotiating on the client's behalf, in the pleadings to the court, and in arguments to the court. Lawyers, overly influenced by adjudication, tend to view these disputes in a narrow, winner-take-all binary way (Riskin 1982). Therefore, as Menkel-Meadow puts it, "[The] '[r]eal' needs of the parties in dispute are not exposed, explored, and resolved" (Menkel-Meadow 1985, p. 33). Her call for lawyers to shift their mindset is the most well-known part of this article.

Andrea Kupfer Schneider, *Counseling about More Than the Law* In: *Discussions in Dispute Resolution*. Edited by: Art Hinshaw, Andrea Kupfer Schneider, and Sarah Rudolph Cole, Oxford University Press (2021). © Oxford University Press.
DOI: 10.1093/oso/9780197513248.003.0014

II. Interdisciplinary Basis

A second contribution from this article is its use of interdisciplinary literature to illuminate how legal negotiations operate. The literature review of empirical studies in psychology, economics, political science, game theory, decision theory, international relations, and others now seems de rigueur. Today, most negotiation textbooks delve into these subjects, affirming that one must understand these disciplines to be a knowledgeable and effective negotiator. This was not the case in the early days of negotiation teaching in law schools, and it arguably took another decade or two before it became mainstream legal negotiation material. From the first client meeting to formulating a negotiation strategy with the client to the negotiation itself, Professor Menkel-Meadow exhorts lawyers to use these empirical findings to become better negotiators.

Professor Menkel-Meadow was also writing at the crossroads of three different streams of legal thought: the clinical movement (based on observation, teaching, and psychological research), the Law and Society movement (with sociology, psychology, and anthropology informing how we perform lawyering tasks), and the nascent alternative dispute resolution (ADR) movement (she mediated in California during the early 1980s). Her impact endures because she weaves these different threads to tell a new story of lawyering skills, processes, and outcomes.

III. The Unheralded Focus on Lawyering Skills to Better Counsel Clients

Yet it is the focus on the client's needs in problem-solving, and the impact of this focus on both client counseling and negotiation, that makes this article so useful and transformative. As Professor Menkel-Meadow defines the importance of the problem-solving approach, she grounds her argument in what was then an evolving approach to client counseling. In the early 1980s, as the clinical movement gained traction, client counseling texts argued for a client-centered approach rather than a more hierarchical approach. Professor Menkel-Meadow's article is strongly anchored in the client counseling literature of the day, quoting Walter Lehman's formative article on client interests (Lehman 1979) and the emerging interviewing and counseling materials from David Binder and others that developed from clinical teaching (see, e.g., Binder & Price 1977).

With this client-centric focus, there are three key lessons: (1) the client's needs are paramount; (2) these needs will potentially be more than merely legal or monetary; and (3) it is the lawyer's job to find this out and explore, with the client, what are those underlying needs and goals. Professor Menkel-Meadow's argument for problem-solving is based on the idea that this approach would likely meet the client's actual needs better than the limited, linear, and narrow thinking required by an adversarial approach.

The article reflects the thinking of the then newly adopted Model Rule 2.1, which states that when giving advice to the client, the lawyer "may refer not only to the law but to other considerations such as moral, economic, social and policy factors that may be relevant to the client's situation" (ABA 1984). (And Professor Menkel-Meadow might have replaced "may" with "should," given her preferences.) The Rule's advice is effectively accomplished through the type of interviewing and counseling skills outlined in the article. In fact, the second comment to the Rule notes that "[a]dvice couched in narrow legal terms may be of little value to the client, especially where practical considerations, such as cost or effects on other people, are predominant" (Comment 2, ABA 1984).

Her call to lawyers to adopt a problem-solving approach and to advise their clients of consequences beyond the narrow legal outcome was an attempt to change the norms of legal practice. This work requires more client interaction and deeper investigation into the client's desires in a potentially different way. One of the article's most important contributions is that plan for *how* attorney-client interactions need to change—from the initial interview to the counseling to the decision to settle—as each of these are stages in a more complex and interactive process.

At the interview stage, Menkel-Meadow outlines that questions need to start with the broad—How would you like to see this all turn out?—before narrowing to the client's issues. Even if the focus becomes monetary, one can remember to continue asking questions—What is the money for? Are there cash substitutes? What are the transaction costs? Is there a desired payment structure? And then the lawyer can delve into the legal claims—Are there relevant regulations? Is an admission of liability necessary? Menkel-Meadow outlines more interview questions illustrating a problem-solving approach—What are the parties' relational concerns, psychological needs (Does one party need vindication?), and ethical worries? All of these suggestions are designed to keep the lawyer focused on client needs versus what the lawyer might assume are the client interests. And this understanding of the client's needs is necessary in order to properly counsel about more than the law.

Once we understand these needs, the move to creating solutions requires more consideration than those produced by a typical adversarial approach. Menkel-Meadow's suggestions—trading off interests, logrolling, expanding the available resources, and looking for solutions based on criteria—are obvious to current readers since these ideas are so well integrated into the negotiation literature today. As Menkel-Meadow notes, in a lease, a typical lawyer might negotiate with a commercial landlord for a low monthly rent based on a percentage of gross income. But your client—starting a new business—might be helped more by a low percentage rate at the beginning of the lease (when cash flow is low) and a higher rate later when the business is predicted to be more successful. Similar examples now are ubiquitous in the negotiation literature—demonstrating how much this thinking is embedded in negotiation training. Yet at the time, the idea that lawyers might do more than advocate for a better position was missing from the legal literature.

The article's next section outlines how "the crux of the problem-solving approach is the conceptualization and planning which precede any execution of the negotiation" (p. 818). In other words, while a typical lawyer and client might plan to engage regarding the positions to take in the negotiation, a problem-solving lawyer will meet with the client to review her needs (as outlined previously) and to start brainstorming the solutions that might satisfy those needs. Additionally, they will assess the other side's needs to recognize any additional information needed from the other side to find a more flexible solution.

Even when only one party uses the problem-solving method, Menkel-Meadow notes that shifting the negotiation is possible through offering several solutions to encourage joint brainstorming. The article further explains that information-sharing must go back and forth. Limiting information as much as possible (as in the adversarial model) or completely sharing all information are both dysfunctional. Menkel-Meadow's reliance on communication and psychological theories to demonstrate this method's utility is persuasive.

Menkel-Meadow closes by noting that the different interpersonal behaviors or approaches used by negotiators—for example, cooperating or compromising or competing—are separate from the analysis of a client's needs. These are distinct choices the lawyer makes after consulting with the client, establishing goals and mindsets, and then considering which orientation will be effective. The point is to identify the problem to be solved and the needs that must be met to achieve a solution. After completing this essential analysis, the negotiator may then choose the interpersonal behaviors that are most likely to help her to continue problem-solving. And, it is not foreordained that the negotiator should behave cooperatively, as that negotiator can undermine effective problem-solving just as much as an overly competitive negotiator.

For me, this article is foundational not only because it makes the claim that problem-solving can achieve better negotiation outcomes but also because it outlines exactly how the lawyer needs to behave to make this happen. And in doing so, it provides an added benefit—illustrating the skill set needed for lawyers to be more complete counselors to their clients to more effectively fulfill their, at that time, new obligations to do so under the Model Rules.

References

David Binder & Susan Price, Legal Interviewing and Counseling (1977).

Roger Fisher & William Ury, Getting to Yes 3–8 (1981).

Walter Lehman, *The Pursuit of a Client's Interest*, 77 Mich. L. Rev. 1078 (1979).

Carrie Menkel-Meadow, *Transformation of Disputes by Lawyers: What the Dispute Paradigm Does and Does Not Tell Us*, 1985 J. Disp. Resol. 25 (1985).

Leonard L. Riskin, *Mediation and Lawyers*, 43 Ohio St. L.J. 29 (1982).

The Origins of Problem-Solving Negotiation and Its Use in the Present

Carrie Menkel-Meadow

I. Multiple Origins of a Search and Hope for a Paradigm Shift

I began teaching, practicing, and researching law in the mid-1970s, first as a legal services and civil rights lawyer, then as a first-generation legal clinician, and then as a theorist and contributor to a variety of "movements" to change law and legal education: poverty law, clinical education, legal feminism, sociolegal studies, critical legal studies, alternative dispute resolution, legal ethics, law, literature and culture, and transnational legal studies. When I first began writing *Toward Another View of Legal Negotiation: The Structure of Problem Solving*, I was motivated by both theoretical and practical concerns.

As a poverty lawyer I had sued many institutions on behalf of my clients: welfare departments, employers, prisons, schools, administrative agencies, housing authorities, retailers, banks—both private and public organizations. In those heady days of litigation, we would often win such lawsuits, often without trial, on summary judgment—for violations of constitutional provisions, statutes, and regulations. Sometimes we would go to trial on the facts and prepare to show that "we" were "right" and "they" were "wrong."

Two major worries spawned my interest in what I came to call "problem-solving negotiation." First, even after "winning" an adversarial legal case, the underlying problem would remain.

Second, the adversarial mindset and assumptions of scarce resources and the need to perform lawyering tasks as if in military battle to win seemed analytically not what socially progressive lawyers should be doing over the long run. Truth was often not so easily arrived at, or there was some "truth or justice" on all sides. Winning "battles" of litigation did not win "the war" on poverty or integrate the schools or provide effective services or fair workplaces. Conflict seemed to beget more conflict, resistance, and hostility. Legal outcomes were, as I came to call them, "brittle"—winner takes all, but losers seek revenge or resistance; damages and injunctions focus on the past, they don't really fix the future. Courts have what I have called "limited remedial imaginations," not because judges don't have good ideas, but because, by law, they are only authorized to preside over limited solutions—simple judgments of guilt, innocence or liability with monetary damages and injunctions as the only remedies. This does not lead to creative solutions to problems or the development of new resources or better ideas.

Carrie Menkel-Meadow, *The Origins of Problem-Solving Negotiation and Its Use in the Present* In: *Discussions in Dispute Resolution.* Edited by: Art Hinshaw, Andrea Kupfer Schneider, and Sarah Rudolph Cole, Oxford University Press (2021).
 DOI: 10.1093/oso/9780197513248.003.0015

I found Howard Raiffa's *The Art and Science of Negotiation* (1982), a mathematically rigorous analysis of what I was arguing in law. The context of a dispute or transaction matters—one must cogitate on a problem and analyze its structures and characteristics *before* one could decide how to behave or what to do in a negotiation. What is at stake? Who are the players? How can their goals be achieved? What resources might be needed to solve the problem? What ideas can be generated to focus on solutions? Science first, then "art." Other sources for me were not only the game theory of John Nash, who looked not only at competitive "games" (for me this was never a good term; in real life they are very serious problems, war, allocation of resources, etc.) but also at "cooperative" ones, and Mary Parker Follett, who studied many ways to "use friction productively" and to "integrate" the parties' interests to achieve solutions that would satisfy both (e.g., the divided orange in *Getting to Yes*, and for me, the vacation in Santa Barbara where there are both mountains and ocean to satisfy a couple with different holiday preferences) (p. 799, n. 169).

So I set out to critique the exclusively "adversarial frame" of much of the legal and nonlegal negotiation literature and develop an alternative model to "solve problems," not "defeat the other side." This involved interviewing clients to see what they really wanted, imagining, and then planning for, the needs of the other side, understanding what the law would provide if the case went to trial or a transaction was challenged, and then, "thinking out of the [legal] box" to see if first, complementary and nonconflicting needs, and then more contested items could be merged, aggregated, disaggregated, or "creatively" managed to find solutions beyond the mere monetization of all legal claims (pp. 794–827).

To "solve a problem" or negotiate a dispute settlement or transaction, one must first consider the substantive goals, consider what mindsets are driving the parties, realize what behaviors develop from those mindsets, recognize what outcomes those behaviors might produce, and consider what kinds of solutions or outcomes are appropriate to the matter; in short, consider which model or approach to negotiation is appropriate to the substantive issue and the context of the negotiation.

There are several other important features of both the origins and (I hope) the continuing impact of *Toward Another View*. First, it was informed by a social welfarist conception of meeting parties' *needs*, in some contrast to the more instrumentalist, economistic, Pareto-optimality of *interests* as described in *Getting to Yes* and general "integrative bargaining" conceptualizations. *Toward Another View* describes a "Model of Problem-Solving Negotiation" as a "Theory of Needs" (pp. 794–804). It explicitly references feminist theory as suggesting that law should meet the "needs" of parties as well as their "interests." The choice of language is important. "Interests" in *Getting to Yes* and elsewhere has an account of efficiency, economistic "utility" functions, and "maximization." "Needs" is broader and includes that which the client might not be aware of herself, until she is counseled by a "problem-solving" trained lawyer, including not only short-term gain, but long-term consequences, as well as what effects negotiated outcomes might have on others, beyond the client (family, employees, competitors, next generations (as in environmental negotiations), and yes even "opponents"). *Toward Another View* explicitly discusses the political and ethical implications of negotiation as a legal process.

This model of a needs-based analysis grew out of my clinical work, especially my work with the first generation of clinicians at UCLA Law School, where we focused on teaching students how to interview and counsel clients to consider multiple sets of "needs"—social, legal, economic, psychological, ethical, and emotional—in a "client-centered" approach influenced by Carl Rogers's psychological counseling models, as recognized in the commentary here by Erin Archerd. Our focus was not to teach lawyers "descriptively" (to conform to the current profession as it was) but to try to teach a new generation, normatively, and prescriptively, to be "better" lawyers (at both skills and with different normative conceptions for the use of those skills). As Professor Archerd suggests, perhaps it is now clients, and not just lawyers, who need to learn about problem-solving, especially in an increasingly harsh competitive, nationalistic, and me-first society.

Second, one of my primary goals in writing the article was to put front and center, in both negotiation conceptualization and legal education, the idea that "creativity" and "synthesis," rather than only analysis, critique, winning (as in debate, legal argumentation, and trial), and individual wealth maximization (as my critique of the reigning law and economics thinking) should be taught in law schools. A good problem-solving lawyer (whether a negotiator, litigator, mediator, or transaction lawyer) should be able to come up with creative ideas to solve clients' "problems," needs, or goals—"defeating the other side" or winning an argument or even a trial is a means, not an "end" in most (not all) cases. This requires, as Andrea Schneider's comment describes, a broadening of legal education and lawyering knowledge to many disciplines outside of legal doctrine. Fortunately, more modern clinical and experiential skills training in law schools now recognizes this—lawyering skills programs, decision-making courses, legal methods programs, legal ethics courses, and even explicit teaching of "problem-solving" in some law schools now focus on economics, statistics, psychology, game theory, sociology, accounting, predictive models, and other disciplines to broaden the knowledge base and the skills necessary to be a good problem-solving lawyer, as in my own course in Problem Solving, Decision Making, and Professional Judgment.

Third, somewhat ironically, given its origins in social justice lawyering and clinical education, *Toward Another View* was quickly taken up by both the Big Law bar and forward-thinking CEOs and GCs of major American corporations. It was the first first-prize winner of "Outstanding Article" in the Center for Public Resources' then new program (1983) to acknowledge scholarly and practical work in the use of "alternative" modes of dispute resolution.

II. Critiques and Legacies?

Russell Korobkin's comment here is titled "We Are All Problem Solvers Now." I wish it were so! Since its publication there have been many critiques of *Toward Another View* and the whole idea of integrative bargaining. In the early years of this "movement," both I and Roger Fisher often debated in person, and in print, noted commercial law professor James J. White (whose masterful article on distributive bargaining ethics is another one of the germinal articles celebrated in this volume), who suggested that empirically there are many more distributive scarce resource legal problems than resource-sharing, pie-expanding, problem-solving opportunities. For the last few decades, other negotiation scholars have taken issue with how often integrative problem-solving negotiation can actually "work," including Russell Korobkin and Gerald Wetlaufer, whose cogent article on the *Limits of Integrative Bargaining* is also included in this volume. But, for me, aside from this important question of how many matters are actually empirically appropriate for integrative bargaining and creative solutions, the most telling critiques have come from other sources.

Herbert Kritzer, not a lawyer, but one of the most prolific researchers of lawyer behavior, noted early in this debate, that with many plaintiffs lawyers being paid through contingent fee arrangements, the kind of nonmonetary solutions to problems I suggested in *Toward Another View* could never come to pass—the economic incentives of lawyer fees required difficult monetization of such creative solutions, such that, he predicted, such creativity would not occur, as being inadequately rewarding for paid lawyers. This critique is correct and prescient, though in more recent times, perhaps less accurate, as some large companies and law firms have utilized some different fee arrangements (e.g., piecework, bonuses for early settlements), and courts require many forms of mandatory alternative dispute resolution (ADR). The critique remains importantly valid to me—it is not enough to focus on individual lawyers or even the whole profession without examining the context in which lawyer work is conducted. What are the incentives, monetary and otherwise, for promoting or inhibiting problem-solving lawyering? This is what we should be studying now.

I am now most interested in other aspects of negotiation theory and practice, also inspired by Howard Raiffa's work, the application of bilateral negotiation theory to multiparty and multi-issued negotiations. When do coalitions form? How is consent determined in more than two-party settings? How can some parties "hold up" other parties? How is decision-making structured with more than two parties?

These questions seem to me to be important for the future of our field and problem-solving negotiation's applications:

1. Under what conditions and in what contexts can we "integrate" parties' needs and interests? When is "integration" or problem-solving not appropriate?
2. When we do have scarce resource or "distributive" issues; how should we best manage the process to achieve the best possible results (For our own clients? For all who might be affected by the negotiated process or outcome?).
3. When are negotiations more "mixed" (as in the hope to create and the need to then "claim") in substance and behavior?
4. How do we negotiate the relationship of lawyers and clients who may have different goals and views about how the negotiation should be conducted and what its purpose is?
5. How do our theories of which models or approaches to negotiation are appropriate change with context and different numbers of participants and increased complexity of issues?
6. How can negotiation theory and practice inform how we solve, not only legal problems but problems of democracy, governance, and peace (the "scaling up" problem)?

This volume of discussions about dispute resolution has enabled us to look to the foundational theories, questions, and issues of the past, in the hope of inspiring new insights, research, and queries about how we can best resolve the disputes and make the transactions of the future. It is a privilege and honor to participate in this conversation, and I thank my commentators for their insights on the values and critiques of my early work in the field.

References

Roger Fisher, William Ury, & Bruce Patton, Getting to Yes (2011).
Mary Parker Follett, Prophet of Management (Pauline Graham ed., 1996).
Herbert Kritzer, *Fee Arrangements and Negotiation*, 21 Law & Soc'y Rev. 341–48 (1987).
John Nash, *The Bargaining Problem*, 18 Econometrica 155–62 (1951).
Howard Raiffa, The Art and Science of Negotiation (1982).

Article 1.4

The Limits of Integrative Bargaining*

Gerald B. Wetlaufer

85 Georgetown Law Journal 369 (1996)

Over the last fifteen years, many of us who study and teach negotiations have been strongly influenced by the possibilities of "win-win solutions," "getting to yes," "problem solving," "value creation," "expanding the pie," "non-zero-sum games," and "integrative bargaining." ... It is now conventional wisdom that opportunities for integrative bargaining are widely available, that they are often unrecognized and unexploited, and that as a result both the parties to negotiations and society as a whole are worse off than would otherwise have been the case....

I reach three conclusions. First, opportunities for integrative bargaining are not nearly as pervasive as is sometimes authoritatively asserted. Second, the claim that opportunities for integrative bargaining make good behavior a simple matter of rational, pecuniary self-interest is not nearly as strong as is sometimes claimed, both because opportunities for integrative bargaining are less pervasive than has been asserted and because, even when such opportunities may exist, the case for good behavior is weaker than has been claimed. Third, and accordingly, the case for good behavior cannot rest entirely on pecuniary self-interest....

I. Distinctions in the Domain of Self-Interest

[T]he nature of "self-interest" invoked by the proponents of integrative bargaining is individual rather than collective, it is pecuniary, and it is immediate and thus independent of reputational or other iterative effects. It is self-interest measured in terms of a person's maximization of her total utility under the common game-theoretic assumptions that she gains no utility from benefits accruing to others (e.g., her adversary) and that she gains no utility from the experience of behaving in an ethical manner.

II. Distinctions in the Domain of Joint Gains

A good deal of confusion arises from the assertion that opportunities for "integrative" or "win-win" bargaining are distinguishable from opportunities for "distributive" or

* Editors' Note: Some of the text of this article as presented herein has been reordered.

Gerald B. Wetlaufer, *The Limits of Integrative Bargaining* In: *Discussions in Dispute Resolution*. Edited by: Art Hinshaw, Andrea Kupfer Schneider, and Sarah Rudolph Cole, Oxford University Press (2021). © Oxford University Press.
DOI: 10.1093/oso/9780197513248.003.0016

"win-lose" bargaining in that the former can "create value" and "expand the pie" while the latter cannot.... [This] causes confusion because, in fact, *all* opportunities for bargaining, including those ... that are solely win-lose ..., present opportunities to "create value" and to "expand the pie."

For ... clarification, I ... distinguish three forms of value creation, only one of which constitutes an opportunity for integrative or win-win bargaining. [In Form I,] the pie can be made larger only in the sense that is true of *all* bargaining including *all bargaining that is merely distributive*.... [T]here is a ... range of possible agreements within which both parties will be better off than they would have been in the absence of an agreement [and, crucially, those] possible agreements are arrayed along a single continuum such that any possible agreement is, in its relationship to any other, better for one party but *worse for the other*.... Form II value creation [shares all these essential characteristics.]

Unlike Forms I and II, Form III value creation involves that kind of pie-expansion or value creation in which the parties can reach a range of different agreements, ... the size of the pie will vary across the range of possible agreements ..., but ... some of those agreements leave *both* parties better off than do others.... [Accordingly,] only Form III value creation offers an opportunity for integrative or win-win bargaining.

III. Assessing Claims Concerning the Nature and Pervasiveness of Opportunities for Integrative Bargaining

The proponents of integrative bargaining usually assert that opportunities for such bargaining are widely, if not universally, available. Lax and Sebenius ... catalogue the opportunities for integrative bargaining. Their list includes differences between the parties in terms of (1) their interests, (2) their projections concerning possible future events, (3) their willingness to accept risks, and (4) their time preferences regarding payment or performance. [A]ll four of these circumstances will sometimes, but only under certain further conditions and with certain important qualifications, afford opportunities for the parties to expand the pie through integrative bargaining. I will argue, however, that such opportunities are less pervasive and less important than is customarily suggested.

A. Differing Interests, including Multiple Issues Differently Valued

[D]iffering interests [will], under ... some ... circumstances, ... create opportunities for integrative bargaining. Imagine, for instance, that a corporate plaintiff sues an airline, that the parties have been exploring the possibility of settlement, and that they have reached a tentative agreement on $80,000. Next assume that the defendant, just back from a seminar on win-win negotiation, proposes an in-kind settlement in which the defendant would provide the plaintiff with $120,000 worth of air travel. Because of the airline's high fixed costs and the frequency with which it carries empty seats, the cost to the airline will be only $30,000. Both parties find the in-kind settlement to be highly preferable to the cash agreement they had tentatively reached.... [The] range of possible agreements [now includes] some [that are] better than others *for both parties* [and] thus there is an opportunity for Form III value creation and ... integrative bargaining.

[A second] example involves a divorce in which there are two issues: money and custody. We will assume, stereotypically, that one party is a work-at-home mom who cares more about custody and the other is a workaholic husband who barely knows his children but cares desperately about the things that money can buy. Then consider [two] possible agreements. In the first, the money is split down the middle and custody is shared on a true 50–50 basis. In the second, the wife gets full and exclusive custody of the children and the husband gets all the money.... Under the first agreement, the parties reach a split-the-difference compromise on each of the two issues, *both* parties will be better off than they would have been in the absence of an agreement and thus we have Form I value creation. But as one moves from the first agreement (compromise on both issues) to the second agreement (both parties get what they value most), both parties will regard themselves as better off than they would have been under the first agreement.... Accordingly, ... multiple issues differently valued [here] creates opportunities for integrative bargaining ... [and] "Form III value creation in that the size of the pie varies across a range of possible agreements and ... some of those agreements are better than others for both parties."

[That said, all exchange transactions—including those that are purely distributive—depend on the parties having differing interests. Thus, we must recognize the limits of this form of integrative bargaining by distinguishing those] circumstances that appear similar to our example[s], [offer] the possibility of Form I value creation [through] *distributive* bargaining, ... and yet ... distinctly ... do *not* present opportunities for integrative bargaining. [These include] [1] a simple exchange transaction ... (for instance, money for a used car), [2] the sale of multiple goods or services ([e.g.,] a new sports car [plus a] "sweeten[er]" [like] a deluxe audio system) [and] [3] the cross-selling of goods or services [like] the purchase of a new car coupled with the "trade-in" of the old.

B. Differing Assessments as to Future Events: Differing Probabilistic Assessments of the Likelihood of Some Future Event or the Likely Future Value of Some Variable

Lax and Sebenius next assert that differences in probabilistic assessments create opportunities for integrative bargaining. It would be more accurate, however, to say that these circumstances will *sometimes* present opportunities for a particular kind of integrative bargaining *if but only if the parties are both willing to bet on their differing assessments*.... Negotiators may exploit these opportunities for integrative bargaining only through a contingent agreement. Differing probabilistic assessments of the likelihood of some future event create opportunities for contingent agreements in the form "if X, then A; if not X, then B." Differing assessments of the likely future value of some variable create opportunities for contingent agreements in ... the form "we agree that A (e.g., price) will be determined in accordance with some future value of X."

[But such differing assessments only present opportunities for integrative bargaining if [1] the differences are properly] aligned, [2] the parties are both willing to bet on their differing assessments, [and [3] the] market [has not—as through a] warranty—[already installed the contingency agreement. Moreover, [4] once the] uncertainty is eliminated and the contingency is resolved, ... all the parties' bets will have been won or lost, the pie will likely return to its original size, ... and at least one party ... will find himself ... much worse off than he had thought. ...

C. Differing Preferences Regarding Risk

Differences in risk aversion may also create opportunities for integrative bargaining. ... If the parties to a negotiation have different aversions to risk and ... the preliminary agreement leaves the risk in the wrong hands, ... that agreement may be modified so as to leave both parties better off. ... Under those circumstances, the party who is not left bearing the risk can be given the risk, the party who will thus get rid of the risk will be better off in more than the amount by which the party acquiring the risk will be worse off, and [that] party will be in a position to compensate the party acquiring the risk in an amount that will leave both parties better off than they were before the compensated shifting of the risk.

D. Differing Time Preferences Regarding Payment or Performance

Differences in time preferences regarding payment or performance sometimes create opportunities for integrative bargaining as well. [If a preliminary agreement is not aligned with the desires of the party with the stronger preference,] the parties can ... expand the pie by altering the time of payment in accordance with the preference of the party who cares more about that aspect of the agreement [and thus permit that party to offer such compensation as will leave both parties better off].

E. Other Differences

Lax and Sebenius argue that ... there are a great many other situations, almost all of them differences, that create opportunities to expand the pie through integrative bargaining. These include [5] "differences in capabilities" between the parties; [6] possible economies of scale; [7] considerations related to continuing relationships; [8] differences in criteria for success; [9] differences in attitudes toward precedent and principle; or [10] differences in constituencies, personal and organizational situations, ideologies, and conceptions of fairness. But none of these circumstances, except those that fall within one of the four categories already discussed, create opportunities for integrative bargaining.

Differences in capabilities and possible economies of scale may create opportunities for joint gains, but not for ... integrative bargaining.... Considerations related to continuing relationships or to reputational effects may provide good reason ... to moderate her reliance on the tactics ... of distributive bargaining, [but do not create] an opportunity for integrative bargaining.

IV. Assessing Claims That It Is in a Negotiator's Self-Interest to Engage in the Tactics of Cooperation, Openness and Truthtelling When Opportunities for Integrative Bargaining Exist

A final claim that can now be evaluated is that opportunities for integrative bargaining necessarily imply that it is in a negotiator's immediate pecuniary self-interest to engage in the tactics of cooperation, openness, truthtelling, honesty, and trust. First, ... opportunities for integrative bargaining are not nearly as pervasive as is sometimes authoritatively asserted. Second, eve ... [where] there are significant opportunities for integrative bargaining, the bargainer must almost always engage in distributive bargaining where the incompatible tactics of truth-hiding and dissimulation are said to be appropriate.... Finally, [even in integrative bargaining] a bargainer's self-interest is never promoted by disclosure for its own sake. Thus, what is true in distributive bargaining is also true where there are opportunities for integrative bargaining: the best possible position is to secure perfect information about the other side's position while disclosing nothing at all about one's own.

V. Conclusion

If there is a general case for cooperation, openness, and truthtelling in negotiations, that case is multidimensional and parts of it are expressly ethica ... There are, of course, times when considerations of ethics may call upon a negotiator to sacrifice a measure of a negotiator's immediate pecuniary self-interest.... It would be appropriate to attend in a systematic way to the facts that, even when it is contrary to our pecuniary self-interest, relationships matter; that we care about our reputations, not just for effectiveness but also for decency and good behavior; that we care about living in—and helping to create—communities in which pecuniary self-interest is not the only language that is spoken.... And it would be appropriate to acknowledge the central importance of the ethical case against certain forms of competitive and self-interested behavior, especially those forms of behavior, central to the process of negotiations, that involve misrepresentations and other conduct that imposes harm upon others.

Comments

Oversimplifying, Overselling, Overreaching

Jennifer Reynolds

Gerald Wetlaufer's *The Limits of Integrative Bargaining* reads like game theory. He speaks in the language of limits and domains. He breaks down value creation into three forms labeled with Roman numerals. He uses simple bilateral transactions between nonrepeat players (e.g., buying a used car) as the foundation for analysis. He assumes that negotiators are rational actors who define their self-interest as immediate pecuniary gain. And then, given these parameters, he argues that the rhetoric of win-win too often overpromises when it comes to value creation. The equation of claims to benefits does not balance.

As an analytical matter, it turns out that this game theoretic problem is fairly easy to solve. Indeed, Professor Wetlaufer solves it himself. He states that either we can ratchet down our value proposition, recognizing that integrative bargaining opportunities are not available in as many negotiation contexts as we thought; or we can define more broadly what we mean by self-interest, to include not only short-term financial gain but also longer-term benefits, financial and otherwise, that may redound to self and others and may include social welfare, personal relationships, community values, ethical behavior, and morality. Put another way, to balance the equation, we need to either promise less (in terms of claims) or allow for more (in terms of what counts as self-interest).

This is interesting, but it's not the most interesting thing about the article. Tucked throughout Wetlaufer's argument for greater precision around terminology are warning signs about the legitimacy and status of integrative bargaining as a practice and as the foundation of the emerging legal field of alternative dispute resolution (ADR). Wetlaufer uses the word "harm" sparingly, referring to potential downsides of competitive bargaining. But implicit in the argument is the larger concern that integrative bargainers might be inflicting harm inadvertently on themselves and others, through their efforts to promote the benefits of integrative bargaining as widely as possible. Reading the article as a meditation on these harms—rather than, say, as an exercise in professional or disciplinary line-drawing—helps unpack the article's enduring appeal and reveals ongoing challenges in negotiation theory and practice.

I. The Harm of Oversimplifying

For example, take Wetlaufer's initial framing of "cooperation, openness, and truthtelling" as negotiation "tactics." Such framing is consistent with his overall

Jennifer Reynolds, *Oversimplifying, Overselling, Overreaching* In: *Discussions in Dispute Resolution.* Edited by: Art Hinshaw, Andrea Kupfer Schneider, and Sarah Rudolph Cole, Oxford University Press (2021). © Oxford University Press.
DOI: 10.1093/oso/9780197513248.003.0017

analytical project, which is to measure the claims about integrative bargaining against the benefits to immediate pecuniary self-interest. This project requires Wetlaufer to distill some of the concepts associated with integrative bargaining (such as cooperation or sharing information) into more manageable "tactics" so that he can assess whether these tactics serve the immediate pecuniary self-interest of a negotiator. He simplifies to analyze, just as negotiation professors and trainers often simplify to teach.

But simplification can quickly turn into undesirable oversimplification. Cooperation, openness, and truthtelling are more than just tactics that can be used or put away as the situation demands. They are complex interactions, often motivated by various normative concerns and not necessarily internally consistent or predictable when it comes to results. Reducing these multifaceted constructions to "negotiation tactics" conflates the complex/moral with the simple/instrumental and erases the relational dimension of negotiation analysis.

Certainly this conflation may have been on Wetlaufer's mind in 1996, when he wrote *The Limits of Integrative Bargaining*. At that time, interest in negotiation was on the rise, and many books, articles, courses, and work-related trainings were emerging at or around that time. Teachers and trainers were busy packaging integrative negotiation (also called "interest-based," "win-win," "principled," or "problem-solving" negotiation) into easily digestible modules for the masses. Like Wetlaufer's article, the first editions of *Negotiation for Dummies* and *The Idiot's Guide to Negotiation*, which espoused light integrative philosophy, were each published in 1996. For the serious scholar of negotiation, the growing popularity of the field must have been validating and also concerning. When something becomes mainstream, after all, the *why* (e.g., deeper concerns, motivations, purposes) can get subsumed by the *how* (e.g., methods of practice), which can stunt intellectual growth and lead to ethical problems.

Clearly Wetlaufer worries about how oversimplification may erode the moral grounding for negotiators, even as he recognizes the pedagogical need for simplification. He argues that "we care about our reputations not just for *effectiveness*"—short-term, results-oriented—"but also for *decency* and *good behavior*." Negotiators thus should think beyond their immediate pecuniary self-interest when developing negotiation strategy and goals, even though such thinking does not easily fit into prepackaged training materials. Oversimplifying notions of value and self-interest, just like oversimplifying the meaning of cooperation and honesty, prevents us from engaging more deeply with the intellectual, interpersonal, and ethical dimensions of negotiation practice.

Wetlaufer's warning about oversimplification resonates still today. Everyone knows that it is hard to be both strategic and moral in negotiation. Negotiation is a complex undertaking that implicates real people in a context that assumes some measure of need, strategy, agency, and self-determination. Such an undertaking calls on and challenges our ethical capacities, as we navigate through interactions that often present opportunities to exploit others—to treat them as levers or obstacles to getting what we want—and to be exploited and objectified ourselves. Avoiding these ethical dilemmas by simplifying away the complexities neglects our responsibilities to ourselves and to other people, and enervates negotiation theory, research, and practice.

II. The Harm of Overselling

Wetlaufer's primary criticism of proponents of integrative negotiation is that they make too many "win-win" promises on behalf of the method. Overselling is harmful in that it creates inaccurate expectations on the part of negotiators and may make it more difficult to respond appropriately to the challenges of real-life negotiations. Put another way, if a negotiator wrongly assumes that all negotiations are Form III, she might misjudge the zone of agreement or fail to recognize other features of the transaction that would be relevant to her aspirations and decision-making.

One might argue, however, that the benefits of overselling outweigh these potential analytical misfires. Most people are overly prone to zero-sum thinking, after all. Without the hard sell from integrative bargaining proponents, these people might never overcome their irrational and self-destructive belief that the pie is always fixed. Put another way, if overselling encourages more people to learn about and use integrative practices, this not only would improve the current adversarial negotiation landscape but also would have positive ripple effects in professional and personal lives. As Wetlaufer observes, an integrative practice like cooperation is intrinsically valuable and promotes better relationships and social welfare. Surely convincing more people to engage in these practices or undertake related coursework and training is therefore worthwhile. On this view, it does not matter that the aspirational claims of integrative bargaining are unattainable—only that they inspire. If integrative negotiation can transform adversarial culture, then the hard sell might make sense.

But herein lies another potential harm. People who engage in constant overselling have to put considerable energy into that effort. They must focus on what has greatest traction with their audience, which, according to Wetlaufer, is often immediate pecuniary self-interest. This means that the less commodified benefits of integrative bargaining are de-emphasized, even though they may be the reason proponents are making the hard sell in the first place. Those of us who study and teach legal negotiation are familiar with faculty and administrator resistance to integrative bargaining, which often sounds "nice" and out of step with the hard-nosed realities of legal practice. Accordingly, many of us stress the non-altruistic pro-selfishness values of integrative bargaining, to bolster institutional legitimacy and our professional stature. We spend a good deal of time and energy framing negotiation and ADR as worthwhile fields of study, which often means overemphasizing and overselling some aspects of the subject at the expense of others.

Too often, such overselling comes at the expense of rigorous critique and intellectual depth. When people are in sales mode, they have less time to engage critically with the field or to develop new theories and directions. Indeed, the modern ADR movement (which includes proponents of integrative negotiation) has its share of high-profile idealists who press a utopian vision of ADR and downplay any possible concerns about alternative practices. This in turn has contributed to some tendencies toward groupthink in the ADR scholarly community, which arguably has made it more difficult for ADR to move beyond its skills-based pedagogical focus toward more robust critical faculties and analysis. In warning against overselling, Wetlaufer reminds us to re-examine the field's assumptions, conclusions, and trade-offs.

III. The Harm of Overreaching

Late in the article, Wetlaufer remarks that "even within the range of circumstances in which there are significant opportunities for integrative bargaining, the bargainer must *almost always* engage in distributive bargaining as well" (emphasis added). Almost always? In fact, in all bargaining scenarios, integrative or otherwise, bargainers must engage in distribution. The pie must be divided. It may be that this distribution feels more or less challenging, depending on the amount of value creation possible and the relational atmosphere of the negotiation, but it must happen nonetheless.

Wetlaufer knows this. His entire article, after all, pushes back on the immoderate overreaching of impassioned integrative bargainers who claim that win-win deals (those that expand the pie such that no division is necessary) are possible in many if not most negotiation situations. It is interesting, then, that Wetlaufer would choose to qualify this statement about integration and distribution in this way. Speculating as to his reasons provides some insight into the early and continuing struggles in the academy around negotiator identity and skill development.

With the publication of *Getting to Yes* and the attendant curriculum developed and promulgated by the Program on Negotiation at Harvard Law School and others, the stakes as to whether you were a "principled" (integrative) or "positional" (distributive) negotiator became more pronounced. Narratives around right and wrong ways to approach disputes and transactions began to emerge, built on promises of value-rich outcomes and asserted benefits of prosocial behaviors. Even those who recognized distribution as an intrinsic part of negotiation downplayed the distributive angle and warned against reaching the distributive point too soon. The skills associated with value creation (creativity, cooperation, building rapport) became preeminent in much negotiation training and scholarship; those associated with distribution (risk analysis, resource allocation, implementation) were correspondingly less of a focus.

The problem is, of course, that by de-emphasizing the difficult distributive parts of negotiation—the reality checks, the compromises—students and practitioners are set up to fail. Overreaching in integrative negotiation practice, as Wetlaufer points out, encourages negotiators to make contingent deals that at first may look valuable but over time turn out badly for one or both parties. Corporate and government actors eager to adopt integrative approaches to decision-making and disputes may not fully recognize the potential downsides of particular options, which could lead them to make poor substantive and/or financial decisions. Critics of integrative bargaining in the legislative context, for example, have pointed out that the desire to get to "win-win" in the face of competing priorities creates an incentive to rack up debts that are pushed onto future generations. When we overreach on the side of value creation—when all we focus on is expanding the pie—we forget our responsibility to evaluate the expanded pie and distribute it sensibly.

IV. Beyond Harm

Ironically, ADR's struggle for legitimacy in the legal academy may mean turning away from those things that made ADR so popular in the first place—outsized promises of quick financial wins in negotiation. By steering negotiation theorists away from the simplifying tendencies of game theory, sales and marketing, classical economics, and pop psychology, Wetlaufer pushes us to see negotiation as something especially suited to legal thought and practice, something with the capacity to order relationships, form path dependencies, build institutions, define professional identities, fashion modes of interaction, express individual and public values, and create law. His critique of the claims around integrative bargaining carve out space for complexity, reflection, and growth.

Integrative Negotiation: Paying the Price of Popularity

Noam Ebner

I. Introduction

While I had read Gerald Wetlaufer's *The Limits of Integrative Bargaining* (*Limits*) early on in my conflict studies, and noticed that my colleagues often included it on their reading lists, I had never realized its profound value—in insight, and in academic approach—until my students taught me its importance.

Excerpts of *Limits* have always appeared in the textbooks assigned in my negotiation courses as well as my introductory course on dispute resolution. It was through tracking my students' work in their first written assignment—selecting and analyzing integrative and distributive negotiation experiences of their own—that I realized that the ones who really "got it" were the ones who were citing those excerpts, specifically. Moreover, I realized that some of them were citing elements of the article *beyond* the excerpts, indicating they had tracked down and read the full article on their own initiative. I only wish my own writing would compel people to delve in beyond any helpfully provided extract of it! These realizations led me to reread the article and appreciate its true import.

In this comment, I will set aside a main thrust of the article—Wetlaufer's breakdown of the opportunities for integrative negotiation and the efficacy of its tools. I greatly admire his careful use of terminology and definitions, to explore and explain notions carefully and precisely rather than engage with generalities. This topic has been comprehensively dealt with by other authors in this section. I will focus, instead, on three areas in which I believe *Limits* bears import not only for understanding negotiation but also for the ongoing process of developing negotiation theory over time, as a community of learners. In *Limits*, Wetlaufer:

1. Discerned between scientific debate and advocacy, in understanding integrative negotiation and its development;
2. Laid a wider and more solid base for considering use of integrative negotiation and its tactics, one grounded in human relations and ethicality rather than solely in rational pecuniary self-interest;
3. Modeled the importance of ongoing critique of axiomatically held views—and the value of doing so respectfully rather than polemically.

Noam Ebner, *Integrative Negotiation: Paying the Price of Popularity* In: *Discussions in Dispute Resolution*. Edited by: Art Hinshaw, Andrea Kupfer Schneider, and Sarah Rudolph Cole, Oxford University Press (2021). © Oxford University Press.
DOI: 10.1093/oso/9780197513248.003.0018

II. Discerning between Science and Advocacy, Specific Effective Strategy and Panacea

In *Limits*, Wetlaufer models scholarly behavior worth emulating: For one, he emphasizes how important it is to separate good sense and good research from advocacy—no matter how enticing the object of such advocacy is. For another, he demonstrates how even when engaging in advocacy for an idea or an approach, it should be lauded for the specific benefits it offers rather than being held out as a panacea. Retaining a very respectful tone toward those who have taken a less careful approach than he recommends, he says:

> We have, in certain respects, allowed ourselves to be dazzled and seduced by the possibilities of integrative or "win-win" bargaining. That, in turn, has led to a certain amount of overclaiming . . . (p. 394)

Limits offers a rebuttal of the shallow, easily trainable messages of integrative negotiation, while clearly expressing the author's own powerful conviction of the profound benefits this approach to negotiation brings to the table. In doing so, *Limits* offers a lesson about ideas, suggesting that truly respecting ideas includes protecting them from populist embrace and co-option. It is a lesson in discerning baby from bathwater in cases where the two might not only be thrown out together, but be confused for one another in the tub.

This approach is not only more academically honest but also, ultimately, serves the advocated purpose better. In the case of interest-based negotiation, it shores up the value-creation rationale with other elements (nonpecuniary interests and ethics, discussed later), providing a stronger foundation overall. I'd suggest that adopting this approach toward other panaceas offered by the field of dispute resolution would be wise. Approaches and tools for making the world a better place—the ultimate goal of many of us who fall into the "advocates" category—would be more effective if grounded in a broad and solid foundation, rather than in a mixture of solid rock and fluff. If we limit the rationale of our work to improving the bottom line, measured in terms of dollars and cents, we are constraining our ability to inspire, and contribute to, deeper conversations and processes aimed at individual and societal improvement.

III. Laying a Wider and More Solid Base for Use of Integrative Negotiation and Its Tactics

Wetlaufer's alternative case for integrative bargaining rests on two foundations: first is that the accepted focus on justifying integrative bargaining through the lens of advancing pecuniary interests ("value creation") is misguided; negotiation behavior is, in fact, guided by nonpecuniary interests as well, and integrative bargaining can satisfy these better than other forms. Second is that behaviors associated with integrative bargaining tend to be more ethical than those associated with other forms of negotiation—and ethicality matters (*Limits*, pp. 392–93).

Wetlaufer unbundles the elements of nonpecuniary self-interest, as well as those of ethicality. He distinguishes between two types of nonpecuniary self-interest: (1) relationships and community; and (2) virtue and the happiness it brings.

He expounds on the first by saying:

> [I]t would be appropriate to acknowledge the ultimate insufficiency of understanding self-interest in narrowly pecuniary terms. It would be appropriate to attend in a systematic way to the facts that, even when it is contrary to our pecuniary self-interest, relationships matter; that we care about our reputations, not just for effectiveness but also for decency and good behavior; that we care about living in—and helping to create—communities in which pecuniary self-interest is not the only language that is spoken . . . (p. 394)

Virtue, the second form of nonpecuniary value, involves living a life in which ethics matter. This provides people with meaning and happiness, both of nonpecuniary worth.

However, Wetlaufer takes virtuous behavior (associated with, as noted previously, the practices of integrative negotiation) one further step forward, grounding its value for negotiators not only in a quantifiable, "this is ethics' nonpecuniary value for you" way—but also in the deeper suggestion that *ethics matter because they matter.*

Wetlaufer suggests two ways in which ethics matter: one is that ethical behavior provides overall communitarian benefit in an economic sense, beyond nonpecuniary gains that any individual might chalk up. The other is that ethics matter because *un*ethical behavior *harms* others.

Shifting the focus from increasing individual gains, or even joint gains, to a perspective taking into account the desire to avoid individual harm is of great significance for negotiation. Wetlaufer suggests that this new perspective should be granted new centrality:

> [I]t would be appropriate to acknowledge the central importance of the ethical case against certain forms of competitive and self-interested behavior, especially those forms of behavior, central to the process of negotiations, that involve misrepresentations and other conduct that imposes harm upon others. (p. 394)

I'll stress, that Wetlaufer promoted specific practices and tactics associated with integrative negotiation by linking them to ethicality:

> If there is a general case for cooperation, openness, and truthtelling in negotiations, that case is multidimensional and parts of it are expressly ethical. (p. 392)

However, he stopped short of deeming integrative bargaining (as an activity, a *brand* if you would) inherently more ethical than any other form. Actions matter, rather than the caption given to them. One might engage in integrative bargaining unethically, and Wetlaufer's writing does not mean to ethicswash that. Negotiators might tell half-truths, share partial information, or cooperate only part of the time, while labeling themselves as integrative. Beyond that, integrative negotiation offers sophisticated methods for behavior that might be considered unethical. Particularly, this is true of the process of exploring and working with interests, the area in which Wetlaufer sees the most potential for integrative behavior:

> Working with interests involves its own range of potentially unethical behaviors. Perhaps the most sophisticated of these is when negotiators, using psychological and rhetorical magic, conjure up a new interest for their counterpart, convince them that it is not only real but also compelling and dominant, and proceed to offer to satisfy that interest—at the price of concessions on other interests that, only a moment ago, seemed of great importance to them. Interest-based negotiators, as well as mediators, do this all of the time. To be sure, the new interest is often "real" in some sense. However, it is not always as real as it is portrayed to be, and it would not necessarily top the counterpart's priority list were it not for the dynamics of the table, manipulated by a skilled interest-based negotiator.

Considering such issues, it would be good to remember Wetlaufer's establishing an ethical foundation for particular actions—openness, truthtelling, and cooperation—rather than endorsing any overall style or model as being ethical. Most importantly, after stating that ethics matters, his closing words set a simple test for easily identifying unethical behavior, its surrounding label notwithstanding: "*conduct that imposes harm upon others*" (p. 394). It is hard to envision a simpler ethical compass.

IV. The Value of Ongoing, Respectful, Critique of Axiomatically Held Views

Limits critiqued the dominant theory of its time, inquiring deeply into integrative negotiation without first accepting that "integrative is always best" and "distributive is always worse." In essence, approach, and tone, this piece opened the door to *further* exploration countering negotiation dogma even as it set the tone for such critique to be respectful and appreciative rather than polemic.

Indeed, acknowledging that integrative negotiation is possible or beneficial only in a limited set of circumstances opened the door for further discussion of the integrative/distributive divide, elaboration of overclaims on either side, and the motivations behind proponents, or advocates, of integrative or interest-based negotiation (e.g., Korobkin, *Against Integrative Bargaining*). It also allowed for legal and social critique of this approach as a movement (e.g., Condlin, *"Every Day and in Every Way We Are All Becoming Meta and Meta"*).

More practically, this acknowledgment, shored up by the critique it engendered, spurred the re-examining of distributive bargaining as a default backup system to use when those circumstances do not exist (e.g., Ebner & Efron, *Moving Up*). Furthermore, it cleared space for exploration of other systems of exchange beyond bargaining, such as bartering

Perhaps more importantly, acknowledging the limited circumstances for application of integrative negotiation serves to lessen the overarching importance of the integrative/distributive dichotomy (e.g., Lande, *A Framework for Advancing Negotiation*

Theory: Implications from a Study of How Lawyers Reach Agreement in Pretrial Litigation), and, in time, new paradigms will form.

The notion that negotiation wisdom needs to be reviewed and reconsidered critically is particularly acute today, given the suggestion that the negotiation field might be overdue for a generational checkup—examining whether existing models and paradigms hold up in practice, given changes in human development, behavior, emotions, cognition, and interaction in the technological age—changes that might include changes in negotiation dynamics and in negotiators (Ebner, *Negotiation Is Changing*).

After a decade and a half exploring the existence of a "canon" of negotiation and a parallel process examining practices in the world of negotiation teaching and training, the negotiation field has reached the point of exploring whether a Grand Unified Theory of negotiation is identifiable (Borbély et al., *A "Grand" Unified Negotiation Theory . . . in Context*). This activity stream explores whether certain negotiation principles and practices are always valid, or whether they are always subject to contextual differences. It is easy to trace elements of this theoretical development of the field back to Wetlaufer's original, respectful rattling of the cage of interest-based negotiation; simultaneously, the legacy of *Limits* is that any Theory—as Grand and as Unified as it may be—inherently poses an invitation for respectful critique.

References

Adrian Borbély, Noam Ebner, Chris Honeyman, Sanda Kaufman, & Andrea Kupfer Schneider, *A "Grand" Unified Negotiation Theory . . . in Context*, 2017 J. Disp. Res. 145–58 (2007).

Robert J. Condlin, *"Every Day and in Every Way We Are All Becoming Meta and Meta," or How Communitarian Bargaining Theory Conquered the World (of Bargaining Theory)*, 23 Ohio St. Journal on Disp. Resol. 231–99 (2008).

Noam Ebner, *Negotiation is Changing*, 2017 J. Disp. Resol. 99–143 (2017).

Noam Ebner & Yael Efron, *Moving Up: Positional Bargaining Revisited*, *in* Rethinking Negotiation Teaching: Innovations for Context and Culture 251–68 (Christopher Honeyman, James Coben, & Giuseppe De Palo eds., 2009).

Russell Korobkin, *Essay: Against Integrative Bargaining*, 58 Case W. Res. L. Rev. 1323–42 (2008).

John Lande, *A Framework for Advancing Negotiation Theory: Implications from a Study of How Lawyers Reach Agreement in Pretrial Litigation*, 16 Cardozo J. Conflict Resol. 1–62 (2014).

Strengthening Integrative Bargaining: How *The Limits of Integrative Bargaining* Sharpened the Work of Negotiation Scholars

Robert C. Bordone

The task of identifying "seminal" works in any field is daunting. Doing this for a field like negotiation where contributions come from diverse disciplines and traditions makes the selection even more complex. Answers to three qualitative questions might determine the extent to which an article might be considered "seminal":

1. To what extent has the piece influenced/impacted its field?
2. What broader lessons might be gleaned from the production of the piece that are unrelated to its substantive arguments or thesis?
3. To what extent are the arguments, frameworks, findings, or substantive ideas themselves paradigm-shifting?

On each of these criteria, Gerald Wetlaufer's *The Limits of Integrative Bargaining* (*Limits*) scores well. With respect to questions one and two above, I argue that *Limits* impact on the negotiation field has been consequential. On the final question, I conclude that, while at times I disagree with Wetlaufer's analysis, his arguments resonate with many. And I agree wholeheartedly with the observation in his reflection piece that naively teaching integrative negotiation to our students without acknowledging the hard realities of distributive issues disserves them by insulating them from the harsh realities of the real world. I use the previous three questions to analyze *Limits* and its legacy on the negotiation field.

I. Influence/Impact of *Limits* on the Negotiation Field

In light of the continued dominance of the integrative approach to negotiation, one might conclude that Wetlaufer's essay had limited impact on the field. An examination of the many times that *Limits* has been cited since its publication reveals that it is most frequently in the spirit of a "But see, e.g.," where the author wants to remind readers that not everyone agrees that the opportunities for integrative negotiation are as pervasive as the author may contend.

In fact, however, *Limits* impacted the negotiation field in at least two important ways. First, it identified for those writing about integrative negotiation the ways in which others might misunderstand the claims they were making about the nature of integrative negotiation. This, in turn, provided an opportunity for clarifying those claims. For example, Wetlaufer's thesis about the limits of integrative opportunities

Robert C. Bordone, *Strengthening Integrative Bargaining: How* The Limits of Integrative Bargaining *Sharpened the Work of Negotiation Scholars* In: *Discussions in Dispute Resolution*. Edited by: Art Hinshaw, Andrea Kupfer Schneider, and Sarah Rudolph Cole, Oxford University Press (2021). © Oxford University Press. DOI: 10.1093/oso/9780197513248.003.0019

in negotiation rests on the assumption that integrative approaches to negotiation are primarily concerned with "immediate pecuniary self-interest" (p. 373). It has never been my understanding that integrative negotiation is concerned primarily (or even mostly) with "immediate pecuniary self-interest," identifying an area where clarification was needed.

Integrative negotiation *is* concerned with advancing one's self interest, where self-interest is understood broadly as a full set of interests. This set includes pecuniary interests in most cases, but also includes a wide array of other concerns unrelated to money. These may be tangible—a good education, housing, security in retirement, health—as well as intangible, such as being treated with respect or feeling heard. In addition, contrary to Wetlaufer's understanding, integrative negotiation is concerned with both *immediate* and *longer-term* self-interest.

Second, *Limits* forced negotiation scholars to be more rigorous in their work. Words carry precise meanings; prescriptions in negotiation are rarely absolute; context in terms of timing, people, issues, systems, and structures all matter: they drive prescription. Wetlaufer's critique forced scholars to sharpen their thinking and be more precise in their diction. For example, Wetlaufer critiques advocates of integrative negotiation for arguing in favor of "cooperation, openness, truthtelling, honesty, and trust" (p. 390). Wetlaufer suggests that advocates of integrative negotiation urged these prescriptions without caveat or caution in any case where integrative opportunities exist. Wetlaufer does not define or distinguish the meaning of these five terms, perhaps because he did not believe that those writing about integrative negotiation differentiated between these ideas either.

In my practice, I often observe students and professionals equate integrative negotiation with "being nice" or "being trusting." But taking a "nice" or "soft" approach is *not* what is meant by integrative negotiation. Moreover, words like cooperation, openness, truthtelling, honesty, and trust have different meanings. As an advocate of integrative negotiation, I would not advise adopting these behaviors without caveat whenever integrative opportunities are present in a negotiation. A more nuanced understanding of how to approach information disclosure now exists at least in part because *Limits* urged scholars to be more careful in how they make the case for openness in negotiation. Literature that describes the tensions between creating and distributing value typically advises negotiators to *consider* being open about some of one's interests while avoiding unilateral and unreciprocated disclosure.

II. Broader Lessons of *Limits*

Quite apart from the merits of Wetlaufer's arguments, *Limits* is seminal for its unique contribution at a singular moment in the history of the field. As Wetlaufer hints in the opening paragraphs of *Limits*, the unquestioned dominance of integrative negotiation over other forms of negotiation was nearly universally accepted dogma in 1996 (p. 370). In addition, the end of the Cold War, the reunification of Germany, and the prosperity of the Bill Clinton presidency (for some, though not all, demographics), all created a hope that cooperation, connectedness, creativity, and value creation might be values that would mark the twenty-first century. Combine these events with an increasing call for "problem-solving" in professional school education, and the case for integrative negotiation seemed incontrovertible. Perhaps excited by the some of the genuine insights that integrative negotiation offered, perhaps moved by the aforementioned developments, and perhaps inspired by the prospect that negotiation could be an activity consistent with noble rather than base goals, advocates of integrative negotiation frequently adopted a nearly religious fervor that blurred the line between academic rigor and popular appeal. As Wetlaufer rightly notes in his reflection, these advocates may have unwittingly disserved students by not apprising them sufficiently of the ever-present reality of distributive questions in negotiation and, at times, the benefits of a more distributional strategy in negotiation. At times advocates of integrative negotiation were too quick to dismiss concerns of power and leverage in negotiation.

To publish a piece that challenged the received wisdom of the day at perhaps the height of its popularity helped restore academic rigor and seriousness to the study of negotiation. The earnest, methodical, and respectful way in which Wetlaufer addresses the claims of integrative negotiation is a model of scholarship. When a certain set of ideas, research methodology, or ideological approach comes to dominate a field, and when one's professional success in that field may depend on accepting the canon and not "rocking the boat," willingness to test and question the ideas can be risky, requiring genuine courage.

Limits accepts this challenge and does it with integrity. It provided cover for others to question orthodoxy and challenge commonly held assumptions. In so doing, it strengthened negotiation as a field of academic inquiry and not simply as a movement of reformers. Every discipline would benefit from voices of dissent that challenge the widely assumed canons of its field.

III. Assessing the Substantive Arguments/Ideas

Earlier, I argued that *Limits* succeeded in pushing negotiation scholars to clarify, contextualize, limit, and hone their claims about negotiation. But what can be said about Wetlaufer's arguments about the limits of integrative bargaining?

Wetlaufer's critique of integrative negotiation is grounded in his understanding that its goal is to advance one's immediate, pecuniary self-interest. He admits that if one adopts a different assumption set, there is a stronger case for integrative bargaining (p. 373). And, in fact, most scholars of integrative negotiation would not share Wetlaufer's assumption that the goal is simply to advance one's immediate pecuniary self-interest.

Wetlaufer describes three forms of value creation—Forms I, II, and III. I have little with which to disagree on his definition of Forms I and II. For Wetlaufer, only Form III, value creation—where *both* parties are made better off—is a genuine opportunity for integrative negotiation (p. 374). *Limits* argues that there are very few negotiations that present opportunities for both parties to be better off. Problematically, his examples primarily assume that money in a single-transaction buy/sell negotiation is the main issue in play for parties. Even in his example of a one-off car purchase, however, parties in the real world often care about more than just the sale price. Integrative negotiation encourages parties to look beyond bottom lines and dollar amounts to convert negotiations that seem to be single-issue/distributive into multiple-issue/integrative ones. For example, some years ago I leased a car from a dealer in Rhode Island. The owner of the dealership needed a record number of sales to receive a bonus from the car manufacturer. For this reason, the monthly lease price he offered me beat the other offers I received. One problem remained: finding someone to drive me sixty miles from my home in Massachusetts to Rhode Island to pick up the vehicle. When the dealer understood my concerns, he offered to have his salesperson deliver the car to my home. This simple, but real, example of integrative negotiation made both the dealer and me better off.

Wetlaufer might argue, however, that my example is not one of integrative negotiation but rather the result of two sequential distributive bargains (p. 378), the first over the cost of the lease price and the second over who should bear the burden of car delivery/pickup. In fact, though, resolving both issues simultaneously was necessary to reach a workable deal. Identifying the respective interests of both parties—selling an additional vehicle at almost any price (for the dealer) and attaining a low price with relative convenience (for me)—helped create a positive bargaining zone where we were both better than if no deal had happened. In his reflection, Wetlaufer argues that the question of who bears the delivery/pickup cost for the vehicle is distributive, not integrative. Perhaps our disagreement on this point can be explained by our perspective in the nature of the transaction. For me, since the shifting of delivery/pickup costs bridged the gap that allowed the transaction to happen for both sides, I see this trade as value-creating: both sides decided that entering into the transaction was better for them than not entering it. So, while the dealer is indeed giving something of value to the buyer, the dealer (assuming he is acting rationally) is also getting something more valuable than his no-agreement alternative would give him. The same is true for me, because but-for shifting in car delivery/pickup costs based on a difference in relative valuation, I would have also gone to my no-agreement alternative, which was to keep looking. As a result, both sides are better off than the no-deal that would have ensued apart from the trade on delivery/pickup costs. This Form III value creation happens only when parties get past seeing negotiation as a single-issue transaction and instead view it as multi-interest and multi-issue.

IV. Conclusion

Toward the end of *Limits*, Wetlaufer suggests that Fisher, Ury, and Menkel-Meadow "had it about right" in their own prescription around unbundling interests and issues, looking for differences in valuation, and engaging in appropriate integrative negotiation (p. 393). This suggests that Wetlaufer's essay may be seen more as a "re-balancing" of the negotiation field at a moment when the mutual gains approaches to negotiation were being viewed, as Wetlaufer himself writes, as the "Holy Grail" of negotiations (p. 394) rather than as an assault on integrative negotiation generally.

Limits profoundly influenced the negotiation field for the good by restoring a healthy skepticism that any single approach or method could be a panacea to solving all the world's problems. The article invited the field to be more rigorous in its analysis, to be more careful in its language, and to be more modest with its claims. Beyond this, by choosing to challenge the dominant dogma of the time, Wetlaufer created space for others to explore and challenge basic precepts in negotiation. In so doing, *Limits* strengthened and sharpened the case for integrative bargaining and earned its place as seminal in the negotiation literature landscape.

Reflections on *The Limits of Integrative Bargaining*

Gerald B. Wetlaufer

My purpose in *The Limits of Integrative Bargaining* was to bring a measure of clarity and discipline to the then-current discussion of integrative bargaining. Specifically, I sought to:

1. clarify the meanings of value creation and integrative bargaining so that the terms could be better put to use in the study, teaching, and practice of negotiations;
2. identify the specific circumstances in which there might be opportunities for value creation and integrative bargaining, as well as those other circumstances to which the term integrative bargaining is sometimes wrongly applied;
3. identify the particular means—the speech acts, tactics, and mechanisms—by which parties might seek to discover and exploit opportunities for integrative bargaining; and
4. examine the case for tactics frequently associated with integrative bargaining including honesty, openness, and good behavior.

As I demonstrated in 1996, any meaningful discussion of integrative bargaining must include the acknowledgment that, in one sense, all successful negotiations—including purely distributive, so-called "win-lose" negotiations—leave both parties better off than they would have been in the absence of an agreement, and, in that weak sense, they "create value" and "expand the pie." Except as a source of frequent confusion, this weak and ubiquitous sense of value creation and pie expansion is entirely irrelevant to our understanding of integrative bargaining. Rather, opportunities for integrative bargaining may only exist when (1) the parties can reach a range of different agreements; (2) the size of the pie will vary across that range of possible agreements; and—crucially—(3) some of those possible agreements will leave both parties better off than do others. Thus, I distinguished between opportunities for purely distributive value creation, where any move from one possible agreement to another leaves one party better off while necessarily leaving the other worse off (Forms I and II value creation), and opportunities for the stronger form of value creation essential to integrative bargaining, where a move from one possible agreement to another might improve the position of both parties (Form III value creation).

With this distinction in place, I identified what I still regard as a comprehensive list of the four concrete and specifiable circumstances that, subject to particular exceptions and qualifications, *may* sometimes offer opportunities for integrative bargaining and Form III value creation. They are:

Gerald B. Wetlaufer, *Reflections on The Limits of Integrative Bargaining* In: *Discussions in Dispute Resolution*. Edited by: Art Hinshaw, Andrea Kupfer Schneider, and Sarah Rudolph Cole, Oxford University Press (2021). © Oxford University Press.
DOI: 10.1093/oso/9780197513248.003.0020

1. Multiple issues differently valued;
2. Differing probabilistic assessments of the likelihood of some future event or the likely value of some variable;
3. Different preferences regarding risks; and
4. Differing time preferences regarding payment or performance.

I further concluded that, except as they might fit into one of these four categories, all claims that other specifiable situations might present opportunities for integrative bargaining are demonstrably false, and I then offered an extensive list of such false claims (p. 372). Having identified the four circumstances that might present opportunities for integrative bargaining, I next specified the means by which the parties could seek to discover such opportunities as well as the formal mechanisms (e.g., logrolling, contingent agreements) by which each such opportunity might be exploited.

As the commentators observe, I found that proponents of problem-solving and integrative bargaining have regularly overstated their case for such bargaining through unwarranted or exaggerated claims concerning the pervasiveness and importance of opportunities for such bargaining. I then further found they had significantly overstated their case for openness, honesty, and good behavior through overbroad and insufficiently qualified claims concerning the necessity of such practices in discovering and exploiting opportunities for integrative bargaining.

The commentators have been generous in their treatment of my paper, and they have said much with which I agree. Specifically, I wholeheartedly accept their criticism of my references to "pecuniary self-interest." I used that term not because I thought those were the only interests relevant to negotiations, but in the mistaken belief that integrative bargaining was being promoted on the ground that it would advance the negotiator's individual pecuniary—rather than general—self-interest. To be clear, I have always understood that a negotiator's interests might go well beyond the pecuniary to include the full range of possible instrumental outcomes as well, for instance, as the negotiator's reputation and, at least potentially, the outcomes for her "adversary" or the vindication of past wrongs. All that being said, I can see no way in which replacing "individual pecuniary self-interest" with "individual self-interest" in any way weakens my larger demonstration that there can be opportunities for integrative bargaining only where there are opportunities for Form III value creation and that the opportunities for integrative bargaining have been greatly overstated.

I come then to Professor Bordone's argument that opportunities for integrative bargaining and "Form III value creation" are present "far more frequently" than I have identified in my list of four and only four circumstances in which such opportunities might be found. In support of his argument, he offers an example involving the lease of a car. In his example, the buyer is negotiating with a distant dealership and comes to realize that he has an interest not just in a low price but also in avoiding the inconvenience involved in picking up the car at the distant dealership. After the second interest has been identified, the dealer altered his existing position by offering to have one of his employees deliver the car to the seller's home. Professor Bordone identifies this as a "simple, but real example of integrative bargaining" and of "Form III value creation" through which both he and the dealer were "both [made] better off than if no deal had happened."

While he accurately observes that this arrangement leaves both parties better off than they would have been in the absence of a deal, what he has shown is true of all successful negotiations and does not mark this as an instance of integrative bargaining. What distinguishes integrative bargaining and Form III value creation is not that both parties are made better off than they would have been absent the agreement but rather that "the parties [can] reach *a range of different agreements*, in which the size of the pie will vary across that range of possible agreements, and in which some of those agreements leave *both* parties better off *than do others*" (p. 374). In his example, agreement was reached only when the dealer took upon himself the cost of delivery, a move that assuredly left the buyer better off but—fatal to the claim of integrative bargaining and Form III value creation—simultaneously left the dealer clearly worse off than he would have been under his earlier offer and before "sweetening his offer" by taking on a burden that otherwise would have fallen on the buyer.

I have in my 1996 article argued that proponents of integrative bargaining have systematically overstated the importance of such bargaining, the prevalence of opportunities for such bargaining, and the utility of honesty, openness, and good behavior. I further believe that we have seriously overstated the case *against* distributive bargaining by understating its pervasiveness and importance and by describing it in the least charitable possible way, altogether ignoring the possibilities that—for all its intractable complexities—it can be conducted with civility and respect, efficiency, in reasonably good faith, and in a way that builds and maintains relationships and leaves the parties satisfied. We have further overstated the incompatibility of distributive and integrative bargaining and framed the debate between distributive and integrative bargaining as a winner-take-all affair by treating both as comprehensive theories applicable in all negotiation situations. As a result, we are left with an understanding of negotiation that is biased and unbalanced, disconnected from practitioners' real-world experiences, and sets our students up for failure.

One result of all this is that we consistently focus our attention on integrative bargaining, where life is relatively easy, and not on distributive bargaining, where it can be quite hard. Should one ever confront an opportunity for integrative bargaining that is not complicated by the need for distributive bargaining (the parable of the orange is a good example), little more is required from the parties than openness regarding their own interests combined with a standard measure of rationality and sometimes a little creativity. It can be conducted quickly, efficiently, and in a manner that is purely rational and totally ethical—at least in part because, while there appears to be a dispute, in truth there is not.

For its part, distributive bargaining is replete with great complexities and sometimes intractable challenges. It is a process to which justice cannot be done without taking full account of its rich range of communicative pragmatics as well as such subjects as power, domination, and manipulation; the rhetoric of persuasion; emotions, cognition, personality, and cultural differences; lying, deception, and manipulation as well as the ability to recognize and defend against such practices; and argument, including arguments from and about principles and objective criteria. Finally, of course, it is dense with ethical complexities, not the least of which is the fact that lying not only works but, in the judgment of some, is essential to a negotiator's effectiveness (see and compare White 1980 and Wetlaufer 1990). Nevertheless, despite all these complexities and challenges as well as the significant potential for "nastiness" and bad behavior, any fair and respectable understanding of negotiation must take full account of distributive bargaining. We simply may not ignore it, understate its significance, or treat it merely as one of the ways in which bad people can interfere with our efforts to expand the pie.

Finally, I argued in 1996 that there are four and only four circumstances in which opportunities for integrative bargaining might exist and then identified six circumstances in which distinguished scholars had mistakenly claimed such opportunities to exist (p. 372). Now, if only to provoke conversation or correction I'll further suggest that opportunities for integrative bargaining will never exist merely because the parties might hold (1) shared interests; (2) interests in their reputations; (3) commitments to principled negotiation and reliance on "objective criteria"; or (4) an interest in ethics as such. While each of these may undeniably lead to valuable prosocial behaviors, they do so only within the domain of distributive bargaining, either by foreclosing some of the harsher tactics of distributive bargaining or, in the case of principled negotiation, by rendering more salient certain points of agreement across the single linear zone of agreement.

In conclusion, I propose that we ought now:

1. Continue attempting precisely to identify the particular, objective circumstances in which there might be opportunities for integrative bargaining as defined in terms of Form III value creation;
2. Identify the exact means by which such opportunities may be discovered and the mechanisms by which they may be exploited;
3. Specify—as narrowly and precisely as we can—the ways in which distributive and integrative bargaining may and may not be incompatible with one another;
4. Begin to do full justice to distributive bargaining, acknowledging its pervasiveness, its interpersonal and ethical complexities, and the fact that it may but need not be "nasty" and unpleasant; and
5. Become clear about the nature of the case for the various prosocial behaviors that have been recommended by proponents of integrative bargaining but which in fact do not aid in "expanding the pie" through Form III value creation.

Only through the pursuit of this work can we develop the hybrid and nuanced approach to negotiations that the real world will require of our students.

References

Gerald B. Wetlaufer, *The Ethics of Lying in Negotiations*, 75 Iowa L. Rev. 1219 (1990).

James J. White, *Machiavelli and the Bar: Ethical Limitations on Lying in Negotiation*, 1980 Am. Bar Found. Res. J. 926.

PART 2
MEDIATION

Article 2.1

Mediation—Its Forms and Functions

Lon L. Fuller

44 Southern California Law Review 305 (1971)

* * *

I

* * *

As for the case method as practiced in American law schools it can indeed be said of it that it combines in a felicitous mixture a study of both process and structure … [S]tructure and process are viewed as interacting, each serving to shape the other.

The trouble with the case method [is that it] is largely confined in practice to a particular kind of law-making… known as "the common law," though a more apt designation would have been "adjudicative law." The adjudicative process is, however, only one way of bringing human relations into a workable and productive order. Other processes include statutory enactment, administrative direction, contractual ordering effected by the parties themselves, and the tacit accommodations that ripen into something equivalent to customary law…

The standard law school curriculum deals with the results of all these forms of social ordering; we do indeed teach students a little bit about customary law and a great deal about statutory law, administrative law and contracts. We do not, however, spend much time exploring the social processes by which these various forms of "law" come into being…

* * *

II

* * *

Lon L. Fuller, *Mediation—Its Forms and Functions* In: *Discussions in Dispute Resolution.* Edited by: Art Hinshaw, Andrea Kupfer Schneider, and Sarah Rudolph Cole, Oxford University Press (2021). © Oxford University Press.
DOI: 10.1093/oso/9780197513248.003.0021

Casual treatments of the subject . . . assume that the object of mediation is to make the parties aware of the "social norms" applicable to their relationship and to persuade them to accommodate themselves to the "structure" imposed by these norms . . . But mediation is commonly directed, not toward achieving conformity to norms, but toward the creation of the relevant norms themselves . . .

It may be suggested that mediation is always, in any event, directed toward bringing about a more harmonious relationship between the parties . . .

But at this point we encounter the inconvenient fact that mediation can be directed, not toward cementing a relationship, but toward terminating it . . .

* * *

III

* * *

Those whose minds are intent on the "structure of authority" . . . are apt to ask of the mediator not, "What does he do?" but, "Whence comes his capacity or authority to arrange the affairs of others?" In this mood the inquiry is likely to be whether his power rests on a tacit contract with the affected parties, or derives from some charismatic qualities possessed by the mediator himself, or should be attributed to some role or office assigned to him by tradition or higher authority . . . [T]aking [such an inquiry] too seriously may lead us to ignore the fact that the mediator's "power" may largely derive from the simple fact that he is there and that his help is badly needed . . .

A serious study of mediation can serve, I suggest, to offset the tendency of modern thought to assume that all social order must be imposed by some kind of "authority." When we perceive how a mediator, claiming no "authority," can help the parties give order and coherence to their relationship, we may in the process come to realize that there are circumstances in which the parties can dispense with this aid, and that social order can often arise directly out of interactions it seems to govern and direct.

* * *

But if it is relatively easy to see that [negotiation] can yield advantages to both parties, it is much more difficult to discern the actual processes of discussion and negotiation that will maximize these gains of reciprocity. Suppose, for example, that one party reveals, intentionally or inadvertently, that he is desperately eager to secure some particular concession from his opposing number. It happens that granting this concession would visit very little disadvantage on the party from whom it is demanded. Does he at once reveal this fact, or does he hold back his concession as a resource on which to draw when he wants something badly that the other party is reluctant to give? Which course of action will, in fact, serve ultimately to maximize the gains of reciprocity for both parties? . . .

* * *

Now it is obvious that [negotiation] can often be greatly facilitated through the services of a skillful mediator. His assistance can speed the negotiations, reduce the likelihood of miscalculation, and generally help the parties to reach a sounder agreement, an adjustment of their divergent valuations that will produce something like an optimum yield of the gains of reciprocity. These things the mediator can accomplish by holding separate confidential meetings with the parties … Armed with this information, but without making a premature disclosure of its details, the mediator can then help to shape the negotiations in such a way that they will proceed most directly to their goal, with a minimum of waste and friction.

* * *

There is another service that a mediator can render when the parties' efforts … have reached the drafting stage[, that of] … "the generalized other." … The negotiators must keep in mind, not only what the words mean to them, but what they may mean to one who was not a participant in their deliberations and tacit adjustments. The mediator can help to supply that perspective.

* * *

The negotiation of a collective bargaining agreement is commonly opened by a general session attended by delegations of persons representing both sides … The result is that the general opening session normally serves only a ceremonial and ritualistic purpose.

What is the next step? If a mediator is available, this is not difficult. Each of the two groups will, in turn, meet alternately with the mediator out of the presence of the other. At these repeated meetings each side will make, perhaps with some initial hesitancy but by degrees more openly, a relatively candid disclosure of the posture of its interests and preferences …

* * *

… Edmund Burke wrote the following lines:

> The world is governed by go-betweens. These go-betweens influence the persons with whom they carry on the intercourse, by stating their sense to each of them as the sense of the other; and thus they reciprocally master both sides.

Burke's remarks contain important implications for the ethos of the mediator's office as well as for that of the agent … Certainly when he receives from one party a statement of his position, the mediator, before conveying it to the other party, will normally strip it of vituperation and recrimination; his duty is to convey the substance of what was said, not its tone or the facial expression that accompanied it. But it is not easy to effect this separation, especially since the depth which a party feels about an issue is something that enters the valuations that shape the final adjustment of diverse interests.

* * *

IV

[The prior analysis] has dealt only inferentially and indirectly with what may be said to be the central quality of mediation, namely, its capacity to reorient the parties toward each other, not by imposing rules on them, but by helping them to achieve a new and shared perception of their relationship, a perception that will redirect their attitudes and dispositions toward one another.

This quality of mediation becomes most visible when the proper function of the mediator turns out to be, not that of inducing the parties to accept formal rules for the governance of their future relations, but that of helping them to free themselves from the encumbrance of rules and of accepting, instead, a relationship of mutual respect, trust and understanding that will enable them to meet shared contingencies without the aid of formal prescriptions laid down in advance...

* * *

Furthermore, it should be remembered that the primary function of the mediator in the collective bargaining situation is not to propose rules to the parties and to secure their acceptance of them, but to induce the mutual trust and understanding that will enable the parties to work out their own rules. The creation of rules is a process that cannot itself be rule-bound; it must be guided by a sense of shared responsibility and a realization that the adversary aspects of the operation are part of a larger collaborative undertaking...

* * *

V

... Some paragraphs back I spoke of [mediation's capacity to reorient the parties toward each other]. This suggests a certain antithesis between mediational processes, on the one hand, and the standard procedures of law, on the other, for surely central to the very notion of law is the concept of rules.

... The crucial problem arises when we ask ... how far and in what respects should [mediation] enter into the administration of laws. A general answer to this question is easy: once a law has been duly enacted its interpretation and enforcement is for the courts; courts have been instituted, not to mediate disputes, but to decide them.

It is not difficult to see why... the standard instrument of dispute settlement should be adjudication and not mediation ... As between black and white, gray may sometimes seem an acceptable compromise, but there are circumstances in which it is essential to work hard toward keeping things black and white. Maintaining a legal system in functioning order is one of those occasions.

It is, then, not in the making of legal rules, but in their enforcement and administration that a certain incompatibility may be perceived between mediative procedures and "the rule of law." ... [W]hereas mediation is directed toward persons, judgments of law are directed toward acts; it is acts, not people that are declared proper or improper under the relevant provisions of law...

* * *

In seeking now to delineate ... the proper domain of mediation, I suggest ... two tests; the first of these tells us when mediation should not be used, the second tells us when it cannot be used. The two tests are as follows: First, is the underlying relationship such that it is best organized by impersonal act-oriented rules? If so, then mediation will generally be out of place except as it is employed to create or modify rules. Second, is the problem presented amenable to solution through mediational processes? Mediation is itself subject to intrinsic limitations; I have discerned two of these: (1) it cannot generally be employed when more than two parties are involved; (2) it presupposes an intermeshing of interests of an intensity sufficient to make the parties willing to collaborate in the mediational effort.

* * *

VI

* * *

If we were to distinguish broadly among the various processes that contribute to social ordering we might discern six: legislation, adjudication, administrative direction, mediation, contractual agreement, and customary "law" ...

* * *

... [Today's] tendency is to convert every form of social ordering into an exercise of the authority of the state, or, among sociologists, into a projection of "norms" by an abstract entity called "society." Legislation, adjudication, and administrative direction, instead of being perceived as distinctive interactional processes, are all seen as unidirectional exercises of state power. Contract is perceived, not as a source of "law" or social ordering in itself, but as something that derives its whole significance from the fact that the courts of the state stand ready to enforce it. Custom ... is viewed by legal scholars as becoming worthy of attention only when it has been recognized by the courts and thus been converted into "law." Only mediation seems to resist this tendency to subsume every kind of ordering under the rubric of "power" or "authority." ...

Comments

Lon L. Fuller: Private Ordering and Mediation

Art Hinshaw

One of the first major law review articles on mediation, published in 1971, Lon L. Fuller's *Mediation—Its Forms and Functions*, is an important piece of dispute resolution scholarship for several reasons. While this commentary focuses upon the article's discussion of private social ordering, Fuller's discussion foreshadows three major dispute resolution developments. In his discussion of the negotiation process, Fuller reveals a remarkable understanding of negotiation as he explains the difficulty of timing the disclosure of information and the gains of reciprocity. Today we view this in terms of the Negotiator's Dilemma—which Lax and Sebenius famously wrote about fifteen years later. Similarly, his discussion of mediation as a means of assisting with the dissolution of marriage presages the first use of mediation in child-custody disputes by approximately ten years. Finally, he even hints at the demise of the joint opening session in mediation when he describes the opening sessions of collective bargaining, with or without a mediator's assistance, as serving "only a ceremonial and ritualistic purpose" (p. 322). If that's all it's for, why not get rid of it? As interesting as it is to find the hints of these developments, a much more integral factor in the article's importance is Fuller's stature as one of the preeminent legal theorists of the twentieth century. According to his biographer, Fuller was "one of the four most important American legal theorists of the last hundred years" (Summers, p. 1) and "the greatest proceduralist in the in the history of legal history" (Summers, p. 151). His jurisprudence, which formed the basis of mid-twentieth-century secular natural law, argued that the purposes of law, the internal reasoning within law, and law's internal morality must be considered when one is engaged in legal analysis. Not only did these notions become central to "thinking like a lawyer" (Powers, p. 221), they also were to be applied to legal processes, including mediation, not solely to abstract notions of law.

Fuller's interest in legal process was rooted in his interest in what he called eunomics—the study of social ordering and its corresponding forms of law. Through this work, Fuller demonstrated that law arises from a variety of sources besides statutes and case law—revolutionary concepts at the time that others have continued to develop. Unlike other processes, such as contracting, he saw mediation as a dual process. On one hand, it was used to resolve questions arising through private ordering and, on the other, it was a form of private ordering itself. Thus, even though this is an article about mediation, it is also about social ordering and legal process.

Fuller thought a critical understanding of social ordering included the uses and limits of the available legal processes, which he identified as legislation, adjudication,

Art Hinshaw, *Lon L. Fuller: Private Ordering and Mediation* In: *Discussions in Dispute Resolution*. Edited by: Art Hinshaw, Andrea Kupfer Schneider, and Sarah Rudolph Cole, Oxford University Press (2021). © Oxford University Press.
DOI: 10.1093/oso/9780197513248.003.0022

administrative direction, mediation, contractual agreement, and customary law. It follows that his mediation discussion most interesting to today's readers is devoted to questions of when mediation should, should not, and cannot be used—issues we still wrestle with today. For Fuller, relationships were key for this determination, and the primacy of relationships gave us the article's most cited proposition.

> [T]he central quality of mediation, namely, it's capacity to reorient the parties toward each other, not by imposing rules on them, but by helping them to achieve a new and shared perception of their relationship, a perception that will redirect their attitudes and dispositions toward one another. (p. 325)

Elsewhere, Fuller describes mediation's purpose as focusing on the relationship itself—providing an efficient means of maintaining, enhancing, and terminating ongoing relationships. Thus, a prerequisite for mediation is that parties have a relationship, but not just any relationship. It needed to be an interdependent relationship where the weight of the relationship itself provided the pressure to reach agreement. The field of labor relations, where Fuller was an arbitrator and mediator, served as the example he used, but he could just as easily have focused on wide range of business and family matters.

The notion of focusing on and repairing or reforming disputing parties' relationship galvanized the field's founders—it offered a different motivation for resolving conflict focused on parties' real needs and interests, one that could lessen adjudication's toll on litigants. As a true alternative to litigation, some thought mediation would transform the judicial system, and the field's founders focused on the relationship angle Fuller trumpeted, both in the field and in the literature. In fact, the early alternative dispute resolution (ADR) movement was an insurgent populist movement—moving away from law, courts, and lawyers to focus on the parties and their needs. Although that transformation did not occur, a mediation explosion did occur and several of Fuller's theories have held true. For example, Waldman (1997) eloquently elaborated on Fuller's observation that mediation provides an opportunity to create norms, including the norms used in structuring and conducting the mediation. She called this the norm-generating model of mediation, focusing upon Fuller's endorsed ideals like empowerment and self-determination.

And while the field's founders focused on relationship repair and other human needs, they ignored what Fuller termed an "inconvenient fact." Besides achieving more harmonious relationships, mediation also serves as a place for the graceful termination of relationships. Legislatures and courts recognized the potential for the orderly termination of relationships resulting in mediation's first foothold within the litigation system—family matters where the focus is creating the "new normal" resulting from the end of marriage.

Fuller's focus on the necessity of a relationship as a mediation prerequisite begs the question of the kinds of relationships that have the interdependence to be ripe for mediation. At one point, he suggested they possess "some strong internal pull toward cohesion" (p. 314), and at another he discussed "an intermeshing of interests of an intensity sufficient enough to make the parties willing to collaborate" in the mediation (p. 330). That narrow band would eliminate a huge percentage of the matters that end up in mediation today. Fuller's article fails to discuss how parties get to mediation, but presumably the parties themselves would determine whether their relationship was of sufficient heft to support a productive mediation. But one thing is clear, a one-time interaction forming the basis of a tort claim would not make a good mediation candidate in Fuller's framework.

Today, civil matters are mediated regardless of relational concerns. There are many reasons for this, but I want to focus on two interrelated concerns touching on this article: mediation's ability to enhance information sharing and the transactional nature of litigation. Mediation conversations typically begin with a focus on the past, the "what happened" conversation. But rather than seeking "the truth," these discussions are meant to further the parties' and the mediator's understanding of the dispute. But this past-focused information typically is not enough to alter the nature of the parties' relationship, particularly when there is little agreement about the past. That's where the mediator comes in. What can a mediator do in these circumstances? Waldman suggests that mediators can act as "norm educators" (Waldman 1997). That is, they help disputing parties understand the norms applicable to their situation, be they legal rules or some other form of norms. For example, many mediators talk about freely giving legal information, information that's publicly available, but not legal advice, applying the law to the facts at hand. Mediators routinely reference all kinds of objective criteria—jury verdicts, relevant similar mediated matters, and child support guidelines to name a few—to assist parties in making and assessing offers and counteroffers. This kind of information moves the parties' focus to the future and provides a vision of how to move on with dignity—a powerful notion. While Fuller argued that norm education was not part of the mediator's role, mediators today consider this a core component of their trade.

Maybe current notions of mediation would make more sense in Fuller's social ordering model if it were included within another legal process—contract formation. As parties engage in the mediation process, they often assume the roles of buyer and seller, at least in legal matters. Claimants and plaintiffs act as sellers who are looking to sell the value of a claim, while respondents and defendants act as buyers attempting to purchase the potential liability associated with the claim. Today, litigation is often thought of in these transactional terms, in part due to a reliance on a cost-benefit analysis of going to trial. In fact, many civil cases are filed without the expectation of a trial.

If Fuller were alive today, he might agree that mediation has at least a foot in the contract formation process. His writings, however, suggest he would disagree with this notion. Fuller saw the process of contract formation as distinct from simply signing a contract. It included bargaining focused on creating and sustaining long-term relationships—labor contracts, partnership agreements, suppliers of goods, and so forth. Thus, he believed that hostile parties, which we believe litigating parties to be, were unable to form relationships necessitating the kind of self-governance document that he saw as the purpose of contracting. Today's notions of contract formation—merely clicking a mouse to signal agreement—are a far cry from what Fuller conceived.

This discussion highlights another major change that has taken place over the last forty-five years: mediation's presence in the adjudicative system itself. Fuller lamented what he saw as a collapsing model of social ordering, one that tried to convert legislation, adjudication, and administrative action solely into exercises of state authority. Contract was important only because of court enforcement, and custom was virtually ignored. He argued that only mediation could resist the state's exercise of power, presumably because it was a system based on relationships. How ironic that mediation has become a routine feature in the adjudicative system and that state power is the primary means of mediation referral today, and yet it is the threat of going forward with adjudicative state action that often pushes parties to settlement.

In his article, Fuller brought a new and unique focus into the legal world, a process dedicated to the needs and relationships of people. Not only did he recognize it, he placed it squarely within his most prominent contribution to posterity, his model for humankind's social ordering. In due course, Fuller's notions that mediation was a relationship-focused process would capture the imagination of policymakers, courts, and academics. And while many of the high-minded notions of mediation's impact on relationships may seem passé and even naïve in today's litigation world, many times it is mediation's unique ability to address human needs, including relationship concerns, that makes the difference in whether a dispute is resolved or not.

References

Lon L. Fuller, The Principles of Social Order (1981).
William Powers Jr., *Lon L. Fuller*, 1985 Duke L.J. 221, 221.
Robert S. Summers, Lon L. Fuller (1984).
Ellen Waldman, *Identifying the Role of Social Norms in Mediation: A Multiple Model Approach*, 48 Hastings L.J. 703 (1997).

The Untethering of Mediation from Relationships

Nancy A. Welsh

I. Legitimization of Mediation

There is no doubt that Lon Fuller contributed mightily to the legitimization of mediation when he chose to identify it as one of six key processes for social ordering, or processes that "bring[] human relations into a workable and productive order" (p. 307). The other processes—legislation, adjudication, administrative direction, contractual agreement, and customary law—were (and are) much more likely to be identified as sources for rules of law.

However, Fuller's legacy is less certain when it comes to his definition of mediation in *Mediation: Its Forms and Functions.*

II. Distinguishing Mediation

Fuller began *Mediation: Its Forms and Functions* by clearly distinguishing mediation from most of the other processes for social ordering. For example, he was careful to point out that mediation was not a process designed to "make the parties aware of the 'social norms' applicable to their relationship and to persuade them to accommodate themselves to the 'structure' imposed by these norms" (p. 307–8). If such an understanding was valid, "the difference between a judge and a mediator [would be] simply that the judge orders the parties to conform themselves to the rules, while the mediator persuades them to do so" (p. 308). In either of these cases, the source of law would remain an external norm as declared by a third party—the judge or the mediator.

For Fuller, mediation was different. It drew its power from parties' relationships. In mediation, parties had the potential to engage in mutual discovery and self-determination (even though Fuller never used that term) to develop their own rule of law. He wrote: "[M]ediation is commonly directed, not toward achieving conformity to norms, but toward the creation of the relevant norms themselves" (p. 308). Almost poetically, he identified the "central quality of mediation" as "its capacity to reorient the parties toward each other, not by imposing rules on them, but by helping them to achieve a new and shared perception of their relationship, a perception that will redirect their attitudes and dispositions toward one another" (p. 325).

Nancy A. Welsh, *The Untethering of Mediation from Relationships* In: *Discussions in Dispute Resolution.* Edited by: Art Hinshaw, Andrea Kupfer Schneider, and Sarah Rudolph Cole, Oxford University Press (2021).
DOI: 10.1093/oso/9780197513248.003.0023

Fuller went on to write about mediation's ability to create a relationship that does not require written rules—a perfect illustration of his thesis that a relationship and its rule of law can be one:

> This quality of mediation becomes most visible when the proper function of the mediator turns out to be, not that of inducing the parties to accept formal rules for the governance of their future relations, but that of helping them to free themselves from the encumbrances of rules and accepting, instead, a relationship of mutual respect, trust and understanding that will enable them to meet shared contingencies without the aid of formal prescriptions laid down in advance. (pp. 325–26)

For Fuller, then, mediation deserved identification as a unique form of social ordering because it facilitated relational human interaction in a manner that led to the spontaneous emergence of customized social norms, social ordering, and law.

Notably, Fuller found it just as important to identify what mediation was *not* as it was to identify what it *was*. Even in the previous passages, Fuller used his descriptions of mediation to reject categorically the notion that social ordering or the rule of law can flow only from the imposition of power or authority. He disparaged scholars' tendency to perceive a contract, "not as a source of 'law' or social ordering in itself, but as something that derives its whole significance from the fact that the courts of the state stand ready to enforce it" (p. 339). Indeed, Fuller rejected the idea that those with power or authority have a monopoly upon the ability to make law or order social relations: "A serious study of mediation can serve, I suggest, to offset the tendency of modern thought to assume that all social order must be imposed by some kind of 'authority'" (p. 315).

III. Mediation's Reliance on Relationships

But mediation's ability to produce a rule of law was entirely dependent upon its unique "person orientation" and thus Fuller was forced to identify certain types of cases as insufficiently relational to be appropriate for mediation. Chief among these were: (1) cases in which there was neither a "felt sense of interdependence" (p. 335) nor "an intermeshing of interests of an intensity sufficient to make the parties willing to collaborate in the mediational effort" (p. 330) and (2) cases in which there was a statutory or judicially created rule of law needed to provide "essential guideposts and boundary markers" to "maintain[] a legal system in functioning order" (p. 328). In other words, what Fuller counseled was that mediation could only produce a rule of law or social ordering within the context of a real, meaningful, substantial relationship.

What, then, would Fuller make of today's mandatory court-connected mediation imposed upon parties involved in all sorts of lawsuits—including parties with no relationships? What would he make of defendants' failure to even attend personal injury and professional malpractice mediations? What would he make of the increasing likelihood of companies' contractual imposition of predispute mediation upon their consumers or employees?

I fear that Fuller would reject these processes' right to claim the status of "mediation."

IV. Mediative Behaviors Identified by Fuller

So let us look beyond Fuller's relational definition of mediation, at the behaviors that Fuller identified as mediative, to determine whether the occurrence of such behaviors could serve as the distinguishing characteristics of mediation. The list is long:

- The mediator is "open-mindedly consultative" (p. 337)
- "[T]he mediator can direct [the parties'] verbal exchanges away from recrimination and toward the issues that need to be faced" (p. 309)
- "[B]y receiving separate and confidential communications from the parties [the mediator] can gradually bring into the open issues so deep-cutting that the parties themselves had shared a tacit taboo against any discussion of them" (p. 309)
- "[H]olding separate confidential meetings with the parties, where each party gives the mediator a relatively full and candid account of the internal posture of his own interests [and a]rmed with this information, but without making a premature disclosure of its details, the mediator can then help to shape the negotiations in such a way that they will proceed most directly to their goal, with a minimum of waste and friction" (p. 318)
- "[W]hen he receives from one party a statement of his position [in caucus], the mediator, before conveying it to the other party, will normally strip it of vituperation and recrimination; his duty is to convey the substance of what was said, not its tone or the facial expression that accompanied it" (p. 324)
- "[H]e can by his management of the interchange demonstrate to the parties that it is possible to discuss divisive issues without either rancor or evasion" (p. 309)
- "[I]nduc[ing] the mutual trust and understanding that will enable the parties to work out their own rules" (p. 326)
- "[H]elping the parties to perceive the concrete ways in which this shared attitude [realizing that the adversarial aspects of their relationship are nonetheless part of a larger collaborative undertaking] can redound to their mutual benefit" (p. 326)

Many of these behaviors are strikingly consistent with what many of us would identify as good mediation practice, regardless of whether the parties have a significant relationship or the mediator urges conformity to preexisting social norms.

These behaviors also are strikingly consistent with the provision of procedural justice—that is, ensuring parties have the opportunity to voice their concerns and thoughts, giving trustworthy consideration to what the parties said, treating the parties in an even-handed and dignified manner, and assuring the parties of a forum that is sufficiently neutral (Lind & Tyler). Mediation should deliver procedural justice, certainly, and it seems likely that mediations characterized by procedural justice are more likely to engender trust, encourage information sharing, foster integrative negotiation, and provide some meaningful form of self-determination—even if it is not quite the heady form of relational self-determination described by Fuller (Welsh, pp. 735–36).

But mediators are not unique in using many of these behaviors. Indeed, Fuller pointed out that administrative decision makers can and should borrow the "open-mindedly consultative" stance of mediators (p. 337). Perhaps it is only when mediators encourage and enable *the parties to behave in a procedurally just way with each other* that mediation is unique. But that returns us, once again, to mediation's grounding in relationships.

V. The Uniquely Mediative Tool of Caucus

Fuller's list of mediative behaviors includes many references to the caucus—the mediator's private meetings with the parties. This technique has been called "uniquely mediative." For Fuller, the caucus was central to the mediator's ability to learn about deeply hidden issues, understand the parties' interests and preferences, shape the parties' negotiations to be as efficient as possible, and accommodate the parties' interests sufficiently in order to help them develop a new charter. According to Fuller, the mediator would use these private disclosures to help the parties "achieve a new and shared perception of their relationship, a perception that will redirect their attitudes and dispositions toward one another..." (pp. 325–26). Once again, Fuller returned to relationships.

What would Fuller think of mediations conducted *entirely* in caucus? What would he make of recent research indicating that in the very personal context of child-custody mediation, mediators' extensive use of caucus has enhanced parents' trust in the mediator but has also left them more hopeless regarding their situation and less confident of their ability to work *with each other*? (State Justice Institute & Maryland Judiciary). These caucuses are untethered from parties' relationships.

VI. The Wisdom of the Mediator

Finally, I turn to Fuller's trust in the mediator and the mediator's understanding and use of what was learned in caucus. Why did Fuller have such trust in the mediator? Perhaps it is because Fuller assumed "naturally-occurring" mediators—that is, people connected in some meaningful way to the parties or their community (whether geographic, professional, religious, or industrial) and wielding authority within that community (Honeyman et al., p. 506). He assumed relationships.

It is important to admit that Fuller was not entirely trusting. At one point, he acknowledged that mediators might, "in communicating the positions of the parties back and forth, ... state 'their own sense to each of them as the sense of the other'" (p. 324). Fuller's remedy, however, relied on the "naturally-occurring" phenomenon he had assumed throughout: real, meaningful, substantial relationships that would serve as both mediation's foundation and its guarantor of effectiveness. Due to these relationships, outcomes would be self-enforcing and sufficiently fair and honest. The outcomes would fall apart if there was too large a discrepancy between the redirection urged by the mediator in a private caucus and the subsequent reality that the parties experienced as they tried to implement the agreement they thought they had reached.

What would Fuller think of today's reality, when meaningful relationships rarely act as the guarantors of mediators' wisdom and mediations' outcomes? What would he think of mediators' enthusiastic embrace of expedited judicial enforcement of mediated settlement agreements? Would mediation continue to deserve its place as a unique process for social ordering?

VII. Conclusion

In the years since Fuller wrote *Mediation—Its Forms and Functions*, mediation has gained increased legitimacy. But the developments described here illustrate mediation's untethering from the relational foundations that Fuller found so essential. He included mediation as one of the key processes for social ordering precisely because it enabled rules to emerge organically from relationships. Today's mediation is not Fuller's mediation. Perhaps it never was.

References

Christopher Honeyman, Bee Chen Goh, & Loretta Kelly, *Skill Is Not Enough: Seeking Connectedness and Authority in Mediation*, 20 NEGOT. J. 489 (2004).

E. ALLAN LIND & TOM R. TYLER, THE SOCIAL PSYCHOLOGY OF PROCEDURAL JUSTICE (1988).

State Justice Institute & Maryland Judiciary, *Administrative Office of the Courts, What Works in Child Access Mediation: Effectiveness of Various Mediation Strategies on Short- and Long-Term Outcomes* (Jan. 2016).

Nancy A. Welsh, *Do You Believe in Magic?: Self-Determination and Procedural Justice Meet Inequality in Court-Connected Mediation*, 70 SMU L. REV. 721 (2017).

Lon Fuller's Influence on the Debate over Mediator Orientations

James J. Alfini

Lon Fuller was one of the most noted legal philosophers of the twentieth century. His 1971 article on mediation is consistent with his writings on the rule of law and the morality of law by identifying mediation's unique character in the array of dispute resolution alternatives. As such, it makes a major contribution to the alternative dispute resolution (ADR) field by providing us with an important theoretical construct that offers us a way of thinking about the mediation alternative, and the mediator's role. Indeed, Carrie Menkel-Meadow has referred to Fuller as "the jurisprude of ADR" (Menkel-Meadow, p. 4).

This comment focuses on how Fuller's article informs later conceptualizations of mediator orientations, particularly Fuller's influence on traditional mediation models, namely, facilitative and evaluative mediation, as well as Bush and Folger's development of transformative mediation theory.

When Fuller was writing in the early 1970s, mediation was widely used in the field of labor-management relations. Thus, he examines the functions that mediation can perform in the negotiation of a collective bargaining agreement. Arguably, that field is less bound by rules of law and may therefore be more conducive than today's civil litigation model to having the parties eschew a rights-oriented approach. In this regard, he states that mediation assists the parties in creating their own norms during the mediation and "mediation is always . . . directed toward bringing about a more harmonious relationship between the parties" (p. 308). Despite considering mediation's use in "marriage therapy," undoubtedly Fuller would be surprised by the extensive use of mediation today in a wide variety of substantive contexts, particularly because he argues against its use in anything other than a dyadic dispute where the parties have a strong relationship (p. 330).

Fuller's commentary on mediation stresses of the mediation process: "For of mediation, one is tempted to say that it is all process and no structure" (p. 307). This overall perspective underscores Fuller's emphasis on mediation's unique quality in the array of dispute resolution processes. To preserve mediation process integrity, he concentrates on the mediator's role, but always in the context of problem-solving in the broader social order.

Fuller sees mediation's central quality as "its capacity to reorient parties toward each other" (p. 325), a conception most consistent with mediation's true character. He thus views the mediator's role as that of assisting the parties "to free themselves from the encumbrance of rules and of accepting, instead, a relationship of mutual respect, trust and understanding . . ." (pp. 325–26). The current literature on mediation would

James J. Alfini, *Lon Fuller's Influence on the Debate over Mediator Orientations* In: *Discussions in Dispute Resolution.* Edited by: Art Hinshaw, Andrea Kupfer Schneider, and Sarah Rudolph Cole, Oxford University Press (2021). © Oxford University Press.
DOI: 10.1093/oso/9780197513248.003.0024

most likely see Fuller's role conception as that of furthering party self-determination, which is the principle that mediation theorists insist is the quality that most distinguishes mediation from other dispute resolution alternatives.

Although Fuller elegantly describes mediation and the mediator's role, he does not offer much in the way of specifics on how the mediator should act to fulfill that role, other than a few examples of what mediators can and cannot do. Over the five decades since Fuller's article, various commentators have described and advocated a variety of mediator practice norms that we might collectively refer to as mediator orientations, of which the most frequently mentioned are facilitative, evaluative, and transformative. Mediator orientations became the dominant conversation in mediation's academic literature for nearly a decade, as academics wrestled with the question of mediation's purpose as the process moved from collective bargaining to a mainstream method of resolving civil litigation. Over time, Fuller has been used as a jurisprudential anchor by each orientation's proponents. But, which of these orientations are more or less consistent with the mediator's role as discussed by Fuller?

The question of the mediator's role and individual mediator's orientations was a long-running discussion, but the debate exploded with the publication of Leonard Riskin's article in 1996, mapping mediator orientations onto a grid. Riskin proposed a system for classifying mediator orientations based on the answers to two questions: (1) Does the mediator tend to define problems narrowly or broadly? (2) Does the mediator think she should evaluate—make assessments or predictions or proposals for agreements—or facilitate the parties' negotiation without evaluating? (Riskin, pp. 24–32). Although Riskin later reconsidered the grid schema and suggested other labels for the mediator orientations, the facilitative/evaluative dichotomy is still widely used in the ADR literature.

Although Riskin did not advocate either mediator orientation, and simply sought to describe the mediator orientations in practice as he saw them, others have been fairly aggressive in advocating one or the other. For example, Lela Love argues that facilitative mediation provides a "genuine alternative to the adversarial paradigm of disputants who fight and a neutral who assesses" (Love, p. 943). She is against the use of the term "evaluative mediation" because she believes that anyone who engages in the activities Riskin describes as "evaluative" is not engaged in mediation. She does not argue that these "evaluative" activities are wrong or unhelpful, but rather that they should not be labeled mediation because they are inconsistent with the distinctive attributes of the mediation process, such as party self-determination. As discussed, Fuller viewed mediation as a problem-solving activity, a characterization that the current ADR literature uses interchangeably with facilitative mediation. Love would therefore draw a line that clearly distinguishes evaluation from mediation.

On the other side, Donald Weckstein presents the counterargument that mediator activism in the form of evaluation or other interventions may actually enhance party self-determination: "Self-determination extends to the disputants' willingness or unwillingness to be exposed to a mediator's educational efforts or evaluations. Accordingly, when consistent with the parties' expectations and the mediator's qualifications, activist intervention by the mediator should be encouraged rather than condemned" (Weckstein, pp. 503–4). Of course, Love (and perhaps Fuller) would respond that such an approach is fine—give the parties what they want, just don't call it mediation.

Some mediation commentaries, practice books, and materials, particularly those authored by members of the legal profession and the legal academy, adopt a more neutral position by distinguishing between facilitative and evaluative mediation and offering advice on when these forms of mediation are most appropriate.

Thus, with the increased entry of lawyers into the mediation field, issues concerning the orientation of the mediator have become more salient. Because lawyer-mediators possess substantive legal knowledge and often have considerable litigation experience, there is a temptation to apply this knowledge and experience during the mediation and offer the mediator's personal evaluation of the case. Again, many have argued that an evaluative orientation is inconsistent with the notion of the mediator as a communication facilitator and that the mediator's orientation should be a strictly facilitative one. However, does the rejection of a protection-of-rights conception become more difficult as mediation is used in substantive areas that are more traditionally defined by the parties' legal rights, particularly where such a dispute has become a court case and has been referred to a lawyer-mediator? To the extent that evaluative mediation may be characterized as advisory arbitration (or where there is no relationship as Fuller envisioned it), Fuller would most likely be opposed to referring to this orientation as mediation, because mixed processes did not fit well into his social ordering construct. In discussing Fuller's concerns about mixed processes, Menkel-Meadow points out that in Fuller's work on social ordering each dispute resolution process has a distinct purpose and morality. Mixing processes like mediation and arbitration would lead to "confusion of role" and "clarity of role within a pure process was essential both for that process' integrity, and for the legitimacy of whatever outcome might be reached" (Menkel-Meadow, p. 19).

Fuller would be more comfortable with the mediator who adopts a transformative orientation, espoused by Baruch Bush and Joseph Folger in their book, *The Promise of Mediation: Responding to Conflict Through Empowerment and Recognition*. In his pre-book article, *Efficiency and Protection, Or Empowerment and Recognition?: The Mediator's Role and Ethical Standards in Mediation*, Bush was obviously influenced by Fuller in developing his "empowerment and recognition" conception of the mediator's role. Bush developed this conception of the mediator's role by first emphasizing the unique character of mediation. He then argues for a conception of the mediator's role that is most consistent with mediation's true character, the capacity to reorient parties toward each other. Just as Fuller views the mediator's role as that of assisting the parties to develop a relationship of mutual respect, trust, and understanding, Bush uses "the special powers of mediation" to develop his "empowerment-and-recognition" conception of the mediator's role: "[mediation] can encourage personal empowerment and self-determination as alternatives to institutional dependency, and it can evoke recognition of common humanity in the face of bitter conflict" (Bush, p. 270). He rejects two popular conceptions of the mediator's role—the "efficiency" conception and the "protection-of-rights" conception—because they are not in line with mediation's unique character, as described by Fuller.

One might ask whether Bush takes a step further than Fuller would anticipate in distinguishing transformative mediation from problem-solving (facilitative) mediation.

He argues that the mediator's activities in a problem-solving mediation are too directed toward achieving the goal of an outcome that will satisfy the parties rather than providing the parties with opportunities for empowerment and recognition (Bush, n.44). I believe Fuller would part company with Bush on this point. Although both Bush and Fuller stress the importance of focusing on relationships in mediation, Fuller is committed to viewing mediation in the context of problem-solving in the social order, while Bush eschews problem-solving mediation.

Since Fuller wrote in 1971, the number of mediator role conceptions and orientations has increased considerably. Would Fuller have embraced this variety, perhaps viewing it as being consistent with the increasing complexity of the field? Or, would he have criticized a more expansive use of the term "mediation" on the grounds that it dilutes mediation's distinctive character? My guess is that, given his penchant for categorization and insistence on process integrity, he would have welcomed the variety, but insisted that some of the orientations not be referred to as mediation, but given other titles. In particular, he would most likely agree with Lela Love that evaluative mediation should be called something else. And, he might also view the transformative model as problematic to the extent that its doctrinaire focus on relationships eschews a problem solving approach to dispute resolution through mediation.

References

Robert A. Baruch Bush, *Efficiency and Protection or Empowerment and Recognition?: The Mediator's Role and Ethical Standards in Mediation*, 41 FLA. L. REV. 253 (1989).

Lela P. Love, *The Top Ten Reasons Why Mediators Should Not Evaluate*, 24 FLA. ST. U. L. REV. 937 (1997).

Carrie Menkel-Meadow, *Mothers and Fathers of Invention: The Intellectual Founders of ADR*, 16 OHIO ST. J. ON DISP. RESOL. 1 (2000).

Leonard L. Riskin, *Understanding Mediators' Orientations, Strategies, and Techniques: A Grid for the Perplexed*, 1 HARV. NEGOT. L. REV. 7 (1996).

Donald T. Weckstein, *In Praise of Party Empowerment—And of Mediator Activism*, 33 WILLAMETTE L. REV. 501 (1997).

Lon Fuller: A Progenitor of the Pedagogy of Skills?

Becky L. Jacobs

This essay examines Professor Fuller's *Mediation—Its Forms and Functions* article for passages that describe a number of the specific skills that students learn in law school mediation courses today and that reflect his recognition of, and admiration for, their essentiality. Professor Fuller passed away in 1978, long before the legal academy's re-orientation toward a pedagogy of skills. Influenced by the MacCrate and Carnegie Reports and Roy Stuckey's Best Practices and by the recommendations of its Task Force on the Future of Legal Education, the American Bar Association (ABA) approved Standard 303 in 2014, pursuant to which law schools must offer a curriculum that requires each student to satisfactorily complete six credit hours of experiential course(s) in the form of a simulation course, a law clinic, or a field placement that "integrate(s) doctrine, theory, skills, and legal ethics, and [that] engage[s] students in performance of ... professional skills. ..." (ABA Standard 303(a)(3)(i), 2017–18).

The question that these influential reports and task forces addressed was whether law schools had genuinely undertaken "to determine what skills, what attitudes, what character traits, what quality of mind are required of lawyers? Are [law schools] adequately educating students through the content and methodology ... to perform effectively as lawyers after graduation?" (MacCrate, p. viii). This introspective curricular soul-searching owes much to Lon Fuller, who also engaged in the serious task of analyzing and defining the object of legal education. His suggestion that "[w]hatever it is we want the student to get, it is something more durable, more versatile and muscular, than a mere knowledge of rules of law" (Fuller, *On Teaching*, pp. 35–36) presages the academy's recent re-evaluation of the efficacy of legal pedagogy to prepare students to competently and responsibly practice law.

Professor Fuller's pedagogical scholarship provides somewhat dissonant messages on experiential learning. In one article, he states "that the core of [a legal education] ought to be the close analysis of cases" (Fuller, *On Teaching*, pp. 35–36), yet in another he provides an acerbic reminder that "[t]here is need to recall that the slogan, 'We teach men to think,' has been the last refuge of every dying discipline from Latin and Greek to ... Common-Law Pleading" (Fuller, *The Making of Lawyers*, p. 190). Fuller's *On Teaching* also contains a declaration that he and other academics are "critical of the appellate case as the exclusive focus of legal education, and would [have included] in [law school] problems of planning, drafting, and legislating" (Fuller, *On Teaching*, pp. 36–37). This was, perhaps, an early acknowledgment by an influential legal scholar of the value of experiential learning.

*****

Becky L. Jacobs, *Lon Fuller: A Progenitor of the Pedagogy of Skills?* In: *Discussions in Dispute Resolution*. Edited by: Art Hinshaw, Andrea Kupfer Schneider, and Sarah Rudolph Cole, Oxford University Press (2021). © Oxford University Press. DOI: 10.1093/oso/9780197513248.003.0025

Mediation—Its Forms and Functions is not an article devoted to legal pedagogy, but rather is one of a series of articles in which Professor Fuller expounds upon the central qualities of a variety of legal processes. To quote another iconic scholar, "[i]n many ways, Lon Fuller remains the only legal philosopher to take theorizing about dispute resolution processes seriously" (Menkel-Meadow, p. 13). The article, however, expounds at length upon the role of the mediator, from both a theoretical perspective and from a more practical one, and contains exegetical passages devoted to the skills that successful mediators bring to the role, skills that are part of the course content of most, if not all, law school mediation clinics and many other alternative dispute resolution (ADR)-related courses.

Consider, for example, the prominence of the theme of mediator impartiality in Professor Fuller's text, wherein he reminds readers that mediators "will generally be at pains to stay out of quarrels arising" between or among the parties and to "preserve[] a posture of detachment. . . ." (p. 310). It is this impartial posture from which mediators derive their "power," which is, according to Fuller, merely that of suggestion. As masters of the process, mediators provide "order and coherence" to this dispute resolution structure, providing coordination and efficiency to previously unsuccessful communications. Teaching law students to master this process, a foundational competency and ethical imperative of which is impartiality, may make mediation-related courses unique in law school curricula that are dominated by the paradigmatic perspective of lawyers in their representative capacities as zealous advocates for their clients.

An impartial stance is the central pose from which mediators, as process-masters, lead the parties into creative spaces where constructive negotiations can occur. This stance and these spaces are similar for all mediators, regardless of individual orientation, a topic discussed in James Alfini's essay. Facilitative mediators, for example, may lead parties to a brainstorming space, asking "why" and "detail" questions; probing concerns and alternatives; seeking multiple options; reality testing; suggesting objective standards, and refocusing the parties on the future. Evaluative mediators might, on the other hand, make a "dramatic suggestion[,]" a reference by Fuller to Thomas Schelling's memorable phrase (p. 315).

Mediator impartiality provides the perspective to identify opportunities for resolution that, for whatever reason, the parties have missed. Fuller reflects upon the mediator's value in maximizing reciprocity, noting the difficulties with which unfacilitated negotiations are often fraught and positing the mediator as the "reasonable man, familiar with the general posture of the utilities on both sides, as a close approximation to something that could be called an optimum settlement" (p. 317). Fuller explores how skillful mediators can assist parties to produce Pareto-optimal (or -neutral) solutions through sequential bargaining and logrolling exchanges that "reduce the likelihood of miscalculation, and [adjust] divergent valuations. . . ." (p. 318). Mediator impartiality also is central to "another service that a mediator can render when the parties' efforts . . . have reached the drafting stage[, that of] . . . 'the generalized other'" (p. 327). This "other" perspective can detect ambiguities and, at a more basic level, may expedite the drafting process.

As Professor Fuller's discussion makes clear, skilled mediators are alert to psychological and strategic barriers to resolving disputes; including *issues related to party commitments*, for example, "[i]f the limitations on the agent's authority are feigned, the mediator can more ... gracefully penetrate the pretense ... []" *or* "[w]hen A refuses ... to consider making a particular concession. ..." (p. 321); *reactive devaluation/attribution bias*, for example, "gratuitous concession ... are apt to arouse suspicions as to their motivation" (p. 317); and *loss aversion*, for example, "one does not necessarily make a gain for himself simply because he denies to the other fellow something he wants" (p. 316). Professors educate students about these and other psychological and neurobiological dimensions of the mediation process in clinics and other ADR-related courses. They also provide instruction regarding the capacities and limitations of mediators in responding to these elements, reinforcing the habit of "reflect[ing] on [a mediator's] proper role and ... sources of ... power" (p. 324).

Fuller also identifies the specific process tools and mechanisms that capable mediators utilize to engage the parties effectively. He characterizes separate confidential caucuses as "a common practice," and descriptions of the skills and themes attendant to their use appear throughout *Mediation—Its Forms and Functions*. For example, his narrative teaches how mediators, or "go-betweens" in this part of the process, use caucuses to explore party perspectives with fewer distractions and with less acrimony.

> [M]ediator[s] can direct [parties'] verbal exchanges away from recrimination and toward the issues that need to be faced, that by receiving separate and confidential communications from the parties[, mediators] can gradually bring into the open issues so deep-cutting that the parties themselves had shared a tacit taboo against any discussion of them and that, finally, [they can by] management of the interchange demonstrate to the parties that it is possible to discuss divisive issues without either rancor or evasion. (p. 309)

This passage describes the masterful use by mediators of caucuses to explore party interests and the careful use of positive reframing to process and reformulate inflammatory language to remove bias or judgment.

Professor Fuller believes that positive reframing in particular is a tool that must be exercised with great finesse on the part of the mediator:

> [W]hen [the mediator] receives from one party a statement of [its] position, the mediator, before conveying it to the other party, will normally strip it of vituperation and recrimination; [the] duty is to convey the substance of what was said, not its tone or the facial expression that accompanied it. But it is not always easy to effect this separation, especially since the depth with which a party feels about an issue is something that enters into the valuations that shape the final adjustment of diverse interests. (p. 324)

This type of meaningful reframing sometimes may require "the experienced mediator ... [to] proceed[] ... to [the] goal ... by circumlocution and indirection" (p. 305), but it also allows [parties] to "proceed most directly to their goal, with a minimum of waste and friction" (p. 319).

This is, perhaps, the most valuable skill that mediators possess: the ability to create an environment—a space—within which parties are able to communicate productively, and it is, according to Professor Fuller, "the central quality of mediation, namely, its capacity to reorient the parties toward each other, not by imposing rules on them, but by helping them to achieve a new and shared perception of their relationship, a perception that will redirect their attitudes and dispositions toward one another" (p. 325). Just as this quote is the most recognizable insight from Professor Fuller's article, mediator impartiality vis-à-vis the parties and any possible resolution and their commitment to the process itself are hallmarks of mediation, regardless of orientation or conception of process. It is their primary function to "induce the mutual trust and understanding that will [create in the parties] a sense of shared responsibility and a realization that the adversary aspects . . . are part of a larger collaborative undertaking" (p. 326). Law school mediation clinics and experiential courses also seek to create a productive space for law students to practice the mediator skills described so eloquently by Professor Fuller.

*****

To conclude, Professor Fuller may not have intended *Mediation—Its Forms and Functions* to be a descriptive, sociolegal analysis of the mediation process and the skills performed by accomplished mediators. Nor is it likely that Professor Fuller intended to be a progenitor of experiential pedagogy in his highly theoretical musings on law teaching. Indeed, in his early writings, he cautioned law schools against placing an overemphasis on skills training.

Regardless, *Mediation—Its Forms and Functions* is replete with references to, and detailed descriptions of, the skills required for a mediator to successfully facilitate the mediational effort, skills that are pedagogically designed into law school mediation clinics and in-class simulations. The article thus not only firmly established Fuller's role in the intellectual history of mediation pedagogy, it also is an homage to adept mediators and to their mastery of the art of the mediation process, praxial scholarship which unites theorists and practitioners.

References

ABA Standards for Approval of Law Schools 303(a)(3)(i) (2017–2018).

Lon L. Fuller, *On Teaching Law*, 3 Stan. L. Rev. 35 (1950).

Lon L. Fuller, *What the Law Schools Can Contribute to the Making of Lawyers*, 1 J. Legal Educ. 189 (1948).

Robert MacCrate, *Foreword* to Roy Stuckey et al., Best Practices for Legal Education: A Vision and a Road Map (2007).

Carrie Menkel-Meadow, *Mothers and Fathers of Invention: The Intellectual Founders of ADR*, 16 Ohio St. J. on Disp. Resol. 1, 13 (2000).

Article 2.2

The Theory and Practice of Mediation: A Reply to Professor Susskind

Joseph B. Stulberg

6 Vermont Law Review 85 (1981)

Introduction

* * *

Professor Susskind touches briefly upon a number of [important] concerns in his article... [H]e asserts [an argument] that the mediator of environmental disputes ... should not be neutral and should be held accountable for the mediated outcome ...

... Susskind's demand for a nonneutral intervenor is conceptually and pragmatically incompatible with the goals and purposes of mediation ... It is precisely a mediator's commitment to neutrality which ensures responsible actions on the part of the mediator and permits mediation to be an effective, principled dispute settlement procedure.

... At a substantive level, Susskind argues that the mediator must ensure that the negotiated agreements are fair ...

[A commitment to neutrality] enables both the mediation process and the mediator to operate effectively[, and] provides ... a principled ... basis for service ...

* * *

I. The Mediation Process: An Overview

The mediation process can be characterized as follows: it is (1) a non-compulsory procedure in which (2) an impartial, neutral party is invited or accepted by (3) parties to a dispute to help them (4) identify issues of mutual concern and (5) design solutions to these issues (6) which are acceptable to the parties ...

* * *

Joseph B. Stulberg, *The Theory and Practice of Mediation: A Reply to Professor Susskind* In: *Discussions in Dispute Resolution.* Edited by: Art Hinshaw, Andrea Kupfer Schneider, and Sarah Rudolph Cole, Oxford University Press (2021). DOI: 10.1093/oso/9780197513248.003.0026

II. The Functions of a Mediator

* * *

... [M]any persons equate a mediator's neutrality with his being a non-entity at the negotiations. Nothing could be further from the truth. Susskind ... notes that the mediator performs some procedural functions and, if necessary, assumes an active role ...

A mediator ... must immerse himself in the dynamics of the controversy to enable him to explain ... the reasons for a party's specific proposal or its refusal to yield ...

... The mediator's role is to convey each party's proposals in a language that is both faithful to the desired objectives of the party and formulated to insure the highest degree of receptivity by the listener ...

* * *

... The mediator is in the best position to inform a party ... that its objective is simply not obtainable through those specific negotiations. He does not argue that the proposal is undesirable and therefore not obtainable. Rather, as an impartial participant in the discussions, he may suggest that the positions the party advances will not be realized, either because they are beyond the resource capacity of the other parties to fulfill or that ... the other parties will not concede ...

* * *

III. Profile of a Mediator

* * *

... The parties at least want the mediator to be intelligent enough to become educated about the matters in dispute as the talks progress. The knowledgeable mediator can ask penetrating questions, be sensitive to when parties are erecting artificial constraints on their conduct ... The mediator does not possess such knowledge, however, [to] serv[e] as an expert who advises the parties as to the "right answers."

... [A] mediator must be neutral with regard to outcome ... If the mediator is neutral and remains so, then he ... invite[s] a bond of trust to develop [with] the parties. [The mediator's] commitment to neutrality ensures confidentiality ...

* * *

[Parties share sensitive information with a mediator including] their priorities, acceptable trade-offs, and their desired timing for demonstrating movement and flexibility ... This type of trust is secured and reinforced only if the mediator is neutral, has no power to insist upon a particular outcome, and honors the confidences placed in him. If any of these characteristics is absent, then the parties must calculate what information they will share with the mediator, just as they do in communicating with any of the parties to the controversy.

* * *

IV. Mediator Strategies for Building a Settlement

* * *

The mediator's job is to structure effective communication among the parties ... He requires the parties to state their concerns and proposed solutions, thereby establishing the criteria against which he can evaluate and quash any attempts to escalate demands.

* * *

B. Moving the Parties Toward an Agreement

* * *

As mediation approaches either an agreement or a breakdown, the mediator forcefully identifies for the respective parties the cost each will pay for not reaching a settlement ... His job ... is to state proposals and arguments so that each party will [understand how others perceive their position], and to press the party to reconsider its needs in light of that new understanding ... The mediator would fail in his job of assisting the parties to reach a resolution if he did not diligently and persistently challenge each parties' own pretensions.

Most of all, the mediator should be guided in pressing the parties by his sense of what is attainable. He should painstakingly listen and search for where the parties have indicated [where] the realm of agreement lies at a given point in time ... He may then shape the discussions and concessions to coincide with these contours that the parties have suggested ...

* * *

V. Environmental Dispute Mediation

* * *

... Susskind ... maintains that [environmental disputes are] such that the mediator must be an "activist" in a ... defined way:

[Mediators should be concerned with the impact of agreements on unrepresented groups, maximizing joint gains, and the agreement's long-term impacts.]

He concludes that an environmental mediator should be committed ... to an outcome that is both just and stable. His second line of argument ... [is] that a "mediator with clout" may be [important when] political pressure is necessary to force concessions from parties ...

A. The Mediator "With Clout"

* * *

Clearly, [the intervention of a Congressman who can prevent a party from reaching its goals through other means] is quite different from that of a mediator who derives his power from his very commitment to neutrality ...

* * *

... [S]usskind should demonstrate how a mediator committed to neutrality cannot render effective service in an environmental dispute ... Is it appropriate, for example, for the "mediator with clout" to threaten a recalcitrant party with political retaliation? ... Susskind should illustrate the value derived, if any, by labeling such intervention "mediation," since it differs in so many striking ways from mediation.

* * *

B. Susskind's "Environmental Mediator"

* * *

... [Susskind argues that the mediator's role is to assure] [t]he widest possible consensus among those who will be affected by the development ... whether or not they possess the power ... to block implementation of the [agreement] ...

This procedure is hardly tenable ... The mediator's role, as traditionally discharged, is to help those [present] reach a resolution and then withdraw. He cannot deal with absent parties. He does not know who they are, what they would have said if they had been present, nor what their priorities are.

* * *

... To suggest that an environmental mediator [protect the public's interest] is comparable to suggesting that ... the mediator [impose] dispositive, enforceable decisions on the parties.

Such a proposal is not simply adding a different twist to the mediation process; it is converting it from mediation to arbitration ...

... Susskind proposes that [the mediator] ... insure [Pareto-optimization—an agreement that secures net benefits for each party without leaving any party worse off than before.] He further suggests that the solution ... have the least possible adverse impact on other aspects of present or future community life. Simply stat[ed] [this is an] awesome ... task ... for the environmental mediator. To [do this], the environmental mediator must ... [ensure] consideration of every possible technical solution ... He must secure demographic information on all persons affected by the dispute and factor their interests, desires, aspirations, preferences and values ... He must project alternative development plans for jobs, tax bases, population trends, aesthetic values, school development and recreational needs for each possible solution. He must calculate the advantages and disadvantages of each solution against retaining the status quo ...

... [T]hese tasks ... involve a host of analytical problems concerning logical theories of probability, measurement, interpersonal comparisons, and contrary-to-fact conditionals. [This suggests] that Pareto-optimal outcomes in the context of an environmental dispute are not, in principle, possible ...

* * *

Susskind apparently contends that [this] responsibility emanates from the nature of environmental disputes, particularly because ... agreements could irrevocably preclude certain options from [later] being entertained. That position ... is not an independent justification for conferring such authority to a mediator.

* * *

If we [accept Susskind's reasoning], then the environmental mediator is simply a person who uses his entry into the dispute to become a social conscience, environmental policeman, or social critic and who carries no other obligations to the process or the participants beyond assuring Pareto-optimality ...

* * *

... The nature of [these tasks] is more akin to our notion of tapping an expert resource to solve a problem than turning to a mediator for assistance in resolving a dispute ...

... It appears that the impetus for Susskind's prescription ... emanates from the understandable reluctance to accord conclusive weight to the preferences of the parties in every conceivable situation ... Although the stated principle is correct, the mediator's role is not thereby converted into that of an advocate, even if the parties [agreement is contrary to public policy].

How should the mediator respond to such a situation? ... The mediator should press the parties to examine whether or not they believe that (1) they would be acting in compliance with the law or with principles they would be willing, as rational agents, to universalize; (2) their activities will be acceptable to their respective constituencies and not overturned by public authorities; and (3) ... their proposed actions are not contrary to their own self-interest. If the parties ... still find the proposed course of action acceptable, then the mediator can simply decide ... that he does not want to lend his personal presence and reputation ... to that agreement and he can withdraw ...

... Each of us has preferences, interests, commitments to certain moral principles ... which ... will prompt us into advocating and acting in a manner that is faithful to these dictates ... What is important is that one keep distinct his personal posture of judgment from the ruledefined practice of the mediator and act accordingly.

Conclusion

... The way to insure the continued integrity and usefulness of mediation as a dispute settlement procedure ... is to be certain that we do not demand that it perform functions beyond the scope of its institutional and conceptual capacity.

... Contrary to Susskind's suggestion, the mediator actually gains his strength ... because of [a] basic commitment to ... neutrality. Susskind's environmental mediator ... assum[es] an intervention posture that differs importantly from that of the traditional mediator. Both roles are important and, in their own ways, useful. They must, however, be distinguished ...

Comments

A Star to Steer Her By

Lela Porter Love

And all I ask is a tall ship and a star to steer her by.
–From *Sea Fever, John Masefield*

I. What Is Foundational?

Perhaps my definition of a foundational work is idiosyncratic, so let me explain. For me, a foundational work is an idea or vision that provides a platform for a field of human endeavor. Such works provide a new, and often better, usually different, understanding of particular phenomena. Memorable foundational statements or formulations seem both simple and game-changing: the earth is round; $e = mc^2$. Other examples include:

The idea of leaderless leadership from the Tao Te Ching, foundational for Taoism—and also for Buddhism (and some mediation trainers).

Charles Darwin's *On the Origin of Species* was a mind-changing work in evolutionary biology.

Freud's work on dreams and their interpretation was a game changer in the field of psychology.

I would call these foundational. All of these new points of departures, in their respective fields, provide an anchor or "a star to steer by" in developing a field.

If we take mediation and ask what pieces are foundational, Stulberg's *The Theory and Practice of Mediation: A Reply to Professor Susskind* falls in that category, as it is groundbreaking, original, and influential—in the portions of the article that explore the meaning of mediation, the boundaries of mediation practice, and the ways that mediation can be differentiated from other processes. Why is that so?

A. A Surprising Departure

Foundational pieces often mark a fork in the road in the way we think about something.

For example, the idea of "turning the other cheek" or giving your cloak to someone who takes your shirt (from the *Sermon on the Mount*) are opposites of existing norms of fairness that call for proportional punishment for crime, and yet the rationality and appeal of these ideas are profound.

Lela Porter Love, *A Star to Steer Her By* In: *Discussions in Dispute Resolution*. Edited by: Art Hinshaw, Andrea Kupfer Schneider, and Sarah Rudolph Cole, Oxford University Press (2021). © Oxford University Press.
DOI: 10.1093/oso/9780197513248.003.0027

In his article, Stulberg was responding to Lawrence Susskind's proposition that a mediator—in the context of environmental disputes—should be committed to an outcome that: is just and stable (Susskind, pp. 6–8), is as optimal as it can be for all involved (Susskind, pp. 46–47), takes all affected parties into account (Susskind, pp. 46–47), and minimizes long-term harms for the environment (Susskind, pp. 46–47). Those propositions are undeniably appealing and describe an understandable norm. Who could contest the correctness or the benefits or the merits of those claims? Everyone in the dispute resolution business is drawn to fairness and ideal closure—or happy endings both for parties to a dispute and for others impacted by its resolution. I would guess that most people signing up to be mediators would believe they are joining cadres of practitioners dedicated to justice and to helping parties end the discomfort and indignities and sacrifices of being in disputes in some ideal fashion.

Stulberg's answer to the question posed by Susskind's perspective on mediation practice is a simple one: mediation is another paradigm and the outcome that the parties chose will be honored by the mediator—whether it is "just" or not, whether it is "ideal" or not, and whether outsiders to the mediation are harmed by it or not. If the resolution is acceptable to the parties, the mediator has done his job, as the mediator's job entails being true to neutrality—that is, honoring party choice—with respect to the outcome.

With respect to Susskind's proposition that environmental disputes involve a special need for high-quality outcomes, that assertion too is plausible and appealing to anyone living on and loving this earth. Susskind warns us that this category of disputes can involve serious harms to "the public health and safety" and the potential for "environmental time bombs" that will negatively impact future generations (Susskind, p. 1). We nod our head in agreement; we share a common interest in the future of the planet. So, the hard case that Susskind posits—agreements in the environmental context that are suboptimal or, worse, harmful to the environment, should not be allowed by a mediator who, instead, should assure quality agreements—is addressed by Stulberg and used as a springboard to define what mediation is and what it can and cannot do: mediation is a process that serves party self-determination; mediated outcomes are outcomes acceptable to the parties.

Stulberg accurately notes that while environmental disputes present an arguably compelling arena for mediators to breach neutrality over the outcome, the same could be said for other case types. In labor management, for example, a "bad" agreement can negatively impact a workplace for many people (e.g., an agreement that allows a toxic manager to keep operating), can retard development with respect to social goods (e.g., an agreement that slows the progress of reforms for women or minorities), or can slow the advancement of social policies (e.g., an agreement that resolves a discrimination claim without bringing it to public light). And, in other areas "bad" outcomes can be potentially devastating, as in family cases. So, there is no "special case" exception to the rule that mediation is about the parties arriving at their own acceptable outcome. This is a clear bright line.

B. Courage

Foundational works involve courage—the courage to make a surprising departure from previously understood norms or understandings and the courage to go out on a limb in taking a potentially unpopular position.

In tackling a hard case (i.e., a mediator who would "allow" an agreement that might cause harm to future generations or degradation to the environment), Stulberg shows courage in embracing a potentially unpopular answer—that "acceptability" by the parties replaces optimality and the conventional understanding of "justice."

C. Clear Vision

In return for shaking our well-ordered notions, foundational works provide a blueprint for another direction, another way of seeing things. They also explain the underlying rationale for the new order.

That Stulberg's article is a clear, well-written, and courageous departure makes it foundational, providing survivability as subsequent generations read, reflect on, and use the idea. The simple idea—mediation is about party choice—provides mediators and society a star to steer by in developing a field and crafting training programs for practitioners, as well as qualifications for practice and ethical codes.

In response to Susskind's assertions, Stulberg provides a vision of mediation as a dispute resolution process with internal cohesion and moral legitimacy. In the article, he lays out mediation's pillars:

Pillar 1: Mediation Is a Process Governed by the Parties

Mediation is about the parties themselves coming to agreements acceptable to them. It is not about fairness as perceived by a justice system external to the parties (though such systems may inform the parties internal norms), nor is it about the most optimal outcome from the point of view of practical considerations—be they environmental, social, or religious. This is radical!

One might think that because the process is governed by the parties themselves it rests on a rung below dispute resolution processes governed by public norms and officials appointed, elected, or chosen to resolve controversies. Not so! According to Stulberg, outcomes that derive from the parties themselves have their own "justice" rationale, which is on par with rights-based dispute resolution processes. Note, however, that mediation is not above the other processes, it is co-equal with them—a part of an array of processes.

Pillar 2: Mediation Is a Process among an Array of Processes All of Which Have Different Rationales and Goals

There is an array of dispute resolution processes that have different moralities and goals. Depending on one's goals, a particular process with that goal in mind should be chosen. This was Frank Sander's point in his seminal article on the multi-door courthouse (Sander). And it is repeated here by Stulberg to ensure Susskind that if neutral expert evaluation and decision is needed in certain environmental disputes—or other types of disputes for that matter—such evaluative input is available, but outside the tent of mediation. Practically speaking, mediation cannot do it all.

Pillar 3: Defining the Key Functions and Attributes of a Mediator

In laying out what mediation means, Stulberg goes on to describe the functions of a mediator—catalyst, educator, translator, resource expander, bearer of bad news, agent of reality, and scapegoat (JS, pp. 91–94). As he explains, each of these functions is utilized to the end of assisting the parties to achieve a self-determined outcome.

Stulberg also lists the attributes of a mediator: ability to understand the dispute and its context, intelligent, good listener, articulate, patient, non-judgmental, flexible, persuasive, imaginative, resourceful, respected, reliable, having access to resources, non-defensive, having integrity, humble, objective, and neutral with regard to outcome. The latter attribute is key to the central thesis of his response to Susskind.

While the lists of functions and attributes, in and of themselves, are not foundational, the exercise of drawing such lists given the overall frame of mediation as a process which helps parties achieve a self-determined outcome is indeed seminal. The picture that emerges from the enumeration of functions and attributes of a mediator is fundamentally different from the picture of a judge or of an expert called in to design a just or Pareto-optimal outcome.

II. Not Foundational in the Paper

Stulberg's paper explores two aspects of the mediator's job—agenda construction and caucus—that are well drawn. Though not "foundational" in the sense put forward here, they are noteworthy. His brilliant discussion of agenda construction (JS, pp. 99–103) sets a remarkably—wonderfully—high bar for both mediation practice and, related to that, mediation training. His discussion of the caucus, however, fails to foresee different schools of mediation—some advocating "no caucus" and others "always caucus" and still others "caucus only for a good reason." The view of caucus in the article focuses on its role in moving parties toward an agreement in an energetic and forceful manner. There are, of course, many other uses of the caucus.

In the thirty-nine years since the article was written, new questions and directions make some of the imperatives seem flawed. Stulberg perhaps did not foresee, for example, that some of his "forceful" directiveness about process would become controversial and is perhaps at odds with the centrality of party choice; or that the goal of mediation that he embraces would be challenged by new theories and scholars (Riskin; Bush & Folger).

Though Stulberg quotes Lon Fuller with admiration, who saw mediation as a process "the central quality of which [is] its capacity to reorient the parties towards each other" (Fuller, p. 325), the larger thrust of the Stulberg piece is that a mediator's job is to move parties toward settlement. In his later writing he included among mediation's goals: enhanced understanding, option development, and agreement—*if* the parties want an agreement (Stulberg & Love).

III. Conclusion

The clarity and precision of Stulberg's article, as it provides a definition of mediation, is what makes this piece foundational. Stulberg gives a "a star to steer by" in our understanding and execution of the mediation process, while stressing that there are other stars in the dispute resolution firmament—each with their own internal rationale and place.

References

Lon Fuller, *Mediation—Its Forms and Functions*, 44 S. Cal. L. Rev. 305 (1971).
Frank E.A. Sander, *Varieties of Dispute Processing*, 70 F.R.D. 111 (1976).
Joseph Stulberg & Lela Love, The Middle Voice (2nd ed.).
Lawrence Susskind, *Environmental Mediation and the Accountability Problem*, 6 Vt. L. Rev. 85 (1981).

Just Settlement? Rethinking the Mediator's Goals

Brian A. Pappas

Lawrence Susskind (1981) famously argued mediation's success should be judged by the agreement's basic fairness or justice. Josh Stulberg (1981) responded that settlement, and not justice, is the mediator's goal (pp. 88, 97, 100–101, 103, 105, 106). In order to achieve settlement, the process must provide self-determination to the parties, that is, be voluntary and noncompulsory, which requires the mediator to be impartial and not focus on the fairness of the outcome (pp. 86, 88–91).

The Stulberg/Susskind debate is about the mediator's goals and effectiveness in achieving them. While Stulberg's response established impartiality as a fundamental mediation tenet, his impartiality definition (requiring the mediator to remain impartial to outcome) is inadequate. Remaining neutral regarding outcome is difficult to achieve when multiple forces operate in the opposite direction, including mandatory mediation, mediators articulating settlement as the goal, and mediators giving suggestions and advice. Each of these elements, while presumably neutral to outcome, create a slippery slope and weaken mediator impartiality. This endangers party self-determination, contributes to eroding the distinctions between formal and informal dispute mechanisms, and ultimately harms our system of justice.

Mediation's foremost principle is self-determination, defined as "the act of coming to a voluntary, uncoerced decision in which each party makes free and informed choices as to process and outcome" (Model Standard of Conduct I). Stulberg links self-determination with impartiality: the voluntary nature of mediation requires mediator impartiality and as a result justice cannot be the mediator's goal. But settlement also cannot be the impartial mediator's goal because mediation is not limited only to those who know they want to settle. Widespread use of mandatory mediation requires parties to attend mediation, but not everyone does so for the purpose of settlement. Stulberg describes mediation as a "tool for resolving disputes" (p. 116), but mediation's true power is as a tool helping people determine whether they want to settle. *Settlement should not be the mediator's goal unless it is the parties' goal.*

What should be the mediator's goal, if it is neither justice nor settlement? A mediator's goal should focus on what will lead to settlement instead of on the settlement itself: fostering effective communication in order to access needed information and help parties figure out what they want. Settlement should not automatically be the goal.

Brian A. Pappas, *Just Settlement? Rethinking the Mediator's Goals* In: *Discussions in Dispute Resolution.* Edited by: Art Hinshaw, Andrea Kupfer Schneider, and Sarah Rudolph Cole, Oxford University Press (2021). © Oxford University Press. DOI: 10.1093/oso/9780197513248.003.0028

Ironically, mediators who state the goal as settlement may make settlement less likely. Stating settlement as the goal erodes mediator impartiality by placing the mediator in opposition to the parties. Stulberg acknowledges this risk: "if the mediator is neutral and remains so, then he … invite[s] a bond of trust to develop between him and the parties." The question is not what settlement will result, but whether there will even be a settlement. A mediator should clearly state the goal of mediation as helping the parties communicate effectively and think through their options. By establishing trust, the parties will share more information with the mediator, including their priorities and acceptable trade-offs (p. 97). Without it, "the parties must calculate what information they will share with the mediator, just as they do in communication with any of the parties to the controversy" (p. 97). Parties will be hesitant to share their true goals and bottom lines, fearful the mediator will pressure them toward those limits. Instead of working with the mediator, the parties may work to "spin" the mediator in an attempt to co-opt them into pressuring the other side. In this way, the mediator's impartiality impacts party self-determination.

The Model Standards of Conduct define impartiality as "freedom from favoritism, bias, or prejudice" and caution mediators to "conduct a mediation in an impartial manner and avoid conduct that gives the appearance of partiality." Stulberg defines impartiality as not imposing a particular outcome on the parties and not evaluating parties' potential solutions. Stulberg is correct about impartiality's impact, but his impartiality definition endangers trust-building and information-sharing.

Just as mediators' goals impact their impartiality and the quality of the mediation, so too, mediators endanger their impartiality by acting on their preferences and evaluating options, making suggestions, and sharing opinions. For example, Stulberg states the mediator should "decid[e] which matters and proposals he believes the parties will find acceptable and … to develop a deliberate strategy for bringing about the desired results" (p. 103). But it is the parties', not the mediator's, assessment of acceptability that matters. Mediators should help the parties decide what they find acceptable and help them in developing a strategy to determine whether they can accomplish their goals in mediation.

Parties often need help organizing information and determining their priorities, requiring the mediator to ask tough reality-testing questions. Stulberg agrees and believes a mediator is irresponsible "if he [does] not diligently and persistently challenge each party's own pretensions" (p. 105). Impartiality allows for more effective "reality testing" as parties who trust the mediator is not going to pressure settlement will honestly share their views and bottom lines. Without trust, as Stulberg suggests, the mediator is merely another party against whom each side must negotiate.

As evaluation endangers impartiality, true impartiality requires the mediator to not share any advice, opinions, or expertise on anything other than process. Stulberg's example describing an employer's resistance (presumably shared during a joint session) demonstrates how evaluation can endanger impartiality. He states to the employee's side in caucus:

> I suggest that you think carefully about how important that matter is to you. Focus, perhaps, on a trade-off with your proposal for taking the day following Thanksgiving

> as a leave day, with the time given back when the immediate supervisor believes it most useful. Such a Suggestion is far more likely to be compatible with the employer's posture than the vacation proposal. (p. 104)

Stulberg defends his example as impartial because the statements are probing each side's flexibility without telling either they were right or wrong, or by characterizing any proposals as reasonable or fair (pp. 104–5). Stulberg argues you can give suggestions as long as you don't evaluate them, but yet he does exactly that.

Stulberg risks his impartiality in several ways. First, he risks the trust of the employee side and them treating him as another negotiation party. Second, he risks the employee telling the employer that it was the mediator's suggestion. If the employee suggests Stulberg's solution, but the employer does not like it, the employee might respond, "Well the mediator liked it, it was his suggestion!" This is unlikely if the mediator is caucusing back and forth, but impartiality is even more important in shuttle mediations because each side's main opportunity to influence the other side is through the mediator. Finally, mediation parties are more likely to comply with agreements they discovered and crafted. Stulberg can employ the same strategy while protecting his impartiality. Consider the same labor dispute:

> From what we heard in the joint session, the employer mentioned they do not have much flexibility on vacation time. How likely do you think it is that they will accept your vacation time proposal? Can you say more about how important that issue is to you compared with your other priorities? What is most important to you, the total time spent working, or the ability to make decisions about how and when work versus vacation time occurs? What ideas do you have that will achieve your interest in vacation time flexibility with the employer's desire for consistency of the numbers of days worked? What would the employer want in return for providing you with flexibility on vacation time? How will [any ideas] meet or not meet the other side's interests and yours?

Instead of violating Stulberg's impartiality rule by evaluating the other side's priorities and making a suggestion, a mediator can use reflective listening, interest identification, and elicitive questioning to help each side determine what they want and make a proposal. Doing so requires an active and engaged mediator. Stulberg believes mediators should not use their substantive knowledge of a dispute "for the purpose of serving as an expert who advises the parties as to the 'right answers'" (pp. 95–96). The difference between suggestions and "right answers" is often unclear. It is a slippery slope to state the mediator is not responsible for justice but then indicate it is acceptable to make suggestions based on the mediator's evaluation of acceptable options. In his opposition to Susskind's justice frame, Stulberg's own impartiality definition still slides toward Susskind's viewpoint requiring evaluation.

A mediator's suggestions are not impartial—they are based on the mediator's desire for settlement and evaluation of what will achieve that end. Any suggestion is likely to benefit one side to the detriment of the other. Instead, mediators should help the parties to communicate, to access expertise, and to determine their walkaway points based on their assessments of their alternatives. Mediators use questioning to help the parties to craft offers by thinking through interests, potential collaborative solutions, and competitive bargaining chips.

Self-determination is what distinguishes mediation from other processes and inadequate impartiality limits party self-determination. Mediation lacks evidentiary and procedural safeguards and so without strong impartiality standards mediation can lead to pressured agreements, weaker self-determination, and a watered-down version of justice (Welsh 2001). Evaluative mediators narrowly define the key principles of mediation, hurting mediation's quality and eroding the distinction between formal and informal mechanisms. The answer isn't to blur the lines between evaluation and facilitation but to strengthen the differences in order to protect formal and informal processes, party self-determination, and advocacy itself.

Justice is not a mediation principle, and it is not available in mediation, as the process includes no formal means of gathering information, no adversarial determination of fact, no neutral expert to apply the law, and no procedural safeguards. If there is justice in mediation, it is an individualized concept that occurs through the self-determination (Nolan-Haley 2012).

Courts look to mediation for settlement, not for justice. Mandatory mediation programs preference mass efficiency and leave attorneys and parties with mediation as the main forum for litigating (Nolan-Haley 2012). Lawyers' professional frame and comfort in litigation leads them to prefer evaluative mediation and lawyer-mediators, which means evaluation and a more legal and formal style of mediation (Welsh 2001). The phenomenon is not limited to lawyer-mediators: "facilitative" mediators (both lawyers and nonlawyers) can be observed pressing settlement, providing options, and evaluating just as much as their "evaluative" cousins. They do so because they correctly believe the courts want settlement, because they view mediation as a better, more correct means of handling conflict than trial, and see their success in terms of how frequently mediations settle. All of which contributes to the formalization of mediation and pushes self-determination to the side (Welsh 2001).

Due to the increased use of mediation and the decline of trial and arbitration, mediation becomes the forum for advocacy, often increasing its adversarial nature (Nolan-Haley 2012). Many parties cannot afford or do not want to hire lawyers, and instead seek lawyer-mediators. This further pressures impartiality as the mediator may feel more responsible for the "justice" of the session. With the courts mandating mediation, lawyers and parties preferring to hire lawyer-mediators, and mediators using a weak impartiality definition, the result is weakened party self-determination.

In his response to Susskind, Stulberg uses impartiality to argue that justice cannot be the mediator's responsibility. Stulberg states we cannot "demand that [mediation] perform functions beyond the scope of its institutional and conceptual capacity" (p. 117). Stulberg's impartiality definition, however, does not go far enough to maintain the correct scope, either at the time he wrote his article or now.

References

Model Standards of Conduct for Mediators (2004).

Jacqueline M. Nolan-Haley, *Mediation: The "New Arbitration,"* 17 Harv. Negot. L. Rev. 61–95 (2012).

Joseph B. Stulberg, *The Theory and Practice of Mediation: A Reply to Professor Susskind*, 6 VT. L. REV. 85–117 (1981).
Laurence Susskind, *Environmental Mediation and the Accountability Problem*, 6 VT. L. REV. 1–47 (1981).
Nancy A. Welsh, *The Thinning Vision of Self-Determination in Court-Connected Mediation: The Inevitable Price of Institutionalization?*, 6 HARV. NEGOT. L. REV. 1–96 (2001).

Neutrality in 2020: A Reply to 1981 Stulberg

Sharon Press and Bobbi McAdoo

Joseph (Josh) Stulberg published *The Theory and Practice of Mediation: A Reply to Professor Susskind* in 1981. His thesis was direct and simple: a mediator's commitment to neutrality is the critical element which "permits mediation to be an effective, principled dispute settlement procedure" (p. 86). Stulberg articulated for all of us—then and now—the centrality of neutrality and impartiality to the very definition of mediation. This articulation continues to be a significant contribution to the dispute resolution field; indeed, the Stulberg article deserves to be labeled "foundational." We question, however, whether the 1981 commitment to neutrality Stulberg articulated is understood by mediator practitioners today in the same way he intended, given the wide range of disputes now subject to mediation. Stulberg wrote in 1981, "[p]aradoxically, while the use of mediation has expanded, a common understanding as to what constitutes mediation has weakened" (p. 85). Ironically, despite Stulberg's very clear thesis, his article contained the seeds that contribute to confusion in the definition of mediation itself.

Stulberg defines mediation as a (1) noncompulsory process in which (2) an impartial, neutral party (the mediator) assists disputing parties to identify issues of mutual concern, and (3) design solutions that are acceptable to the parties (p. 88). Thirty-nine years later, not only has the field evolved in such a way as to render portions of this definition outdated, each component requires a nuanced review and discussion. We will look at each component in turn.

First, is mediation a "non-compulsory process"? Given the development of court-connected and court-mandated mediation programs, this definitional component of mediation is no longer true. In 1981, Stulberg's frame of reference mostly included labor, employment, and community disputes, which shared several common characteristics, most notably that disputants voluntarily sought the assistance of a mediator and had some type of relationship which was likely to continue. Fast forward thirty-nine years and we have a significant number of court-mandated mediations of civil disputes which have neither of these characteristics.

Secondly, Stulberg's definition of mediation includes both impartiality and neutrality, but he really focuses his discussion around the concept of "neutrality," and in particular, outcome neutrality. In a 2012 article, Stulberg revisited his 1981 piece and underscored his belief that "[a] mediator must be neutral with respect to negotiated outcomes but not neutral with respect to process" (Stulberg 2012). The mediation field has struggled with defining and differentiating the terms impartiality and neutrality. A common understanding in 2020 is that *neutrality* refers to outcome, that is, the mediator's commitment not to have a stake in how the parties choose to resolve (or not) their dispute; while *impartiality* has to do with personal biases, that is, the

Sharon Press and Bobbi McAdoo, *Neutrality in 2020: A Reply to 1981 Stulberg* In: *Discussions in Dispute Resolution*. Edited by: Art Hinshaw, Andrea Kupfer Schneider, and Sarah Rudolph Cole, Oxford University Press (2021).
DOI: 10.1093/oso/9780197513248.003.0029

mediator's commitment not to let personal opinions affect how the mediator conducts a mediation. With the knowledge and acceptance that no one can ever be completely unbiased, the field has coalesced around the belief that mediators are ethically bound to *act* "impartially" regardless of personal reactions to the disputants or the dispute, even as the Model Standards of Conduct for Mediators specifically state that impartiality "means freedom from favoritism, bias or prejudice" in terms of how the mediation is conducted *and* with regards to the outcome (Model Standards II). Stulberg's thesis, listing "neutral with regard to the outcome" as one of the "desirable qualities and abilities" of a mediator, has more than survived the test of time. Stulberg's intent, however, regarding the appropriate role of the mediator *during* the mediation is less clear (e.g., what exactly does it mean to *not* be neutral with respect to process and how does this relate to the ethical directive to be impartial?) and may have unintentionally contributed to some confusion for the unsophisticated reader.

The final component of Stulberg's definition of mediation is the mediator's role in "design[ing] solutions that are acceptable to the parties." Here, Stulberg, intentionally or not, plants seeds for *both* transformative and evaluative mediation. A central point in Stulberg's article is that the mediator, while knowledgeable, "does not possess such knowledge . . . for the purpose of serving as an expert who advises the parties as to the 'right answers'" (p. 96). He bristles against the assertion that the mediator knows what is optimal for the participants in the dispute. This concept, which later was framed as honoring "self-determination," became a foundational element of mediation and the role of the mediator. It is the core of transformative mediation which is premised on the notion that people in conflict are in a state of weakness and confusion. The mediator's role is to support participant moves toward finding clarity and strength (empowerment and recognition) and *not* to disempower them by providing answers or making decisions for the participants *throughout* the mediation.

While these transformative constructs exist, however, the piece is littered with references, noted in bold, which support the mediator acting in a very directive role during the mediation. For example, Stulberg states, "[b]y **forcing** the parties to speak through selective spokespersons, the mediator restricts potential grandstanding, reduces interruptions . . ." (p. 98). In describing the use of caucus, he states: "Meeting separately with the parties enables the mediator to **force** a party to consider the merits of its proposals or alternative settlements without the party displaying any weakness or group dissension to the other parties" (p. 103). And "[the mediator] can **force** a party to determine if the proposals reflect the needs of its constituents or simply the preferences of one or two members of the bargaining team. If the latter, he can frequently embarrass the team into modifying its position . . ." (p. 105). "As mediation approaches either an agreement or breakdown, the mediator **forcefully** identifies for the respective parties the cost each will pay for not reaching a settlement" (p. 105). "The mediator would fail in his job of assisting the parties to reach a resolution, however, if he did not diligently and **persistently challenge** each party's own pretensions" (pp. 105–6). Most of all, "the mediator should be guided in **pressing the parties** by his sense of what is attainable" (p. 106).

Stulberg recognizes that from the perspective of the party "who is subjected to these persuasive tactics, it may appear that the mediator has joined forces with the other party and has become its advocate in trying to extract concessions from him" (p. 105). Despite this recognition, Stulberg brushes this aside by stating that "sophisticated" negotiators would understand that the mediator really is impartial.

From Stulberg's 1981 frame, this may have been true, but in 2020 we find these suggestions to be problematic and to be overly directive (and evaluative) moves which run afoul of the mediator's obligation to be impartial/neutral *and* to honor party self-determination. In 2020, the growth and development of court-connected/mandated mediation and its use in a range of disputes means that often parties are not "sophisticated." This contrasts with Stulberg's example of parties who had voluntarily entered into mediation and were equally aware that the alternative to an agreement was a strike and a company shutdown. We leave aside whether these type of directive moves are appropriate in circumstances when everyone is in agreement that the most important outcome is to prevent a strike and shutdown; but the types of disputes mediated 2020 now include those where settlement may not be the optimal or desired outcome. A participant may want a day in court rather than settle for what someone on the outside may view as a "good settlement." The assumption that settlement is the desired and appropriate outcome for every mediation is no longer (if it ever was) accurate. In addition, when Stulberg advances the point that the mediator "should be guided in pressing the parties by [the mediator's] sense of what is attainable" (p. 106), this points to a very omniscient mediator who appears to be more similar to Susskind's non-neutral mediator than Stulberg believes.

It would be helpful in analyzing Stulberg's piece if we had empirical research results to draw on for guidance. Specifically, is there any evidence that the techniques described by Stulberg (or Susskind) contribute to "good" mediation? In 2012, a Task Force on Research on Mediator Techniques (the "Task Force") was convened by the ABA Section of Dispute Resolution to examine empirical studies that linked specific mediator actions (e.g., mediator evaluation of the case, eliciting disputant ideas) either to enhanced mediation outcomes or to detrimental effects of the mediation process. The Task Force was established, in short, to "identify, assess, and distill the findings of empirical research on the effectiveness of mediator techniques" (Task Force Report).

The examination of forty years of empirical studies by the Task Force yielded no definitive answers. The Report only concludes that some mediator actions appear to have a greater potential for positive effects than negative effects on both settlement and disputants' relationships and on perceptions of mediation. Indeed, a substantial likelihood of no effects for any given technique was also prevalent.

A few striking conclusions from the work of the Task Force might be apt here.

With regard to settlement, most studies found mediator styles or specific actions considered pressing or directive (with some element of pressure or coercion) either increased settlement or did not affect settlement. These same pressing actions, however, were found to have no effect or were associated with more negative views of the mediator, the process, the outcome, and the ability to work with the other disputant.

When the mediator's actions involved recommending a settlement, suggesting options, or offering case evaluation, these actions also either increased or had no effect on settlement. The related data on the effects of these actions on disputants' perceptions and relationships, however, was mixed—positive, negative, and no effect.

Other categories of mediator techniques such as eliciting disputants' suggestions and solutions, and addressing disputants' emotions or relationships, leaned toward the positive in the category of effect on disputants' perceptions and relationships. Eliciting disputants' suggestions and solutions also increased or had no effect on settlement; addressing disputants' emotions or relationships had the potential to increase settlements but also the potential to reduce settlement. Other mediator actions, including building trust and rapport with disputants, and using pre-mediation caucuses focused on establishing trust, leaned positive but from a small number of studies.

Eliciting disputants' suggestions and solutions appears to have the most potential to be positive in both effect on settlement and effect on disputants' perceptions and relationships. This empirical evidence, scant as it may be, supports Stulberg's thesis—a profound element of mediation is the mediator's commitment to outcome neutrality; to trust the participants' sense of what should happen in their conflict is essential. It is indeed part of the definition of mediation.

Considering what we now know about how the field has developed, we believe that Stulberg did not go far enough. He was absolutely right in his clarity and commitment to *outcome* neutrality, but we believe the mediator also needs to be neutral/impartial throughout all of the process. Specifically, we question whether the directive role of the mediator Stulberg seems to endorse carries with it too much risk of subverting the mediation process and the accepted role of the mediator. A mediator who is (too) evaluative might bring about settlement, but the parties in that mediation might conclude that procedural justice norms have been violated and leave the mediation with little trust in the mediator or mediation process for the future.

It is a testament to Stulberg that this article continues to raise important and relevant points of discussion; there is no question that it is a foundational publication. Our reply to 1981 Stulberg is a mighty thank you for his insight. We are energized to pick up and expand where he left off—to ensure that the important thesis he articulated in 1981 continues to be relevant in 2020.

References

Report of the Task Force on Research on Mediator Techniques (2017).

Joseph B. Stulberg, *Must a Mediator Be Neutral? You'd Better Believe It!*, 95 MARQUETTE L. REV. 854 (2012).

Revisiting Mediator Neutrality

Joseph B. Stulberg

I. Introduction

I am honored and humbled to have my previously published article included as a subject for discussion in this volume. The remarkable bonus, of course, is to receive thoughtful, insightful—and, might I observe, extremely generous—comments and critiques on it by professional colleagues and friends; their insights are rich and valuably advance the analysis and practice of mediation.

I believe that the reason the article might warrant a place in this volume relates not particularly to my analysis but to its topic: mediator neutrality. To this day, I believe that clarifying and defending a compelling conception of mediator neutrality remains the most important intellectual and practical subject for work in this area: party participation in mediation compels it and public confidence in mediation's process integrity depends on it.

Each commentator thoughtfully raises distinct challenges to the manner in which I treated this general topic. I want to respond to selected aspects of each contribution by trying to identify the questions that I believe their comments trigger; that leaves to the current and rising generation of scholars and practitioners, quite confidently from my vantage point, the arduous but rewarding task of answering those questions. I want to begin, however, by setting the context—the commanding need—to which these questions and potential responses are directed.

II. Context of Investigation

I believe that mediation is a social process for resolving disputes among persons, and that participating in mediation for all stakeholders, including the mediator, is a justice event. Its integrity, therefore, lies in its supporters providing a compelling account of its fundamental components, including such matters as party self-determination, mediator neutrality, and process confidentiality. In Dworkin terms, any proponent of a theory of mediation must offer an interpretative, albeit objective, account of this social practice (Dworkin 2011).

It is critical that we acknowledge this setting. Doing so rules out as implausible, because not supported by compelling theory, some immediate claims about mediator neutrality, including assertions that a mediator's being neutral is analogous to adding a "neutral" chemical to a mix that itself does not alter the interaction among the other elements, or that mediator neutrality requires the mediator "to leave her values at the

Joseph B. Stulberg, *Revisiting Mediator Neutrality* In: *Discussions in Dispute Resolution*. Edited by: Art Hinshaw, Andrea Kupfer Schneider, and Sarah Rudolph Cole, Oxford University Press (2021). © Oxford University Press.
DOI: 10.1093/oso/9780197513248.003.0030

entrance to the mediation room." Those assertions simply beg the question of what constitutes mediator neutrality.

I believe it possible to provide a sound, persuasive interpretative theory of mediation. In responding briefly below to the penetrating insights of my thoughtful commentators, I do not explicate such an account here, although I am doing so in a forthcoming manuscript (Stulberg, forthcoming). At this point, I simply want to highlight and reaffirm the need for it and to emphasize that my comments, as do those of the commentators, presumes one.

III. Response to Commentators

A. Process versus Outcome

Professors McAdoo and Press thoughtfully press me to clarify my claim that "[a] mediator must be neutral with respect to outcomes but not neutral with respect to process." Is that possible, they query, and how, if at all, does the concept of impartiality relate to my discussion?

They highlight a crucial consideration, and perhaps with the passage of time I have gained greater clarity myself. Here is what I continue to believe: there is an important difference between the concepts of *impartiality* and *neutrality*. In my judgment, maintaining a posture of *impartiality* requires that individual to apply agreed-upon rules, principles, and norms to a particular situation in a manner that respects the concept of "relevant consideration" embedded in them. For instance, if the governing rule is that one party speaks at a time, then applying or abiding by that rule *impartially* requires a person to acknowledge that the rule should be applied to cut off interruptions, even when the interrupter claims, "But what he said is not truthful," or "He does not know what he is talking about—let me clarify matters."

One can impartially apply a rule, whether its content is unwise, burdensome, or even unfair. Since every procedural rule has substantive implications, the mediator must attend to them, confident that each rule supports party participation in the mediation process as a justice-event. Stated strongly, I believe that a mediator has the responsibility for developing and applying a range of procedural guidelines for guiding the mediation conversation that reasonable persons would view as fair and that are made known to and embraced by the parties. If one or more parties propose a rule that the mediator finds troublesome—ranging from "meet only in caucus" to "only men get to speak during the mediation"—then the mediator must decide whether he or she wants to proceed with conducting the session; without apology, there is no mediator neutrality on such process matters.

By contrast, a mediator must maintain a neutral posture of judgment regarding outcomes. This posture is deeply embedded in and supported by our historical political tradition in which we recognize and celebrate that each person, as a dimension of human dignity, has the autonomy to shape and choose for herself those life events and values that enrich her human experience. It is the mediator's role to try to understand, not displace, those decisions. It is central to promoting human freedom in a democratic society. For example, suppose in a divorce mediation that a child's mother states that her daughter's interests are best served by having the child's father unilaterally make significant decisions regarding the child's religious practices, school training, and social experiences, and the father immediately accepts the proposal. What should the mediator do? A mediator might personally bristle at the mother's deference to the father's role in parenting and want to encourage that mother to assert and assume her right and responsibility to parent the child. The mediator can bristle—internally—but presuming the parties understand the arrangements and are capable of effectively implementing their terms, a mediator must support their party choice.

B. Is a Mediator's Focusing on Securing a Settlement Inconsistent with a Mediator Being Neutral?

Professor Pappas engagingly challenges my claim that a mediator's goal is to assist parties reach settlement. He thoughtfully writes:

> But settlement also cannot be the impartial mediator's goal because mediation is not limited only to those who know they want to settle. Widespread use of mandatory mediation requires parties to attend mediation, but not everyone does so for the purpose of settlement.... Settlement should not be the mediator's goal unless it is the parties' goal.

His comments, echoing a theme that McAdoo and Press also note, helpfully point to a distinction that I need to clarify. Pappas notes, convincingly, that it is not always the case that every party to a mediation session wants to reach a settlement; he then posits that the more appropriate mediator posture should be to help people, through conversation, "to determine whether they want to settle." Lawrence Watson Jr., a preeminent mediator of civil litigation cases, has advanced a somewhat similar point, though his important insight is that the mediator's task is to help parties identify possible settlement terms so that they can then decide whether it is in their interest to settle; to state Watson's comments in Fisher/Ury terms, the mediator's duty is to help parties identify possible resolution terms and compare those to their best alternative to a negotiated agreement (Fisher, et al.).

I welcome and endorse Pappas' perspective but continue to ask the following question: Isn't it the mediator's duty, when conducting the conversation, to shape it as a problem-solving dialogue? And if the answer to that is affirmative, then isn't it a significant part of the mediator's job to advance participant conversation so that they are discussing negotiable issues and developing possible solutions that might be acceptable, thereby distinguishing a mediator from a meeting facilitator, a panel moderator, or a mental health professional conducting a therapy session? There are many valuable types of conversations, ranging from those occurring during organizational annual meetings to town hall gatherings, "public conversations," legislative debates, or judicial trials. All contribute importantly to sustaining democratic participation in our public life. But none of these are, nor pretend to be, what mediators have a particular duty to advance. It is in that sense that I continue to believe that a mediator, in principle, has the distinctive responsibility to prompt and prod mediation parties to develop and consider possible settlement terms.

C. Is Party Acceptability of Outcome Disconnected from Justice Principles?

With characteristic clarity, Professor Love highlights the powerful appeal of Susskind's challenge:

> With respect to Susskind's proposition that environmental disputes involve a special need for assurance of high quality outcomes, that assertion is too plausible and appealing to anyone living on and loving this earth. Susskind warns us that this category of disputes can involve significant harms to "public health and safety" and ... negatively impact future generations. We nod our head in agreement; we share a common interest in the future of the planet.

That, poignantly portrayed, is what makes for a hard case.

Love accurately notes that I challenge Susskind's conclusion that the mediator in such instances is responsible for ensuring that such negative outcomes do not occur. I claimed, I believe accurately, that comparable choices arise in multiple settings; the examples I used involved labor-management negotiations in the public sector, but as Love notes, the principle applies to settings ranging from family matters to complex civil litigation.

But the attraction of Susskind's example, understandably and with justification, still leaves mediators uneasy. Why? Love suggests, as have others, that those, including myself, committed to sustaining party choice through mediation might be jettisoning, perhaps cavalierly, public norms and rules. To me, that points to the signal theoretical and practical challenge for mediators: What is or should be the relationship between a mediator's promoting party autonomy and a mediator's obligation, as a member of a political community, to securing fidelity to norms of fairness and justice?

To observe that this is a complicated question is to state the obvious. I have been persuaded that the most compelling brief for using mediation to resolve disputes within our social community is that mediation can, in principle, comport closely with what Rawls has described as a procedure reflecting principles of *pure procedural* justice (Rawls 1999); that is, *if* the rules of participation and engagement reflect a commitment to our basic moral principles regarding justice as fairness—persons are participating and making decisions without coercion, no one is privileged or disadvantaged by his or her racial, gender, or religious background, and so forth—then any outcome that parties generate by participating in that process will be fair. There is no independent criterion, such as greatest happiness for greatest number of persons, that trumps party choice. It is in that important sense that I believe that "party acceptability" should constitute the governing criterion for assessing mediated outcomes.

IV. Conclusion

I believe there is something majestic and noble about the mediation process and the privilege of serving as a mediator within it. That majesty is tied to the dominant democratic values and principles—equality, personal responsibility, and dignity—that structure participant engagement in it. But sustaining public confidence in mediation comes only by having reflective, responsible persons participate in it and who, informed by that experience, thoughtfully examine and adjust mediation's format to incorporate developing social innovations and practices to ensure that mediation's use continues to meet the unmet and emerging social needs of our fellow citizens. That responsibility remains the work for its twenty-first-century practitioners, policymakers, and scholars, of which these commentators and book editors are members. As long as I am able, I eagerly look forward to learning from their contributions and insights.

References

Ronald Dworkin, Justice for Hedgehogs (2011).
Roger Fisher, William Ury, and Bruce Patton, Getting to Yes 99 (3d ed. 2011).
John Rawls, A Theory of Justice 73 (Rev. ed. 1999).
Joseph B. Stulberg, Lectures on Mediation Theory and Practice (forthcoming).

Article 2.3

The Mediation Alternative: Process Dangers for Women

Trina Grillo

100 Yale Law Journal 1545 (1991)

Introduction: The Promise of Mediation

* * *

There is little doubt that divorce procedure needs to be reformed, but reformed how? Presumably, any alternative should be at least as just, and at least as humane, as the current system, particularly for those who are least powerful in society. Mediation has been put forward, with much fanfare, as such an alternative . . .

* * *

Nonetheless, I conclude that mandatory mediation provides neither a more just nor a more humane alternative to the adversarial system of adjudication of custody, and, therefore, does not fulfill its promises . . .

* * *

I. The Rise of Mandatory Custody Mediation in California

* * *

. . . California's mandatory mediation law . . . requires that all custody and visitation disputes be mediated prior to being considered by the county Superior Court . . .

In practice, the qualifications of mediators provided by the California courts vary widely . . . [And their] services offered are frequently inadequate at best . . .

* * *

. . . More than half of California counties [require mediators to make recommendations to the court if mediation does not result in settlement] . . . I have observed that the recommendations of mediators are almost always accepted by the

Trina Grillo, *The Mediation Alternative: Process Dangers for Women* In: *Discussions in Dispute Resolution.* Edited by: Art Hinshaw, Andrea Kupfer Schneider, and Sarah Rudolph Cole, Oxford University Press (2021).
DOI: 10.1093/oso/9780197513248.003.0031

judge; indeed, some mediators [use this fact] to pressure the parties into reaching an agreement.

II. The Betrayal of Mediation's Promises

* * *

[In most legal settings a system of norms emerges in which those who violate those norms are sanctioned. But in mediation, the participating parties are unaware of these norms. They look to mediators to provide them cues, and mediators typically do this, and mediators sanction those who violate these norms. One such norm is that mediators typically insist that parties refrain from complaining about their spouse's conduct and blaming each other and rather focus on the future. Doing so destroys the context of the parties situation and the notions that mediating couples are to be treated equally.]

* * *

[While mediation is a place where emotions can be expressed, expressions of anger are often overtly discouraged, thereby silencing a woman who may have, for the first time in her life, found a voice for her anger. For a woman who has just found her anger, the suppression of the very force that that has driven her forward is a devastating message. And this message is particularly damaging to African-American women whose anger is already delegitimized by society and suffer from free-floating hostility by virtue of the color of their skin.]

* * *

[Furthermore, when mandatory mediation is a part of the court system, the idea that parties are engaging in self-determination is illusory. For example, mediation where abuse has occurred is troubling. Mandatory mediation programs do not always allow parties to opt out of the process, and where such provisions exist, abused women may have trouble showing they meet the opt out provisions because her word about her predicament is doubted. In such cases, she is then required to meet with her abuser to determine child custody.]

* * *

[In California the problem is exacerbated because lawyers are typically excluded from mediation sessions. Furthermore, California law permits courts to allow mediators to make custody recommendations to the court based on information acquired during the mediation. Where this practice occurs, failing to embrace a proposal that the mediator favors or to disavow an agreement before it is approved by the court—especially in a jurisdiction where mediators' recommendations are almost always accepted—is likely to be an empty gesture. The mediator will make the recommendation, and lawyers who see the proposal upon its submission to the court may be reluctant to be perceived as saboteurs of the agreement. It is unclear why a mandatory system would encourage the exclusion of lawyers, nevertheless excluding lawyers from the process makes parties more vulnerable to the mediator's authority.]

* * *

III. Mandatory Mediation and the Dangers of Forced Engagement

* * *

For [a victim of physical abuse], the direct confrontation with her husband, with the safety of her children and herself at stake, would surely be psychologically traumatizing and might also put her in physical danger. Because of these possibilities, the chance—even the substantial one of a beneficial result cannot justify the sort of intrusion by the state that occurs when mediation is mandatory.

* * *

A. The Ethic of Care in Mediation

… [F]eminist scholars have suggested that women have a more "relational" sense of self than do men … The female mode is characterized by an "ethic of care" which emphasizes nurturance, connection with others, and contextual thinking. The male mode is characterized by an "ethic of justice" which emphasizes individualism, the use of rules to resolve moral dilemmas, and equality … Nevertheless, it is clear that those who operate in a "female mode"—whether biologically male or female—will respond more "selflessly" to the demands of mediation.

* * *

… Above all, she will be asked to put the well-being of the children before her own, as if she and her children's well-being were entirely separate. Her problem in addressing her future alone, however, may be that she reflexively puts her children before herself, even when she truly needs to take care of herself in order to take care of her children …

… She is likely, in mediation, to be susceptible and afraid once again … [She], and not her husband, will be susceptible to any pressure to compromise, and to compromise in her situation might be very dangerous for both her and her children.

B. Sexual Domination and Judicial Violence

Women who have been through mandatory mediation often describe it as an experience of sexual domination, comparing mandatory mediation to rape. Catharine McKinnon's work provides a basis for explaining why, for some women, this characterization is appropriate. MacKinnon has analyzed gender as a system of power relations, evidenced primarily with respect to control of women's sexuality ... It is precisely the potential for connection that permits invasion into the integrity of women's bodies ...

... It may seem a large leap, from acts of physical violence and invasion to the apparently simple requirement that a woman sit in a room with her spouse working toward the resolution of an issue of mutual concern. But that which may be at stake in a court-ordered custody mediation—access to one's children—may be the main reason one has for living, as well as one's hope for the future. And because mandatory mediation is a forced engagement, ordinarily without attorneys or even friends or supporters present, it may amount to a form of "psychic breaking and entering" or, put another way, psychic rape.

The reality of this background of judicial violence cannot be discounted when measuring the potential trauma of the mandatory mediation setting. Although the mediation system is purportedly designed in part to help participants *avoid* contact with the violence that must come from judicial decisions, in significant ways the violence of the contact is more direct ... Mediation is described as a form of intervention that reflects the *disputants'* view of the quarrel. But having a mediation take place on court premises with a mediator who might or might not inject her prejudices into the process may make it unlikely that the disputants' view will control. ...

* * *

When I have suggested to mediators that even being forced to sit across the table and negotiate, unassisted, with a spouse might be traumatic, their reaction has been almost uniformly dismissive ... A few hours of discomfort seems not so much to ask in return for a system that, to their mind, serves the courts and the children much better than the alternative. But a few hours of discomfort may not be all that is at stake; the trauma inflicted upon a vulnerable party during mediation can be as great as that which occurs in other psychologically violent confrontations. As such, it should not be minimized ...

Moreover, because the mandatory mediation system is more problematic for women than for men, forcing unwilling women to take part in a process which involves much personal exposure sends a powerful social message: it is permissible to discount the real experience of women in the service of someone else's idea of what will be good for them, good for their children, or good for the system.

IV. Alternatives to Mandatory Mediation

* * *

... [R]ather than representing a change in the system to accommodate the "feminine voice," in actuality, mandatory mediation overrides real women's voices saying that cooperation might ... be detrimental to their lives and the lives of their children ...

... The legislative choice to make mediation mandatory has been a mistake.

* * *

Any reform proposals, of the adversarial system or of a mediation alternative, should be rejected if they result in further disempowerment of the disempowered ... Any reforms should evince a concern for the personhood of the mediation clients, a concern that is lacking under current mediation practices.

... [A]n adequate mediation scheme should not only be voluntary rather than mandatory, but should also allow people's emotions to be part of the process, allow their values and principles to matter in the discussion, allow parties' attorneys to participate if requested by the parties, allow parties to choose a mediator and the location for the mediation, allow parties to choose the issues to mediate, and require that divorcing couples be educated about the availability and logistics of mediation so as to enable them to make an intelligent choice as to whether to engage in it.

... [T]he mediator must learn to respect each client's struggles, including her timing, anger, and resistance to having certain issues mediated, and also must learn to refrain, to the extent he is capable, from imposing his own substantive agenda on the mediation.

Conclusion

... When mediation is imposed rather than voluntarily engaged in, its virtues are lost. More than lost: mediation becomes a wolf in sheep's clothing. It relies on force and disregards the context of the dispute, while masquerading as a gentler, more empowering alternative to adversarial litigation ... Seen in this light, mandatory mediation is especially harmful ...

... [I]f mediation is to be introduced into the court system, it should provide a better alternative. It is not enough to say that the adversary system is so flawed that even a misguided, intrusive, and disempowering system of mediation should be embraced. If mediation as currently instituted constitutes a fundamentally flawed process in the way I have described, it is more, not less, disempowering than the adversary system—for it is then a process in which people are told they are being empowered, but in fact are being forced to acquiesce in their own oppression.

Comments

Trina Grillo: Productive Rage

Carol Pauli

Trina Grillo's article was powerful because it conveyed a woman's anger, rising from deep inside the field. Writing as a woman of mixed race and as a mediator, Grillo critiqued mediation by enlisting its own methods: she drew her insights from behavioral and social sciences and from women's stories of lived experience. Grillo wrote that mandated mediation in the intimate field of family law could trap a woman in an impossible dilemma. Forced to face her opponent at the informal mediation table, she could be "good"—cooperative, responsible, and calm. Or she could be "bad"—bitter, vengeful, and raging. Either way, silent or screaming, the woman was losing her voice.

This dilemma echoed one posed by psychologist Harriet Lerner, then at the Menninger Clinic. At one extreme, the stereotypical good woman took care of others to such a degree that she lost track of her own vital needs. At the other, the bad woman was aware of her own anger but expressed it in a way that was easily ridiculed and dismissed. Lerner had produced several academic papers on women's anger, as well as a best-selling self-help book, *The Dance of Anger*. Grillo cited Lerner, in both forms of literature, in no fewer than fifteen footnotes. Lerner's research and clinical work supported Grillo's observation that women had learned in girlhood that their anger would be demonized in a patriarchal system. Like Grillo, Lerner wanted to change that system, "to bring the old roles and rules into question" (Lerner, *Dance of Anger*, p. 223).

Ironically, mediation was supposed to be part of that change. It had been nurtured by feminists as a womanly alternative to the patriarchal, combative world of litigation and abstract formalities handed down by the white men Carrie Menkel-Meadow called the "lawgivers" (Menkel-Meadow, p. 29). Mediation meant to bring a justice of healing to people in conflict, and no conflict seemed a better fit than the familiar, often tearful, wrangling over child custody and visitation. Mediation promised to take account of the context of women's individual stories, provide room for their feelings, and honor their ability to speak and decide for themselves.

So Grillo's critique must have seemed like a betrayal to many of her colleagues. Given the sublime promises of mediation, a reader could practically hear Grillo's chiding as she recounted the way mediation had arrived "with much fanfare" (p. 1548) and then had been "heralded" and "touted" and finally imposed (p. 1552). In California child-custody and visitation disputes, parties were now required to mediate. They could not choose their own mediators or protest the court's choice without risk. Although the sessions were confidential, a mediator could make recommendations directly to the court, so what parties said and did "in confidence" could hurt them. There was, indeed, a betrayal, said Grillo: forcing mediation on parties betrayed

Carol Pauli, *Trina Grillo: Productive Rage* In: *Discussions in Dispute Resolution.* Edited by: Art Hinshaw, Andrea Kupfer Schneider, and Sarah Rudolph Cole, Oxford University Press (2021). © Oxford University Press.
DOI: 10.1093/oso/9780197513248.003.0032

its defining promises. At the extreme, when a woman was fighting for access to her own children, forced mediation was "psychic rape" (p. 1606).

Grillo was not the first person to write that mediation could be distorted by power and prejudice. She cited predecessors from the decade before. Owen Fiss, for example, in his *Yale Law Journal* article, *Against Settlement*, had warned that, where one party had more power than the other, mediation could be coercive and unjust. In *Fairness and Formality: Minimizing the Risk of Prejudice in Alternative Dispute Resolution*, Richard Delgado and his colleagues wrote of the cruel irony that stripping away the formalities of the courtroom could increase the risk of prejudice against the poor and disempowered, the very people mediation had hoped to help. Janet Rifkin's *Mediation from a Feminist Perspective: Promise and Problems* even asked whether mediation, rather than heralding a new, feminist jurisprudence, might be merely reinforcing the old one. Fiss and Delgado had written abstractly. Rifkin had told stories, but their plots were benign. Grillo's stories were different.

Grillo told the kinds of stories that had provided the foundation of feminism, stories of women's experience of being dominated. She told them much as those stories had been told to her. The men in her vignettes were familiar characters. The unfaithful husband had left his wife. The untrustworthy father had failed to return his son to his ex-wife on time and had lied about placing him in a harsh, unlicensed day-care center. The distraught women in the stories also rang true. One feared that the mediator would see her as a bad mother. She feared her own anger, an emotion she had little experience in managing or using. Another woman could not even articulate her injury. In the mediation process, the women tried to be "good." They managed to remain cooperative and calm. They listened as they were counseled to stop blaming, to look to the future rather than the past, and to be less controlling. The women nodded. They made concessions. They quietly agreed. Their agreements could make a reader's blood boil.

What tormented these women, Grillo wrote, was not the unfeeling rigidity of patriarchal rules but the complete lack of rules. Adrift in the informality of mediation, the women were subjected again to the same unspoken societal norms to which they had always been vulnerable. But now the psychological barriers that had hindered them took on the added authority of the state. A "microlegal system" (p. 1556) of subtle and powerful messages told a woman what could be said and what could not be said, which feelings were appropriate and which were not. Angry memories were in the latter categories, and the norms were enforced through a concomitant set of "microsanctions" (p. 1556).

This unspoken legal system was eerily invisible. The powerful parties, including the mediators, were unable to see or feel the outlines of the system. The shape of the constraints could even be obscure to the subjected weaker party. For her, the only indication might be the recurring ache of losing once again. Mediation, Grillo wrote, could be just as disempowering as the patriarchal courts and even more personally damaging to a woman.

Although Grillo's focus on California family courts was laser-like, her direct hit illuminated more than its target. Many of the disturbing dynamics that she found in mandatory mediations could arise as well in processes that were ostensibly voluntary. To begin with, a reader had to wonder whether any weaker party's agreement to settle—or even to mediate—could be entirely free of subtle coercion. Social constraints, particularly for women, were so pervasive that a woman in any dispute might not see them clearly enough to name them, to articulate her concerns, or to access the legitimate questions trying to surface in her mind. Mediation's fundamental dedication to self-determination might be meaningless for a woman whose very selfhood had been systemically stunted.

Furthermore, if a woman's anger was delegitimized in this system, Grillo said, the wrath of a minority woman was even more delegitimized because it was routinely rejected along multiple fronts. For example, an angry Black woman would be dismissed by men, both Black and white. But she would also be rejected by whites, both male and female. So the silent social norms unleashed in mediation were uniquely disabling to those at intersections of disempowerments. As a woman of Cuban, Black, and Italian heritage, Grillo knew such intersections firsthand.

To write that Grillo was angry is a risk for someone who never knew her. By all accounts, Grillo was a joyful, passionate, brilliant, and caring professor and mediator. Yet in her remarks to the Southwest People of Color Conference in1992, edited and published after her death, Grillo said that she struggled at times with anger. In this case, she was talking about her experience of demeaning, subtle, micro-aggressions against minority women in the legal academy. "I worry that this anger will leak out in some way that will feel inappropriate to me.... that it will leak out where it can do the most damage—expressed as an unkind comment to another person in a relatively powerless position" (Estate of Trina Grillo, p. 749).

It is possible that, in researching women's anger, Grillo found Lerner's work to be a useful personal guide. Lerner's insight was that both the "good" woman and the "bad" woman were unwittingly preserving the system that oppressed them. After all, the good woman's compliance did not demand change, but neither did the bad woman's outbursts. Both served instead to protect and even rigidify the unspoken, oppressive rules. A woman who wanted change would need to use her anger in a new way. She would need to listen to it and see what dissatisfaction it was revealing to her. Then she would need to use anger as a tool to clarify her own selfhood, accepting her separateness and individuality, taking responsibility for the things she could control, and then taking action.

Such a woman would also need to brace for what would follow. This time, she would not likely be dismissed. Instead, she would find that her self-defining moves had the power to provoke real responses in others. Among those responses would be forceful opposition. Lerner counseled women to expect this and to stay the course over the long term, even while forgiving their own inevitable missteps. She likened the process of real feminist change to a kind of dance in which a woman learns how to put her feet down in different steps, one at a time, and thereby prompts her counterpart to make reciprocal adjustments.

In the twenty-nine years since Grillo's article, social science has learned more about subtle social norms. New research has found that unconscious stereotypes, implicit bias, and racial anxiety affect almost everyone, undermining even the fundamental neutrality of mediators (Izumi, p. 689). Power imbalances can happen in many directions, sometimes surprising ones. Contacted for this essay, Lerner expanded on a point that both she and Grillo had acknowledged briefly years ago: in their own way men, too, may be hurt in unstructured family talk. "[I]t is true that women have been denied the expression of healthy anger and protest. It is also true, based on my decades of clinical experience, that men are as likely, or more likely, to lose their voice in marriage" (Lerner, email exchange). A justice of healing will require humility.

Trina Grillo's foundational work stirred other scholars because she used her anger effectively. In the optimistic early days of mediation, when she saw signs of trouble, she did what the women in her stories could not do. She distinguished her own selfhood and said clearly what she saw happening. She did not play the "good" woman and suppress her anger. She also did not play the "bad" woman and rant uselessly. Instead, she listened to her own discomfort. She clarified and communicated her own separate position within the field that she still loved. She put her foot down, and the field continues to respond.

References

Estate of Trina Grillo, *Tenure and Minority Women Law Professors: Separating the Strands*, 31 U.S.F. L. Rev. 747 (1997).

Carol Izumi, *Implicit Bias and Prejudice in Mediation*, 70 SMU L. Rev. 681 (2017).

Harriet Lerner, The Dance of Anger: A Woman's Guide to Changing the Patterns of Intimate Relationships (1985).

Harriet Lerner, Email exchange (2018).

Carrie Menkel-Meadow, *Excluded Voices: New Voices in the Legal Profession Making New Voices in the Law*, 42 U. Miami L. Rev. 29 (1987).

Grillo's Rigorous Path to Intentional, Mindful Mediation

Karen Tokarz

Trina Grillo's critique of the "promises of mediation" in her article, *The Mediation Alternative: Process Dangers for Women*, was influential during the formative years of mediation practice in this country—when state and federal courts across the country were exploring and expanding mediation's use. Mediation was heralded as an informal, contextual, noncoercive forum where parties could have their voices heard and keep decisions in their own hands, and as a viable alternative to the adversarial, patriarchal, objectivist trial system.

Grillo's article, however, raised critical questions and highlighted serious risks of mediation, especially for women in court-ordered family cases—what she called "the betrayal of mediation's promises" (p. 1555). Grillo's reach ultimately extended far beyond the realm of divorce and custody mediation on which she focused and, as I discuss in this essay, continues to this day.

In this essay, I share how Grillo's article resonated with me personally and professionally at a moment in time when I was skeptical about the evolution of mediation, and how it informed my later teaching, scholarship, and practice of mediation. In the essay, I also try to share points on the rigorous path, what some would call a more mindful and feminist path, that Grillo illuminated for mediators to follow in hopes of doing mediations more responsibly and intentionally.

In the early 1990s, about the time Grillo's article was published, I was repeatedly approached to mediate cases, especially employment and civil rights cases, given my experience as an employment discrimination professor. For quite a while, I resisted the call. I was hesitant for multiple reasons, including concerns about the impact of mediation on self-determination of parties, on parties' ability to air their stories, and on the public narrative about case outcomes.

I eventually agreed to undertake a voluntary, non-court-ordered employment mediation in which both parties were represented by counsel, assuming that would balance the scales. The plaintiff was a female who claimed she was not hired for a job due to her disability. Unfortunately, the plaintiff's attorney was woefully unprepared and totally unaware of the employer's per se statutory violation in asking applicants on the company application form: "Do you have any handicaps?" Intimidated by threats in the opening session from the company's male human resources officer and male attorney, the plaintiff's male attorney aggressively and repeatedly urged the plaintiff to accept the defendant's minimal offer because he mistakenly believed there was a great likelihood that the defendant would get summary judgment.

Karen Tokarz, *Grillo's Rigorous Path to Intentional, Mindful Mediation* In: *Discussions in Dispute Resolution*. Edited by: Art Hinshaw, Andrea Kupfer Schneider, and Sarah Rudolph Cole, Oxford University Press (2021). © Oxford University Press.
DOI: 10.1093/oso/9780197513248.003.0033

Throughout the mediation, I felt greatly conflicted. It wasn't just that I knew that the plaintiff's counsel was dead wrong on the law and on the likelihood of summary judgment for the defendant. I was conflicted about my role and the mediation process itself. I struggled with the disparate levels of attorney competency and competitiveness, the power imbalance between the plaintiff and the plaintiff's counsel, and the plaintiff's obvious deference to all of the men in the room. I worried about my own underdog and gender biases. I must have asked myself a dozen times over a few hours: "What exactly is my role here? "What does it mean to be impartial and neutral?" "Is this process procedurally and substantively fair for the parties?" "Will this process produce better justice than a trial?"

That day confirmed my instinctive fears about the dangers of mediation. I came away with serious doubts about the role of the mediator and the mediation process, and about myself. As I sought to come to grips with my questions about mediation, I refrained from doing mediations for almost two years. I spoke with mediators and participants about my concerns. I participated on panel discussions at the bar association on the dangers of mediation, especially court-ordered mediation, including the informality and lack of procedural rules, the impact of directive and evaluative mediators, the potential death of the jury system, and the loss of public narrative.

Somewhere along the line, a colleague suggested that I read Trina Grillo's article. I remember wondering how it could be helpful to me, given that I never anticipated handling family mediations, and certainly not custody mediations. (Over the years, I have handled over 800 mediations, only one of which was a family mediation.)

But my colleague persisted, for which I am most grateful. The article provided a feminist critique "focused primarily on what happens in situations where people of unequal bargaining power directly confront each other, with either no or little legal protection" (Menkel-Meadow 1997, p. 1418). The article was invaluable in raising questions crucial to mindful mediation and reflective practice that eventually gave me the insights and confidence to return to mediation, and have sustained me since.

Interestingly, given Grillo's thoughtful and harsh criticism of the risks of mediation, the article restored my hope and faith in the process. I have recommended Grillo's article to mediators, lawyers, law students, and even judges as a source of reflection and self-questioning as they engage with people who find themselves seeking justice in the legal system. The stakes are too high, and people's lives too precious, to not be as aware and intentional as Trina Grillo demands in her article.

While much of Grillo's thinking and, indeed, passion derive from divorce and child-custody mediation, and from certain features specific to California's family court system as it was in 1991, the essence of her critique carries over to other areas. There are distinct commonalities with cases involving discrimination, harassment, and abuse against women (and other marginalized groups) by employers, teachers, coaches, family members, and police, including emotional vulnerability, social group responsibility, power imbalances, financial inequality, and discomfort with the mediation process. It is not a large leap at all from treasuring her article as influential and pioneering in family mediation to valuing it for parties and mediation in other areas of law.

Over the years, with the help of others, I developed a list of questions/reflections for myself drawn from the issues raised by Grillo and other feminist mediators and scholars, in hopes of warding off being a well-meaning, but unmindful, mediator. I try to reflect on these concerns about myself and the process before and after my mediations. I/we are all aware of these issues, but Grillo pushes us to be more intentional and rigorous in our examination.

First, Grillo asks whether the parties are clear that participation is voluntary, or does one or both of them feel s/he cannot really choose to go to trial? Did I make it clear to the parties that participation is voluntary? Did the desire of some of the parties, the attorneys, the court, or the mediator overshadow the needs of the individual parties? Grillo warns us that we cannot take this for granted:

> When mediation is imposed, rather than voluntarily engaged in, its virtues are lost. More than lost: mediation becomes a wolf in sheep's clothing. It relies on force and disregards the context of the dispute, while masquerading as a gentler, more empowering alternative to adversary litigation. Sadly, when mediation is mandatory it becomes like the patriarchal paradigm of light it is supposed to supplant. (p. 1610)

Second, Grillo asks how best to protect the autonomy and self-determination of the parties at all stages in the mediation through settlement, making space for the parties' "authentic voices." In movement toward settlement, she asks if the "claiming rights" of the parties and the attendant empowering benefits, especially for those who do not share societal power, are being attended to, or are they sidelined, as the mediator and the lawyers work toward getting the dispute settled? (pp. 1556–58). Was I mindful of allowing the parties to speak for themselves (and their groups) and assert their self-determination, recognizing, as Grillo suggests, that some parties may feel particularly powerless, may not feel free to speak in their authentic voice for fear of making their situation worse, and may feel controlled in mediation? (p. 1550). How to balance these needs against the needs of other parties to resolve the dispute and move on?

Third, Grillo challenges us to be conscientious about the mediation process from the smallest to the biggest details. Did I pay attention to unwritten norms of the "microlegal" system and "microsanctions" by myself or others present in the mediation—for example, who talks when, even small talk, and how much; did I allow room for expressions of emotion; and who is enforcing the norms and how? In simple terms, is either party, or both, silenced or intimidated by norms of which others in the room may not be aware? In particular, she asks, what effect does this have on the plaintiff, who may already be feeling disempowered because of her unfamiliarity with the norms and because she is the one who has lost her job or has been discriminated against, harassed, or abused? (pp. 1556–57).

Fourth, Grillo urges us to attend to bias, given that implicit bias exists in all of us and that "mediator neutrality is a myth." As Carol Izumi highlights, "Extensive research and analysis related to mediator behavior, the dynamics of the mediation process, and the science of implicit social cognition reveal a huge gap between the vision of mediator neutrality and the realities of biased mediator thoughts and actions" (Izumi 2010, p. 153). Did I scrutinize my biases and pursue deliberate and self-conscious practices to avoid what Grillo calls "the dangers of unacknowledged perspective and unrecognized partiality" (pp. 1586–93) and Richard Delgado cites as the "risk of prejudice in mediation"? (Delgado 1985, p. 1387).

Last, and perhaps most importantly, Grillo challenges us to examine whether the mediation denies or squelches the parties' sense that "what transpires is at least partially a matter of right and justice." Did the process of mediation and settlement facilitate what the parties might get from a trial if they won, or even if they did not win but still had a public airing of their story, that is, the experience of telling their story and claiming, if not winning, their rights? (pp. 1556–57).

This last question Grillo raised goes to the heart of intentional, mindful mediation. One might argue that this is less relevant now that mediation is such an accepted and entrenched part of our dispute resolution system. Indeed, the answer for some might be a hearty, "who cares?" But that cannot be the answer. Parties have the right to get a sense that the mediator (and the judge) has considered these issues.

In no small part due to Grillo's wake-up call, mediators are more aware of the issues she raised almost thirty years ago. And, while she focused on changing the institutions and rules that govern divorce and custody mediation with sensitivity to women, her path for revisioning the role of the mediator and the mediation process has had lasting impact on mediation in all areas of law. Her arguments that mediators "must learn to respect each client's struggles, including her timing, anger, and resistance to having certain issues mediated, and also learn to refrain to the degree s/he is capable, from imposing one's own substantive agenda on the mediation" remain relevant today (p. 1610).

For all these contributions and more, Grillo has my enduring gratitude, respect, and appreciation.

References

Richard Delgado et al., *Fairness and Formality: Minimizing the Risk of Prejudice in Alternative Dispute Resolution*, Wis. L. Rev. 1359 (1985).

Carol Izumi, *Implicit Bias and the Illusion of Mediator Neutrality*, 34 Wash. U. J.L. & Pol'y 71 (2010).

Carrie Menkel-Meadow, *What Trina Taught Me: Reflections on Mediation, Inequality, Teaching and Life*, 81 Minn. L. Rev. 1413 (1997).

The Grillo Effect at Thirty

Douglas N. Frenkel

Trina Grillo's 1991 sounding of alarm bells concerning the impact on women of participating in mediation came as momentum was growing in a nationwide effort to incorporate informal dispute resolution mechanisms in family courts. Her critique was not the first, following on well-known warnings of the effect of an unchecked march toward "alternatives" on economically disadvantaged and racial minority disputants, civil rights enforcement, and society's general need for court-articulated public norms. Nor was she the first to raise concerns about the vulnerability of women as participants in mediation. So why is her article so noteworthy?

Its timing—at the crest of the first wave of the feminist movement and as alternative dispute resolution courses gained curricular traction—was propitious. Its placement in arguably the nation's most prestigious law journal did not hurt. But it is the passion of Grillo's advocacy that both lingers and may explain the impact her article may have had—and not had—on dispute resolution policy, practice, and research.

Illustrating her assertions with stories based on actual California custody mediations, Grillo examined the process from the inside, depicting the interplay of efficiency-driven, uninsightful, or overtly biased mediators with women who could not or would not assert themselves in face of the manipulative (or worse) fathers of their children. The combination of more and less subtle mediator control in limiting the discussion of past fault-based conduct and women displaying societally expected emotional passivity, Grillo asserted, yielded a proceeding that denied them a needed outlet for their rage and deprived them of custodial or other legal rights to which they would otherwise be entitled. Acknowledging the impact of recently enacted formal gender equality in family law doctrine, Grillo portrayed mediation as having veered from its promise of quasi-therapeutic contextual decision-making to a trap for women, especially when the process was imposed upon them.

Grillo's micro-analytic depiction of what can go wrong in a family mediation made for powerful reading and surely caused some neutrals to rethink their ways.[1] Modern trends in training family mediators—increased sensitivity to and training about power imbalances generally, and domestic violence in particular; growing appreciation for the need and time to allow, and, indeed, encourage some emotional unpacking of a couple's past—were certainly responsive (if not responses) to the process concerns Grillo's piece highlighted. The same might be said of the increasing acceptance of mediator interventions that provide legal or other professional information or that terminate a proceeding in the face of a problematic negotiation or outcome. And it may be no coincidence that some of the structural problems she assailed

[1] *See* Karen Tokarz's comment *supra* for an excellent exposition of this.

Douglas N. Frenkel, *The Grillo Effect at Thirty* In: *Discussions in Dispute Resolution.* Edited by: Art Hinshaw, Andrea Kupfer Schneider, and Sarah Rudolph Cole, Oxford University Press (2021). © Oxford University Press.
DOI: 10.1093/oso/9780197513248.003.0034

as settlement-pressuring—exclusion of lawyers from the process, mediators making custody determination recommendations to judges in cases that do not settle, severe limitations on time allotted for mediation—were eliminated or greatly ameliorated in the years after her article was published.

But Grillo's piece did not confine itself to raising awareness or improving the process. Hers was a broader critique, in which mandatory (and much voluntary) mediation must be seen through the lens of a broader inequality and powerlessness suffered by women, which renders them vulnerable to being exploited in a private, informal setting. When viewed against the larger landscape of trends in mediation research, scholarship, and policy over the last quarter century, however, this part of her thesis can be viewed as having been largely refuted or repudiated. Consider the following.

While individual abuses of the sort Grillo chronicled surely occur, the existing contemporaneous and more recent empirical data—including studies of the very California mediation scheme she decried—fail to support claims that the process oppresses women or leaves them feeling oppressed. Although they are neither voluminous nor consistent enough to support broad generalizations, this research includes the following findings: mandated mediations in California both settle and terminate via impasse at the same rates as in voluntary submissions both nationally and in the state, suggesting that coercion and submissiveness are not major factors (Depner et al., p. 195; Kelly & Duryea, p. 41; Kelly, p. 375). While they may not fare as well as men in terms of objective outcomes in mediation generally, there is no evidence that, in family mediation, women are compelled to yield custodial entitlements (compare Bachar & Hensler, p. 829, with Kelly, p. 377). On subjective measures, women express significantly more process and outcome satisfaction with family-based mediation than litigation and give mediation the same, if not higher, satisfaction ratings as men (Bachar & Hensler, p. 830; Kelly & Duryee, p. 42). A comprehensive "snapshot" study of California mandatory custody mediations undertaken in the same year as Grillo's publication yielded widespread favorable responses from both fathers and mothers: 92 percent of parents agreed that "the mediator listened to my concerns," with only a small minority feeling "too intimidated to say what I really felt" or "pressured [by the mediator] to go along with things that I did not want" (Depner et al., pp. 198, 200). In a study of both voluntary and mandated proceedings published the following year, California women reported significantly greater confidence than did men in being able to assert themselves with their ex-spouse as a result of participating in the mediation (Kelly & Duryee, p. 42). Perhaps most significantly, compared with litigated outcomes, mediation improved long-term relationships between noncustodial parents (mostly fathers) and their children (Emery et al., p. 30).

Second, while reverberations of Grillo's arguments may have yielded selective policies limiting the use of mediation in certain contexts—for example, the controversial Obama-era Department of Justice prohibition of even voluntary mediation in cases of alleged campus sexual assault—such results are the exception rather than the rule. Indeed, Grillo's major target, mandatory custody mediation, rather than being slowed in the wake of critical feminist scholarship, spread nationally (although with varying opt-out approaches and exclusions for cases of violence or impairment). By 2014, over two-thirds of the states had instituted or authorized mandatory mediation—three times the number in 1996.

Third, at the academic level, perhaps in recognition that the alternative dispute resolution train has left the station, serious political critique of the informal justice movement, including those based on gender, has slowed to a trickle.

What might explain the contrast between the article's broader policy concerns and the world of mediation thirty years later? Given the push to "alternatives" in the early 1990s, Grillo may have been swimming against a tide that no scholarship—regardless of its rigor—could have stopped. It may also be that, over time, gradual but positive shifts in women's (and men's) roles in society and in families—which she presumably would have applauded—may have taken some of the wind out of her argument's sails.

But it may also be that the fervor of Grillo's advocacy undercut its message and even invited pushback. She used selective anecdotal evidence that depicted only incompetent mediators to urge an end to an entire system. She oversimplified and overgeneralized, speaking of women and men in sweeping and stereotypic terms. The same might be said of her treatment of the psycho-dynamics of family dissolution—and how power can be defined or exercised in the intimate space of a mediation. Its one-dimensional and static view of power (as vested in the more knowledgeable, competitive or assertive party, i.e., the male) seemed at odds with what was known about the subject at the time.

Beyond methodology, Grillo's central portrayal of women's likely behavior in mediation—especially as to family disputes—was itself logically puzzling. If, for example, as Grillo and others argue, women are better than men at emotional, relational discourse, why does it follow that, unprotected, they will be silent (or easily silenced) victims of a spouse or a mediator? And even when a woman is silent, might that not reflect a choice to set aside her anger in service of other goals? Is it necessarily a deficit in negotiating ability or a sign of victimization to seek harmony or accept "less" if that will spare a child from her parents' ongoing hostilities or increase the odds of a father's future generosity to and involvement with his kids? Indeed, a related and similar illogic might attach to her prescription for the problem of mandatory mediation: If the debilitating social problem is women's inability to express their (productive) anger or otherwise stand up for themselves, why is litigation or negotiation through surrogates more likely than mediation to promote their future agency?

Finally, one cannot reflect on the article's impact without taking note of Grillo's choice of rhetoric. Labeling inept or bureaucratic mediator process control an "act of violence" (p. 1573) and calling mandatory family mediation the "psychic rape" of women (p. 1606) was certainly attention-gathering. But the use of such hyperbole may have gone too far, undermining her thesis and prompting reactance.

The juxtaposition of such arguable methodological and advocacy shortcomings with developments in the last three decades may suggest the most enduring (if unintended) contributions of this and similar pieces to the dispute resolution field.

First, mere claiming about informal processes no longer suffices. Those who want to create or challenge policy about how or whether to conduct mediation need to produce evidence to support their positions. Ideology alone no longer carries the day in a maturing field.

Second, most participants in our modern litigation system now at least consider how to talk about difficult subjects with those with whom they are embroiled in conflict. This is no small matter, especially when it comes to families and the very individuals Grillo championed. While Grillo failed to stem the growth of mandatory custody mediation, women's prowess in navigating that process appear to be on the ascent.

Indeed, this may yet be a case of losing the battle but winning the war.

References

Gilat J. Bacha & Deborah R. Hensler, *Does Alternative Dispute Resolution Facilitate Prejudice and Bias? We Still Don't Know*, 70 SMU L. REV. 817 (2017).

Charlene E. Depner, Karen V. Kannata, & Marlene B. Simon, *Building a Uniform Statistical Reporting System: A Snapshot of California Family Court Services*, 30 FAM. & CONCILIATION CTS. REV. 185–206 (1992).

Robert E. Emery, David Sbarra, & Tara Grover, *Divorce Mediation: Research and Reflections*, 43 FAM. CT. REV. 22–37 (2005).

Joan B. Kelly, *A Decade of Divorce Mediation Research*, 34 FAM. & CONCILIATION CTS. REV. 373–85 (1996).

Joan B. Kelly & Mary A. Duryee, *Women's and Men's Views of Mediation in Voluntary and Mandatory Mediation Settings*, 30 FAM. & CONCILIATION CTS. REV. 34–49 (1992).

Post-Grillo: New Family Mediation Protections and Revised Dangers

Kelly Browe Olson

Until Professor Trina Grillo's article warned readers of its process dangers, the family mediation process was viewed as a positive antidote to extensive and costly litigation and as a valuable opportunity for families to work together informally to resolve their custody, support, and property issues. Grillo, an academic and a practicing mediator, asserted that family mediation was not living up to its potential, that mediators hurt women and minorities by mandating participation without lawyers, and that its use created a false sense of empowerment. She was concerned that some mediators were not neutral, failed to focus on clients' individual needs, and were unable or unwilling to deal with women's emotions, especially reasonable anger and frustration.

Grillo's article was a major rebuke of family court mediation and sparked positive change, especially in how mediation programs screen cases for participation. This comment examines how some important issues from her article have been addressed and how other concerns remain.

I. The Decrease in Mandatory Mediation and Increase in Screening and Other Training

Grillo posited that mandatory mediation referrals were worse for participants than litigation because mediation's informality led to a lack of procedural protections for vulnerable parties. She suggested that mediators had little or improper training and that oversight was lacking to determine whether cases were appropriate for mediation.

Today mediation is more presumptive than mandatory, but these concerns are still relevant. Since 1991 screening protocols for dispute resolution programs and training on the appropriateness of various processes have greatly improved both for mediators and other family law professionals. This impact can be traced to Grillo's article. Her concerns led to greater awareness and more training, which in turn led to more information about the potential biases in the process. For example, Grillo was very much concerned with mediators making custody recommendations to courts. Except in one California county, family mediators no longer make recommendations. Mediators are now providing a confidential opportunity for party communication without the pressure of knowing that if they fail to reach a settlement the mediator will become their de facto decision maker. Several of Grillo's other concerns, such as mediators' neutrality and ability to deal with strong emotions, power imbalances, and intimate partner violence (IPV), are now included in mandatory mediator training

Kelly Browe Olson, *Post-Grillo: New Family Mediation Protections and Revised Dangers* In: *Discussions in Dispute Resolution*. Edited by: Art Hinshaw, Andrea Kupfer Schneider, and Sarah Rudolph Cole, Oxford University Press (2021). © Oxford University Press. DOI: 10.1093/oso/9780197513248.003.0035

and continuing education. While jurisdictional training and education requirements vary in quality and quantity, all family mediators now have more required training than before Grillo's article.

Despite more use of alternative dispute resolution processes and more training opportunities than in Grillo's day, some court personnel (including judges) and family attorneys are still poorly informed about the particular suitability of the available dispute resolution processes for individual families. This is especially so with regard to the impact of IPV, power imbalances, and family dynamics that influence their clients' capacity to negotiate or to make informed decisions. Grillo advocated for better information on these topics and for cases to include assessments of a family's strengths and weaknesses in order to help clients determine the right process for their particular needs. This lack of individualized screening has not been adequately addressed.

II. Identifying and Responding to Power Imbalances and Intimate Partner Violence

Grillo also expressed concern about inadequate mediator training to recognize IPV or other power imbalances and information on how to mediate once they have been identified. As a result, she believed mediation was re-victimizing women, punishing them for the anger they were experiencing, and failing to acknowledge their real concerns. In the decades since her article, scholars and practitioners have developed numerous screening tools to help program administrators, attorneys, and mediators identify whether families and individuals are capable of negotiating effectively in mediation, of participating in mediation with special protocols, or if they would be better served with a more formal litigation process.

Today meaningful screening protocols identify problematic behavior and coercive acts and provide opportunities for the screeners to talk with parties about how these negative communication patterns may impact their ability to negotiate effectively with each other. Also, importantly, screening processes may help parties learn to identify negative patterns in their behavior, which leads to better understandings of their relationship dynamics and how those dynamics will impact their custody negotiations.

Even though IPV and its impact on parties in family law cases is much more widely known and understood today and IPV is regularly the subject of advanced training and continuing education programs, mediation programs and family law courts still struggle with its definitions and how best to manage IPV impacted families. The legal definitions, which typically require recent physical threats or assault (see AR Code § 9-15-103 (4) (2017)), are far narrower than the social science definition: physical violence, sexual violence, stalking, and psychological aggression (including coercive tactics) by a current or former intimate partner (i.e., spouse, boyfriend/girlfriend, dating partner, or ongoing sexual partner) (Braiding et al.).

Previous legal intervention should never be the only basis for opt-out provisions, yet state laws, judges, and mediators usually require recent restraining orders, protective orders, or criminal charges in order for participants to invoke IPV-based mediation opt-out provisions. Victims of coercive controlling behavior without evidence of recent physical threats or harm, those who were not granted protective orders, and those who never sought help before, are frequently ineligible to opt-out of mediation, leaving them vulnerable to re-victimization in the process.

Furthermore, IPV screening is not a one-time event. It must continue throughout the case because IPV is not static; it may develop or escalate as parties separate and go through their divorce process. Screening tools are most effective when administered by professionals who understand IPV and capacity issues as well as how mediation processes work. Additionally, professionals must speak with the parties individually and follow up with both written and oral questions. Where IPV is a concern but does not require court intervention and both parties want to mediate, ongoing screening and safety protocols must be a part of the process. Grillo's worry about how mediation's informality fails to protect victims suggests that only highly skilled and specially trained mediators—those who know how to identify more subtle types and patterns of violence—should facilitate when pervasive IPV has been identified. Modern IPV-related protocols Grillo would appreciate include: shuttle mediation, video conferencing, asynchronous meetings, and other uses of technology. A recent federal study found that some IPV-categorized case participants were more satisfied and had more successful outcomes when the parties used shuttle or video conferencing mediation instead of litigation (Adams et al.). Even with these modifications, coercion or violence can happen outside of the process. And while mediator understanding of IPV is increasing and advanced training on IPV in family mediation is required in multiple jurisdictions, parties still must be provided opportunities to make their own informed choices about the type of court-based or private dispute resolution process that is best for their family.

Another issue arises when courts overprotect and limit the ability of litigants to opt in and participate in alternative processes because of previous violence or power issues. Oftentimes parties with protective orders are barred from choosing mediation even if it is their preference. While forbidding mediation is an improvement over requiring it in these cases, Grillo and many others see this limitation as another constraint on parties' choices.

Grillo wrote in her article that mediators and family courts need to focus on empowering parties, not using mandatory processes to disempower them. To do this, all modern family dispute resolution processes, including litigation, need to provide safe environments and minimize the risk of coercion and the potential for future violence. Judges, administrators, attorneys, and mediators must screen cases and be attentive for signs of ongoing abuse as families traverse the court system and alternative processes. All jurisdictions should allow parties to opt out of mediation. If, however, screening fails to reveal patterns of coercive control or process concerns, attorneys and self-represented litigants should be able to choose to use mediation and, where available, a variety of interventions, including early neutral evaluation, arbitration, and litigation. Traditional courts are not a panacea, but they do provide more protections through formal processes, restraining orders, enforcement mechanisms, and the judicial authority to make decisions.

III. Continuing Concerns about Safe and Appropriate Alternative Resources

As courts have expanded and family mediation has grown, some programs have seen severe fiscal cutbacks forcing them to prioritize efficiency. Time-restrained mediators may be less focused on the parties' self-determination, ability to negotiate, and basic understanding of the process. Additionally, they may persuade or manipulate families to enter into inappropriate agreements. Grillo's concerns for families pushed into these processes are still relevant, they may have mediators who are not neutral, who limit the parties' self-determination, and who push too hard for agreements, especially when these shortened processes become hyperfocused on settlement statistics.

Furthermore, the large disparities between impoverished court-connected mediation programs and those with abundant resources and between families who can or cannot afford private options, have created very different socioeconomic-based mediation structures. One is focused on parties' needs and available at their request, and the other struggles with limited time and assistance and more generalized ADR processes.

Another resource-based difference is the availability of other dispute resolution options, including early neutral evaluation, arbitration, private judging, and collaborative or cooperative law processes. The availability of more processes helps to expand family options, but utilizing them without adequate and ongoing screening simply repeats the errors Grillo sought to rectify. Her concerns continue to serve as a warning to all dispute resolution programs—they fail their clients if their mediators cannot recognize severe inequities caused by power imbalances or coercion because of a lack of adequate training, limited time and resources or a failure to focus on the dynamics of coercive control.

IV. Conclusion

Over the last twenty-nine years, family courts have seen an exponential increase in their caseloads and in the number of self-represented parties, resulting in overwhelmed family court dockets. To address these issues, many courts have embraced alternative resolution processes, including mediation, for timely resolution of cases. Family courts and dispute resolution programs need to implement Grillo's idea of discarding "one size fits all" standards that rarely fit anyone and instead focus upon tailored solutions to address the conflict and the capacity levels of individual families. To accomplish this, programs need to prioritize universal screening, emphasize mediator training, neutrality, confidentiality, and party self-determination, and provide families sufficient time to understand and consider their options.

After writing her article, Professor Grillo continued to mediate. She favored the transformative model that focuses on empowerment and recognition and provides a safe space for the expression of emotions. She wrote optimistically about family mediation. Through her articles and actions, she indicated the importance of continuing to engage in difficult discussions about family mediation practices and to examine which processes are appropriate, available, effective, and beneficial. When used correctly, facilitative and cooperative processes provide families an appropriate basis for future cooperative decision-making. Dispute resolution academics and practitioners must continue to work toward more empirical and ethnographic research on the family court systems to ensure that dispute resolution processes are meeting their stated objectives, and that all families have access to a variety of dispute resolution processes. If we keep working to create alternatives to litigation that are responsive and mindful of the unique needs of individual families who have experienced IPV, then we have truly listened and responded to Grillo's concerns.

References

Jeannie M. Adams et al., *New Services for Families in the DC Superior Court*, at https://www.americanbar.org/groups/dispute_resolution/publications/dispute_resolution_magazine/2019/spring-2019-family-matters/9-adams-et-al-dc-superior-court/ (last accessed June 29, 2019).

AR Code § 9-15-103 (4) (2017).

M.J. Breiding et al., Intimate Partner Violence Surveillance: Uniform Definitions and Recommended Data Elements, Version 2.0 (National Center for Injury Prevention and Control, Centers for Disease Control and Prevention, 2015).

Article 2.4

Understanding Mediators' Orientations, Strategies, and Techniques: A Grid for the Perplexed

Leonard L. Riskin

1 Harvard Negotiation Law Review 7 (1996)

Introduction

... [A] bewildering variety of activities fall within the broad, generally-accepted definition of mediation—a process in which an impartial third party, who lacks authority to impose a solution, helps others resolve a dispute or plan a transaction ... And there is no comprehensive or widely-accepted system for identifying, describing, or classifying them ...

For these reasons, almost every conversation about mediation suffers from ambiguity, a confusion of the "is" and the "ought." ...

The largest cloud of confusion and contention surrounds the issue of whether a mediator may evaluate [claims].

* * *

... I hope [to provide clarity through] a system for categorizing and understanding approaches to mediation. I try to include in my system most activities that are commonly called mediation and arguably fall within the broad definition of the term ...

* * *

II. The Proposed System

The system I propose describes mediations by reference to two related characteristics, each of which appears along a continuum. One continuum ... measures the scope of the problem or problems that the mediation seeks to address or resolve ...

The second continuum ... measures the strategies and techniques that the mediator employs in attempting to address or resolve the problems that comprise the subject matter of the mediation ...

Leonard L. Riskin, *Understanding Mediators' Orientations, Strategies, and Techniques: A Grid for the Perplexed.* In: *Discussions in Dispute Resolution.* Edited by: Art Hinshaw, Andrea Kupfer Schneider, and Sarah Rudolph Cole, Oxford University Press (2021).
 DOI: 10.1093/oso/9780197513248.003.0036

* * *

A. The Problem-Definition Continuum: Goals, Assumptions, and Focuses

The focus of a mediation—its subject matter and the problems or issues it seeks to address—can range from narrow to broad . . .

1. Level I: Litigation Issues
In very narrow mediations, the primary goal is to settle the matter [approximating the result in trial or other decision-making process] . . .

. . . Discussions would center on the strengths and weaknesses of each side's case and on how the judge or jury would likely determine the relevant issues of fact and law.

2. Level II: "Business" Interests

* * *

[These mediations] might consider more fundamental business interests, such as both firms' need to continue doing business, make profits, and develop and maintain a good reputation . . . [B]y exploring . . . business interests, both companies [may] improve their situations in ways they might not have considered but for the negotiations prompted by the dispute.

3. Level III: Personal I Professional I Relational Issues
"Level III" mediations focus attention on more personal issues and interests. . . . [M]ediation participants often must address the relational and emotional aspects of their interactions in order to pave the way for settlement of the narrower economic issues . . .

. . . Focusing on such issues may be important even if the mediation does not produce a solution to the narrower problems . . . In addition, the parties might repair their relationship by learning to forgive one another . . . They might learn to understand themselves better, to give up their anger or desire for revenge . . . or to otherwise improve themselves.

4. Level IV: Community Interests
"Level IV" mediations consider an even broader array of interests, including those of communities or entities that are not parties to the immediate dispute. For example, . . . the participants might consider ways to clarify the law . . . or to produce a model contract provision. In other kinds of disputes, parties might focus on improving, or "transforming," communities

Of course, mediations that employ broader problem-definitions can include resolution of narrower problems that appear to the left on the continuum . . . As the problem broadens, however, the distributive issue could become less important . . . In other words, in moving from narrow to broad definitions of the subject matter of a mediation, one's view of the conflict can change from that of a problem to be eliminated to that of an opportunity for improvement.

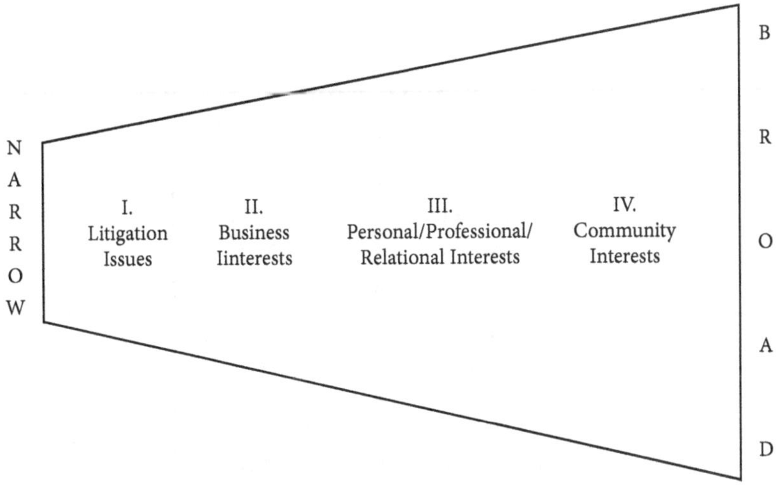

Figure 1 Problem-Definition Continuum

* * *

B. The Mediator's Role: Goals and Assumptions Along The Facilitative-Evaluative Continuum

The second continuum describes the strategies and techniques that the mediator employs to achieve her goal of helping the parties address and resolve the problems at issue. At one end of this continuum are strategies and techniques that evaluate issues important to the dispute or transaction. [This includes behaviors to direct some or all of the mediation's outcome.] At the other end of the continuum are beliefs and behaviors that facilitate the parties' negotiation. [This includes conduct to assist the parties to communicate with and understand one another.]

The mediator who evaluates assumes that the participants want and need her to provide some guidance as to the appropriate grounds for settlement... and that she is qualified to give such guidance by virtue of her training, experience, and objectivity.

The mediator who facilitates assumes that the parties are intelligent, able to work with their counterparts, and capable of understanding their situations better than the mediator and, perhaps, better than their lawyers... Thus, the facilitative mediator assumes that his principal mission is to clarify and to enhance communication between the parties in order to help them decide what to do.

To explain the facilitative-evaluative continuum more fully, I must demonstrate how it relates to the problem-definition continuum. The relationship is clearest if we show the problem-definition continuum on a horizontal axis and the facilitative-evaluative continuum on a vertical axis, as depicted in Figure 2. The four quadrants each represent a general orientation toward mediation: evaluative-narrow, facilitative-narrow, evaluative-broad, and facilitative-broad.

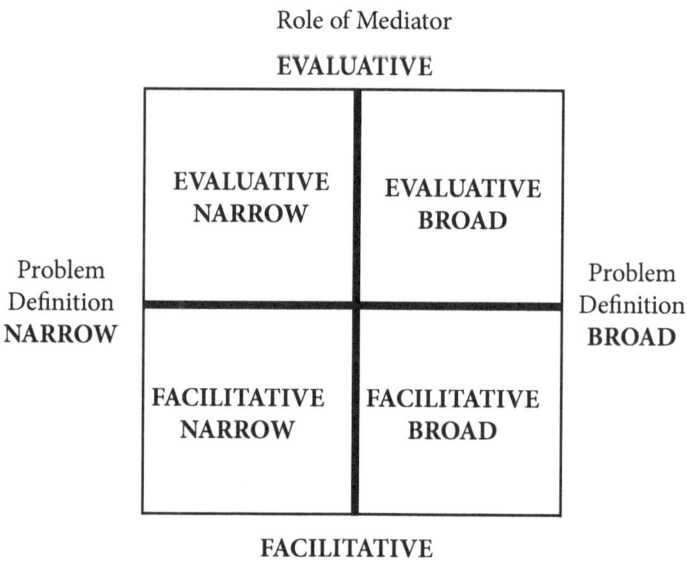

Figure 2 Mediator Orientations

C. The Four Orientations: Strategies and Techniques

* * *

1. Evaluative-Narrow

A principal strategy of [this] approach is to help the parties understand the strengths and weaknesses of their positions and the likely outcome of litigation . . . [M]ost mediation activities take place in private caucuses in which the mediator will gather additional information and deploy evaluative techniques, such as the following . . .

[These techniques include: assessing the strengths and weaknesses of each side's case, predicting court outcomes, proposing position-based compromise agreements, and urging or pushing the parties to settle or to accept a particular settlement proposal or range.]

2. Facilitative-Narrow

[This] mediator shares the evaluative-narrow mediator's general strategy—to educate the parties about the strengths and weaknesses of their claims and the likely consequences of failing to settle . . . He does not use his own assessments, predictions, or proposals. Nor does he apply pressure.

* * *

The facilitative nature of this mediation approach might also produce a [few opportunities for party] education or . . . transformation . . .

3. Evaluative-Broad

* * *

[This] mediator's principal strategy is to learn about the circumstances and underlying interests of the parties and other affected individuals or groups, and then to use that knowledge to direct the parties toward an outcome that responds to such interests. To carry out this strategy, the evaluative-broad mediator will employ various techniques, including the following . . .

[These techniques include: educating herself about the parties' underlying interests, predicting the impact of non-resolution on the parties' interests, offering broad interest-based proposals, and urging the parties to accept the mediator's or another's proposal.]

4. Facilitative-Broad

[This] mediator's principal strategy is to help the participants define the subject matter of the mediation in terms of underlying interests and to help them develop and choose their own solutions that respond to such interests . . . To carry out such strategies, the facilitative-broad mediator may use techniques such as the following.

[These techniques include: helping the parties understand their interests and their counterpart's interests, assisting the parties to develop and propose broad, interest-based options for settlement, and aiding the parties in their evaluation of settlement proposals and non-settlement.]

* * *

D. Movement Among the Continuums and Among the Quadrants: Limitations on the Descriptive Capabilities of the Grid

* * *

. . . [M]ost mediators . . . generally conduct mediations with a presumptive or predominant orientation . . .

Yet many mediators employ strategies and techniques [making] it difficult to fit their practices neatly into a particular quadrant. First, some mediators deliberately try to avoid attachment to a particular orientation. Instead, they emphasize flexibility . . . based on the participants' needs or other circumstances in the mediation.

* * *

III. Effectiveness of the Grid, Especially in Selecting Mediators

* * *

The grid can help us envision an ideal mediator for any individual case. She would be sufficiently flexible to employ the most appropriate orientation, strategies, and techniques as the participants' needs present themselves. This would require the ability (1) to both evaluate and facilitate, and (2) to see things both narrowly and broadly. She would have subject-matter expertise and she would be impartial . . .

* * *

A. The Potential Advantages and Disadvantages of the Various Approaches to Mediation

* * *

1. The Problem-Definition Continuum

a. *Narrow Problem-Definition.*—[It] can increase the chances of resolution and reduce the time needed for the mediation. The focus on a small number of issues limits the range of relevant information, thus keeping the proceeding relatively simple . . .

. . . [It] can [also] increase the chance of impasse because it allows little room for creative option-generation or other means of addressing underlying interests, which, if unsatisfied, could block agreement . . .

b. *Broad Problem-Definition.*—[It] can produce an agreement that accommodates the parties' underlying interests, as well as the interests of other affected individuals or groups . . .

In some situations, however, [it] can have the opposite effect: it can increase both the probability of an impasse and the time and expense required for mediation by focusing the parties on issues that are unnecessary to the resolution of the narrow issues . . .

* * *

2. The Mediator Role Continuum

a. *The Evaluative Approach.*—The evaluative mediator … removes some of the decision-making burden from the parties and their lawyers. [Sometimes] this makes it easier for the parties to reach an agreement. [Mediator evaluations] can give a participant a better understanding of his "Best Alternative to a Negotiated Agreement" (BATNA), a feeling of vindication, or an enhanced ability to deal with his constituency…

Yet, in some situations an assessment, prediction, or recommendation can make it more difficult for the parties to reach agreement by impairing a party's faith in the mediator's neutrality or restricting a party's flexibility…

* * *

b. *The Facilitative Approach.*—[It offers many advantages] if the parties [can understand] both sides' interests or developing potential solutions… [It] also offers greater potential for educating parties about their own and each other's position, interests, and situation … [However,] a poorly-conducted facilitative approach might waste a great deal of time if it does not respond to underlying interests either in the process or in the outcome.

* * *

IV. Conclusion

* * *

One cause of [the confusion about what constitutes mediation] is the absence of any widely-shared comprehensive method for describing the various approaches to mediation practice … I mean to provide such a method. My goal is to facilitate clear thinking about processes that are commonly called mediation and fall, at least arguably, within the usual understanding of mediation…

* * *

Comments

"True Enough"

Michael T. Colatrella Jr.

Of the many contributions that Professor Leonard Riskin introduced in his landmark article *Understanding Mediators' Orientations*, none is more profound than the educational value of the original Riskin Grid (the "Grid") as a mental model to aid in understanding the mediation process. Describing a phenomenon through use of a simple model so that it can be systematically studied is a well-established and valuable scientific method. To be effective, however, good models must be calibrated to an appropriate level of sophistication for the student. The Grid is an effective model to help students new to mediation to conceptualize what mediators do and how they do it. Indeed, Riskin states that clarifying the mediation process is the Grid's primary purpose. Along these lines, Riskin emphasizes one of the article's primary aims is "to facilitate discussions and help to clarify arguments by providing a system for categorizing and understanding approaches to mediation." Although some have criticized the Grid as being too simple, incomplete, and even misleading, it is the Grid's simplicity that enables Riskin to illuminate the mediation process so brightly. Riskin himself, in a later article, attempted to address the Grid's so-called weaknesses and limitations by suggesting a more dynamic Grid system (Riskin). The Grid persists magnificently as a fundamental model of understanding of what mediators do. It remains a central feature of mediation education because it is a clear and simple conceptual framework of the mediation process that a mediation novice, whether a law student, an attorney, or a professional interested in mediation from any number of other disciplines, can understand. The Grid endures, in other words, not because it is perfect, but because it is "true enough."

The Grid presents a model—a mental paradigm of understanding—specifically set out to "describe processes that were commonly called mediation . . ." by illustrating how mediators approach their work (Riskin, p. 7). For our purposes, a model is a representation of a "system or phenomenon which is said to exist in common experience" (Golbert, pp. 891–92). Any model created to describe an endeavor as varied and messy as the process of dealing with interpersonal conflict must be oversimplified to be useful. Models are effective precisely because they distort the reality of the very phenomena they describe as a means to highlight the phenomena's salient features. This is akin to building a Tinkertoy model of a carbon atom. It is nothing like the real thing, but helpful in understanding important aspects of the atom nonetheless. The Grid succeeds and endures because, like many other successful scientific models, it captures something fundamental about mediation in part by ignoring much else about it. Harvard Philosophy of Education Professor Catherine Elgin explains this idea elegantly as follows:

Michael T. Colatrella Jr., *"True Enough"* In: *Discussions in Dispute Resolution.* Edited by: Art Hinshaw, Andrea Kupfer Schneider, and Sarah Rudolph Cole, Oxford University Press (2021). © Oxford University Press.
DOI: 10.1093/oso/9780197513248.003.0037

> [S]cience routinely transgresses the boundary between truth and falsehood. It smooths curves and ignores outliers. It develops and deploys simplified models that diverge, sometimes considerably, from the phenomena they purport to represent. Even the best scientific theories are not true." (Elgin, p. 113)

So, when evaluating the utility of a scientific model, the correct question to ask is not whether it is true, "but whether it is true enough."

Whether a model is true enough turns on the question of whether it advances useful knowledge about the phenomena. Learning theory tells us that in no place are symbols and models more important than in educating novices in a system or skill (Mayer 1989, pp. 1019–21). These are two areas where the Grid shines. A concrete example of one way the Grid makes teaching mediation easier to beginners is that it provides an excellent structure for distinguishing between the overarching steps in the mediation process and the narrower strategies and techniques that mediators might deploy within that overarching structure. Teaching this feature of mediation is challenging because mediators who ascribe to different overarching philosophies of mediation may use similar steps in the mediation process, but for different purposes. For example, the facilitative mediation model, which, in part, relies on participants assessing the merits of their claims for themselves, is generally comprised of five steps: (1) the mediator's opening statement; (2) the parties' opening statements; (3) identifying issues; (4) problem-solving/negotiation; and (5) finalizing the mediation. Yet more evaluative mediators, who often provide opinions on the merits of parties' arguments and, perhaps, the value of a case, might use this same overarching structure to conduct a *very* different type of mediation than one conducted by a more facilitative mediator. For instance, using the same general mediation process just described, a more evaluative mediator might provide a prediction of whether a judge would exclude certain evidence relevant to the dispute if the case went to trial. This could significantly affect the balance of power between the parties in the mediation. A purely facilitative mediator, however, would never use this more directive technique. Rather, she might address the same issue by asking the parties to articulate the strengths and weakness of their arguments on the issue of the admissibility of this evidence. Accordingly, the Grid is an immensely effective teaching tool because it helps demonstrate that the strategies and techniques that mediators use in assisting parties to manage, resolve, or transform interpersonal conflict are connected to a mediator's "orientation" or broader mediation philosophy, which is among the most important variables for students of mediation to understand.

Of course, the Grid famously (and to some, infamously) incorporates only four variables—facilitative and evaluative orientations and narrow and broad orientations. A particular utility of this two-axis approach is that these four variables make a continuum of possible mediator orientations across vertical and horizontal axes, rather than rigid "boxes" or "styles." In other words, a mediator may be any combination of these variables to varying degrees. Facilitative and evaluative mediator orientations are described briefly earlier. But broad versus narrow mediator orientations refers to how expansively the mediator defines the problem. In narrower problem definitions, a mediator in a legal dispute might focus only on helping the participants resolve the specific legal claim that the plaintiff articulates in the complaint. In a broader problem definition, the mediator might expand the problem's scope to incorporate business interests, personal interests, and even community interests that go well beyond the explicit legal issues. An example of the broader mediator philosophy would be that a mediator working with participants to resolve an employment discrimination allegation might, in addition to addressing the legal claims at hand, facilitate a discussion among the parties to find ways to modify the promotion process at issue so that it would be seen by the organization's employees as more transparent and equitable. So, depending on her problem-solving "orientation," a mediator might adopt any number of combinations of Riskin's four variables. For example, a mediator might be *very* narrow in problem definition and *slightly* evaluative. Or, she may be *very* broad in problem definition and *moderately* facilitative, or some other combination of the four variables. Using this approach, the model captures at least two fundamental features about mediation and mediators. One is that people called "mediators" can differ widely in their dispute resolution strategies from each other. Two, in most cases, mediation is a dynamic process in which mediators can, and do, utilize various "orientation" strategies and techniques even within the same mediation, not fitting neatly into any one quadrant of the Riskin Grid.

The Grid also helps mediation teachers discuss various strategies and techniques in connection to a simple framework that makes understanding the strategies and techniques easier. Mediator "reality testing" is a good topic to demonstrate this point. Reality testing is a notoriously difficult topic to teach because, like mediation itself, it contemplates many different strategies and techniques that often diverge dramatically from each other, yet fall under the common nomenclature "reality testing." But one way students can begin to understand the complexity and richness of this topic is to provide them with a list of reality testing tactics or mediator behaviors, either in the form of an exercise or discussion, and then ask them where these tactics and behaviors might fall on the Grid. Here are a few examples of such questions:

- Where on the Grid might a mediator technique of asking parties to discuss the strengths and weakness of their case be positioned?
- Where on the Grid would they place a technique like a mediator providing procedural information about how the court process might unfold if the matter is not settled?
- Where on the Grid might the technique of a mediator providing legal information that sets out the legal requirements of fraud without applying those elements to the facts of the case be positioned?
- Where on the Grid might mediator behavior fall in a dispute over employment discrimination in a promotion claim where the mediator asks the parties to create a list of possible solutions to make the promotion process to be, and be seen, as fairer going forward?

For all these questions, the Grid provides a meaningful mental structure to understand how these different techniques and behaviors relate to one other. Absent this simple paradigm, these techniques are unmoored. They are like a list of characters without a narrative. But with the model, they form a comprehensible constellation of techniques that relate to one another and thus impart greater meaning to the student of mediation. When students are working from a simple model like the Grid, effective learning happens because students have a solid scaffolding on which to build greater understanding.

Finally, *Understanding Mediators' Orientations* is a classic piece of scholarship because it explains the Grid model in a way accessible to those new to mediation. A common pitfall that instructors strive to avoid is communicating about their discipline with undue complexity. The popular author and Harvard professor, Steven Pinker, in his book on academic writing, calls this phenomenon the "curse of knowledge." Pinker describes the curse of knowledge as a state of mind where the teacher or writer "has a difficulty in imagining what it is like for someone else not to know something that you know" (Pinker, p. 59). An extreme example of the curse of knowledge in action is a presentation or article aimed at a novice that is littered with unexplained technical terms, concepts, and acronyms. But Riskin's article on *Understanding Mediators' Orientations* is the apotheosis of this because it is so accessible. Clarity is a particularly important quality in mediation teaching and scholarship because those interested in understanding mediation come from a wide array of disciplines that include not only lawyers and their clients but also business people, clergy, social workers, psychologists, and many more. The Grid's success and the article's lasting influence is thus also a product of its ability to reach this wide audience with its clear thinking and writing. Riskin assumes that the reader has little or no knowledge of the mediation process, and consequently, he draws the reader into the world of mediation and mediator orientations and teaches him or her something important about the mediation process.

Among the important lessons that the article provides to students of mediation is a reminder that observing and describing are first principles of science. Although mediation as a process is thousands of years old, it is still a young science. The Grid was among the first conceptual models of mediation and thus provided a common language to understand and describe it. The Grid's conceptual model formed the foundation of how we think and talk about mediation in much of the scholarly discourse that has come after it, even among those who are critical of it. Mediators and mediation scholars continue discuss and debate categories of mediator orientations in terms of facilitative, evaluative, broad, and narrow that Riskin introduced in the article. These terms have become part of the mediation lexicon and have allowed us to communicate more clearly and think more systematically about the mediation process in ways that have advanced the discipline of mediation. As importantly, Riskin has equipped us to educate subsequent generations of mediators more effectively and more "scientifically" because of the elegant, accessible, and useful taxonomy that he created with the Grid.

References

Catherine Z. Elgin, *True Enough*, 14 PHIL. ISSUES, EPISTEMOLOGY 113–31 (2004).

Janice D. Gobert, *Introduction to Model-based Teaching and Learning in Science Education*, 22 INT'L J. SCI. EDUC. 891–94 (2000).

Richard E. Mayer, *Models for Understanding*, 59 REV. EDUC. RES. 43–64 (1989).
STEVEN PINKER, THE SENSE OF STYLE: THE THINKING PERSON'S GUIDE TO WRITING IN THE 21ST CENTURY (Reprt. ed. 2015).
Leonard L. Riskin, *Decisionmaking in Mediation: The New Old Grid and the New New Grid System*, 79 NOTRE DAME L. REV. 1, 3–53 (2003).

Dismantling the "Facilitative" "Evaluative" Dichotomy: Reflecting on Riskin's Grid and Predicting the Future

Alyson Carrel

Leonard Riskin's foundational article *Understanding Mediators' Orientations, Strategies, and Techniques*, in which he presented a new model of mediator approaches, commonly known as Riskin's Grid, has survived the test of time. More specifically, Riskin's use of the terms "facilitative" and "evaluative" to describe the role of the mediator has endured multiple critiques and attempts at revision. Today, nearly twenty-five years later, practitioners, educators, service providers, and users of mediation still rely on these terms to describe and analyze a mediator's approach to her craft. This response piece describes how the terminology has evolved and predicts that in the face of new and renewed challenges, the terminology may finally lose its false dichotomous relationship.

Riskin was not the first to attempt describing the array of mediator approaches. Before Riskin's Grid, other scholars attempted to describe these approaches by using colorful terms such as "trashing, bashing, and hashing," metaphors such as "orchestrators and dealmakers," and goal-oriented terminology such as "settlement frame" and "communication frame." In Riskin's article, he instead created a simple model comprised of two perpendicularly intersecting continua. Each continuum describes different mediation characteristics creating a four-quadrant grid and an infinite number of coordinates reflecting a variety of mediator approaches. Riskin was not trying to define ideal mediator behaviors or best practices, but instead capture the realistic mediator behaviors and practices he observed and that users were likely to encounter.

Although broadly adopted, Riskin's Grid was not universally adored. The grid, specifically his use of the descriptive term "evaluative," provoked a fervent and unyielding debate. Critics worried that it legitimized the behavior of some mediators who acted more like arbitrators, telling parties what would happen if they failed to settle their claims, why they should settle, and how they should settle. Critics further feared that the inclusion of the term, and its place opposite the term "facilitative," would destroy the central tenant of mediation as a facilitative process. Scholars even called the term "evaluative mediator" an oxymoron, arguing that a mediator who evaluates legal claims should not be called a mediator at all (Kovach & Love 1996). These ongoing debates critiquing the inclusion of "evaluative" mediator approaches skewed the original construct of a continuum between the "facilitative" and "evaluative" approaches and turned it into a false dichotomous relationship where one was deemed either a "facilitative" mediator or an "evaluative" one. In addition, this intense debate, and the resulting spotlight on the "facilitative" and "evaluative" terminology, entirely pushed

Alyson Carrel, *Dismantling the "Facilitative" "Evaluative" Dichotomy: Reflecting on Riskin's Grid and Predicting the Future*
In: *Discussions in Dispute Resolution.* Edited by: Art Hinshaw, Andrea Kupfer Schneider, and Sarah Rudolph Cole, Oxford University Press (2021). © Oxford University Press. DOI: 10.1093/oso/9780197513248.003.0038

aside the second continuum, focusing on the problem definition. In effect, the four-quadrant grid turned into a singular dichotomy with only one question: whether or not the mediator could provide a case evaluation.

Riskin's thinking evolved as exhibited in several smaller articles in mediation trade magazines laying out iterative revisions to the grid, resulting in a second major piece on this subject published in 2003. In this paper, Riskin reflected on his grid article, responded to the original grid's critics, and proposed new revisions to address the limitations of the original grid and how it was applied. In his first revision, which he called the New Old Grid, Riskin addressed the debate about the term "evaluative" by removing the terms "facilitative" and "evaluative" altogether and replacing them with new terms, "elicitive" and "directive," respectively. By using the term "directive" instead of "evaluative," he hoped to capture the same evaluative behavior mediation users might experience without de-emphasizing the essential facilitative nature of mediation. Secondly, Riskin sought to reiterate that the relationship between the two approaches was meant to be a spectrum of choices, not a dichotomy, and so, once again, he used the continuum construct. He also reminded readers of the grid's second dimension and reiterated the importance of his problem-definition continuum. However, within the same article, Riskin made a second revision, believing both the original grid and the New Old Grid were too static. He called this second revision, the New New Grid. In the New New Grid, Riskin kept the new "elicitive" and "directive" terminology and continua but revised the second continuum to address far more than the problem definition, and instead explore decision-making at various points in time during the mediation regarding substantive issues, process, and even meta-process decisions. He turned the singular two-dimensional grid into a series of grids, with each one describing decision-making at distinct points in time during a mediation, as a series of frames in a film capturing individual moments through time.

Although this new (new) construct was (and is) infinitely better at accurately describing the nuance of mediation, neither the construct nor the new "elicitive" and "directive" terminology has permeated the field lexicon like the original grid's "facilitative" and "evaluative" terminology. Nearly twenty-five years later, mediators, service providers, membership organizations, educators, as well as court rules and state statutes, utilize the original grid's terminology to define mediation approaches and define expectations (albeit slightly more nuanced than in the 1990s). Even with Riskin's push to reassert the entirety of the construct—that it is a two-dimensional grid consisting of a spectrum of behaviors that describe more than just the role of mediator—the field is stuck in the dichotomous "facilitative" and "evaluative" terminology construct.

To understand the negative impact of this dichotomous construct, it might help to place it in the context of other foundational articles featured in this book discussing the impact of mediation neutrality, mediation with marginalized populations, and private settlement processes for public disputes more generally. For instance, Trina Grillo questioned the use of mediation in the divorce context because she feared women negotiate away their rights when a mediator expresses an opinion that settling is better than going through the lengthy and emotionally draining court process. Josh Stulberg questioned Larry Susskind's assertion that mediators have a duty to ensure parties considered the impact of their settlements on the broader public constituency. And Owen Fiss worried more generally that the act of privately settling disputes hides the harm from the public's understanding of wrongdoing. Moreover, it seems these same concerns, that dispute resolution systems mistakenly prioritize privacy over publicity, exist today. Following the explosive revelations of Hollywood producer Harvey Weinstein's long-standing sexual misconduct and private, confidential settlements, people wondered how and why his actions and the sexual harassment at the hands of others in Hollywood, business, and government had remained secret such a long time. What would Grillo, Stulberg, or Fiss say about the use of mediation to settle individual sexual harassment or assault cases against a repeat sexual predator and the impact that settlement has on future women working with that individual? Furthermore, what impact would it have on future sexual harassment and assault victims more generally?

Some might argue that case evaluation provides value and addresses the issues raised by Grillo, Stulberg, and Fiss, without undermining the facilitative nature of mediation. For instance, if a divorce mediator asks parties to compare their potential settlement with their inherent legal rights, would Grillo have worried that women were (and maybe still are) disadvantaged in mediation? Additionally, if a mediator makes it a practice to ask parties to consider the impact of potential settlement terms on unrepresented parties and constituents not at the table, would there even be a debate between Stulberg and Susskind? Further, if a mediator asked a party to consider the ramifications of privately settling compared to pursuing litigation and making the dispute public for the benefit of a larger group, would Fiss be as concerned about the personal choice to settle? Some might call these actions simply good mediation practice, regardless of whether the mediator was acting in an evaluative or facilitative manner. However, through the lens of Riskin's Grid model, and more specifically the "facilitative"/"evaluative" dichotomy construct that it symbolized, the mediator seems left with one of two choices: whether or not to evaluate the claim's legal merits to assist parties to determine whether or not it is a good idea to settle. The idea that a facilitative mediator can incorporate evaluative concepts is not new, and may not address all the concerns that Stulberg, Grillo, and Fiss raise. However, it demonstrates that absent the dichotomous construct within Riskin's Grid, these terms, in and of themselves, can be less polarizing.

But there is hope. Although the "facilitative" "evaluative" language has been cemented in the field's lexicon, new technological advancements may finally dismantle the faulty dichotomous construct Riskin, and others, tried to correct. For instance, will the phrase "evaluative mediator" become an anachronism with technology advances such as predictive analytics? Predictive analytics rely on vast databases of information to glean trends, gain insights, and predict outcomes. Platforms such as Bloomberg's Litigation Analytics or Lexis Nexis's Lex Machina and Ravel Law use predictive analytics to provide attorneys with insights into case trends, judge behaviors, and most likely court outcomes. Where on the grid would a mediator be placed if she refuses to give an evaluation, but offers parties the use of Lex Machina to receive case insights and evaluation through predictive analytics? Although not drastically different than other hypotheticals Riskin posed in his 2003 article, this hypothetical makes it much clearer that a mediator can maintain a facilitative approach while recognizing the value and need for an expert case evaluation. And in doing so, more clearly demonstrate that the terms are not opposites.

In this way, the terminology may still endure even as the dichotomous construct falls aside, or this might simply inform a new debate in the future. Although we affectionately still refer to the concepts in Riskin's article as the Riskin Grid, it is not the two-dimensional model of the grid that has permeated our lexicon, it is the "evaluative" "facilitative" terminology Riskin used in the grid that has come to define the mediation field, which is why this is a foundational article. And yet it may be that advancing technology is what finally dismantles this dichotomous construct and prompts users to apply these terms as Riskin originally intended.

References

Kimberlee K. Kovach & Lela P. Love, *"Evaluative Mediation" Is an Oxymoron*, 14 ALT. TO THE HIGH COST OF LIT. 31 (Mar. 1996).

Leonard L. Riskin, *Decision-Making in Mediation: The New Old Grid and the New New Grid System*, 79 NOTRE DAME L. REV. 1 (2003).

The Riskin Grid: A Mixed Legacy

Donna Erez-Navot

I. Is Riskin's Grid Formative?

In considering whether Len Riskin's *Understanding Mediators' Orientations, Strategies and Techniques: A Grid for the Perplexed* is a formative piece, I start with the definition of "formative." Formative is defined as "helping to shape, develop or mold." For me, the grid is formative in that Riskin's original grid idea became fertile ground for criticism of his model, which together resulted in a productive debate that in some ways is more important than the grid itself. The grid should be credited with shaping the framework for conversations integral in the development of the mediation field for at least a decade, if not more.

In his article, Riskin used a simple and straightforward grid to organize what was occurring in processes billed as mediation. The grid consisted of a horizontal axis depicting a problem definition as a continuum from narrow to broad and a vertical axis depicting the spectrum of mediator behavior continuum from facilitative to evaluative. The most important quadrant for this commentary is the one on the top left called the evaluative-narrow quadrant, where the mediator behavior concentrates on very narrow, litigation-focused settlements and the mediator predicts court or other outcomes for the parties during the session.

In this commentary, I first review the debate that the grid article sparked. Then I discuss the relationship of the organizing principles of the grid to current model standards, guidelines for mediation programs, ethical guidelines, and quantitative research methods. These subsequent sections will show how the field of mediation has grappled, and perhaps begun to come to terms, with the contradictory practices included within the definition of mediation as conceptualized by Riskin's grid.

II. The Original Debate: Uproar of the 1990s

The grid quickly caused controversy and became the focus of academic debate for nearly ten years. Critics' fundamental concern surrounded the inclusion of evaluation as an accepted mediator practice. They argued that the practice was antithetical to the field of mediation. Professors Lela Love and Kimberly Kovach were alarmed, calling evaluative mediation an "oxymoron" (Love & Kovach 1996). Professor Josh Stulberg argued that "any orientation that is 'evaluative' as portrayed on the Riskin grid is conduct that is both conceptually different from, and operationally inconsistent with, the values and goals characteristically ascribed to the mediation process" (Stulberg 1997). Much of the focus of the concern with evaluation fell on two issues: first, whether

Donna Erez-Navot, *The Riskin Grid: A Mixed Legacy* In: *Discussions in Dispute Resolution*. Edited by: Art Hinshaw, Andrea Kupfer Schneider, and Sarah Rudolph Cole, Oxford University Press (2021). © Oxford University Press.
DOI: 10.1093/oso/9780197513248.003.0039

parties to the mediation process could pursue self-determination if their process included evaluation and, second, whether mediation outcomes could go beyond the rigidity of the adversarial process if they were defined in a narrow, legalistic approach. In other words, if mediation can include narrow and evaluative approaches, how could it be distinct from the traditional judicial process?

According to many, Riskin's model was problematic because it adopted an overinclusive definition of mediation. The subsequent debate focused on the way actions along the evaluative-narrow quadrant violate mediation's core principles of party self-determination and mediator impartiality. For example, in caucus, when a mediator identifies a monetary range that one side is likely to receive in damages in subsequent litigation or that they will not be able to prevail on a certain motion, the mediator is putting into question whether the parties will be able to make their own decision (party self-determination) and whether the mediator is being biased toward one party (mediator neutrality). By defining mediation so broadly, Riskin's inclusiveness assisted in mediation's adoption into a wide and diverse set of programs. Part of the continuing relevance of Riskin's grid lies in the fact that many dispute resolutions systems in operation today embody the contradictions that the grid contained.

As mediation was adopted widely and institutionalized, evaluative mediation was not only accepted, but became the norm in mediations involving lawyers as mediators or representatives. For example, today, in high-end commercial cases, it is common to employ a caucus-only model led by mediators who focus on legal issues. Parties are never in the same room, the conversation is extremely narrow, and the mediators are constantly evaluating the client's legal claims (Galton & Allen 2014). This current model falls squarely into the top left quadrant, which may rob parties of the opportunity to come up with creative and unique solutions that are not based on legal doctrine.

To respond to the criticism, Riskin followed up the grid with an article describing two mediation models. The first model was the "New Old Grid." Here, the problem definition (narrow and broad) stayed the same, but the approaches of the mediator were now described as elicitive and directive. For his final model, Riskin proposed the "New New Grid," which used a series of grids that focused the attention not only on the mediator but also on the participants, the parties, and the lawyers. It also took into consideration time and the dynamics of decision-making. Although these follow-up models were helpful in addressing some concerns, they certainly did not resolve the problem.

III. The Grid Debate and Its Influence on Dispute Resolution

Practitioners of conflict resolution believe that out of conflict and intense debate can come beauty and innovation. This sentiment rings true for Riskin's article. For the past twenty-five years, the debate his article engendered has influenced the field tremendously and led to innovation and clarification in three major areas: (1) model standards of practice for mediators; (2) guidelines for mediation programs and ethical guidelines; and (3) quantitative research methodology.

A. Model Standards

While drafting model standards for mediators, the debates about the grid were analyzed to determine what constitutes high quality mediation. The discussions while drafting the Model Standards of Practice for Family and Divorce Mediation (2000) and the Model Standards of Conduct for Mediators (2005) grappled with the question of whether the mediator's obligation to foster party self-determination was possible in evaluative narrow mediations.

With regard to civil claims, the public comment indicates that the drafters of the 2005 ABA Model Standards of Conduct for Mediators tried to address the debate to ensure that evaluation was curtailed and self-determination was paramount. The Joint Committee specifically altered the definition of mediation from the one in the 1994 Standards to respond to the "raging" debate in the mediation world over the facilitative versus evaluative mediation. In the 2005 ABA Standards, the three main goals remain constant (to guide the conduct of mediators; to inform the mediating parties; and to promote public confidence of mediation as a process for resolving disputes), but the definition of mediation was revised to reflect the overarching importance of party self-determination.

Similar to the 2005 ABA Model Standards of Conduct for Mediators discussed earlier, the 2000 Model Family Mediation Standards recognize that "[s]elf-determination is the fundamental principle of family mediation. The mediation process relies upon the ability of participants to make their own voluntary and informed decisions." Nonetheless, these Standards allowed a mediator "to provide the participants with information that the mediator is qualified by training or experience to provide" (Sheppard 2001), and evaluating legal claims were allowed in family law mediation. The Family and Divorce Mediation Standards gave permission for evaluation and left the decision about a lawyer-mediator evaluating a case to the parties, who would hopefully choose wisely as to which process they desired.

B. Guidelines for Mediation Programs and Ethical Guidelines

In many states, mandatory court annexed mediation is the norm in civil and family disputes. Parties are unable to choose their mediator and are instead assigned one by the court. In light of the fact that mediators (including evaluative-narrow mediators or "muscle" mediators) are being assigned without party input, the local rules and state ethical guidelines are vital to ensure a fair process where parties can feel free to make their own decisions in an informed way.

Although the evaluative-facilitative debate has been seen by many as a purely academic endeavor, some states have grappled with these questions in their ethical guidelines. For example, Florida and Minnesota both permit mediators to use evaluative techniques while incorporating mechanisms to "tame" such evaluation and ensure it does not violate party self-determination. Minnesota's mediators are permitted, under the ethical rules, to evaluate. These rules also state that a mediator should withhold his/her suggestions or opinions until after the parties had requested this evaluative service.

Professor Nancy Welsh later analyzed the concept of self-determination in the court annexed mediation context (Welsh 2001). She concluded that the provisions in various states, like the ones described in Minnesota and Florida, will not adequately safeguard party self-determination or protect parties from coercive evaluation by mediators. Welsh offers the idea of a three-day nonwaivable cooling-off period before mediated settlement agreements, whether oral or written, become binding. She believes that this would serve "as an effective antidote to high pressure tactics [from mediators], both because the cooling-off period protects those who have already been subjected to high pressure tactics and because the threat of easy rescission makes it less likely that rational actors will choose to use high pressure tactics." In the mediation context, both of these effects imply that the introduction of a cooling-off period would be an effective means to protect party self-determination.

C. Quantitative Research Methods

Today, the grid and subsequent debate also continues in the quantitative analysis of mediation programs. In 2012, the ABA convened a Task Force on Research on Mediator Techniques to examine empirical studies that linked specific mediator actions (e.g., mediator evaluation, eliciting ideas from parties) to either enhanced mediation outcomes or to detrimental effects. Although the research overall was not conclusive, five facilitative techniques were found to have had a positive effect both on settlement and on disputants' relationships and perceptions of mediation. These were: (1) facilitating disputants' suggestions or solutions; (2) giving more attention to disputants' emotions, relationships, and sources of conflict; (3) working to build trust and rapport; (4) expressing empathy or praising the disputants; and (5) structuring the agenda and using pre-mediation caucuses focused on establishing trust.

Similarly, the Maryland Courts engaged in a comprehensive quantitative study in 2016, finding that clients had negative perceptions of fairness for mediators who offered evaluations, opinions, and solutions. With regard to outcomes working for the long term, clients reported higher satisfaction when mediators used facilitative practices. Another recent article compared mediator behaviors that fell in different quadrants of the grid. It found that more facilitative techniques were associated with positive outcomes, while evaluative ones had significant negative effects. Also of interest is that greater time spent in caucus was associated with increased participant trust in the mediator but more negative attitudes among participants.

IV. Is the Debate Over?

We may have come to a point where practitioners have accepted the grid and its application to the field. According to Eric Galton and Tracey Allen, when summarizing the debate of the 1990s, "[e]veryone has begun to recognize that mediators deploy a variety of styles, often in the same case, searching to apply an approach that is effective for the specific case and participants" (Galton & Allen 2014). The movement of mediation in the shadow of the law and the exponential increase of court-annexed mediation programs has led us to a point where the grid is an accepted framework and evaluative mediators sit on court panels side by side with facilitative ones. Perhaps the mediation marketplace, which is directed by lawyer consumers of mediation, have led us to accept diverse mediator orientations (including evaluative ones). In the final analysis, the debate itself, spurred by Riskin's grid—and the way that debate has been institutionalized—hopefully continues to safeguard our end users and ensures high quality mediation.

References

Eric Galton & Tracy Allen, *Don't Torch the Joint Session*, 21 Disp. Resol. Mag. 25 (Fall 2014).

Lela P. Love & Kimberlee K. Kovach, *"Evaluative" Mediation Is an Oxymoron*, 14 Alternatives to High Cost Litig. 31 (1996).

Andrew Schepard, *An Introduction to the Model Standards of Practice for Family and Divorce Mediation*, 35 Fam. L.Q. 1 (2001).

Joseph B. Stulberg, *Facilitative Versus Evaluative Mediator Orientations: Piercing the "Grid" Lock*, 24 Fla. St. U. L. Rev. 985, 986 (1997).

Nancy A. Welsh, *The Thinning Vision of Self-Determination in Court-Connected Mediation: The Inevitable Price of Institutionalization?*, 6 Harv. Negot. L. Rev. 1, 3 (2001).

Growth from the Grid?

Kimberlee Kovach

Professor Len Riskin's effort to categorize mediators' work certainly provided the stimulus for ongoing and engaging discussions and debates about the very essence of the mediator's role. The piece was essentially the first time since the advent of the "modern mediation movement" that the field had a foundation upon which to center process debates (Riskin 1994). That is, the focus was not on the mediation process generally, or its use, but rather on the specifics of the tasks, tools, and skills used by mediators in their work. In his article, Riskin identified approaches to the mediation process grounded in precise activities of the mediator. While other articles such as that by Trina Grillo, which is a part of this volume, engendered controversy with regard to mediation use generally, it was Riskin's positioning of mediation into four distinct quadrants, and placing the mediator's activities in a dichotomy, that generated debate. This centering of these discussions alone provides the article the basis for its identity as one of the most influential in the field. And of course, the *Grid* (along with the initial responses) was the genesis for many additional articles dealing with the topic of mediator conduct, and specifically the evaluative approach to mediation. Although the discussions and debates that followed were at sometimes contentious, at other times they served as the focal point for contemplation, reflection, and growth.

At the time of the article's publication, the concept of mediators evaluating claims was not addressed in any teaching, training, or other literature. In fact, I doubt that many teachers and trainers even discussed the topic. The subsequent articles addressing mediator evaluative techniques were both critical and supportive, and in many instances the debate continues today. And I would venture to say that experts differ in terms of whether this debate was (or still is) helpful or harmful with regard to the continued development and evolution of mediation practice. Although Riskin has since revised the Grid and included other descriptors of the mediator's work (Riskin, *The New Old Grid*, 2003), it is the first rendition that has garnered far more attention and focus.

While the original article was quite influential and served to ignite the controversy, without which many experts would not have highlighted these aspects of mediation, it has also been viewed somewhat critically for polarizing the field. Of course, Riskin acknowledged that he did not anticipate such reaction or the resulting difficulties and divisiveness. At the same time, however, it was the intense debate and criticism of approaches that resulted in focused attention to the specifics of the mediator's work. That focus was, and remains today, beneficial and constructive. This analysis of specific conduct in our work forced us to look at ourselves and engage in a deeper examination of the specific actions or moves mediators make, and the skills and tools they

Kimberlee Kovach, *Growth from the Grid?* In: *Discussions in Dispute Resolution.* Edited by: Art Hinshaw, Andrea Kupfer Schneider, and Sarah Rudolph Cole, Oxford University Press (2021). © Oxford University Press.
DOI: 10.1093/oso/9780197513248.003.0040

employ. Upon reflections, I see three distinct aspects relating to this article that could spark further conversations.

The first issue concerns the disjunction between the practice of mediation and the theory and teaching of the process. One only need go to the article's second page to note that Riskin's example of the differing views of the process comparing the lawyer—mediator (practice orientation) as in the evaluative quadrant with the facilitative approach urged by academics. Even today, a deep schism remains between what is taught in mediation classes and trainings and what is practiced on a day-to-day basis. Would being more deliberate in recognizing and discussing this detachment be helpful? If so, in which direction? Should academics be more inclusive of practice changes? Or should practitioners adhere to the mediation model taught? So to change this disjuncture, or bridge the gap, should we attempt to increase regulation of practice? Can a state or other entity, as some have suggested during the height of these debates, require those who practice "evaluative mediation" to label their work as neutral case evaluation and not mediation? Or should academics reassess what they are teaching? Should trainers, as some do, include more case evaluation tools and techniques as integral components of the basic mediation process? While most of these questions could have been asked shortly following the article's publication, they were not, and clear answers have not surfaced in the last twenty-five years.

The second issue concerns the impact of the space in which the mediation operates. Directly related, and nearly absent from the original piece—and absent from much of the literature generally—is the consideration of how much influence the legal system (and lawyers specifically) have had in shaping the mediation process. From the beginning, what was described by Frank Sander as a Multi-door *Center* was nearly immediately changed to *Courthouse*. Although as I have noted elsewhere, this alternative system of dispute resolution, and particularly mediation, was to be *apart* from the legal system, nearly immediately these alternative processes were taken in and subsumed so that it became *a part of* that very system. Even with early warnings that alternative dispute resolution would be co-opted, it was still transformed to fit within the legal paradigm. Others have noted this impact, and examined whether this change was beneficial or harmful—or perhaps both. (Would mediation have been as viable as it is today if it stayed apart from the legal system?) (Press 1997). Of course, in many jurisdictions, lawyers did not readily accept mediation—at least not the more facilitative model. Upon reflection, if the legalization of mediation was necessary for its acceptance, was it worth it? For whom?

Yet because lawyers play a dominant role in much of mediation practice, this impact, and particularly any adverse influence, is rarely, if at all, mentioned. Even today, the mediation process continues to be shaped and even dictated by the lawyers who regularly participate in mediation as party representatives. A more recent example is the disappearance of a joint session or meeting from the mediation process. This mutation has been dictated by lawyers, who apparently do not have the skills necessary to engage in such discussions in a productive manner or are not comfortable with their clients speaking to one another. In many jurisdictions today, mediation looks nothing like the process described or taught—especially with parties never seeing one another during the entire day. Removal of this early stage of mediation, with all participants together and sharing at least some minimal information, was the result of mediators catering to lawyer demands. And in this *adaptation* of mediation, the process loses some of its potential for problem-solving and empowerment. The importance of the roles of the parties is diminished a great deal when they are not permitted to really participate in the way originally envisioned. Lawyers, who admittedly are the gatekeepers for much of mediation practice, continue to be dominant in shaping the mediation process.

Another reflection when considering the Grid was the limited nature of the subsequent discussions about the evaluative-facilitative axis. Most, if not all, of the considerations about evaluation were law-centric. When evaluation discussions occurred, an implicit (maybe at times explicit) presumption existed that the evaluation had to do with potential legal outcomes. Little literature has addressed the role of the mediator in evaluating the financial impacts of either continuing litigation or resolving the dispute, and there is similarly little discussion of mediators' evaluating the social implications of interpersonal relationships in the workplace when employees sue their employers. Mediators rarely provided an evaluation to the parties about the psychological aspects involved in conflict engagement—and failing to resolve disputes. Even in family mediations, I have seen little written about mediators providing mental health assessments about the divorcing process and its impact upon children. And when considering competing visitation arrangements, shouldn't mediators, if they are evaluating, then discuss how different options might have different psychological impacts upon adolescents, tweens, and toddlers? Even in those instances where we know that litigation takes a psychological toll on people, the discussions usually surround what a judge or jury might do if the matter goes to court, and not how one's spouse or children will be impacted by three years of litigation. Shouldn't someone also help parties evaluate the psychological aspects and mental health implications of continued and escalating conflict?

Perhaps these considerations are absent because most mediators employing evaluative techniques were, and are, lawyers. And the lawyers who are hiring the mediators are focused on one kind of outcome—a resolution to a lawsuit. But generally, there was a dispute before a lawsuit was filed, and the parties involved have financial, social, and psychological considerations, to name a few. If evaluation is indeed part of the process, then shouldn't it be much broader and include more than one factor?

Finally, a third issue focuses on the overlooked axis of problem definition. Although Riskin's work was quite influential in sparking the discussions of mediator orientations in the evaluative-facilitative quadrants, little has been said about the definitional component. For many of us, the old adage that "the mediator controls the process, the parties control the content" was so dominant that, in our view, problem definition decisions would actually lie with the parties. So it seemed, I think, there was little to debate. Or perhaps, it could also have been a result of those, including this author, who took issue with the Grid focused nearly exclusively on the facilitative-evaluative aspect, with very little consideration of problem definition. Perhaps it was not viewed as controversial although in many ways, how the matter is viewed can impact the tasks and work of the mediator.

It seems that more emphasis and discussion should be placed on the problem-definition component in terms of the mediator's role. For example, when cases are in litigation, is the *matter* really resolved if the *lawsuit* is settled? I venture to say that in many instances, there is a vast difference between lawsuit settlement and resolution of the matter. Yet for many, whose work is dictated by lawyers, the primary, perhaps even exclusive, objective of mediation is settlement of the case. Why shouldn't relationship repair be considered an important part of the process when an ongoing relationship exists? Riskin has even brought up this point (Riskin & Welsh 2007), but the issues related to the problem-definition continuum have been largely ignored.

Perhaps it is time to examine the mediation process with the focus on its purpose: simply settling lawsuits or resolving disputes in ways that allow parties to have closure, to repair relationships, and to engage in creative problem-solving. With that point in mind, we could work in reverse to design a process that would include actions and activities to best achieve those end goals. What comes may look like the traditional notions of mediation.

Many years ago, a wise and experienced mediator in commercial practice, noted in his first book that mediators should be chameleon-like. And we now know that mediators often adapt the process to the individual case needs. In fact, it is that ability to recognize needs and make process modifications that makes mediation so effective in reaching resolution across a large variety of dispute types and widely diverse people. I now believe that in creating quadrants, Riskin was acknowledging this movement potential.

Yet even the chameleon has limitations. It cannot transform into a caterpillar. Likewise, the mediation process must retain its core characteristics. We have gained a great deal of experience and knowledge in the twenty-five years since the publication of the Grid. It is now time to use that in assisting the chameleon to define its core.

References

Trina Grillo, *The Mediation Alternative: Process Dangers for Women*" 100 Yale L.J. 1545 (1991).

Sharon Press, *Institutionalization: Savior or Saboteur of Mediation?*, 24 Fla. St. U. L. Rev. 903 (1997).

Leonard L. Riskin, *Decisionmaking in Mediation: The New Old Grid and the New New Grid System*, 79 Notre Dame L. Rev. 3 (2003).

Leonard L. Riskin, *Mediator Orientations, Strategies, and Techniques*, 12 Alternatives to High Cost Litig. 111 (1994).

Leonard L. Riskin & Nancy A. Welsh, *Is That All There Is? The "Problem" in Court-Oriented Mediation*, 14 Geo. Mason L. Rev. 863 (2007–08).

PART 3
ARBITRATION

Article 3.1

The New Federal Arbitration Law

Julius Henry Cohen and Kenneth Dayton

12 Virginia Law Review 265 (1926)

ON FEBRUARY 12, 1925 President Coolidge signed the United States Arbitration Law, which became effective January 1st, 1926. By this Act there is reversed the hoary doctrine that agreements for arbitration are revocable at will and are unenforceable, and in the language of the statute itself, they are made "valid, enforceable and irrevocable" within the limits of Federal jurisdiction.

The Evil to Be Corrected

... The evils which arbitration is intended to correct are three in number: (1) The long delay usually incident to a proceeding at law, in equity or in admiralty, especially in recent years in centers of commercial activity, where there has arisen great congestion of the court calendars. This delay arises not only from congestion of the calendars, which necessitates each case awaiting its turn for consideration, but also frequently from preliminary motions and other steps taken by litigants, appeals therefrom, which delay consideration of the merits, and appeals from decisions upon the merits which commonly follow the decision of any case of real importance. (2) The expense of litigation. (3) The failure, through litigation to reach a decision regarded as just when measured by the standards of the business world. This failure may result either because the courts necessarily apply general rules which do not always fit a specific case, or because, in the ordinary jury trial, the parties do not have the benefit of the judgment of persons familiar with the peculiarities of the given controversy.

Making an agreement to arbitrate is not always sufficient, however. If both parties are strictly honorable and if there is no misunderstanding between them as to the scope and effect of the agreement which they have made, they will carry out the contract to arbitrate and perform the award entered upon it, and there is no necessity for a statute. Unfortunately, this situation does not commonly exist. The party refusing to proceed may believe in good faith that for one reason or another his agreement to arbitrate does not bind him (i.e., he may assert that he made no such agreement or that it was not intended to cover the particular controversy).

Even without this, after a dispute has arisen, one party or the other ordinarily has a certain technical advantage which may be impaired if he submits the controversy to arbitration rather than to the courts. It may be in the application of a settled rule of law. It may be in some procedural peculiarity, or it may be merely in the delay of which

Julius Henry Cohen and Kenneth Dayton, *The New Federal Arbitration Law* In: *Discussions in Dispute Resolution.* Edited by: Art Hinshaw, Andrea Kupfer Schneider, and Sarah Rudolph Cole, Oxford University Press (2021).
DOI: 10.1093/oso/9780197513248.003.0041

he is assured by the congestion of the courts before he has to meet his obligation. The result is that this party is usually loath to surrender his supposed advantage. His unwillingness is not necessarily due to dishonesty or bad faith. Unfortunately, business has become so used to the doctrine of revocability of arbitration agreements that these clauses are not regarded in the same light as other contractual obligations, and the party who refuses to perform his agreement frequently does not realize that he is violating his plighted word. He has no conscious intention of defaulting upon his agreement, but the rule of law has blinded him to the fact that this is an agreement. While our American courts have usually declared a friendly attitude toward arbitration, they have felt themselves bound by the long standing decisions holding that arbitration agreements were revocable at will and would not be enforced by the courts. The result has been that any party who wished to avoid an agreement which he had made to arbitrate had only to declare his refusal to proceed and the courts would not order specific performance of the contract while the alternative of a damage suit was inadequate.

Furthermore, after the completion of an arbitration proceeding and the rendition of an award, the remedy open to the successful party if his opponent refused to perform the award was not in all respects satisfactory. To be sure, the award was usually considered a determination of the merits of the controversy, and the successful party had only to plead and prove the award to recover judgment upon it. Even this remedy, however, left room for an extended law suit because of the collateral issues of fraud and misconduct and other impropriety in the proceeding which might be introduced and which meant that the delay in finally recovering judgment was substantially as great as though action had been brought upon the original dispute. The one advantage lay in the fact that proof became simpler.

Legal Justification

It has been suggested that the proposed law depends entirely for its validity upon the exercise of the interstate-commerce and admiralty powers of Congress. This is not the fact. It rests upon the constitutional provision by which Congress is authorized to establish and control inferior Federal courts. So far as congressional acts relate to the procedure in such courts, they are clearly within the congressional power. This principle is so evident and so firmly established that it cannot be seriously disputed. The statute as drawn establishes a procedure in the Federal courts for the enforcement of certain arbitration agreements. It is no infringement upon the right of each State to decide for itself what contracts shall or shall not exist under its laws. To be sure, whether or not a contract exists is a question of the substantive law of the jurisdiction wherein the contract was made. But whether or not an arbitration agreement is to be enforced is a question of the law of procedure and is determined by the law of the jurisdiction wherein the remedy is sought. That the enforcement of arbitration contracts is within the law of procedure as distinguished from substantive law is well settled by the decisions of our courts.

. . . It seems probable, however, that Congress has ample power to declare that all arbitration agreements connected with interstate commerce or admiralty transactions shall be recognized as valid and enforceable even by the State courts. In both interstate commerce and admiralty the Federal power is supreme. Congress may act at its will, and having acted, no law or regulation of a State inconsistent with the congressional act can be given any force or effect even in the courts of the State itself. They are as much bound to carry out the provisions of such a Federal statute as though it was an act of their own legislature. This rule is so well settled that it is no longer subject to question or discussion. It has been enforced in innumerable instances . . .

Public Policy and the Relation of Law and Arbitration

. . . Sound public policy demands specific enforcement of arbitration agreements by the law. To argue that such enforcement should receive only the sanction of business opinion and should remain extra-legal, is unsound. An agreement for arbitration is a business contract. It should be as inviolable as any other business contract, and once it is violated the law should give an adequate remedy. There is a difference between an arbitration agreement and the ordinary contract in the fact that there is no adequate remedy for a breach of the arbitration agreement except through specific performance. Damages are not and cannot be compensatory. It was not so long ago that even the remedy of damages was denied to certain forms of contract which are among the commonest in the business world. No one in this day of commercial activity could argue that the ordinary contract of sale or that commercial paper should not be recognized by the law and that obligations assumed thereby should be enforced only so far as the obligor felt the force of business opinion . . .

. . . Arbitration is not a radical innovation. To be sure, it reaches the settlement of controversies by routes much more direct, much less hedged about by technicalities, much more with an aim to homespun justice, than do actions in the courts. But arbitration has too long a history, too long a connection with Anglo-Saxon mercantile life, to leave room for any fear of its ultimate value when it is understood and used intelligently . . .

. . . Neither is the relation of the lawyer to arbitration generally understood. We cannot stress too strongly the need for lawyers promptly equipping themselves with knowledge of this field. No lawyer is competent to give advice in this field until he has made the study of it which he makes of every other phase of the law with which he deals, but subject to this necessity for initial study and the occasional help of a specialist, needed in every branch of the law, the new arbitration statute has opened up to the general practitioner a new instrument through which he can offer to his clients a service and a result formerly denied them. Clients must be educated in the use of arbitration, and it is in this education that the opportunity of the lawyer lies . . .

. . . Not all questions arising out of contracts ought to be arbitrated. It is a remedy peculiarly suited to the disposition of the ordinary disputes between merchants as to questions of fact-quantity, quality, time of delivery, compliance with terms of payment, excuses for non-performance, and the like. It has a place also in the determination of the simpler questions of law-the questions of law which arise out of these daily relations between merchants as to the passage of title, the existence of warranties, or the questions of law which are complementary to the questions of fact which we have just mentioned. It is not the proper method for deciding points of law of major importance involving constitutional questions or policy in the application of statutes.

Speaking generally, it is a proper remedy for the determination of those classes of disputes which arise day by day in the common experience of the disputants and the individuals to whom the dispute is to be referred, where all meet upon a common ground. It is not a proper remedy for what we may call casual questions-questions with which the arbitrators have no particular experience and which are better left to the determination of skilled judges with a background of legal experience and established systems of law . . .

. . . The lawyer is needed in arbitration proceedings. Experience proves this. His training in proper presentation and in the differentiation of essentials and non-essentials is invaluable. The lawyer who will *forget technicalities* and who is equipped to handle business matters *understandingly* and expeditiously has open to him an entirely new field of practice. We should think it strange indeed if the courts were found supporting or advocating a system which was against the interests of the law or of the profession from which the judges are drawn. Nevertheless, our own courts, while declaring that arbitration agreements were unenforceable, have been most insistent that the policy of arbitration was wise and that it should be encouraged and extended . . .

. . . The arbitration law has now been in effect in New York for five years. Despite the inertia which had to be overcome before the statute could become properly effective, phenomenal progress has resulted, and the attitude of the courts toward the law and toward proceedings under it has been most encouraging. Almost without exception the courts have done their utmost to facilitate procedure by the support of the act, have upheld the power of the parties to make such agreements, have recognized their duty to abide by them, have given the strongest support to the powers of the arbitrators thereunder and to the finality of their awards, and have refused to permit the invasion of technicalities in the application of the law or the determination of rights under it. There is no less reason to believe that the Federal courts will give equally sincere support in the application of the Federal statute.

New York City, *Julius Henry Cohen. Kenneth Dayton.*

Comments

A Robust History of Arbitration in Early America: Commentary on *The New Federal Arbitration Law*

Carli N. Conklin[1]

Julius Henry Cohen and Kenneth Dayton's 1926 article, *The New Federal Arbitration Law*, is primarily an apologetic in favor of the Federal Arbitration Act, which Congress passed in 1925. Cohen and Dayton drafted their article as a response to real or anticipated criticisms that the new Federal Arbitration Act was "a radical innovation." What makes their article a formative article in the field of dispute resolution is not their argument that, instead of being "a radical innovation," arbitration had a long-standing history in American law. In fact, their explicit claims on this point seem, at first glance, to be fairly anemic, with only passing references to arbitration's Anglo-Saxon roots or its robust presence in more recent English and American legal history. The historical richness of this article is found not in what Cohen and Dayton explicitly assert, but in what they assume in their assertions. In other words, Cohen and Dayton could make seemingly anemic claims regarding the robust history of arbitration in the Anglo-American legal tradition convincing to their readers only if they were speaking to an audience whose understanding of that history was as rich as their own. In that context, each historic claim serves as a shorthand reference to a rich history of arbitration that Cohen and Dayton could fairly assume was common knowledge among their readers—including early twentieth-century arbitrators, lawyers, judges, and legal scholars—whose vantage point for understanding the history of early American arbitration was nearly a century closer in time than our own.

This comment explores six of Cohen and Dayton's historic claims, revealing the rich history of arbitration behind each shorthand reference. These claims are: (1) the common law right to submit one's dispute to arbitration; (2) the robust nature of state-level arbitration in early America; (3) the benefits, and historical use, of arbitration within the merchant community; (4) the historic tensions between lawyers and arbitrators, and between litigation and arbitration as a means of resolving disputes; (5) the procedural interplay between arbitration and the courts;

[1] For a more complete discussion of the historical themes addressed in this comment, see Carli N. Conklin, *A Variety of State-Level Procedures, Practices, and Policies: Arbitration in Early America*, 2016 J. Disp. Resol. 55 (2016); Carli N. Conklin, *Lost Options for Mutual Gain? The Lawyer, the Layperson, and Dispute Resolution in Early America*, 28 Ohio St. J. on Disp. Resol. 581 (2013); and Carli N. Conklin, *Transformed, Not Transcended: The Role of Extrajudicial Dispute Resolution in Antebellum Kentucky and New Jersey*, 48 Am. J. Legal Hist. 39 (2006).

Carli N. Conklin, *A Robust History of Arbitration in Early America: Commentary on* The New Federal Arbitration Law
In: *Discussions in Dispute Resolution*. Edited by: Art Hinshaw, Andrea Kupfer Schneider, and Sarah Rudolph Cole, Oxford University Press (2021). © Oxford University Press. DOI: 10.1093/oso/9780197513248.003.0042

and (6) the public policy goals articulated in support of a more widespread use of arbitration.

I. The Common Law Right to Submit One's Dispute to Arbitration

One of the most prominent, and most important, aspects of Cohen and Dayton's article is their assertion that the creation of a federal statute governing arbitration would not eliminate one's right to a jury trial. Implicit in their argument is the flip side of this discussion, which is that resorting to arbitration, instead of the courts, for the resolution of one's dispute was a disputant's right under the law. This right to arbitrate had its roots in the English common law, with John Cowel, in his seventeenth-century legal dictionary *Nomothetes, The Interpreter: Containing the Genuine Signification of Such Obscure Words and Terms Used Either in the Common Or Statute Lawes of this Realm*, and William Blackstone, in his eighteenth-century *Commentaries on the Laws of England*, both defining common law arbitration and outlining its procedures in terms that would have been strikingly familiar to Cohen and Dayton as they promoted a federal, statutory form of arbitration in the twentieth-century United States.

II. The Robust Nature of State-Level Arbitration in Early America

In a similar juxtaposition, Cohen and Dayton's argument that federal arbitration legislation would not usurp state arbitration assumes the presence of state-level arbitration in the first place. A common law form of arbitration had existed at the colonial and then state levels as early as the seventeenth century. Early colonies and then American states also adopted the English practice of reference, where parties to litigation could have their dispute referred to arbitration, with the resulting award entered as a judgment of the court. Finally, in 1698, England passed the Arbitration Act, known as the Locke statute, to encourage arbitration by allowing parties to secure an arbitration award as a judgment of the court without first commencing litigation, thereby combining the extrajudicial benefits of common law arbitration with the judicial enforcement of reference. American states followed suit, passing their own versions of the Locke statute throughout the late eighteenth and early nineteenth centuries. A review of state statutes and court opinions suggests that each of these three forms of arbitration were robustly utilized by disputants throughout the antebellum period. Cohen and Dayton seem to acknowledge not only this presence of state-level arbitration but also the importance of its practice, as they explicitly assure their audience that the new federal arbitration law was intended to operate alongside, but not usurp, arbitration law and practice at the state level.

III. The Benefits, and Historical Use, of Arbitration within the Merchant Community

In seeking to advance arbitration under the new federal statute, Cohen and Dayton argue for the benefits of arbitration particularly for early twentieth-century businesspeople. In so doing, they are tapping into a long-standing tradition of merchant use of arbitration. Interestingly enough, Cohen and Dayton argue in favor of arbitration for the same reasons—speed, cost savings, simplicity of process, and expertise—that motivated merchant use of arbitration from the Middle Ages forward. These policy arguments in favor of merchant arbitration seem to be a perennial favorite, as they formed the basis of a long-running, and oftentimes vitriolic, debate over the use of arbitration or litigation as the best means of resolving merchant disputes in the post-Revolutionary United States.

IV. The Historic Tensions between Lawyers and Arbitrators, and between Litigation and Arbitration as a Means of Resolving Disputes

Cohen and Dayton's attempt to appeal to lawyers evidences the continuation of a historic tension between lawyers and arbitrators, and between litigation and arbitration as a means of resolving disputes. Interestingly enough in light of their statutory triumph, Cohen and Dayton attempt to mitigate that historic tension; instead of pitting the arbitrator against the lawyer in their support of arbitration, they explain how arbitration could be a financial and professional boon *for lawyers* and how arbitration itself could benefit from the lawyers' presence in arbitration proceedings. In this argument, Cohen and Dayton cleverly take one of arbitration proponents' most historically provocative arguments—that arbitration promotes a level playing field and, as a result, equal access to justice through the *absence* of lawyers in the dispute resolution process—and turn it on its head, seeking to gain the legal profession's support of arbitration by claiming that both the arbitration process and the lawyers' own clients would benefit from the presence of lawyers before, and during, the arbitration proceeding.

V. The Procedural Interplay between Arbitration and the Courts

Cohen and Dayton not only emphasize the potential interplay between arbitrators and lawyers but also the potential interplay between arbitration and the courts. The procedural benefits they identify—such as judicial enforcement of the arbitration award—and the questions they consider—such as the revocability of arbitration agreements or arbitration awards, the hostility or friendliness of courts to arbitration agreements or arbitration awards, and the grounds for appeal of an arbitration award—are not suggestions for a new relationship between arbitration and the courts but, instead, a recognition of the foundational elements of a relationship between arbitration and the courts that had existed from the colonial era forward. In other words, the relationship that Cohen and Dayton envisioned between arbitration under the Federal Arbitration Act and the federal courts is a relationship that had been playing out on the state level for more than a century. Instead of laying new statutory ground rules for the relationship between arbitration and the courts, Cohen and Dayton seem to be suggesting that the long-standing rules that had governed court treatment of arbitration in the antebellum period—where common law arbitration, reference, and statutory arbitration had been widely upheld by states' highest courts, each under their own terms—would now apply to the specific form of arbitration outlined in the federal statute. It is an approach that both mitigates the perception of judicial hostility toward arbitration and encourages judicial support for arbitration in the years to come.

VI. The Public Policy Goals Articulated in Support of a More Widespread Use of Arbitration

This brings us to the final place where Cohen and Dayton echo a deeper historical understanding of arbitration, which is in their articulation of arbitration as good public policy. When Cohen and Dayton pivot toward this discussion at the end of their article, they are not articulating new ideas but, instead, are emphasizing arguments in favor of arbitration that had been commonly articulated throughout early American history. These arguments include cost savings, time savings, simplicity, finality, arbitrator expertise, and the possibility of remedies that, unlike judgments in a court of law, could be specifically tailored to the dispute at hand. Underlying each of these arguments is a vigorous historical conception of what it means to achieve justice in resolving disputes. Historically, justice was conceived of both in terms of procedure and in terms of outcome. So, for example, we see late eighteenth- and early nineteenth-century Kentuckians advocating for arbitration due to its speed and cost savings *and* for the finality of its outcome—especially in the settling of land title disputes. Similarly, eighteenth- and nineteenth-century New Jersey Quakers built arbitration into their meeting house rules—and required it of their members. Their reasons for doing so combined the perceived amicability of the arbitration process with an outcome that favored a communal conception of justice; they believed that arbitration, as opposed to litigation, was best suited to restoring harmony both between the disputants and within the larger community. In antebellum Massachusetts, merchants used arbitration in part due to arbitrators' expertise in commercial law. In fact, late eighteenth- and early nineteenth-century policy debates in Massachusetts reveal the rising legal profession's attempts to convince merchants that the courts were increasingly competent enough to rule on commercial disputes in a way that would both reflect, and assist in the development of, a cohesive body of commercial law.

VII. A Formative Article in the Field of Dispute Resolution

On the surface, Cohen and Dayton's article provides a summary of the key issues and debates surrounding the passage of the Federal Arbitration Act in the mid-1920s. But perhaps even more interesting is what is happening beneath the surface. The arguments summoned by Cohen and Dayton in favor of the Federal Arbitration Act were not new but, instead, were a continuation of long-standing support for, and debates over, the use of arbitration throughout American history.

By the end of the twentieth century, the rich history of arbitration in the early American legal tradition that is implied within Cohen and Dayton's apologetic would be largely lost in the field of legal scholarship, obscured by claims of judicial hostility to arbitration at the state level that stemmed, in part, from the language of the Federal Arbitration Act. As more recent scholars seek to rediscover that early history, Cohen and Dayton's article provides an intriguing suggestion that knowledge of this robust history existed, if, at times, under the surface, in the place we might least expect it: an article promoting the act that came to almost solely define our twenty-first-century understandings of arbitration in American history.

The Federal Arbitration Act in Its Infancy: Cohen and Dayton's *The New Federal Arbitration Law*

Imre S. Szalai

Julius Henry Cohen, the principal drafter of the Federal Arbitration Act (FAA), together with Kenneth Dayton, another lawyer who worked at Cohen's firm, published a landmark article announcing the FAA's enactment in February 1926, one month after the FAA's effective date. An interesting history surrounds the writing of the article, which stands as a milestone in the field of arbitration law for several reasons, including: its introduction and justification of a statute that has had a far-reaching impact on America's civil justice system; its contextualization of the FAA; its acknowledgment of concerns regarding the FAA; and its recognition that private parties should promote arbitration. The article is significant for celebrating the birth of a landmark statute and capturing a small snapshot of the rich legal history of the FAA. Also, in retrospect, the article has taken on a new meaning and serves as a reminder that the FAA, now almost one hundred years old, needs reform.

I. Why the Article Was Written

Cohen wrote the article for two primary reasons. First, at a general level, its publication was consistent with progressive philosophies of reformers who desired to modernize America's arbitration laws. Second, the article addressed concerns raised during a congressional hearing regarding the FAA.

Charles Bernheimer, a merchant with the New York Chamber of Commerce known as the "Father of Commercial Arbitration," was the visionary and driving force behind the FAA's enactment during the 1920s. Through the Chamber, Bernheimer hired attorney Cohen as the legal mind to effectuate Bernheimer's dreams for a modern commercial arbitration statute. Working closely with Bernheimer in a multiyear campaign, Cohen became the FAA's principal drafter and a key lobbyist for its enactment.

The FAA was enacted during the closing years of the Progressive Age, a tumultuous period of change in American society, with rapid industrialization, urbanization, waves of immigration, and a growing national economy. To cope with these changes, progressive philosophy embraced the role of experts serving as decision makers. Thus, arbitration, with its possibility of having experts serve as decision makers, resonated with progressive reformers. Also, when suggesting reforms, many progressives understood the value of public relations campaigns, to help create perceptions and correct misunderstandings.

Imre S. Szalai, *The Federal Arbitration Act in Its Infancy: Cohen and Dayton's* The New Federal Arbitration Law In: *Discussions in Dispute Resolution*. Edited by: Art Hinshaw, Andrea Kupfer Schneider, and Sarah Rudolph Cole, Oxford University Press (2021).
 DOI: 10.1093/oso/9780197513248.003.0043

Cohen's article should be understood against the backdrop of the Progressive Age. The FAA's drafters engaged in extensive lobbying and publicity campaigns. They were passionate about arbitration, with sincere, deeply held beliefs in its value to resolve commercial disputes, and they used every opportunity to evangelize about arbitration. For example, Bernheimer wrote editorials and obtained interviews with media outlets such as the *New York Times* and *Saturday Evening Post* to spread the gospel about arbitration. Additionally, Bernheimer and the New York Chamber hired Cohen to engage in extensive research for a three-hundred-page book on why the English ouster doctrine was flawed, and this book laid the groundwork for the FAA's enactment. Similarly, the article can be viewed as part of the reformers' broad publicity campaigns to inform the public and correct misunderstandings about the scope of the statute. The article provides an overview of the FAA, along with justifications for its enactment and a call for private initiatives to support arbitration.

The more specific reason for writing the article involves a failed congressional hearing. There were two congressional hearings regarding the FAA, in 1923 and 1924. The reformers, especially Bernheimer, viewed the 1923 hearing as a failure; the bill died in committee with the close of Congress that year. Also, during the 1923 hearing, Montana Senator Thomas Walsh was skeptical, even antagonistic toward the bill, asking difficult, leading questions suggesting the bill was unjustified. To make matters worse, Bernheimer was flustered during the 1923 hearing because he was in a rush to leave the hearing in Washington, D.C., and catch a train to New Jersey to lobby for a New Jersey arbitration statute. In the weeks following the 1923 hearing, Bernheimer, the visionary behind the FAA, replayed the testimony from the hearing in his mind, wishing that he would have answered a question differently or realizing he did not fully explain the proposed statute as he desired, especially in the question-and-answer format used by Senator Walsh, a skilled trial attorney whose pointed, leading questions were critical of the bill.

In light of this less-than-successful first hearing in 1923 and given some opposition that had arisen from labor interests, Bernheimer and Cohen prepared a written brief for the second congressional hearing in 1924, to provide full, detailed explanations and justifications for the bill and to help alleviate any concerns regarding the bill. The brief, which became a part of the public record of the 1924 hearing, provided backup support in case the reformers again failed to tell their full side of the story during the 1924 hearing.

The article was lifted, virtually verbatim, from Cohen's brief submitted during the 1924 congressional hearing. Thus, the text's initial intent was to persuade, to correct misunderstandings, and to lobby Congress to enact the FAA. When the article was published in 1926, the purpose of the text was only slightly modified. It still served a purpose of convincing, justifying, and instructing, but not to enact the FAA. Instead, the language of the 1926 article helped promote the use and implementation of the newly enacted FAA, which in turn would help support the reformers' continued efforts in lobbying states to enact their own arbitration statutes. Furthermore, the reformers had just created the American Arbitration Association in January 1926, immediately before the publication of the article. The reformers were also promoting arbitration and getting the fledgling organization off the ground—which would grow to become a leading arbitration organization in America, and the article helped advance these interests.

II. The Article's Significance

This article is a milestone publication because it introduces and justifies the statute with the most far-reaching impact in the field of American arbitration, and this article comes from the legal mind of the legislation's key drafter.

The FAA is a landmark statute. It reversed the ouster doctrine and common law hostility against the enforcement of predispute arbitration agreements. Through the statute, the government in effect entrusted its people to take certain disputes out of the courthouse so that they could resolve disputes privately, on their own, with the same effect as if the arbitral decision were coming from a court. The FAA embodies the democratic values of a society respecting freedom and personal autonomy. It also reflects a progressive belief that experts, instead of generalist courts, are appropriate decision makers to cope with a complex, ever-changing society. The FAA's enactment can be understood as a small, intermediate, evolutionary step between a court-centered, common law system dominating American society in the 1800s and the growth of the administrative state during the 1900s. Furthermore, enacting the FAA allowed arbitration to spread beyond small organizations or trade groups so that arbitration could be used more expansively in a growing, interconnected economy. In sum, the FAA is a landmark statute on multiple levels, and the article's primary significance is in introducing and justifying this landmark statute for the legal and business communities.

The article also provides a broader context for understanding the FAA. The article's introductory paragraphs recognize that the FAA's enactment was part of a broader movement for procedural reform. The early 1900s was an age of procedural reform because American courts were broken, a labyrinth of complex and confusing procedures. During this period, a movement to create uniform federal court procedures arose, and the push for the FAA was part of this broader movement for procedural reform. Understanding that the FAA was part of a broader reform movement helps provide a different perspective regarding the FAA. For example, by contextualizing the FAA as part of a larger movement, one can more easily see that it serves as a safety valve for an overburdened, broken court system. A robust arbitration system is healthy for a smoothly functioning court system. Through the existence of competing systems, a private arbitration system and a public court system, each system can improve and learn from the other. The procedural reformers of the early 1900s recognized the interrelatedness regarding different methods of dispute resolution. This same dynamic or interrelatedness exists today, with court procedures influencing arbitration, and arbitration developments influencing court procedures.

Cohen's article also alludes to misunderstandings or "murmurs" about the statute. Interestingly, the article does not define all the suspicions or misunderstandings, and, unfortunately, concerns and suspicions are still with us today. For example, during the 1923 congressional hearing, Senator Walsh raised concerns about the potential for abuse with take-it-or-leave-it, non-negotiable arbitration clauses. Also, labor expressed concerns about the FAA's applicability in the labor context. Senator Walsh and the labor unions were prophetic with their concerns, as the applicability of the FAA to consumer and employment disputes in more recent decades has created a backlash and calls for curtailing the FAA's scope. Although not directly addressed in the article, the FAA's drafters recognized and perceived the fear that Senator Walsh and others had about the statute. There was a concern at the time of the FAA's enactment that the statute would become like a river jumping its course and expanding beyond its narrow, originally intended confines of commercial, contractual disputes. Although the article does not address modern debates about the statute, the article indirectly suggests an answer to one of the pressing problems regarding modern, expansive interpretations of the FAA. In discussing the FAA, the article refers exclusively to commercial disputes and commercial arbitration. The FAA was never intended to cover employment disputes.

The article is also significant for recognizing the need to promote arbitration. At the very end, the article concludes by recognizing that arbitration institutions should supervise and administer arbitration and, with experience, improve it. In other words, even though the FAA exists, private parties must still implement and promote arbitration. These statements reveal the nature of the FAA; it does not create arbitration or force the process upon parties. Instead, the FAA establishes a legal framework to facilitate arbitration when chosen by parties. For the growth of arbitration, the article recognizes that private institutions are invaluable for training, instructing, and promoting arbitration's proper growth.

During the 1920s, the progressive reformers engaged in aggressive, large-scale educational campaigns, including speeches about the benefits of arbitration at churches, synagogues, and movie theaters. (Can you imagine today seeing a commercial at the beginning of a Hollywood blockbuster movie about the benefits of arbitration?) The article recognizes the need for private initiatives to promote arbitration, and this need still exists today. In more recent years, attention-grabbing headlines regarding arbitration have been negative and one-sided, focusing on abuses without recognizing arbitration's potential benefits.

The article serves as a reminder of the need for educational campaigns about arbitration's benefits.

Finally, the article captures a snapshot of legal history, the birth of a landmark statute in the 1920s, and some parts of the article seem quaint in retrospect. For example, the article mentions the FAA will operate to facilitate arbitration "within a few days"; the FAA was intended to create summary proceedings to enforce arbitration agreements. However, in more recent times, FAA proceedings can last for years, and in this respect, the FAA no longer seems to promote speedy resolution of disputes. The article captures the FAA in its infancy, in a purer, simpler stage of its existence, before the many circuits splits and controversies of today regarding arbitration law. Viewed from today's perspective, there is a strong contrast between today's legal environment and the article's portrayal of the FAA's infancy, and this striking contrast serves as a reminder of how much the FAA needs reform.

The New Federal Arbitration Law: A Call to Ethical Practice Not Yet Realized

Kristen Blankley

The 1926 essay about the Federal Arbitration Act (FAA) authored by Julius Henry Cohen and Kenneth Dayton contains numerous insights into the purposes of arbitration, the promise of the FAA, and the intent of Congress in enacting the legislation. But tucked into this essay is also a statement about lawyer self-interest potentially leading them away from counseling clients to draft arbitration clauses or using arbitration services out of risk of earning lower fees.

The authors' predictions were simultaneously right and wrong. The authors incorrectly predicted that lawyers would not counsel their clients to arbitrate. On the other hand, the authors correctly noted that lawyer self-interest would have an effect on arbitration practice. This interest—incorporating litigation techniques into arbitration—is what has the undesirous effects the authors feared. This essay first describes Cohen and Dayton's concerns about lawyer self-interest, and then discusses how modern practice has fulfilled some of the authors' predictions and created new ethical problems. Ultimately, this essay endorses returning to the initial intent of the FAA for ethical and practical reasons.

I. The Underlying Concern—Lawyer Self-Interest

Cohen and Dayton understood the competing financial interests between attorney and client and the implications of a streamlined process on both sides. New practices can lead to financial concerns, and the lawyer "has a pecuniary interest in the practice of his profession, and in a situation of this sort, it is better to face this fact and its implications and remove misunderstandings which, without warrant, stand in the road of progress" (p. 282). Lawyers may be uninterested in arbitration because settling cases may be significantly less expensive and less time consuming—thus leading to lower attorney fees. By contrast, litigation process at the turn of the twentieth century involved (before the passage of the Federal Rules of Civil Procedure) significant technical procedural mechanisms and delay, that is, the "waste motion," contributing to the lawyer's bottom line. At best, the lawyer truly believes that litigation leads to good client outcomes, with the lawyer simultaneously earning high fees. At worst, the lawyer churns fees through expensive legal work with low probability of success.

Cohen and Dayton's statements were revolutionary and well ahead of their time. They recognized that lawyers feel pressure to engage in every litigation tactic available, in part, because of self-interest. Yet they also wisely recognize that "it is more

Kristen Blankley, The New Federal Arbitration Law: *A Call to Ethical Practice Not Yet Realized* In: *Discussions in Dispute Resolution*. Edited by: Art Hinshaw, Andrea Kupfer Schneider, and Sarah Rudolph Cole, Oxford University Press (2021). © Oxford University Press. DOI: 10.1093/oso/9780197513248.003.0044

profitable to settle matters in dispute rather than fight them to the end" because the goal of a lawyer is to "attain the ends of justice as nearly, as quickly and as economically has he can" (p. 282). Arbitration meets the needs of economical dispute resolution, and the "lawyer's real return" comes from resolving disputes "to the client's satisfaction" (p. 282). The authors considered that commercial arbitration "more nearly attains" client goals "than does an action at law," leading to more satisfied clients and a better business model (p. 283). Presumably, resolving cases in the client's best interest will ingratiate the client to the lawyer, and the lawyer would receive additional business from the client when the client needs additional legal services or when the client refers new business to the lawyer.

At the time of the essay's publication, the proper role of lawyers in arbitration was still evolving. Cohen and Dayton recognized lawyers' skepticism of arbitration because clients could decide to represent themselves in arbitration or employ a nonlawyer advocate—thus, weakening the market for legal services—due to arbitration's relaxed procedures. Cohen and Dayton, however, strongly asserted that the "lawyer is needed in arbitration proceedings" (p. 283).

Lawyers understand the technicalities and arguments necessary to present a case in an adjudicative manner, and they provide a valuable service that can and should be utilized in the arbitration forum. Ultimately, many of these ideas gained further traction more than fifty years later.

II. The Trend in Favor of Arbitration and Client Interests

The ideas that Cohen and Dayton discussed regarding client satisfaction and discovering the true needs of the clients came to the forefront in 1981 when Roger Fisher and William Ury first published *Getting to Yes: Negotiating Agreement Without Giving In*. Of course, *Getting to Yes* is a seminal text on negotiation, but its focus on interests, as opposed to positions, is highly consistent with Cohen and Dayton's teachings decades prior.

Fisher and Ury's second (of five) principles is to "focus on interests" (Fisher & Ury, p. 40). Interests are the "silent movers" that "motivate people" (Fisher & Ury, p. 41). Interests are not necessarily the wants or desires of a negotiator, client, attorney, or the like, but the underlying reasons the person is interested in the stated objective. For example, a person might want to negotiate for a Ford automobile (the position), but the buyer's underlying interests could range from wanting reliable transportation, hoping to save money, supporting an American company, and looking for a four-door sedan. When considering the interests, a Ford might not be the only car that the buyer would find satisfying, and a successful purchase might encompass many makes and models of vehicle.

Today, legal ethics urge lawyers to consider client interests underlying their stated objectives. In addition to the lawyer's role as advocate, the lawyer also has a duty of serving as a counselor. Model Rule of Professional Responsibility 2.1 states: "In representing a client, a lawyer shall exercise independent professional judgment and render candid advice. In rendering advice, a lawyer may refer not only to law but to other considerations such as moral, economic, social and political factors that may be relevant to the client's situation." The American Bar Association (ABA) promulgated this rule as part of the 1983 changes to the Model Rules of Professional Conduct (Garwin, p. 407). At the time, fifty years after the Cohen and Dayton article and contemporaneous with the publication of *Getting to Yes*, such a rule was controversial, and the ABA Section of General Practice unsuccessfully sought to block this rule from becoming part of the Model Rules (Garwin, p. 407). Today, client-centered advocacy is a model of lawyering that is more popular, with a focus on client interests and resolving those interests in a way that meets clients underlying needs, as opposed to their outward legal issues.

For this reason, Cohen and Dayton were well ahead of their time. By 2004, the ABA finally added a sentence to Comment 5 of Rule 2.1, stating: "[W]hen a matter is likely to involve litigation, it may be necessary . . . to inform the client of forms of dispute resolution that might constitute reasonable alternatives to litigation" (Garwin, p. 410). In many ways, this comment appears to be exactly what Cohen and Dayton would have recommended. This comment recommends that lawyers understand different types of dispute resolution and how those processes can best meet client needs.

III. Arbitration's Increasing Use of Litigation Techniques and Expense

Unfortunately, despite the philosophical benefits of interest-based decision-making and client-centered representation, attorneys have been reluctant to use them. Instead, lawyers often focus on their traditional duties as zealous advocates (Zitrin & Lanford, pp. 65–66). Cohen and Dayton discussed the "waste motion," a tactic that produces little good for the client and creates a lot of fees for attorneys. Today, those procedural mechanisms include both motion practice, as well as the discovery process.

Litigation attorneys have found many ways to manipulate the discovery process in the name of zealous advocacy. In some instances, lawyers find "creative" ways to withhold documents from lawful production requests to the other side (Zitrin & Lanford, pp. 63–64). In other instances, lawyers produce so many documents—notably electronic documents—in order to try to bury particularly damaging information. Document discovery can easily occupy hundreds of hours of attorney time, and of the tens or hundreds of thousands of documents produced, only dozens are actually used in a trial.

This type of litigation behavior has spilled into the arbitration forum, potentially destroying any cost or time savings that arbitration offers parties. The College of Commercial Arbitrators studied this issue and reported that "business-to-business arbitration has taken on the trappings of litigation—extensive discovery and motion practice, highly contentious advocacy, long cycle time and high cost" (Stipanowich, p. 1). Clients, in particular, are disappointed that arbitration "now costs just as much, and takes just as long, as litigation" (Stipanowich, p. 1). For the most part, these increased procedures give clients little advantage, especially compared to the legal fees generated.

After all of this time, why do lawyers have such a difficult time solving client problems in an expeditious and cost-efficient way? Many reasons likely contributed to the import of litigation tactics into arbitration. First, as alternative dispute resolution (ADR) options came into fashion, lawyers did not give serious consideration into changing their behavior in the different forums. Instead, they continue to act as trial lawyers, whether they are negotiating, mediating, or arbitrating. Second, lawyers fear malpractice, whether such fear is justified or realistic. They may employ a "scorched earth" approach to prosecuting or defending a claim out of fear of opening themselves up for liability. Third, lawyers may believe they have an ethical obligation to leave "no stone unturned." Although the Model Rules no longer include "zealous advocacy" in the text of any rule, many lawyers still believe this to be a cornerstone of ethical practice. Finally, lawyers may be acting out of greed. Discovery and motion practice is expensive, and importing these types of procedures into ADR processes could greatly increase the number of available billable hours.

IV. A Return to the Aims of the FAA

The way to actually meet client needs would be a return to the primary aims of the FAA as discussed by Cohen and Dayton. Even a cursory examination of the FAA uncovers Congress's intent that arbitration be an expedited process to quickly meet the needs of the parties. The FAA contemplates little court intervention and gives great deference to arbitrators and their awards.

At the time, the FAA did not regulate the arbitrator's behavior because arbitration in the 1920s *was streamlined and cost-efficient.* Only when lawyers became more involved did arbitration begin to import some of litigation's worst attributes.

To curb lawyer behavior, arbitrators, provider organizations, clients, and attorneys must be more deliberate about the discovery and motion practice. The College of Commercial Arbitrator's 2010 *Protocols* gives good advice, such as: "Limit discovery to what is essential; do not simply replicate court discovery," "Set specific time limits," and "Control motion practice" (Stipanowich, pp. 26, 36). Of course, these sentiments are not self-executing. Lawyers and arbitrators need better education about managing an expeditious process. Further, clients (particularly business clients) hold considerable influence over the proposed arbitration budget and encouraging counsel to stay within such a budget.

At its beginning, arbitration held tremendous promise as a process to better meet client needs for efficient, cost-effective, and even interest-based dispute resolution. Lawyers had a key role to play, but rather than lawyers adapting to arbitration's promise, arbitration adapted to lawyers' basest instincts. Arbitration can still meet this promise, but doing so will require a conscious effort on the part of all stakeholders and a commitment to participant interests.

References

Roger Fisher & William Ury, Getting to Yes: Negotiating Agreement Without Giving In (1981).

A Legislative History: The Development of the ABA Model Rules of Professional Conduct, 1982–2013 (Art Garwin ed., 2013).

Thomas J. Stipanowich et al. eds., *Protocols for Expeditious, Cost-Effective Commercial Arbitration: Key Action Steps for Business Users, Counsel, Arbitrators & Arbitrator Provider Institutions, College of Commercial Arbitrators* (2010).

Richard Zitrin & Carol M. Langford, The Moral Compass of the American Lawyer (1999).

Emphasizing Efficiency in the Digital Age

Amy J. Schmitz

Arbitration systems provided quick, private, and final determinations in an efficient manner that avoided "the strict course and tedious ceremonies of Law Suits." Julius Henry Cohen spoke these words in his 1918 book, *Commercial Arbitration and the Law*. At that time, Cohen already saw the power of self-contained systems for resolving disputes. He saw how Quakers in Pennsylvania established a citizen arbitration system, while communities in Connecticut, Massachusetts, South Carolina, and Georgia developed arbitration mechanisms for certain private disputes, including neighbor trespass squabbles.

Meanwhile, the New York business community developed arbitration systems, and the New York Chamber of Commerce became a hub for arbitration during the American Revolutionary War.

But these arbitration systems threatened the courts, leading courts to deny enforcement of arbitration agreements. As an arbitration apologetic, Cohen stepped up to submit testimony on behalf of what is now the Federal Arbitration Act (FAA) (Arbitration of Interstate Commercial Disputes, Joint Hearings Before the Subcommittees of the Committees on the Judiciary, 68th Cong., 1st Session, S. 1005 and H.R. 646, p. 36 (Jan. 9, 1924)). Cohen's focus was on ensuring that courts enforce arbitration agreements and promote efficient dispute resolution. Furthermore, Cohen emphasized that arbitrators were called not to apply strict judicial "law" but instead to allow merchants to settle their questions in accordance with custom and norms.

Cohen's testimony was the foundation for Cohen's and Kenneth Dayton's article, *The New Arbitration Rule*, which came out in print just after President Calvin Coolidge signed the FAA into law on February 12, 1925 (p. 265). The FAA was a monumental step toward what later became the "ADR" movement and the push for establishing more efficient dispute resolution procedures. Before the FAA's enactment, arbitration was binding only in states such New York and New Jersey, where business groups had lobbied for enforcement of arbitration agreements in the early 1920s (p. 266).

Cohen and Dayton, therefore, wrote their article as an advocacy piece for the FAA and for enforcing arbitration agreements and awards. They emphasized that the New York Chamber and the American Bar Association should be free to conduct arbitration without judicial intrusion. They feared courts would judicialize the process and interfere with arbitration's ability to quickly resolve disputes with minimal disruption of commercial relations (pp. 285–86). Thus, they set a foundation for promoting efficient dispute resolution for fact-based contract disputes.

Amy J. Schmitz, *Emphasizing Efficiency in the Digital Age* In: *Discussions in Dispute Resolution*. Edited by: Art Hinshaw, Andrea Kupfer Schneider, and Sarah Rudolph Cole, Oxford University Press (2021).
DOI: 10.1093/oso/9780197513248.003.0045

I. Focusing on Efficiency

This comment focuses on this recurrent theme of efficiency in ADR, and how it has evolved into the new world of "ODR," online dispute resolution. Cohen and Dayton astutely surmised that courts are not necessary for resolving all disputes. In their pre-internet *lex mercatoria*, arbitration was particularly apt for quickly resolving merchants' contract disputes because the courts were congested and the issues were fairly basic. Reputation, facts, and community norms were more important than wrote "law" in resolving these contract disputes. Cohen and Dayton also emphasized that such contract disputes do not require the time and publicity associated with judicial dispute resolution. Courts, they argued, should focus attention on major questions about law, the constitution, or policy (pp. 267–86).

Today, the same focus on efficiency rings loud and clear in the "legal tech" and ODR movements. The marketplace has moved online, and so have disputes. Accordingly, dispute resolution systems have moved online. Consider the traders in cotton markets or chambers of commerce when Cohen and Dayton wrote their article: they thought their disputes were business matters best handled without costs and complexities of courts. Juxtapose these traders with online buyers and sellers who similarly seek to resolve disputes without court costs and complexities.

II. Creating Contained Dispute Resolution Systems

Online traders are multiplying. For example, eBay is a thriving digital market with buyers and sellers who share common understandings and norms. Like merchants in the 1920s and chambers of commerce, eBay traders also know that reputation is king. Sellers will quickly go out of business on eBay under the weight of bad reviews. Sellers and buyers also realize that they must find ways to resolve disputes quickly, to avoid trade disruptions and costly dispute resolution procedures.

It is therefore no surprise that eBay was an ODR pioneer. eBay saw little need for courts in its business. Instead, it sought to resolve disputes through eBay's private and self-contained ODR system. After using outside ODR providers as incubators, eBay set up its own ODR system and launched the Resolution Center in February 2004. With the new system, eBay resolved up to 60 million disputes per year by 2011. At this rate, eBay has likely resolved 500–600 million disputes through ODR. The aim is toward fairness and efficiency.

Furthermore, eBay built its forum to "fit the fuss" and created a stepped process, similar to how merchant communities set up arbitration systems to fit the context of the disputes at hand. eBay's system begins with problem diagnosis, works through steps of direct technology assisted ODR, to online mediation, and finally to an evaluation phase where eBay decides the case if the transaction partners cannot do so. Each party decides unilaterally when it wants the process to move to the next phase. The system's goal is to prevent as many disputes as possible, amicably resolve as many as possible, and then decide the remainder as quickly and fairly as possible.

eBay's ODR system is only the tip of the ODR iceberg. Now, we see similar projects occurring throughout the world. Again, the focus on efficient resolution of fact-based disputes remains a common theme. It harkens back to the larger movement toward procedural reform instigated with the FAA.

III. Resolving Cross-Border Claims

The ODR movement has become most pronounced with respect to cross-border claims, as was true at the dawn of the FAA with its focus on providing overarching enforcement with respect to cross-state-border claims. Creating ODR for cross-border claims was of such concern that the UN Commission on International Trade Law (UNCITRAL) convened its Working Group III on Online Dispute Resolution to advance guidelines on ODR for cross-border e-commerce. This Group met twice a year from 2010 to 2016 and created a global community of ODR enthusiasts. Although member states never reached consensus on ODR rules, meetings ended with a clear charge to continue movement toward the goal of creating a global ODR system.

The ODR movement is therefore at a stage similar to that of the arbitration movement at the time of the Cohen and Dayton article. The FAA signaled a push for universal enforcement of arbitration agreements and awards, as proponents of ODR are similarly crafting legal infrastructure for online mediation and arbitration. We see this in the European Union's Directive on Alternative Dispute Resolution for Consumer Disputes (the "ADR Directive") and Regulation on Online Dispute Resolution for Consumer Disputes (the "ODR Regulation"). These provisions work in tandem to require member states to implement ODR systems for consumer claims. Accordingly, all EU member states must designate ODR providers and have a monitored presence on the European Union's central ODR platform to provide consumers the option of using ODR to resolve issues regarding their intra-EU cross-border purchases.

Beyond the European Union, there is also a move toward greater uniformity and fluidity in ODR systems themselves. This again reminds one of Dayton's and Cohen's call for self-contained arbitration subject to limited judicial review. For example, I have proposed a single global ODR portal with Colin Rule, the architect of eBay's ODR system. This proposal is for a global ODR platform called "NewHandshake.org." This system would be unified so that it could affordably scale alongside the expansion of global e-commerce. This would call for a single hub that powers the overall system. There would be hundreds of routes into this home base, or core platform. These routes would derive from ODR providers, merchants, and consumer protection authorities around the world. Merchants would visit the Newhandshake.org site and fill out a form to register in the system. At that time, merchants also would have to specifically agree to abide by due process and fairness standards of the program.

This simple ODR platform would not rely on the courts. Instead, it would provide a self-contained means for obtaining redress in consumer cases. It would live on a "cloud" accessible via computer or mobile device. In this way, it would open new avenues to remedies for consumers while lowering costs of customer service and dispute resolution for companies. Most consumers would rather file claims and obtain remedies with a few clicks and swipes on a mobile device, than via frustrating phone calls or filing in-person claims. At the same time, merchants using an ODR system garner goodwill and customer loyalty, while cutting costs of training and maintaining customer service representatives that may issue uneven support. Furthermore, merchants benefit from gathering information about their products and services in a more usable manner than they do through telephone and general email complaints. NewHandshake.org could also use anonymized data regarding similar cases to suggest settlements where the parties have reached an impasse.

This focus on opening new avenues to remedies lurked behind the FAA as well. Cohen and Dayton applauded arbitration as providing cheaper and faster means for obtaining remedies and resolving disputes in merchant communities. NewHandshake.org would similarly open new avenues to remedies for consumers in small dollar claims. Rules of equity, fairness, and commercial norms would have special meaning in this ODR platform. This again reminds one of the special meaning of such standards and "rules" in arbitration as envisioned by Cohen and Dayton. Not all claims need a judicial remedy.

IV. Confronting Concerns

Of course, there are many details that would need to be worked out for such a global ODR system.

There will be repeat player advantages, questions of fairness, and all the other concerns that arise with new dispute resolution systems. We saw this in the wake of the FAA. Who would have expected at the time Cohen and Dayton wrote their article that predispute arbitration clauses would become enforceable in consumer and employment contexts? This has now become problematic, especially where there is no true consent. Similarly, arbitrators who were "insiders" were simply seen as experts in the early days of the FAA, but now we worry about collusion with repeat players such as large companies that are continually hiring the arbitrators.

In a similar vein, public policy and ethics issues arise with respect to ODR. For example, one of the central debates in UNCITRAL Working Group III was the enforcement of predispute agreements requiring online arbitration. Accordingly, any global ODR system should be voluntary for consumers to pursue postdispute. Furthermore, a trigger mechanism could be added to catch dangerous products (i.e., if there are high levels of claims regarding the same product). Internal checks also should be added to the ODR system to prevent merchants and consumers from "getting away with" fraud or other abuses. For example, system data would show whether a particular merchant continually fails to reply to claims. That merchant could then be removed from the system after a certain number of violations. Similarly, a buyer may be "flagged" for filing fraudulent claims, or violating other ethical norms.

V. FAA Fast Forward

Cohen and Dayton envisioned a niche for arbitration in dispute system design. They saw the importance of efficiency and reserving courts for public policy and other conflicts that require public resolution. They also emphasized arbitration as a self-contained system that provides remedies with limited judicial review.

Fast forward to current debates regarding ODR. Like arbitration in the 1920s, ODR presents more efficient means for resolving fact-based disputes. It promises to save time and money in resolving ecommerce disputes in particular. Moreover, like arbitration in the 1920s, it is the only reasonable means for seeking redress in cross-border contexts.

Of course, dispute system design will continue to evolve, and the multi-door courthouse will expand. We are only at the threshold for ODR and what is to come. Who knows—someday we may be discussing an "ODR Act" or treaty.

Article 3.2

Commercial Arbitration

Soia Mentschikoff

61 Columbia Law Review 846 (1961)

***

[T]he structure and the process of commercial arbitration are determined by the different institutional contexts in which it arises.

***

The simplest [institutional context or setting] is when two persons in a contract delineating a business relationship agree to settle any disputes that may arise under the contract by resort to arbitration before named arbitrators or persons to be named at the time of the dispute. In this, which can be called individuated arbitration, the making of all arrangements, including the procedures for arbitration, rests entirely with the parties concerned.

***

A second type of arbitration arises within the context of a particular trade association or exchange. The group establishes its own arbitration machinery for the settlement of disputes among its members, either on a voluntary or compulsory basis. . . .

The third setting for commercial arbitration is found in administrative groups, such as the AAA[1] which provide rules, facilities, and arbitrators for any persons desiring to settle disputes by arbitration. . . .

In a survey of trade associations in which we received 547 relevant responses, 34 per cent of the associations indicated that their members made individual arrangements for arbitration; 29 per cent indicated that they used some type of organized machinery, . . . and 26 per cent reported that their members never arbitrate. These differential responses [indicated] that there were rational reasons for the existence of these differences.

***

[I]t is useful to distinguish between those factors that can be said to produce a *need* for arbitration machinery in commercial groups and those factors that merely make it desirable. The reasons commonly given for arbitration—speed, lower expense, more expert decision, greater privacy—are appealing to all businessmen, and yet not all

[1] AAA is used as a shorthand for American Arbitration Association throughout the article.

Soia Mentschikoff, *Commercial Arbitration* In: *Discussions in Dispute Resolution.* Edited by: Art Hinshaw, Andrea Kupfer Schneider, and Sarah Rudolph Cole, Oxford University Press (2021). © Oxford University Press.
DOI: 10.1093/oso/9780197513248.003.0046

utilize arbitration. It seems reasonably clear, therefore, that for some trades these factors are of greater importance than for others, and that for some trades there must be countervailing values in not resorting to arbitration. We postulated three factors as being theoretically important in determining whether or not a particular trade needed institutionalized use of arbitration. . . .

The first factor was the nature of the economic function being performed in relation to the movement of the goods by the members of the association. We postulated that persons primarily buying for resale [merchants] were much more likely to be interested in speed of adjudication, and that since price allowance would be a central remedy for defects in quality or, indeed, for nondelivery, the speed and low cost characteristics of arbitration would be particularly attractive to them, thus leading to the creation of institutionalized machinery. The trade associations in which such merchants constitute all or part of the membership reported as follows: 48 per cent use institutionalized machinery, 34 per cent make individual arrangements for arbitration, and only 18 per cent never arbitrate. These figures are to be contrasted with the reports from those trade associations that stated that their memberships did not include any merchants. In those groups 23 per cent reported the existence of institutionalized arbitration, 44 per cent reported individual arrangements, and 33 per cent reported no arbitration whatever.

[The second major factor was the participation of the members of the association in foreign trade where resort to the formal legal system poses uncertainty and relative unpredictability of result for at least one of the parties.]

***

The third factor . . . relates to the kind of goods dealt with by the members of the association. One of the major areas of dispute among businessmen centers on the quality of the goods involved. If, therefore, the goods are such as not to be readily susceptible of quality determination by third persons, arbitration or, indeed, inspection, is an unlikely method of settling disputes.

Self-contained trade group arbitration is, therefore, an extremely important method of settling buyer-seller disputes, . . . [and the] major issue is usually one of either interpretation of the contract or the measurement of performance.

***

The AAA was the American response to the delays and difficulties that could result from procedural defects in the arbitration process in situations where the economic sanctions of some of the trade groups were not available. This organization from its beginning held itself out as an expert in matters that went to the enforceability of an award and set up its rules and regulations with the primary aim of rendering awards that would not be set aside by the courts. It has succeeded greatly in the accomplishment of this goal, and as a result, it is now one of the most important forums for the determination of commercial disputes by arbitration.

***

[AAA arbitration] differs substantially from arbitration at the self-contained trade groups. The decisions that are rendered by the arbitration committees of self-contained trade associations do have precedential value. This is achieved in two ways: in some associations opinions are written and circulated to the membership; in others awards can be appealed or referred to other committees for the establishment of general standards. Most important, however, in all of these associations there is a continuity in the membership of the deciders, which means that the system of precedent operates automatically, for a question decided in one case on the basis of consideration of competing norms is unlikely to be decided differently in the next case by the same people. However, the casual system of arbitration used by the AAA, is designed to discourage the use of precedent. The Association puts enormous pressure on its arbitrators not to write opinions but to merely state the award in dollar amounts. It also tries very hard and very successfully not to have any one person sit as an arbitrator more than once or twice a year.

... 40 per cent [of the trade association groups] explicitly discourage or forbid the use of attorneys, and in the remaining 60 per cent attorneys very rarely appear. The AAA, on the other hand, encourages the parties to use attorneys. This difference reflects the basic proposition that in the self-contained trade groups the norms and standards of the group itself are being brought to bear by the arbitrators, and the incursion of lawyers with their potential emphasis on general legal norms and standards is viewed as a factor deflecting expeditious hearing and wise decision. At AAA, theoretically, substantive legal rules are welcome as norms for decision, and therefore attorneys are welcome. In fact, however, relatively few arbitrators or counsel feel bound by the substantive rules of law, although most feel it should be "considered."

The third difference between self-contained trade association systems and the casual arbitration at the Association lies in the methods by which awards are enforced. The ultimate sanction in many of the self-contained associations and in almost all of the exchanges is a disciplinary proceeding and thus, potential legal problems with respect to procedure are not seriously considered in these groups. The ultimate sanction at the Association is the rendering of judgment on the award by a court of competent jurisdiction, and therefore problems of procedure are always uppermost in the minds of the tribunal clerks, who are charged with the duty of policing the arbitrators sufficiently, so that the award rendered will be legally enforceable.

***

In almost all self-contained trade associations ... lawyer participation is either forbidden or discouraged, and very few of the arbitrators are lawyers or law-trained. The emphasis in these groups is on the utilization of norms and standards of the trade for deciding without regard to their similarity to or difference from the norms or standards that would be imposed by substantive rules of law. We frequently heard ... that lawyer participation was not desired for two reasons: (1) lawyers did not understand the business usages and practices that were typically involved in adjudicating the dispute and were therefore not helpful; and (2) lawyers made the proceedings unduly technical and tended to create unnecessary delays. This second complaint about lawyers has some support in our analysis of the Association records. Both delays in the selection of arbitrators and postponements between hearings occur more frequently in cases in which the parties are represented by attorneys. Of course, the figures also showed that attorneys were more likely to be employed as the amount involved in the case became larger. Personal observation at the Association leads me to the reluctant conclusion that in the great majority of the cases observed, lawyer participation not only failed to facilitate decision but was so inadequate as to materially lengthen and complicate the presentation of the cases....

... Court actions are typified by the absence of expertise as to the particular business or trade involved, on the part of both the judge and the jury, but in the self-contained trade group arbitration mechanisms, the arbitrators all have this expertise. In many of the cases at the Association, [arbitrators] have no peculiar expertise in the particular trade or business involved in the dispute that is before them for decision....

... The most important similarity of Association arbitration to the formal legal system is found in the attitudes with which the arbitrators come to the proceedings. First and perhaps most significant, the Association explicitly urges its arbitrators to adopt a judicial attitude that will lead to decision on the merits rather than to a compromise award. "Compromise" is used here in its invidious sense of arriving at decision by, as one arbitrator expressed it, "giving a little and taking a little." It does not mean that legitimate clashes of interest are not resolved in a way that seems fairest to both sides, a process that lies at the foundation of any attempt to evolve a rule of law.

... [W]hen the 180 [AAA] arbitrators were asked to agree or disagree with the proposition that "arbitrators are expected to find a way of satisfying both parties in a dispute by finding compromise solutions," more than two-thirds disagreed with the statement. In addition, over half accepted the following proposition: "An arbitrator should try to decide for one party or the other and not try to look for ways of compromising."

Another aspect of the judicial attitude inculcated in the arbitrators by the Association is exemplified by the responses of the arbitrators used in the experimental study to questions about the utilization of substantive rules of law. Eighty per cent of the experimental arbitrators thought that they ought to reach their decisions within the context of the principles of substantive rules of law, but almost 90 per cent believed that they were free to ignore these rules whenever they thought that more just decisions would be reached by so doing.

***

Arbitrators as a class act according to logical reasoning in terms of issue, fact, and norm. When they disagree with the award, they disagree for as logical reasons as dissenting judges. The difficulties in arbitration are the same as those in the courts—how to provide the deciders with the norms and standards that are best suited to wise decision. Some of these difficulties arise out of the use of an adversary system of adjudication with its emphasis on party control. That system has values of importance for a democratic society but, whether exemplified by court cases or Association arbitration, it also has the obvious disadvantage of being no better than the calibre of the presenters and the deciders and the knowledge that is or becomes available to the deciders by virtue of prior experience or the procedures of the trial. Whether we have yet evolved the best procedures for providing such knowledge either in arbitration or in the courts without sacrificing the other real values of an adversary system seems open to question.

Comments

Everything Old Is New Again

Sarah R. Cole

Soia Mentschikoff wrote *Commercial Arbitration* nearly sixty years ago, yet, like all great articles, it continues to offer lessons and guidance for today. The article was one of the first to recognize that the term "arbitration" actually covered a variety of related, but importantly different, types of mechanisms. Through her exhaustive empirical study, Mentschikoff developed a taxonomy for describing these differences, categorizing arbitration into two basic subsets: individuated and administered, with the latter category in turn comprising two separate subtypes, one where the trade group provided the administration and one where the administrator was a third party. It was in exploring the differences among these types of arbitration that Mentschikoff made her most long-lasting contributions. This is true in two regards. First, she noted that one key way in which arbitral subtypes varied was in the extent to which lawyers played a role, and she warned that increased lawyer involvement may have dramatic negative impacts on the utility of arbitration. Second, in studying the various different types of arbitration and the parties' techniques for choosing among them, Mentschikoff confirmed that different types of disputes may be better suited to one form of arbitration than another. This observation takes on increased urgency in a world where there seems to be an ever-increasing rush to one-size-fits-all or monolithic arbitration. In both of these regards Mentschikoff was ahead of her time, and her article remains both an important and fascinating read.

Mentschikoff's study involved a survey of commercial arbitration practices at 547 different trade associations. Arbitration, according to Mentschikoff, was a sensible resolution process for parties involved in a commercial transaction because customs and norms, as applied by an expert decision maker, were more likely to yield acceptable final results than was the court system. Moreover, commercial parties generally recognized that arbitration offered greater speed, lower cost, and more privacy than the court system. Thus, not surprisingly, Mentschikoff found that 74 percent of commercial parties chose to arbitrate and, depending on the presence of certain factors, tended to prefer one *form* of arbitration over another. More specifically, the survey revealed that 34 percent of trade association members made individual arrangements for arbitration, while the remaining 29 percent used some kind of organized machinery administered either through the trade group itself, or through a third-party administrator like the American Arbitration Association (AAA). For the purpose of this comment, though, the specific reasons why members might opt for one form of arbitration over another is less important than Mentschikoff's observation that the form of arbitration mattered. That is, Mentschikoff's study explained that the parties were not merely choosing to arbitrate in general, but rather were selecting a particular

Sarah R. Cole, *Everything Old Is New Again* In: *Discussions in Dispute Resolution*. Edited by: Art Hinshaw, Andrea Kupfer Schneider, and Sarah Rudolph Cole, Oxford University Press (2021). © Oxford University Press. DOI: 10.1093/oso/9780197513248.003.0047

type of arbitration, and that the decisional framework for choosing among these dispute resolution mechanisms was multifactored, meaning that the parties recognized that a single form of arbitration was not suitable for every dispute.

The article also explored the differences among these arbitral subtypes. For example, Mentschikoff compared self-contained trade group arbitration with the emerging administered arbitration model dominated both then and now by AAA. Mentschikoff marveled at the dissimilarity of trade group and AAA-administered arbitration, highlighting a variety of differences—AAA decisions lacked precedential value, repeat arbitrators were rare, and written reasoned opinions rarer still. In this part of the piece, she also provided a critique of one aspect of AAA arbitration—the introduction of lawyers. Mentschikoff did not view the introduction of lawyers to arbitration as a salutary event. She worried that lawyer involvement would turn the focus in arbitration from customs and norms to law. This change, in turn, might lead to undesirable results that departed from settled commercial understandings among trade group members. Even more worrisome was that lawyer involvement could lead to increased procedure, bogging down the arbitral process without providing a commensurate benefit in terms of outcome. To use Mentschikoff's words, "in the great majority of cases ... lawyer participation not only failed to facilitate decision but was so inadequate as to materially lengthen and complicate the presentation of the cases." While Mentschikoff noted that lawyers could help the arbitrator by educating him about legal standards in cases where those standards were relevant, she emphasized that commercial disputes typically turned on application of norms and customs developed in business and, thus, would be unlikely to benefit from lawyer participation.

Mentschikoff's point about lawyer participation continues to resonate, and her fears have come to fruition in a variety of ways. As predicted, lawyers transformed the commercial arbitration process both substantively and procedurally, converting it to a virtual private trial, often complete with substantial discovery. Substantively, the increased use of lawyers pushed arbitration from a custom-based dispute resolution process, to one based on law (an area in which lawyers have greater expertise and familiarity). Procedurally, increased lawyer utilization resulted in burdening a streamlined process with discovery and motion practice, thereby slowing it down and increasing costs. Compounding this problem, as more businesses came to rely upon arbitration agreements with their customers and employees, the nature of the disputes directed to arbitration has become increasingly more legal, with the role for lawyers in arbitration (and their desire for expansive process) growing concomitantly.

Today, in most arbitration, disputants proceed with lawyers, and occasionally pro se (in consumer and employment). In both repeat player commercial arbitration as well as repeat-player versus one-shot player arbitration, lawyer participation led to increased process and greater focus on law, rather than on customs and norms. Ironically, in the original birthplace of arbitration, commercial disputes, this "proceduralization" of arbitration has resulted in a documented move away from arbitration. Companies now dislike arbitration because it is cumbersome and costly, and they have voted with their feet, turning to mediation in their predispute agreements and to litigation for postcontractual disputes. This method of resolving disputes is not much more expensive than arbitration, and there is opportunity for judicial review. In that way, Mentschikoff's concerns about lawyers in commercial arbitration have come to fruition—the participation of lawyers reimaged commercial arbitration into a full-blown trial, albeit without a jury.

But Mentschikoff's article proved prophetic in another way in an entirely different type of arbitration: one-shot versus repeat player arbitration. As companies expanded arbitration into this context, consumer and employment advocates expressed concern that arbitration at best compromised individual rights and, at worst, suppressed legitimate claims. Noting that such disputes often turn on statutory interpretation, arbitration critics argued that lawyers are a virtual must. But, in pressing such claims, critics may be giving insufficient due to the concerns that Mentschikoff raised about the "lawyerization" of arbitration. After all, lawyers are expensive, and the prevalence of lawyers in this kind of arbitration has made it virtually impossible for a consumer with a small claim to obtain representation. Thus, lawyerizing arbitration in this context, coupled with the virtual end of class arbitration (see *AT&T v. Concepcion*, where the Supreme Court held that the Federal Arbitration Act preempted California's ruling that class waivers in arbitration are unconscionable under certain circumstances) has resulted in claim suppression, rather than creating a venue where the one-shot player can obtain justice.

Yet, for that one-shot player, arbitration *should* hold great promise. Arbitration provides a forum that should not require excessive process or, necessarily, lawyers. As the success of labor arbitration demonstrates, well-trained advocates who understand the law and customs as they apply to the world of grievances can provide exactly the kind of representation needed, at a relatively low cost, in a speedy and fair forum. Mentschikoff might well argue that arbitral opponents, in asserting the need for *more* lawyers have it exactly *wrong*. Instead, she might say, we need to return to low-cost representation, focusing on educating nonlawyers to provide representation in the kinds of disputes brought in arbitration by consumers and employees. We need to return a world where the parties' arbitration process suits the parties using the process and the stakes at issue. This was the world of arbitration that Mentschikoff's article deftly portrayed, and one that arbitration's critics, with their cries for ever-more process, appear to ignore.

Mentschikoff's study revealed that parties care about tailoring, and that they often prefer different types of forums for different types of disputes, with "types of disputes" understood at a fairly granular level. For example, if the trade group members were involved in foreign trade, they typically wanted to "create their own set of substantive rules or standards of behavior as the controlling rules for their members." Of course, then, the decision makers would have to be familiar with the standards to be applied. Created in the shadow of an uncertain legal landscape for international commercial disputes, this kind of institutionalized private machinery was workable because no judge understood what rules to apply as well as did the expert decision makers.

Mentschikoff noted that different concerns often drove those who were using arbitration to resolve disputes over the quality of goods. Drilling down, she distinguished among type of goods (raw, softs, and hards) in an effort to explain why businesspeople might want third-party adjudication for some disputes (raws—which are fungible) as compared to other disputes (hards—where the remedy is often repair or replacement—were less susceptible to the arbitration process).

Of course, consumer and employment arbitration were not even a glimmer in Mentschikoff's eye at the time she wrote her article on commercial arbitration. But arbitration proponents and opponents might learn from her analysis the importance of adapting the particulars of a given arbitration process to fit the kinds of disputes arbitrators now adjudicate. Some arbitration critics (see, for example, the authors of the Arbitration Fairness Act) oppose the use of arbitration for all one-shot versus repeat player statutory disputes. As I have said elsewhere, though, arbitration is here to stay, and we would be better off adapting the arbitration process to suit the kinds of disputes arbitrators are asked to adjudicate, rather than try to eliminate arbitration entirely. In many ways, consumer and employment arbitration are more similar to labor arbitration than they are to commercial arbitration. While consumer and employment arbitration lack the bilateral repeat player (at least viewed from the perspective of union and management as compared to individual grievant and management) structure of labor arbitration, many of labor arbitration's innovations, including reasoned written opinions, learned and experienced nonlawyer advocates, and diverse arbitrator panels would benefit those one-shot players who agreed by contract to arbitrate their disputes. I have advocated many of these changes elsewhere, but, in this limited space, I encourage those who design and offer arbitration processes (i.e., AAA and Judicial Arbitration and Mediation Services (JAMS)) to consider carefully who is arbitrating, who (lawyer or nonlawyer) represents the parties, how much discovery is necessary, if any, whether motions are appropriate (under any circumstances), who decides the disputes, what standards guide the decision maker, and how to determine if the arbitrator complies with those standards. All of these questions can be answered at a relatively low cost and would likely make arbitration more accessible to parties with limited resources who lack knowledge about the arbitral process.

Through her commercial arbitration study, Mentschikoff created a taxonomy of arbitration processes for commercial disputes. A similar taxonomy could be created for modern arbitration, with different procedures applicable to the arbitration depending on who the parties are and what disputes are at issue. Mentschikoff debunked a one-size-fits-all process for commercial arbitration. Developing a modern menu of arbitral forms for the myriad disputes and parties currently compelled to arbitrate would give Mentschikoff's brilliance currency again, and appropriately so.

The Legacy of Soia Mentschikoff's *Commercial Arbitration*

W. Mark C. Weidemaier

What is the legacy of Soia Mentschikoff's 1961 article *Commercial Arbitration*? Judged by objective metrics like citation count, or by the esteem in which scholars of arbitration and commercial law hold it, the article would have to be rated one of the most influential in the arbitration canon. A deeply realist exploration of how commercial arbitration was practiced among trade association members and before the American Arbitration Association, *Commercial Arbitration* is, among many other things, an early model for the empirical study of alternative dispute resolution processes. Mentschikoff rejected the stylized view of arbitration as an ad hoc process in which precedent played no role and procedures bore no relation to those observed in court.

Commercial Arbitration delivered on the promise of an earlier article, *The Significance of Arbitration*. Both articles reject easy generalities, such as assertions that arbitrators routinely consider nonjusticiable claims and disregard state-supplied law, do not generate precedent, and are not influenced by the rules of evidence and procedure (a view Mentschikoff dismissed as "patent nonsense" (Mentschikoff, *The Significance of Arbitration*, p. 706)). Both articles also anticipate questions that remain central to modern thinking about arbitration and about contracts. For example, although Mentschikoff recognized that arbitration could generate precedent, she expressed doubt that arbitrators would create socially optimal rules (Mentschikoff, *The Significance of Arbitration*, p. 706). That insight became central to the classic law and economics justification for public funding of courts. She was also keenly aware of the relationship between contract drafting and dispute resolution procedure, especially when it came to the use of form contracts (p. 853). Most fundamentally, Mentschikoff was deeply interested in questions of institutional context. The core insight underlying her empirical work was that "both the structure and the process of commercial arbitration are determined by the different institutional contexts in which it arises" (p. 848). Though derived from the study of trade association arbitration, this insight promised to shape arbitration scholarship in other areas as well.

It is here, however, that we see the limits of *Commercial Arbitration*'s legacy.

Contemporary arbitration scholarship often demonstrates little interest in context. By this, I mean that arbitration scholarship rarely focuses on how arbitration regimes are shaped by structural considerations—defined broadly to include the rules and training procedures of arbitration institutions; the characteristics, training, and professional norms of arbitrators; the conditions of the market for arbitrators' services; and the relational (or nonrelational) nature of the interactions between the disputants. It is not that such questions are ignored entirely. For the most part, however, they occupy the periphery of arbitration scholarship. This is especially true if we look for scholars who

W. Mark C. Weidemaier, *The Legacy of Soia Mentschikoff's* Commercial Arbitration In: *Discussions in Dispute Resolution.* Edited by: Art Hinshaw, Andrea Kupfer Schneider, and Sarah Rudolph Cole, Oxford University Press (2021). © Oxford University Press. DOI: 10.1093/oso/9780197513248.003.0048

share Mentschikoff's interest in commercial law. There are exceptions, to be sure. Lisa Bernstein and Barak Richman leap to mind, both for the close study of dispute resolution processes and the focus on relational commerce. And certainly there has been empirical interest in arbitration and in arbitrators, especially, but not only, in the context of international disputes. But despite Mentschikoff's outsized reputation among scholars of arbitration and commercial law, *Commercial Arbitration* does not seem to have significantly influenced the course of arbitration-related scholarship. Why might that be so?

An important part of the answer derives from a development that probably would have surprised and alarmed Mentschikoff: the widespread use of arbitration clauses in consumer and employment contracts. The overriding objective of many scholars writing about this development has been to highlight the dangers arbitration may pose to individual claimants and to the public values embodied by law. But this salutary goal inclines observers to pay little heed to questions of institutional context. To the contrary, the literature often reduces arbitrator behavior to the product of crass financial incentives, such as the desire to please the repeat-play businesses that wield outside influence over an arbitrator's future income.

Although not entirely inaccurate, this conception of arbitrators and their incentives is incomplete. Consumer and employment arbitration regimes are not monolithic. They too are shaped by institutional context, including rules of arbitrator ethics, voluntary "due process" rules, the presence (or absence) of repeat-play claimant's lawyers, the extent to which the business identifies and settles valid claims before arbitration begins, and so forth. Yet the arbitration literature demonstrates relatively little interest in such factors. I do not mean to be overly critical. The primary concern animating much scholarship in this area is the dramatic growth of consumer and employment arbitration. The architects of that development often justify it by invoking stylized empirical facts about arbitration and about the litigation process it replaces— say, by the assertion that arbitration offers quick justice to consumers and employees with low-value claims. That assertion appears not to be true—at least, claimants do not seem to take advantage of the benefit or cannot find lawyers to help them do so (e.g., Horton & Chandrasekher). In any event, for participants in this debate, the stakes are not about whether arbitration has "generative power" (Mentschikoff, *The Significance of Arbitration*, p. 698) or about how institutional context shapes consumer and employment arbitration regimes. The stakes are about whether arbitration agreements should be enforced at all. The resulting empirical work tends to measure the prevalence of arbitration in consumer and employment contracts, arbitration outcomes, and similar matters. Perhaps the urgency of these questions has diluted interest in questions of institutional context and diverted attention away from commercial arbitration.

Speaking of stylized empirical facts: of course, I am generalizing, offering a contestable description of arbitration scholarship. Certainly there has been interest in how arbitration procedures evolve and are shaped by institutional forces (e.g., Bingham [Amsler]), though even here the focus is rarely on commercial arbitration in the classic sense important to Mentschikoff. Space constraints and the format of this essay do not permit a thorough review of this literature. The broader point is simply that concern over the social and individual costs of consumer and employment arbitration has substantially displaced interest in arbitration as a *process* and drawn attention away from arbitration in commercial transactions between merchants.

If many arbitration scholars have been preoccupied by the growth of consumer and employment arbitration, what about scholars of commercial law and contracts? Some of the most important contracts scholarship of the past fifty years has been founded on the insight that contracts—and the institutions they create—exist in a thick web of social relations, which are themselves worthy of study. Obvious examples include Stewart Macaulay, Ian Macneil, and, more recently, Mark Suchman and others. Observers of financial markets might think of the work of Annelise Riles in this context. And certainly contracts scholarship has not overlooked arbitration. Yet most empirical work on contracts examines the express terms of written contracts, rather than engage in close study of the transactions they embody or (in the case of arbitration) the institutions they create. Again, I acknowledge the overgeneralization. There are prominent and abundant exceptions—consider, as just one example, experimental work into what one might call the psychology of contract formation (e.g., Wilkinson-Ryan & Hoffman).

More recently, contracts scholarship has begun to examine how institutional context shapes contract design and collaboration. Yet this development has not yet had a significant influence on arbitration-related scholarship, which remains largely focused on the prevalence and express terms of arbitration agreements. Part of the explanation likely stems from the fact that arbitration hearings are private and often confidential, meaning that researchers interested in arbitration as a process must leverage social and professional connections to facilitate study.

Part of the explanation, too, may stem from the dominance of economic theory, which has played an outsized role in shaping contracts scholarship. To oversimplify, economically oriented contracts scholars tend to view dispute resolution through the lens of contract design, asking, for instance, how the ex ante choice between contract rules and standards is shaped by the choice of dispute resolution regime. But these important questions have largely been asked by scholars interested in how parties write contracts, not by those interested in how arbitration actually works.

I began this essay by noting that, despite her emphasis on trade association arbitration, Mentschikoff was remarkably prescient in anticipating questions that remain important today. These include, among others, questions about the role of precedent, about the extent to which public court procedures influence practice norms in arbitration, and about the role arbitration and arbitrators can play in interpreting (and also influencing the design of) form contracts. On each question, Mentschikoff resists the urge to essentialize, recognizing that dispute resolution procedures both shape and are shaped by institutional context. To put this insight in somewhat different (if a bit narrower) terms: arbitrators may be agents empowered by contract, but they also have *agency*. How they exercise that agency, and the consequences for commercial relations, remains an important, often overlooked, area of study.

References

Soia Mentschikoff, *The Significance of Arbitration—A Preliminary Inquiry*, 17 Law & Contemp. Prob. 698, 698 (1952).

David Horton & Andrea Cann Chandrasekher, *After the Revolution: An Empirical Study of Consumer Arbitration*, 104 Geo. L.J. 57 (2015).
Lisa B. Bingham [Lisa Blomgren Amsler], *Self-Determination in Dispute System Design and Employment Arbitration*, 56 U. Miami L. Rev. 873 (2002).
Tess Wilkinson-Ryan & David A. Hoffman, *The Common Sense of Contract Formation*, 67 Stan. L. Rev. 1269 (2015).

Inside the Black Box: A Short Comment on Soia Mentschikoff's *Commercial Arbitration*

David Horton

Soia Mentschikoff's *Commercial Arbitration* is a great article for two reasons. First, it asked a novel question: What actually happens in arbitration? Second, it demonstrated that the answer varies with the context. In this short comment, I'll try to explain why this kind of nuanced empirical research is particularly important today. Then I'm going to take the self-centered step of explaining why one of my current projects owes a debt to Mentschikoff's classic piece.

I.

To appreciate Mentschikoff's contribution, it's helpful to step back. When she published *Commercial Arbitration*, the FAA was only thirty-six years old. According to the conventional wisdom, arbitration was a pale substitute for litigation. Even the FAA's draftsman, Julius Henry Cohen, cautioned that arbitration was not necessarily an appropriate forum for statutory questions. Likewise, in *Wilko v. Swan*, the US Supreme Court held that Congress did not intend plaintiffs to resolve claims under the Securities Act of 1933 outside of the court system. The Justices reached this conclusion, in part, by rattling off a list of arbitration's deficiencies:

> Even though the provisions of the Securities Act, advantageous to the buyer, apply, their effectiveness in application is lessened in arbitration as compared to judicial proceedings
>
> ... This case requires subjective findings on the purpose and knowledge of an alleged violator of the Act. They must be not only determined but applied by the arbitrators without judicial instruction on the law. As their award may be made without explanation of their reasons and without a complete record of their proceedings, the arbitrators conception of the legal meaning of such statutory requirements as "burden of proof," "reasonable care" or "material fact," ... cannot be examined. (*Wilko*, pp. 435–36)

Despite consensus that arbitration generated results that differed from the output of judges and juries, we simply didn't know what happened behind the black curtain of the arbitral forum. I'm aware of just one previous piece of scholarship that might be

David Horton, *Inside the Black Box: A Short Comment on Soia Mentschikoff's* Commercial Arbitration In: *Discussions in Dispute Resolution*. Edited by: Art Hinshaw, Andrea Kupfer Schneider, and Sarah Rudolph Cole, Oxford University Press (2021). DOI: 10.1093/oso/9780197513248.003.0049

called an empirical study of arbitration. In 1948, a Note in the *Harvard Law Review* analyzed three hundred recent cases from the American Arbitration Association (AAA) (Note, p. 1033 n.7). The anonymous student author began by explaining that "the legal profession ... is uninformed and suspicious of the results which arbitrators reach" (Note, p. 1022). Nevertheless, the author's review of the AAA awards led him or her to conclude that arbitrators generally follow the law, except when a particular rule contradicts an entrenched business norm (Note, p. 1044). Other than this snapshot, courts' and commentators' conclusions relied upon anecdote and intuition.

Enter Mentschikoff, who sharpened our understanding of private dispute resolution. The heart of her article is her comparison of arbitration among trade associations with its counterpart in the AAA. Mentschikoff highlighted ways in which the practices diverged. For starters, trade association awards had precedential value. Some merchant groups circulated awards among their members. Similarly, because trade association arbitrators were drawn from a small pool of experts, "a question decided in one case on the basis of consideration of competing norms [wa]s unlikely to be decided differently in the next case by the same people" (p. 857). In sharp contrast, the AAA discouraged the use of previous awards. One of the institution's goals was to generate arbitral rulings that survived judicial review under the FAA. In general, courts must confirm an award if there is any support for it in the record. Thus, from the AAA's perspective, the less an arbitrator said, the better. Indeed, as Mentschikoff put it, the AAA "puts enormous pressure on its arbitrators not to write opinions but to merely state the award in dollar amounts" (p. 857).

In addition, Mentschikoff observed that the two forums varied in their allegiance to substantive rules. In trade associations, merchants selected industry luminaries—not lawyers—as arbitrators. Likewise, cases hinged on customs, not legal arguments. As a result, 40 percent of these groups banned lawyer participation. But at the AAA, the picture was more complex. Arbitrators tended to be generalists, like judges. In theory, black-letter principles controlled outcomes, which encouraged lawyer involvement (p. 858). In reality, though, "relatively few arbitrators or counsel fe[lt] bound by the substantive rules of law, although most fe[lt] it should be 'considered'" (p. 858). Mentschikoff illustrated this point with her most celebrated finding:

> Eighty per cent of the [AAA] arbitrators thought that they ought to reach their decisions within the context of the principles of substantive rules of law, but almost 90 per cent believed that they were free to ignore these rules whenever they thought that more just decisions would be reached by so doing. In other words, what they were saying is that rules of law were entitled to very heavy respect but could be reexamined in the interests of justice. (p. 862)

Finally, Mentschikoff discussed how parties enforced awards in each sphere. Trade associations self-regulated by using disciplinary hearings as "[t]he ultimate sanction" (p. 858). Conversely, an AAA award could easily end up under the microscope of a court. As a result, AAA personnel actively "police[d] the arbitrators" to ensure that their handiwork was "legally enforceable" (p. 858).

In sum, Mentschikoff broke new ground by describing how arbitration operated from the inside. She also established that "arbitration" is malleable and context-dependent, not monolithic. As I discuss next, this insight proved to be prescient.

II.

In the decade after *Commercial Arbitration* appeared, new providers began to challenge the primacy of the AAA. In the early 1970s, Kaiser Permanente, the nation's largest health maintenance organization, mandated that its patients resolve medical malpractice claims within its own arbitration system. For-profit companies like ADR Services, Inc., Alternative Resolution Centers, Endispute, and the National Arbitral Forum (NAF) opened their doors. In 1978, H. Warren Knight, a former trial judge, created Judicial Arbitration and Mediation Services (JAMS). JAMS marketed itself as the forum of choice for complex, high-stakes cases. It aggressively recruited arbitrators who, like its founder, had once served on the bench. These entities expanded the options available to parties who wished to settle conflict privately.

Then, in the 1980s, "alternative" dispute resolution went mainstream. The Court backtracked from its view that arbitration was inferior to litigation. Reasoning that the process had matured, the Justices overruled *Wilko*, opening the door for the arbitration of claims under important federal statutes. As the Justices explained, the choice between venues did not affect the ultimate result of a case:

> By agreeing to arbitrate a statutory claim, a party does not forgo the substantive rights afforded by the statute; it only submits to their resolution in an arbitral, rather than a judicial, forum. It trades the procedures and opportunity for review of the courtroom for the simplicity, informality, and expedition of arbitration. (*Mitsubishi Motors Corp.*, p. 628)

Arbitration clauses spread throughout the economy, sparking debate. Businesses argued that extrajudicial dispute resolution was quick and economical. They contended that they passed on their lower litigation costs to their customers, workers, and patients. This view resonated with the Court, which saw arbitration as an outlet for self-represented plaintiffs with small claims. For example, as Justice Breyer remarked in *Allied-Bruce Terminix Companies, Inc. v. Dobson*, the sleek and informal process was helpful to consumers who wanted to complain about a product. But critics cast arbitration as a lawless vacuum that should not be entrusted with important statutory rights. In their eyes, the process was "an inferior system of justice, structured without due process, rules of evidence, accountability of judgment, and rules of law" (*Stroh Container Co.*, p. 751 n.12).

In the 1990s, several arbitration providers responded to these critiques by self-regulating. As concern grew about the propriety of arbitrating medical malpractice claims, Kaiser commissioned a Blue Ribbon Panel to revamp its arbitration system. The AAA went even further, announcing that it would not handle healthcare disputes stemming from a predispute arbitration agreement. Finally, both the AAA and JAMS altered their approach to mandatory arbitration. Each institution announced that it would refuse to administer a case under any consumer or employment contract that did not comply with basic principles of due process. In addition, the AAA and JAMS adopted internal rules that tried to level the playing field by capping fees, authorizing broad discovery, and giving both parties a voice in arbitrator selection.

These changes cut in two directions. In many ways, they benefited plaintiffs. For example, they reduced the risk that arbitration fees and costs would deter claims. Under the newly minted institutional rules, corporate defendants paid most of the tab. Similarly, robust discovery increased the likelihood of an aggrieved consumer, employee, or patient uncovering some smoking gun document or telling admission. Yet these developments also had a flip side. By encumbering arbitration with complex regulation, they arguably made the process less hospitable to self-represented plaintiffs. Even something as benign-seeming as the mechanism for choosing an arbitrator could tilt the scales toward repeat players by rewarding parties who were familiar with a potential decision maker's background, demeanor, and philosophy. This new system was great for plaintiffs with seasoned lawyers, but it only magnified the informational gap between corporations and the archetypical *pro se* individual complaining about a product.

Recently, this fraught relationship between arbitration and informality mutated again. In 2011, with *AT&T Mobility LLC v. Concepcion*, and in 2013, with *American Express v. Italian Colors Restaurant*, the Court effectively made class arbitration waivers bulletproof, tasking customers and employees with initiating their own two-party arbitrations rather than riding the wake of class proceedings. Businesses and their advocacy groups defend these opinions by arguing that arbitration is superior to the class action. For example, the US Chamber of Commerce asserted that arbitration empowers regular people to act *pro se* and pursue their own low-value causes of action:

> For many employees with individualized complaints against their employer—whether involving wrongful discharge, unlawful discrimination, or other grievances—arbitration is the only viable means of recovery, because the employees' claims are too small to justify the expense of court litigation or to attract a contingency-fee lawyer A small claim is more viable in arbitration because costs in arbitration are lower—and because in an arbitral forum, "it is feasible for employees to represent themselves." (Brief, *32–*33)

Thus, more than ever, arbitration is torn in two directions. On the one hand, it must absorb complicated, court-like procedures in order to safeguard substantive rights. But on the other hand, it has been pressed into service as a kind of private small claims court—a rough-and-tumble method of adjudication that must be accessible to lay plaintiffs.

III.

To help policymakers and courts navigate this new landscape, it's important to engage arbitration the same way Mentschikoff did. I'm working on a study with my colleague

Andrea Cann Chandrasekher of every consumer, employment, and medical malpractice arbitration filed between 2010 and 2016 in the AAA, JAMS, ADR Services, and Kaiser.

One preliminary takeaway is that each of these institutions offers its own distinctive brand of arbitration. For example, the AAA sets the gold standard for fast and cheap dispute resolution. Fees are low. Parties often argue by phone or submit a case on the papers. The overwhelming majority of arbitrators are practitioners, not retired judges. Conversely, in JAMS and the Kaiser Office of Independent Administration, the process moves deliberately, features dispositive motions and full-fledged hearings, and often involves decision makers who are former judges.

These differences seem to affect results in awarded matters. Even controlling for other variables, the most reliable determinant of a plaintiff victory in JAMS and Kaiser is having a lawyer who boasts arbitration experience. At the risk of oversimplifying, this suggests that there is tension between the goals of protecting substantive rights by (1) making arbitration more formal, and (2) encouraging *pro se* plaintiffs to pursue their own small claims. That these objectives may be incompatible is sobering and defies an easy solution. But if we do find a way forward, it will be through the kind of thoughtful empirical research that Mentschikoff pioneered.

References

Note, *Predictability of Result in Commercial Arbitration*, 61 HARV. L. REV. 1022 (1948).

Brief of the Chamber of Commerce of the United States of America as Amicus Curiae Supporting Petitioners in Nos. 16-285 and 16-300 and Respondents in No. 16-307, Nos. 16-285, 16-300, 16-307, 2017 WL 2644688 (U.S. June 16, 2017).

Wilko v. Swan, 346 U.S. 427 (1953).

Mitsubishi Motors Corp. v. Soler Chrysler-Plymouth, Inc., 473 U.S. 614 (1985).

Stroh Container Co. v. Delphi Indus., Inc., 783 F.2d 743 (8th Cir. 1986).

Lasting Lessons from Mentschikoff's *Commercial Arbitration*

Stephen J. Ware

Soia Mentschikoff's seminal 1961 article, *Commercial Arbitration*, includes lasting insights about commercial arbitration, commercial law, and even about commerce. Key to these insights is Mentschikoff's empirical study of trade association arbitration and her comparison of such industry-specific arbitration with the more general commercial arbitration exemplified by the American Arbitration Association. This comparison shows arbitration's ability—especially in the "core commercial" context of trade associations—to privatize substantive law, adjudication procedure, and even enforcement of the adjudicator's decision. Mentschikoff thus leads us from the humble context of routine sales disputes to grand questions about the roles of private parties and governments in the production, application, and enforcement of law.

Mentschikoff's survey of trade associations may be *Commercial Arbitration*'s most important contribution for what it teaches us not only about commercial arbitration but also about commercial law and, indeed, about commerce. By "us," I mean later scholars of commercial arbitration and commercial law. As fellow commercial law professor Chris Drahozal and I wrote (citing *Commercial Arbitration*), "going back to Soia Mentschikoff's pioneering research, the commercial arbitration literature has focused on sales of goods as the leading place to find arbitration clauses between businesses" (Drahozal & Ware, pp. 463–64). We wrote this while cautioning against reading data collected by Theodore Eisenberg and Geoffrey Miller to suggest that "given their choice, most businesses that negotiate contracts would prefer a judicial dispute resolution system over arbitration" (Drahozal & Ware, p. 464). While Eisenberg and Miller saw a "surprisingly low frequency of arbitration clauses" in the contracts they studied (Eisenberg & Miller, p. 335), Drahozal and I drew on Mentschikoff's *Commercial Arbitration* to note that Eisenberg and Miller did not appear to study sales of goods and other "types of contracts that the arbitration literature commonly identifies as likely to include arbitration clauses. As a result, their study likely significantly understates the use of arbitration clauses in contracts between sophisticated parties" (Drahozal & Ware, pp. 463–64). In short, sale-of-goods disputes have long been the core of "commercial arbitration," and one of *Commercial Arbitration*'s great strengths is its emphasis on goods, as opposed to land, services, credit, intellectual property, or information.

While the word "commercial" is sometimes used to describe any activity with a business purpose, transactions in goods differ from other business transactions because goods, as tangible movables, differ from both land—which is tangible, but immovable—and intangibles like services, credit, intellectual property, and

Stephen J. Ware, *Lasting Lessons from Mentschikoff's* Commercial Arbitration In: *Discussions in Dispute Resolution*. Edited by: Art Hinshaw, Andrea Kupfer Schneider, and Sarah Rudolph Cole, Oxford University Press (2021). © Oxford University Press. DOI: 10.1093/oso/9780197513248.003.0050

information. Such differences cause transactions in goods to raise legal issues not raised by other business transactions. For example, Uniform Commercial Code Article 2—which governs sales of goods, but generally not sales of land, services, or intangibles—has rules on risk of loss while goods are in possession of a carrier or other bailee, as well as rules on the seller's tender of goods and the buyer's acceptance or rejection of those goods. None of these rules has a close analog in sales of land, services, or intangibles.

Moreover, cross-border transactions in goods grew earlier in history and remain larger than most other types of cross-border transactions, so the case for uniform law across jurisdictions grew earlier and remains stronger with respect to transactions in goods than transactions in land and services. In fact, uniform law—both within the United States and internationally—advanced earlier and further with respect to transactions in goods than in land or services. One of the advantages of uniform law across jurisdictions is that it reduces disputes about which jurisdiction's law governs. When law is nonuniform, each party to a dispute may argue for its own jurisdiction's law, which is presumably more familiar and perhaps more favorable to that party. So uniform law can relieve a party of the costs of complying with the presumably less familiar and favorable law of the opposing party's jurisdiction.

Similarly, arbitration can relieve a party of the costs of litigating in the courts of the opposing party's jurisdiction. These include fear of a court's possible bias for its own fellow citizens litigating against foreigners. Such fears can be avoided with a neutral arbitral forum. So this advantage of arbitration, like the advantage of uniform law, is more significant with respect to transactions in goods, which are more likely to be cross-border, than transactions in land and services. Thus, we should not be surprised that Mentschikoff found that the organizations of parties who most often deal in goods—trade associations—created arbitration systems to resolve disputes among their members.

Mentschikoff's survey of these trade associations found 34 percent of the associations "indicated that their members made individual arrangements for arbitration," while 29 percent "indicated that they used some type of organized machinery, including the American Arbitration Association," and 26 percent "reported that their members never arbitrate" (p. 849). Mentschikoff's analysis of this data yields *Commercial Arbitration*'s key insight: "These differential responses from trade associations as to the utilization of arbitration was not on a random basis, but indicated instead that there were rational reasons for the existence of these differences" (pp. 849–50). Mentschikoff's empirical data on the prevalence of arbitration distinguishes among the types of goods involved; and she classifies parties according to their roles in the production and distribution of goods, with particular emphasis on "merchants," which she defines as "persons primarily buying for resale" (p. 850). Mentschikoff made three findings:

1. Where members of a trade association buy primarily for resale the rate of institutionalized arbitration machinery is higher than associations without these types of merchants.

2. Associations dealing in foreign trade, especially importers, were more likely to use an institutionalized arbitration system.
3. Raw/fungible goods associations are more likely to develop an institutionalized arbitration system than hard/finished goods like cars or appliances. (pp. 850–52)

Mentschikoff further adds that when all three factors—merchants (buy for resale), international trade, and raw goods—are present, the rate of institutionalized arbitration approaches 100 percent (p. 852). She concludes that "[s]elf-contained trade group arbitration is, therefore, an extremely important method of settling buyer-seller disputes," and the "[m]ajor issue is usually one of either interpretation of the contract or the measurement of performance" (pp. 852–54). With those two phrases, Mentschikoff concisely captures the core of "commercial" arbitration and, I believe, the core of "commercial" law: a dispute between merchants in the same industry over the interpretation or performance (as opposed to the formation) of their contract for the sale of goods.

If commercial law professors and even commercial arbitration professors rarely see such "core commercial" disputes—even though we read lots of commercial cases and lots of commercial arbitration cases—then Mentschikoff explains why: such disputes do not produce much litigation. These disputes often go to trade association arbitration with no litigation needed to enforce the predispute arbitration agreement or to vacate the arbitration award. Parties to these disputes rarely go to court, Mentschikoff writes, because they are repeat players in the same industry and thus are vulnerable to nonlegal pressures (culminating in expulsion from the trade association) if they challenge the arbitration agreement or the arbitration award (p. 854).

These "core commercial" disputes are further removed from lawyers' notice because they typically do not involve lawyers representing the parties in arbitration or serving as arbitrators (p. 859).

In contrast, Mentschikoff shows, commercial arbitration involving parties not in the same trade association tends to be very different (pp. 857–58). This general commercial arbitration—often administered by the American Arbitration Association (AAA)—is much more like litigation. While lawyers often do not appear in trade association arbitration because merchants play all the necessary roles, general commercial arbitration usually has lawyers representing the parties and often serving as arbitrators. Mentschikoff observed AAA hearings and writes: "Personal observation at the Association leads me to the reluctant conclusion that in the great majority of the cases observed, lawyer participation not only failed to facilitate decision but was so inadequate as to materially lengthen and complicate the presentation of the cases" (p. 859).

Moreover, Mentschikoff illuminatingly emphasizes that a big part of the AAA's mission is to produce arbitration awards that courts will confirm rather than vacate (p. 856). She describes AAA procedures including a clerk whose job is to draft the award and prevent the arbitrators from writing a reasoned opinion, because the AAA believes a very short award—with no reasoning that could tempt a court to find flaws—is less likely to be vacated (p. 865).

Relatedly, because the AAA is more concerned than trade associations about how an arbitration will appear to a reviewing court, the AAA is more concerned about arbitration procedure, thus further "lawyer-izing" AAA arbitration compared to trade association arbitration (p. 858).

While the short awards desired by AAA may deter vacatur, they lack the reasoning of a good precedent that can be relied upon in future cases. This fits Mentschikoff's observation that AAA arbitrators' decisions are rarely used as precedents, while, in contrast, trade association arbitrators' decisions often have precedential value (p. 857). Trade associations, she writes, maintain continuity in their arbitrators and circulate their opinions to members or allow for some form of appeal. *Commercial Arbitration*'s discussion of arbitration awards includes one of Mentschikoff's most cited passages, which is her finding that "[e]ighty per cent of the experimental arbitrators thought that they ought to reach their decisions within the context of the principles of substantive rules of law, but almost 90 per cent believed that they were free to ignore these rules whenever they thought that more just decisions would be reached by so doing" (p. 861).

Mentschikoff's finding that most arbitrators feel free to ignore substantive rules of law highlights the degree to which arbitration can privatize law. At the extreme of privatization, Mentschikoff shows us trade association arbitrations that privatize all three of:

1. substantive law (through arbitrators applying industry trade rules rather than governmental law, and through the precedential effect of arbitrators' reasoned awards);
2. adjudication procedure (through arbitration procedures quite different from courts' rules of procedure and evidence); and
3. enforcement of the adjudicator's decision (through private sanctions culminating in expulsion from the association).

By contrast, the general commercial arbitration typical of the AAA often includes only the second of these three forms of privatization. So Mentschikoff's comparison of two types of commercial arbitration leads us from the mundane context of ordinary sales disputes to fundamental questions about the roles of private parties and governments in the production, application, and enforcement of law.

In sum, Mentschikoff's *Commercial Arbitration* continues to teach us about commercial arbitration in ways that also teach us about commerce and about the private production, application, and enforcement of law. While merchants arbitrating their disputes before fellow merchants—largely free of the substantive law, adjudication procedures, and enforcement tools provided by government—may initially sound like something lost in the mists of time since the medieval Law Merchant, Mentschikoff showed it to be thriving in the mid-twentieth-century United States.

References

Christopher R. Drahozal & Stephen J. Ware, *Why Do Businesses Use (or Not Use) Arbitration Clauses?*, 25 Ohio St. J. on Disp. Resol. 433 (2010).

Theodore Eisenberg & Geoffrey P. Miller, *The Flight from Arbitration: An Empirical Study of Ex Ante Arbitration Clauses in the Contracts of Publicly Held Companies*, 56 DePaul L. Rev. 335 (2007).

Article 3.3

Panacea or Corporate Tool?: Debunking the Supreme Court's Preference for Binding Arbitration

Jean R. Sternlight

74 Washington University Law Quarterly 637 (1996)

***

III. The Court's Preference for Binding Arbitration Is Not Supported by Legitimate Policy Arguments

. . . There are two major flaws with the argument that binding arbitration is necessarily better for all parties. First, although most would agree that arbitration can often be superior, as an empirical matter it is not clear that binding arbitration is necessarily faster, cheaper, and otherwise better than litigation. ***

Second, even assuming for the sake of argument that arbitration is cheaper, quicker, and even better for society as a whole, it may still not serve the interests of all parties This Article asserts that any social gains achieved by forcing binding arbitration on unknowing little guys are outweighed by the distributional inequities and injustices also incurred.

***

1. Procedure Influences Substance

Every litigator knows that procedural rules affect substantive outcomes. Litigators learn that judges' determinations on such matters as venue, discovery, whether a matter may proceed as a class action, and whether a claim should be dismissed on summary judgment will likely determine the outcome of the case. [P]rocedural mechanisms can be used as a "litigation weapon."

2. The Drafter of the Agreement Will Attempt to Draft the Procedures to Take Advantage of its Opponent

. . .

***

Jean R. Sternlight, *Panacea or Corporate Tool?: Debunking the Supreme Court's Preference for Binding Arbitration*
In: *Discussions in Dispute Resolution*. Edited by: Art Hinshaw, Andrea Kupfer Schneider, and Sarah Rudolph Cole, Oxford University Press (2021). © Oxford University Press. DOI: 10.1093/oso/9780197513248.003.0051

The company might discourage the consumer from using the arbitration remedy not only by reducing the consumer's expected recovery, ... but also by increasing the consumer's own transaction costs. . . . For example, the agreement might require the consumer to bring the action in a distant forum, under laws different from those applicable in the consumer's own jurisdiction, or even in a language foreign to the consumer. If the consumer cannot afford to hire a distant lawyer or travel to a distant location, the consumer may drop the claim. Also, the company might ensure that the consumer has to pay a substantial amount for the arbitrator's time. As one lawyer noted, at least when one goes to court the judge is free. Finally, the company might seek to prevent consumers from joining together in a class action Often, suits that cannot be brought as a class action cannot economically be brought at all.

***

Second, the companies can be expected to structure the arbitration to minimize their liability exposure if claims are brought. The company would rationally seek to reduce the likelihood of a plaintiff victory and also to decrease a plaintiff's recovery in the event of a verdict. One way defendants can decrease a consumer's expected return is to prevent the consumer from engaging in adequate discovery. Because the consumer will be more needful of discovery than will the company, which maintains the relevant records and has continuing access to the decision makers, even a seemingly neutral restriction on discovery will affect consumers adversely.

Large companies will also attempt to select a decision maker likely to decrease their likely payout. Beyond avoiding the jury trial, the company will also seek an arbitrator or panel favorably disposed toward the company. Arbitration agreements frequently provide that the arbitrator shall be a current or former manager from the company's field of business, and courts have repeatedly held that mere selection of a former manager from a particular industry is not evidence of bias. Although such an individual may well do her best to decide the case fairly, she will probably be able to see the company's position more easily than the little guy's position. In addition, arbitrators may be consciously or unconsciously influenced by the fact that the company, rather than the consumer, is a potential source of repeat business. An arbitrator who issues a large punitive damages award against a company may not get chosen again by that company or others who hear of the award. Finally, even if the arbitrators are not biased, the consumer, likely a "one-shot" player, will be less able to make an informed selection of arbitrators than will the "repeat-player" company. . . .

***

Finally, having used the arbitration agreement to limit discovery, to pick favorable decision makers, and to select favorable substantive law, the company can consolidate these gains by depriving the consumer of a significant opportunity to appeal. The appeal right is most important to the party likely to have been disadvantaged in the original proceeding. Therefore, the strict limit on appeals contained in the FAA and possibly enhanced in private arbitration agreements also cuts against the consumer.

3. Competitive Market Forces Will Not Be Able to Prevent Businesses from Gaining an Advantage over Consumers

Some defenders of mandatory binding arbitration, while recognizing that businesses would perhaps like to use form contracts and binding arbitration to benefit themselves at the expense of the consumer, argue that competitive market forces will prevent companies from achieving those goals. These free marketeers argue that if the terms of consumer contracts were in fact unduly and inefficiently biased toward the supplier, then other suppliers, in order to benefit themselves, would step in and offer a contractual provision that treated the consumer more generously. The free marketeers further contend that the market will ensure that any benefits secured by the suppliers through imposition of an arbitration provision will be passed on to the consumers. Thus, if mandatory arbitration provisions are common in form contracts, it is because the greater speed and lower cost of arbitration benefits all parties and is therefore efficient and preferable.

***

This story of "free market to the rescue" is significantly flawed. . . . Most importantly, the competitive defense of form contracts depends on an assumption that consumers read, understand, and evaluate the cost of the binding arbitration clause being imposed by the seller. Instead, it seems generally true that while consumers may be well informed about certain key contractual terms, such as price or color or engine size, they generally know very little about the subordinate contract terms, commonly known as "boilerplate." If the consumer is not aware of the existence or significance of the clause, the supplier is free to impose a term that benefits the supplier but significantly harms the consumer.

***

C. No Net Societal Gains Attributable to the Imposition of Binding Arbitration Justify Imposing Costs on Individual Consumers

***

To assess the comparative societal values of binding arbitration and litigation one must analyze both the costs and benefits of the two alternatives. From a cost standpoint, not everyone would agree that binding arbitration is cheaper and quicker than litigation. As arbitrations become more complex they become more like litigation and just as expensive. Further, even to the extent one can show that resolving a case through arbitration is cheaper than resolving the case through trial, the fact is that most claims never make it to trial. To the extent that parties choose to take a case to arbitration that either would not have been litigated or would have settled quickly had it been litigated, arbitration may actually increase societal costs.

Nor is it necessarily true that there would be more widespread access to justice if all claims were resolved through binding arbitration rather than through litigation. On the contrary, the authors of arbitration agreements enter into binding arbitration agreements in order to pay out less money in arbitration than they would have paid out in litigation. At least absent regulation there seems to be no valid reason to assume that consumers as a whole will do better in arbitration than in litigation, and the seller's preference for arbitration suggests that the seller does better.

Even if binding arbitration were clearly cheaper than litigation, many would argue that the benefits society gains through avoiding litigation are not sufficiently great to justify the additional expense. Arbitration may not provide certain public goods that are provided by litigation. For example, Professor Owen Fiss, Professor Judith Resnik, and Judge Harry Edwards argue that our existing system of justice serves a public purpose. By closing off access to proceedings, eliminating judicial precedent, and allowing parties to write their own laws, we compromise society's role in setting the terms of justice. . . .

Moreover, denying consumers adequate compensation may itself be a social cost. If one party is able to dominate the process of setting the terms for arbitration, that party may be able to secure an unfair advantage over its opponent. Such inadequate recoveries may hurt not only the consumers themselves but also their families, thereby affecting overall social cohesiveness and productivity. Persons who were not able to recover compensation against a seller of consumer goods might have to be supported by all of society. . . .

Finally, assuming binding arbitration is preferable to litigation for society as a whole, having considered both the costs and benefits of the two systems, it is not necessarily fair or just to force a loss on certain individuals to bring about a benefit for society as a whole. As first-year economics students learn, there is a difference between efficiency and equity. It could be that society as a whole would be better off if a particular nasty individual were gagged, locked up, or even thrown off a cliff. Still, most would argue that the individual's rights of free speech, liberty, and life make it wrong to harm the individual, even if society as a whole would gain. Applying this same reasoning, it may be wrong to force a detrimental system of justice on consumers merely to obtain a gain for society as a whole. It is particularly egregious to allow this imposition where, as discussed above, the net social benefits of arbitration have not been proven.

More specifically, the Constitution provides all of us with the right to a jury trial for claims "at common law" for an amount in excess of $20. While the Court has recognized that constitutional rights may voluntarily be waived, waiver should not encompass forcing a consumer unknowingly to relinquish her right to pursue a claim through a fair jury trial solely to benefit other consumers.

. . .

V. Reassessing the Preference

It is time for the Supreme Court to reassess its extreme preference for mandatory binding arbitration over litigation, and to replace its current preference with the more limited acceptance of binding arbitration initially intended by Congress when it enacted the FAA. Rather than numbly repeat the mantra that arbitration is to be favored over litigation, the Court should instead look upon arbitration with favor in appropriate circumstances. Specifically, it should distinguish between those arbitration agreements entered voluntarily and knowingly by two or more parties of comparable strength, and those imposed by a stronger party on a weaker party that is ignorant of the clause's terms and implications. Further, the Court should not permit its assessment to be controlled by the interests of court administrators in hiring fewer judges and building fewer courthouses. To the extent that the Supreme Court refuses to recognize that unregulated mandatory binding arbitration agreements can be detrimental to consumers, employees, and other little guys, Congress should step in to protect their interests.

Like many of arbitration's strongest advocates, I believe that binding arbitration can be quicker, cheaper, more harmonious, and fairer than litigation. However, whereas some believe binding arbitration is necessarily superior to litigation, I believe only that arbitration can be superior to litigation, depending on the circumstances. Two or more merchants, with roughly equal bargaining power, should be permitted to select binding arbitration over litigation if they believe that selection serves their best interests. Consumers and employees, as well, should be permitted to opt for binding arbitration if they believe binding arbitration is preferable. However, companies should not be permitted to mandate that consumers or other little guys unknowingly waive their jury trial, due process, and Article III rights in favor of a possibly unfair arbitration process. Court should interpret the FAA to allow both state legislatures and lower courts to protect consumers from injustice.

Comments

Rethinking the Debunking: On Arbitration Myths, Preferences, and Legal Theory

Jill I. Gross[1]

Early in her academic career, Professor Jean Sternlight identified and critiqued what she called the Supreme Court's "preference for binding arbitration" over litigation. She published *Panacea or Corporate Tool?: Debunking the Supreme Court's Preference for Binding Arbitration* in 1996 in an attempt to "debunk" that preference. This commentary engages in a Sternlightian exercise, assessing the success (or failure) of her own debunking. Ultimately, though her article did not alter the Court's preference, it laid the groundwork for future scholars to infuse concepts of justice and fairness into the debate about mandatory arbitration.

I. Sternlight and the Preference Myth

In *Panacea or Corporate Tool*, Sternlight's historical road map through the Supreme Court's arbitration jurisprudence demonstrates how the Court's preference for arbitration over litigation developed. Though seeds of that preference appeared earlier, Sternlight marks 1983—the year the Court in *Moses H. Cone* mandated lower courts to apply a presumption of arbitrability when enforcing arbitration agreements—as the year the preference emerged (p. 660). She then argues that the Court's preference was derived from three principal myths. First, despite language and legislative history suggesting that Congress's intent in passing the Federal Arbitration Act (FAA) in 1925 was to direct courts to treat arbitration agreements as *equal* to any other contract, the Court interpreted the FAA to reflect *Congress*'s express preference for arbitration over litigation in commercial cases, including in the adhesive clause context, what Sternlight calls the "preference myth" (pp. 660–62). The Court, according to Sternlight, then adopted this mistaken view of congressional preference as its own. Other myths she identified include the "scope" myth—that Congress intended the FAA to apply in state courts (as opposed to federal courts only)—and the "substance" myth—that there is no difference in substantive outcomes in arbitration from those likely obtained in litigation (because procedure influences substance) (pp. 664–73).

[1] I am eternally grateful to my colleague Bridget Crawford for helping me develop the ideas in this commentary.

Jill I. Gross, *Rethinking the Debunking: On Arbitration Myths, Preferences, and Legal Theory* In: *Discussions in Dispute Resolution.* Edited by: Art Hinshaw, Andrea Kupfer Schneider, and Sarah Rudolph Cole, Oxford University Press (2021).
 DOI: 10.1093/oso/9780197513248.003.0052

Sternlight urged the Court to reconsider its FAA interpretation in light of these three myths.

Though the Court has utterly ignored Sternlight's call to reassess its preference for arbitration (or her call in a 1997 companion piece to rethink its constitutionality), scholars consider *Panacea or Corporate Tool* foundational in the arbitration field. Why? Sternlight was certainly not the first scholar to criticize mandatory arbitration, nor was she the first scholar to try to dispel the myth that Congress intended the FAA to apply to mandatory arbitration. Indeed, the Court continues to ignore scholars' strong historical evidence of congressional intent when passing the FAA (Szalai) and instead elevates the FAA from an "equal treatment" of arbitration contracts statute to a "super-statute" strictly enforcing arbitration agreements against virtually all challenges (Gross, p. 124).

II. The Article's Influence

Panacea or Corporate Tool is highly influential for two reasons. First, as a doctrinal matter, Sternlight was the first scholar to put several pieces of the puzzle together: she combined a comprehensive chronology of Supreme Court cases, a thorough examination of the intent of Congress, policy arguments, and forceful recommendations. In so doing, she gave future scholars a solid doctrinal road map and new tools for arguments against mandatory arbitration, fueling the "forced arbitration" movement that brought the scholarly arguments against adhesive arbitration into the mainstream media.

Consider the empirical impact of *Panacea or Corporate Tool*: according to Westlaw, the 75-page article has been cited 469 times, including by nine courts between 1997 and 2017, ranging from the US Supreme Court (in dissent) to the Alabama Supreme Court, 370 law review articles from publication to present day, and in 76 briefs or petitions filed in any court.

These citations support arguments by lawyers, legislators, and scholars that the FAA should not apply to adhesive arbitration agreements, one-shot players are at a disadvantage in arbitration, and arbitration may deprive claimants of their ability to vindicate their statutory rights.

Second, as Hiro Aragaki argues in his contribution, Sternlight's thesis draws on critical legal theory—without labeling it as such—to push back on the law and economics foundation of the Supreme Court's FAA jurisprudence of the 1980s and 1990s. As a threshold matter, why did law and economics theory have such a tremendous impact on arbitration law starting in the 1980s? The answer, at least in part, is timing. Though the study of economics as a distinct discipline has its origins in the eighteenth century, the introduction of economics into the study of law is a uniquely twentieth-century development. The 1970s witnessed a dramatic proliferation of scholarly work applying economic theories and methodologies to the study of law. By the late 1980s, many legal scholars integrated concepts and approaches such as game theory, Pareto efficiency, strategic bargaining, and prisoners' dilemmas into their teaching and scholarship.

Undoubtedly, these developments in the legal academy had a tremendous impact on how lawyers developed arguments for the strict enforcement of arbitration agreements, as multiple generations of law students were exposed to economic theories at various law schools for several decades. It is no surprise, then, that the Court's 1980s watershed decisions interpreting the FAA heavily relied on a law-and-economics-based analysis of those agreements. As *Panacea or Corporate Tool* explicitly acknowledges, "[v]iewed in a broader context, the Court's decisions in these cases can be seen as expressing a law and economics philosophy favoring the alienability of court access rights" (p. 674). Sternlight keenly observes that the Court's preference for binding arbitration is rooted in its view that arbitration is a net benefit for society because it facilitates contracting efficiency.

III. Inviting a Critical Legal Studies Perspective

Given this framework, Sternlight's article also should be understood as an invitation to the Court to incorporate into its arbitration jurisprudence the thinking of another paradigmatic-shifting approach to legal scholarship—critical legal studies. In US law schools, the Critical Legal Studies (CLS) movement, typically dated to the first Conference on Critical Legal Studies in 1977, challenged law's objectivity; instead CLS adherents viewed law and legal structures as mostly (if not entirely) politically motivated. The absence of race and gender diversity among the Crits in turn gave rise to feminist legal theory and critical race theory in the last decades of the twentieth century. A third generation of critical theory, including Critical race feminism, the LatCrit movement, and even a subfield known as critical tax theory, developed in the twenty-first century in turn because of perceived gaps in those intellectual movements and to bring more nuanced analyses to their areas of inquiry.

Despite these variations, all critical theory and its progeny, at the core, embrace "perspective" as relevant and important. Yet, the Court's arbitration law decisions patently omit any discussion of such perspective, an omission that trickles down to lower courts when they examine the enforceability of adhesive contracts containing arbitration clauses. For example, later scholars, critiquing courts' lax requirement that a consumer who enters into an arbitration contract manifest assent merely by clicking an "I agree" button on an app, acknowledge the limitations of seeing arbitration agreements through the narrow law and economics lens. The "[f]ocus on classical contract with a law and economics bent produces a market and efficiency focus that dissuades courts from considering contextual factors such as parties' gender and race" (Schmitz, pp. 263–64).

Sternlight's article attempts to steer the law and economics focus in a different direction.

By using language of perspective and other CLS concepts without naming them as such, she "debunks" the Court's four main law-and-economics-based policy justifications for the Court's preference for mandatory arbitration. First, she argues, the freedom of contract justification is belied by the reality of the adhesive nature of problematic predispute arbitration clauses.

Second, the political justification that, collectively, the parties to these clauses benefit from a cheaper, faster process is not supported by empirical evidence. As a corollary, she protests that Pareto-optimal efficiency does not necessarily equal justice. Third, she contends that underlying assumptions regarding the role of market forces in preventing sellers from taking advantage of consumers are flawed, as they completely ignore how parties behave in fact. Though Sternlight circa 1996 could not have foreseen the twenty-first-century rise of the application of behavioral economics to the law, this argument plainly injects into the conversation observations about the behavior of ordinary consumers. (Notably, behavioral insights greatly factor into Sternlight's later writings, e.g., Sternlight & Robbennolt 2012.) Finally, there is no evidence to support the justification that, even if a few parties are harmed, society as a whole benefits. Sternlight argues that we should not sacrifice justice in any individual case for the mere *possibility* of a benefit to society as a whole.

IV. The Law and Economics Approach to Arbitration Law Prevails

To be sure, Sternlight's arguments have not changed the course of arbitration law. Even recent Supreme Court decisions, particularly those enforcing class action waivers in arbitration agreements, reflect the Court's continued reliance on law and economics thinking. As Professor Blalock wrote, "In the Court's reasoning in *Italian Colors*, we see the neoliberal model of choice insofar as it refuses to account for the ways material realities and inequalities constrain choice" (Blalock, p. 98 n.139). And though Sternlight desperately wants to debunk this thinking, she was remarkably prescient about the unlikelihood of doing so. In *Panacea or Corporate Tool*, almost as a side note, she recognized how courts' enforcement of class action waivers in consumer and employment agreements (an issue that was percolating in the lower courts at the time) can suppress consumer claims (p. 683). And, despite her subsequent coverage in later pieces of the perils of class action waivers, the resulting scenario she most feared came true two decades later: in both *American Express Co. v. Italian Colors Restaurant*, 570 U.S. 228 (2013), and *AT&T Mobility LLC v. Concepcion*, 563 U.S. 333 (2011), the Supreme Court twice upheld class action waivers in predispute arbitration clauses in consumer contracts against unconscionability and effective vindication challenges.

In those class action waiver cases, the Supreme Court made clear that it is not interested in *perspective*. Justice Kagan wrote in her dissent in *Italian Colors* (p. 240): "The monopolist gets to use its monopoly power to insist on a contract effectively depriving its victims of all legal recourse. And here is the nutshell version of today's [majority] opinion, admirably flaunted rather than camouflaged: Too darn bad."

It is difficult to hypothesize why law and economics has had such a strong influence on arbitration law, and contract law, more generally, while critical legal studies and its progeny have not. If one views the Court's strict enforcement of adhesive arbitration clauses as an intentional judicial docket-clearing mechanism, then considerations of individual justice cannot occur. If one views the outcome as merely an irrefutable interpretation of the language of the FAA, it must be true that "perspective," or the disadvantaged bargaining position of a particular party, is irrelevant.

V. Reframing the Debunking

Perhaps this is why reframing Sternlight's "debunking" as a stealth attempt to apply a critical perspective to the Supreme Court's arbitration decisions deserves attention. She wrote her *Panacea or Corporate Tool* article through the lens of what she calls "the little guy" (defined somewhat awkwardly by Sternlight as a "gender neutral" term, but one that "refers to small companies as well as humans"). She asks courts to consider the impact of a strict application of the FAA on a variety of cohorts—not just the so-called rational company acting in society's collective interests: "This Article asserts that any social gains achieved by forcing binding arbitration on unknowing little guys are outweighed by the distributional inequities and injustices also incurred" (p. 679).

Her emphasis on the "little guy" attempts to import critical perspectives into the analysis of arbitration clauses, without ever naming it as such or citing to the ever-increasing body of critical legal scholarship. By taking this approach, Sternlight brings concepts of justice and fairness to the forefront of the debate about mandatory arbitration that traditional law and economics discourse ignores. In my view, that is a significant contribution to the field and deserves recognition by all who understand human beings as more than the sum of their economic transactions.

References

Corinne Blalock, *Neoliberalism and the Crisis of Legal Theory*, 77 LAW & CONTEMP. PROBS. 71 (2014).

Jill I. Gross, *Justice Scalia's Hat Trick and the Supreme Court's Flawed Understanding of Twenty-First Century Arbitration*, 81 BROOKLYN L. REV. 111 (2015).

Amy J. Schmitz, *Sex Matters: Considering Gender in Consumer Contracting*, 19 CARDOZO J.L. & GENDER 437 (2013).

JEAN R. STERNLIGHT & JENNIFER ROBBENNOLT, PSYCHOLOGY FOR LAWYERS: UNDERSTANDING THE HUMAN FACTORS IN NEGOTIATION, LITIGATION AND DECISION MAKING (2012).

IMRE STEPHEN SZALAI, OUTSOURCING JUSTICE: THE RISE OF MODERN ARBITRATION LAWS IN AMERICA (2013).

The Critical Theory Legacy of Jean Sternlight's *Panacea or Corporate Tool?*

Hiro N. Aragaki

No one can deny the seminal role that Jean Sternlight's *Panacea or Corporate Tool?: Debunking the Supreme Court's Preference for Binding Arbitration* has played in helping to define a distinct strand of domestic arbitration law scholarship. While earlier works treated in this volume, such as that of Julius Henry Cohen or Soia Mentschikoff, had approached the subject through the lens of commercial arbitration, *Panacea* underscored the importance of a very different context in which domestic arbitration law was being both applied and formed: "mandatory binding arbitration," which is to say arbitration that takes place not between two commercial parties but between a commercial party and a consumer or employee. It did so by tackling a number of key issues with Professor Sternlight's characteristic passion and acumen: the unfairness of enforcing arbitration clauses against the proverbial "little guy" or the comparative lack of procedural safeguards in arbitration as compared with litigation, to name a few.

When I was originally asked to write this commentary I wanted to demonstrate that the critique of mandatory binding arbitration had actually originated in *Panacea*, and thus that *Panacea* had effectively set the terms of the debate for the ensuing two-plus decades. But in fairness to other scholars writing at the time as or just before, such as Rita Cain, Sarah Rudolph Cole, Michael Z. Green, G. Richard Shell, and Katherine van Wezel Stone, I realized that I could not in good conscience make such a claim. So while *Panacea* has endured as one of the most influential contributors to the debate,[1] it was not the debate's progenitor.

There is, however, one very significant way in which *Panacea* represented a turning point, and it has to do with what I consider to be *Panacea*'s critical method. Articles written around the time of *Panacea* or earlier were examples of what I shall call first-order critique: they unpacked flaws in the Court's legal reasoning, pointed out overlooked policy considerations germane to the mandatory binding arbitration context, and explained how the US Supreme Court's decisions were contrary to the history of arbitration or the legislative history of the Federal Arbitration Act (FAA). *Panacea* also advanced these first-order critiques, but it was unique in that it took them to another level by gesturing—albeit imperfectly—toward what is sometimes referred to as "Critical Theory," a Left scholarly tradition heavily influenced by post-Marxist theory and whose pedigree can ultimately be traced to the Enlightenment (Geuss, *passim*). In

[1] For some persuasive reasons why, see the contributions of my co-commentators Michael Green and Jill Gross.

Hiro N. Aragaki, *The Critical Theory Legacy of Jean Sternlight's* Panacea or Corporate Tool? In: *Discussions in Dispute Resolution.* Edited by: Art Hinshaw, Andrea Kupfer Schneider, and Sarah Rudolph Cole, Oxford University Press (2021). © Oxford University Press. DOI: 10.1093/oso/9780197513248.003.0053

law, Critical Theory received its fullest exposition in the Critical Legal Studies (CLS) movement.

CLS famously took aim at the idea of the autonomy of law—the idea that law was a complete, independent, and internally coherent system that yielded definite answers to specific problems based on reason or logical deduction. It did so in a number of important ways. First, CLS (like Legal Realism before it) contended that law was fundamentally indeterminate and contradictory, thus making it possible for judges to reason backward and reach almost any conclusion they wished. The upshot was that law could no longer claim to be a field of scientific inquiry; instead, it was essentially indistinguishable from raw politics. Second, for these reasons CLS maintained that law is especially susceptible to being instrumentalized by powerful interests, and in this way is complicit in perpetuating structures of domination in society, such as the system of capitalism. Third, and perhaps most importantly, CLS sought to expose the law's ideological character—that is, its ability to legitimize inequality and oppression by making them appear to be necessary, correct, or desirable. Fourth, CLS scholars intended for their research to produce not just more knowledge but also more action. Roberto Unger referred to this as CLS's "transformative" moment (Unger, pp. 600–02, 670–73).

To be sure, *Panacea* does not self-consciously locate itself within the Critical Theory tradition, nor do I think Professor Sternlight intended for it to do so. Nonetheless, I argue that *Panacea* can and should be understood as a work of Critical Theory because it touches on the four central themes of legal indeterminacy, power, ideology, and transformation previously identified.

First, *Panacea* underscored the radical **indeterminacy** of arbitration law by showing how the Court's jurisprudence took contradictory positions over time on issues such as the FAA's purpose or whether arbitration differed from litigation in outcome-determinative ways. Second, more so than other articles published in the same period, *Panacea* drew attention to the plight of the "little guy." The point was not just to claim that the practice of mandatory binding arbitration was a "corporate tool," and thus to point the finger at corporate employers or investment banks; instead, it was to underscore the role that law—and, crucially, the Court—played in ossifying those relations of **power** (p. 712). Third, *Panacea* exposed arbitration law's **ideological** character. One of its main contentions, after all, was that FAA doctrine was little more than an elaborate "myth" spun by the Court. The *Oxford English Dictionary* defines a myth as an idea that is both false and widely held, which at the very least suggests how myths have the potential to legitimize subordination through false consciousness. *Panacea* highlighted the way that the Court's decisions did just that, by claiming on the one hand to further the original intent of the FAA or unobjectionable social policies such as freedom of contract, while simultaneously concealing the reality that arbitration was being foisted on consumers without their genuine consent and without any real evidence that it was socially beneficial on efficiency or fairness grounds. Fourth, *Panacea* was pitched as a wake-up call—to consumers who remained blissfully "unaware" of arbitration clauses, to legal commentators who were only just "beginning to take note" of them, and to a Congress that had the power to stand up to the Court and make things right (pp. 637–38, 644). In this way, *Panacea* betrayed an almost utopic faith in its own potential to produce **transformation**.

The novelty of *Panacea*'s critical method at the time it was published appears in sharp relief when one compares *Panacea* with another seminal critique of mandatory binding arbitration that entered the scene in the same year: Paul Carrington and Paul Haagen's *Contract and Jurisdiction*. Unlike *Panacea*, *Contract and Jurisdiction* essentially imports all of the positivist assumptions about law's autonomy that CLS rallied so hard to debunk. This is apparent in the way the authors faulted the Court for failing to grasp the true purpose behind the FAA, for erroneously believing that arbitration's streamlined procedures "do not entail any consequential restriction on substantive rights," and for being oblivious to the consequences of its decisions on weaker parties (Carrington & Haagen, pp. 343–45, 349, 367). Rather than see the Court as a political institution invested in maintaining the machinery of capitalism, Carrington and Haagen portrayed it as a victim of its own myopia. In other words, the law is still determinate and rule bound; it is "out there" waiting to be discovered by the judge *qua* scientist, like the law of gravity or the movement of celestial objects. The problem was merely that the Justices of the Court were bad scientists, who were either too biased or misguided to apply the law correctly. This outlook is moreover consistent with Professor Carrington's well-known skepticism toward CLS at the time.

By contrast, *Panacea* gave us the first glimpse of a radically different way of understanding and critiquing the same basic set of problems. For *Panacea*, the Court was not a group of bungling scientists who had misapprehended the inner logic or practical realities of domestic arbitration law. *Panacea* instead took the much bolder, CLS-inspired position that arbitration law *was* politics, and it sought to expose how the apex institution for the production of that law—the Court—had a self-interested, purposive hand in creating a state of affairs (FAA preemption, the demise of the nonarbitrability doctrine, etc.) that managed at once to oppress consumers *and* legitimize that oppression behind the aura of that thing we call "Law." No other domestic arbitration law article at the time had put itself so squarely in this Critical Theory camp.

I think it's fair to say that *Panacea*'s critical approach has won out over the first-order critique exemplified by *Contract and Jurisdiction* and other articles of the period. The Left is now much more cynical about arbitration law's claim to autonomy and much more apt to view the Court's decisions as ideological—as result-oriented justifications in the service of commercial self-interest.[2] But lest we forget, when *Panacea* was first published back in 1996, this way of seeing things was far from self-evident. It took a certain prescience, daring, and depth of thought to connect the field of arbitration with Critical Theory, which is one of the reasons why *Panacea* has earned its place as a classic in the domestic arbitration canon and why Professor Sternlight has earned a place as one of the most influential scholars in our field.

At the same time, the Left has largely failed to follow through with the full Critical Theory implications of *Panacea*. It is easy to grasp the arbitrary and hegemonic nature of a decision such as *AT&T Mobility v. Concepcion* that lacks almost any principled rationale; it is far more difficult to pierce through legal doctrines or arguments that appear legitimate on their face but that may have the same oppressive effects as *Concepcion*. Rather than take up the mantle of this much more radical type of critique,

[2] Nowhere is this cynicism clearer than in the class arbitration context, where the Court has made it all but impossible for consumers with small dollar claims to vindicate their rights.

however, commentators have been content to rehash the same basic arguments that were in circulation even prior to *Panacea*. As a result, the debate suffers from a certain repetitiveness and even polarization, with complex questions being reduced to easy categories of good versus evil.

Let me give an example from scholarly debates about mandatory binding arbitration. Consider the oft-repeated contention that arbitration is unfair to consumers because it is not sufficiently law-like—for instance, because there is no discovery or appellate review, or because arbitrators are not bound by the substantive law or the rules of evidence. The Left uniformly takes arbitration's informalism to be problematic because it assumes that only formal rules can constrain self-interest and speak truth to power (Aragaki, pp. 143–55). And here it certainly has a point. But in doing so, the Left also reveals its own naïve faith in the law's autonomy and, by extension, in public and rule-bound adjudicative processes. What's missing is any recognition of the Critical Theory insight that law and legalism are sometimes not the solution but rather the problem; that binarisms like right/wrong or good/evil typically obscure more than they elucidate; that things sometimes appear necessary or intuitively persuasive not because they truly are but because they are the product of false consciousness.

My hope is that this contribution will stimulate the Left to go even further than *Panacea* by embracing Critical Theory's skepticism about law and legal consciousness in general, not just by criticizing the idiosyncratic and almost contrived FAA jurisprudence of the Burger, Rehnquist, and Roberts Courts. Doing so has the potential to take the debate to a new level, one at which the focus is less about private arbitration versus public courts and more about the particular formal *and* informal processes that traverse both domains and, most importantly, the ways in which they each have the capacity to mask injustice, structural domination, and the ugly side of capitalism. In a distant future, this may even yield some much needed common ground between the Left and more traditional supporters of arbitration, since CLS and alternative dispute resolution were both born of a distrust of the law and they both have a long history of association with Left ideals such as Progressivism and access to justice.

References

Hiro N. Aragaki, *Constructions of Arbitration's Informalism: Autonomy, Efficiency, and Justice*, J. Disp. Resol. 141–69 (2016).

AT&T Mobility v. Concepcion 563 U.S. 333 (2011).

Paul D. Carrington & Paul H. Haagen, *Contract and Jurisdiction*, Sup. Ct. Rev. 331–402 (1996).

Raymond Geuss, The Idea of a Critical Theory: Habermas and the Frankfurt School (1981).

Roberto Mangabeira Unger, *The Critical Legal Studies Movement*, 96 Harv. L. Rev. 561–675 (1983).

Framing the Debate to Show How Big Guys Insist That Little Guys Arbitrate as a Corporate Tool

Michael Z. Green

Professor Jean Sternlight's 1996 article, *Panacea or Corporate Tool?: Debunking the Supreme Court's Preference for Binding Arbitration*, attempted to capture and critique what was a somewhat novel phenomenon at that time, the expansion of the Federal Arbitration Act (FAA) as an enforcement tool by big businesses. Sternlight exposed those big businesses and their desires to limit the right to seek court relief for those with less bargaining power in our society or what Sternlight termed "little guys" (p. 637). The article identifies three purported myths about FAA enforcement. These three myths, which Sternlight seeks to debunk, include: (1) a preference for resolving disputes through arbitration over litigation even when it involves agreements with little guys lacking bargaining power; (2) the FAA was intended to apply in state courts; and (3) the results in arbitration do not differ from results obtained in the courts (pp. 641–43).

While the second and third myths add overall value to Sternlight's thesis, this comment addresses what I believe to be the most seminal impact of the article: the focus on debunking the myth that arbitration should be enforced as a preference for resolving disputes when agreed to by corporate parties requiring adherence by parties lacking bargaining power. This bargaining power argument was articulated most forcefully at the time by Justice Stevens as a dissenter in the key cases that Sternlight emphasizes (pp. 702–4). However, Sternlight's article encapsulates just how much the Court's preference for arbitration involving weaker parties was theoretically and empirically unsupportable. In framing her analysis to focus on consumers, employees, and franchisees as little guys compelled to arbitrate their disputes as a result of adhesion agreements, Sternlight's article became a beacon and a starting citation for all those critical of the Supreme Court's expanded enforcement of the FAA.

When the Sternlight article was published, it inspired me as a new scholar already invested in critiquing so-called mandatory arbitration of employment discrimination claims. Sternlight's article became the road map for criticizing adhesion agreements to arbitrate statutory employment discrimination claims as a condition of employment. Another article by Katherine Van Wezel Stone, *Mandatory Arbitration of Individual Employment Rights: The Yellow Dog Contract of the 1990s*, published in the same year as Sternlight's article, also accentuated the concerns with employers forcing employees to enter arbitration agreements whether as individuals or represented by unions (Stone, pp. 1030–36). An important critique and direct response to

Michael Z. Green, *Framing the Debate to Show How Big Guys Insist That Little Guys Arbitrate as a Corporate Tool* In: *Discussions in Dispute Resolution*. Edited by: Art Hinshaw, Andrea Kupfer Schneider, and Sarah Rudolph Cole, Oxford University Press (2021).
 DOI: 10.1093/oso/9780197513248.003.0054

Stone's article by Roberto Corrada (Corrada, pp. 1051–52), together with Stone's and Sternlight's articles, became a lightning rod in challenging adhesion contracts subjecting employees to arbitration agreements as a condition of employment. Overall, Sternlight's article provided a seminal analysis that not only highlighted the power differential for employees but also for consumers and franchisees, all lumped together as little guys, being required by the big guys to arbitrate their disputes instead of being able to pursue litigation.

Specifically, for scholars exploring the expanded application of the FAA in both labor and employment arbitration, Sternlight's article developed an argument for fundamental fairness in bargaining that still resonates today, even if those little guys are millionaires being required to arbitrate in a way mandated by billionaires in professional sports disputes (Green & Carney, pp. 407–8). While Sternlight was debunking the Supreme Court's preference for arbitration in her 1996 article, she inspired me to debunk an employer's preference and advantage in arbitration versus the courts four years later (Green, pp. 443–62). I personally cited to her thoughtful and prescient analysis four more times within the next ten years after the publication of Sternlight's article as part of my repeated efforts to raise concerns about lack of bargaining power when enforcing agreements to arbitrate.

Many others recognized the seminal aspects of the Sternlight article by citing it in more than 350 secondary sources and at least 8 cases. Even in 2018, the concerns that Sternlight was so perceptive about have proven still to be valid issues. Big guys have made little guys accept arbitration on the terms of the big guys in the employment, consumer, and franchise setting. Congress has done little to stop this except with a few actions limiting the application of mandatory arbitration clauses to the military and federal contractors. Generally, if big guys want to use arbitration rather than litigation, they can do so unless dealing with another big guy who has the bargaining power to negotiate around an arbitration clause. And, in 2018, as the last-ditch efforts to at least suggest that big guys should be stopped from prohibiting little guys from joining together to use their collective strength as a balance to the big guys in arbitration, the Supreme Court decided to allow big guys to stop class claims from getting to arbitration.

As state legislatures, state courts, some members of Congress, and a few dissenting Supreme Court Justices have found, nothing seems to stop the big guys from imposing their arbitration will and preference on the little guys as a matter of course under the unyielding and overwhelmingly supportive Supreme Court FAA jurisprudence. As a result, we can pretty much believe that the answer to Sternlight's question is that arbitration is a corporate tool. Nevertheless, arbitration should not be thrown out completely as representing a totally ineffective system for little guys. The primary alternative, litigation, may actually provide a more reprehensible dispute resolution process even if arbitration certainly does not represent a panacea for the little guys.

We had recently hired a new law faculty colleague with mostly international arbitration experience. As he prepared to teach arbitration for the first time, I contemplated what readings I would recommend to him in discerning what the big deal is when it comes to understanding the mandatory arbitration juggernaut in the United States. I immediately thought of Sternlight's article. Moreover, I decided to tell him that the underlying theme throughout the existence of mandatory arbitration in the United States has been a battle of the big guys versus the little guys.

Although the little guys have attempted many creative legal theories to thwart this process, they have failed to gain any traction in defeating the big guys' efforts to insist upon using arbitration to resolve disputes with them. Some of those inventive (but still unsuccessful) legal challenges have included raising contract doctrines to prevent enforcement, attempts to reverse legally erroneous awards, and the prevention of class waivers. Others had hoped that a broad agency tasked with addressing consumer finance issues, the Consumer Finance Protection Bureau, might be able to level the playing field. Nevertheless, that agency has failed to change the enforcement of arbitration agreements. Alternatively, there was some hope that Congress might pass legislation, the Arbitration Fairness Act, to right the wrongs that little guys face in being required to arbitrate. Unfortunately, Congress has failed to establish any comprehensive legislation that would protect little guys subjected to arbitration agreements. Even the aggressive anti-arbitration media campaign reflected in the series of stories in the *New York Times* has not stalled the arbitration train from moving forward. Rather, the big guys have forced the little guys to get on board the arbitration train.

As mentioned, to date every one of the unique legal challenges to mandatory arbitration has failed. This fact leads back to the significance of Sternlight's article more than twenty years later. If a scholar could do any two of these three things—delve into a relatively new legal topic, highlight the problems that it would present, and predict the myriad ways this problem might play out over the next twenty years—it would be a career highlight. Sternlight did all three in this article. Hence, it made a unique mark on all of us who write about and are concerned about how the big guys continue to require the little guys to arbitrate any statutory, consumer, employment, franchise, or other dispute because of the Supreme Court's extraordinary enforcement of that agreement.

Despite political forces coalescing to thwart any resounding legal change as a result of Sternlight's article, her voice is still being heard today. Movements, like #MeToo, have started new efforts to make gains that would ban mandatory arbitration. More specifically, through the use of social media, the #MeToo movement has used its overall power to help the little guys by convincing some big guys, including major law firms, to agree to abolish their mandatory arbitration policies. As Sternlight helped us all understand, the real solution to the forced arbitration problem involves providing bargaining power for the little guys regardless of what the Supreme Court or Congress decides.

References

Roberto L. Corrada, *Claiming Private Law for the Left: Exploring Gilmer's Impact*, 73 Denv. U. L. Rev. 1051–70 (1996).

Michael Z. Green, *Debunking the Myth of Employer Advantage from Using Mandatory Arbitration for Discrimination Claims*, 31 Rutgers L.J. 399–471 (2000).

Michael Z. Green & Kyle T. Carney, *Can NFL Players Obtain Judicial Review of Arbitration Decisions on the Merits When a Typical Hourly Union Worker Cannot Obtain This Unusual Court Access?*, 20 N.Y.U. J. Legis. & Pub. Pol'y 403–50 (2017).

Jessica Silver-Greenberg and Robert Gebeloff, *Arbitration Everywhere, Stacking the Deck*, N.Y. Times Series on Arbitration Clauses, Dealbook Behind the Fine Print, Part 1, Oct. 31, 2015, available at https://www.nytimes.com/2015/11/01/business/dealbook/arbitration-everywhere-stacking-the-deck-of-justice.html.

Katherine Van Wezel Stone, *Mandatory Arbitration of Individual Employment Rights: The Yellow Dog Contract of the 1990s*, 73 Denv. U. L. Rev. 1017–50 (1996).

Panacea or Corporate Tool?: The Sequel

Jean R. Sternlight

It seems so long ago. Rereading my article, now more than twenty years later, is like rewatching the beginning of an old long war movie. I was so young, optimistic, and naive. When I wrote the article I saw myself as something of a prophet Isaiah, crying in the wilderness. My goal was to alert the world to the dangers I saw in the then-new phenomenon of mandatory contractual arbitration, and to fight back against that phenomenon. I thought, or at least hoped, that if I alerted the world to the dangers I saw, surely someone would step in to protect consumers and employees. Instead, while the world has certainly been alerted, so far corporate use of mandatory arbitration remains largely unchecked and indeed has expanded beyond what I ever imagined in my worst nightmares. One recent study found that more than 50 percent of nonunion employees have been deprived of their right to sue their employer in court, and we all know that mandatory arbitration is rampant in the consumer setting. In addition, companies have used mandatory arbitration to insulate themselves from class actions in many contexts.

Did mandatory arbitration turn out to be the "corporate tool" that I feared? Sadly, yes. I accurately predicted that companies would use such arbitration both to discourage claims and to minimize payouts, and that powerful economic and psychological forces would prevent the free market from magically ensuring fair and efficient results. Recall those prior scenes when companies used mandatory arbitration to direct claims to biased arbitrators and arbitration providers (*Hooters* & National Arbitration Forum) to create a process that would maximize consumers' and employees' costs while minimizing their benefits (think *Gateway*—class action waivers, distant fora, low likelihood of success, and low payout arbitrations). Such processes have suppressed or limited claims by victims of sexual harassment, fraud, and personal injury, to give a few examples (remember *Fox News*, Equifax, Wells Fargo, nursing homes, and for-profit schools). And, by limiting "little guys'" access to justice, the clauses not only harmed individual claimants but also negatively impact our public system of justice by preventing adequate enforcement of our laws and keeping claims private. Yet I did fail to imagine a few extreme excesses. For example, I failed to anticipate that collection companies would use arbitration to pursue claims against debtors and persons accused of crimes such as writing bad checks, thereby denying the accused access to court.

While there is still much more we would like to know about the largely secret world of mandatory arbitration, some excellent empirical research has been conducted in these past twenty plus years by both organizations and individual professors. One of the most impressive pieces of work was the multiyear study the Consumer Financial Protection Bureau conducted. Although this study was focused on the use of forced arbitration in the financial sector, its conclusions are similar to those reached in other

Jean R. Sternlight, Panacea or Corporate Tool?*: The Sequel* In: *Discussions in Dispute Resolution.* Edited by: Art Hinshaw, Andrea Kupfer Schneider, and Sarah Rudolph Cole, Oxford University Press (2021).
DOI: 10.1093/oso/9780197513248.003.0055

settings. While some studies by business-supported researchers claimed to show that forced arbitration is that "panacea"—quicker, cheaper, and better for consumers and employees than litigation—I think it is fair to say that the weight of research does not support this claim, but rather comes out on the side of mandatory arbitration generally being a "corporate tool." This is understandable given that the companies are the ones writing the clauses.

As the horror stories began to pour in, the war over mandatory arbitration became more serious, involving many actors, many ups and downs, and many fronts. The forces amassed against mandatory arbitration have included numerous legal academics, pro-consumer groups, and plaintiff-side employment lawyers. The National Academy of Arbitrators and the ABA Section on Dispute Resolution have also spoken out against the worst excesses of forced arbitration, rightly fearing that the tarnished reputation of mandatory arbitration might infect the public perception of international or commercial arbitration, or even mediation. The press also played a key role, providing coverage of the forced arbitration war in print (*New York Times*, *Wall Street Journal*, *USA Today*) and on television.

At several points along the way it appeared that mandatory arbitration might be defeated or at least sharply curtailed, whether in Congress, the courts, by administrative agencies, in the press, or on the now ever-present internet. As I laid out in 1996, mandatory arbitration could be attacked using arguments based on the Constitution, the Federal Arbitration Act (FAA), other federal statutes, contract law, state law, and public policy. Some of these arguments fared far better than others, but at least to date, none has come close to defeating mandatory arbitration. While the constitutional arguments intuitively appeal to many, courts have generally found that jury trial rights are waived (albeit perhaps unknowingly) when people "agree" to arbitration, and courts have similarly generally refused to find the state action that would be predicate to a viable Due Process challenge. Nor have arguments based on Article III succeeded to date, even though arbitration impinges on the turf of Article III judges.

Attempts to use the text and history of the FAA to rein in the excesses of mandatory arbitration have also failed, despite excellent historical and policy work by many. Scholars have tried to convince courts that the FAA should not apply to most employment cases, that the FAA should only apply in federal court, or that the FAA should not preempt state constitutions and statutes designed to ensure that arbitration is agreed to voluntarily. Yet even with text and history on critics' side, the Supreme Court has time after time interpreted the FAA to allow companies to use extreme and abusive forms of mandatory arbitration, and even to prevent critics from undercutting such arbitration using state statutes or common law. In *AT&T Mobility v. Concepcion* (2011), for example, the Supreme Court found that reliance on state unconscionability doctrine was preempted by the FAA. Many commentators and also some Supreme Court Justices have critiqued the Court's approach to the FAA. Indeed Justice O'Connor, no radical, observed that "the Court has abandoned all pretense of ascertaining congressional intent with respect to the Federal Arbitration Act, building instead, case by case, an edifice of its own creation" (*Allied-Bruce Terminix Cos. v. Dobson* (1995)). Nonetheless, while the Supreme Court may not be right, it does have the last word.

Realizing that the Supreme Court's interpretations of the FAA itself were not going to be useful in regulating mandatory arbitration, critics turned to the language of other existing federal statutes regulating consumer protection, Medicare, securities, antitrust, and labor law. A few lower courts accepted arguments under some of these statutes for a time, but ultimately the attacks generally have not worked, or have not worked in significant ways. For example, in *American Express Co. v. Italian Colors Restaurant* (2013), the Supreme Court found, 5–3, that companies could use forced arbitration clauses to prevent plaintiffs from bringing class actions to enforce their antitrust rights, even if this meant that plaintiffs could not effectively protect their rights under the law. As Justice Kagan put it, the majority's decision amounted to "too darn bad." The McCarran Ferguson Act does apparently allow states to regulate arbitration with respect to insurance, but the Supreme Court has held that the National Labor Relations Act does not prevent companies from using arbitration to prevent collective action by workers, including class actions (*Epic Systems*), and other federal statutes have not been found to block companies from using forced arbitration to insulate themselves from claims.

Advocates seeking to protect consumers and employees also turned to traditional contracts arguments—not only unconscionability but also doctrines defining agreement (or lack thereof), consideration, duress, fraud, waiver, estoppel, and much more. But while these kinds of arguments have occasionally defeated some particularly extreme arbitration clauses, they too have failed to stop the onslaught of mandatory arbitration, for three main reasons. First, it is expensive to challenge a supposed arbitration agreement on contractual grounds, and most consumers, employees, and even their attorneys lack the resources to gather necessary evidence, legal research, and possibly expert testimony. Second, the Supreme Court has used its broad interpretation of FAA preemption to block some of the contractual arguments. And third, in a move I did not anticipate, the Supreme Court has held that contractual challenges must often be made to the arbitrators themselves, rather than courts, even though the arbitrators have an incentive to rule in favor of arbitration.

Thus, critics of mandatory arbitration have called upon Congress to pass new legislation that would change the ending of the story by limiting or eliminating mandatory arbitration in various contexts. Congress has not yet passed the most comprehensive such statute, the proposed Arbitration Fairness Act, which would prohibit companies from imposing mandatory arbitration in employment, consumer, and (depending on the version of the proposed bill) sometimes other contexts. However, some narrower statutes have been adopted when interest group politics have properly aligned. Legislation, for example, now protects automobile dealers from arbitration imposed by sellers (but allows dealers to impose arbitration on customers); members of the military from arbitration imposed by payday lenders; poultry and livestock farmers from mandatory arbitration imposed by dealers; victims of sexual assault or sexual harassment from mandatory arbitration imposed by government contractors; and home purchasers from mandatory arbitration imposed by lenders. Critics have also asked administrative agencies to use their powers under various statutes to limit or eliminate the use of mandatory arbitration in contexts such as education, Medicaid, and consumer financial services, but these efforts have now failed after at first making great progress.

Still, the war now continues on other fronts, as mandatory arbitration critics have impressive stamina as well as creativity. The FAA preempts state legislatures from directly restricting mandatory arbitration, but inventive state legislatures have sometimes sought to act indirectly, for example, by requiring arbitrator or arbitration providers to at least disclose certain information about past practices.

Critics have also asked arbitration providers to adopt Due Process protocols that would (if complied with) police the fairness of mandatory arbitration or perhaps proscribe it altogether in particular settings, such as medical treatment. And, the power of the internet is now being employed to confront companies directly, such as when Starbucks was pushed to back down from forcing discontented gift card purchasers to arbitrate their claims, when employees have used picketing and social media to demand that major companies cease requiring their employees to resolve sexual harassment claims through mandatory arbitration, or when Harvard Law students pushed major law firms to stop forcing summer associates into arbitration.

We opponents have had our moments of exhilaration. I remember believing that President Barack Obama and a Democratic Congress would pass the Arbitration Fairness Act. I recall thinking that the Consumer Financial Protection Bureau under a President Hillary Clinton would lead the way to administration regulation of the anti-class-action waiver aspect of mandatory arbitration. I thought the National Labor Relations Board would be able to protect workers' rights to participate in class actions. I even felt good about the occasional Supreme Court cert grant or decision that could begin to turn the tide and protect against corporate excess (remember *Green Tree Financial Corp. v. Bazzle* (2003)? And *Green Tree Financial Corp. v. Randolph* (2000)??). Yet for the most part it feels as if the war has been lost, and that the Supreme Court and Congress have allowed mandatory arbitration to become that corporate tool I so greatly feared.

I can only hope that Martin Luther King Jr. was right and that the long arc of the moral universe bends toward justice. If so, perhaps we will one day be rid of the scourge of mandatory arbitration. But now, being far more cynical than twenty plus years ago, I think we had better continue to fight hard, in any venue we can think of, and not just count on that arc of the moral universe to take us to justice. Instead, perhaps we can call on Joan of Arc to make an appearance in the next sequel, and let's hope she is not burned at the stake this time.

Article 3.4

Employment Arbitration: The Repeat Player Effect

*Lisa B. Bingham [Lisa Blomgren Amsler]**

1 Employee Rights & Employment Policy Journal 189 (1997)

Introduction

Employment arbitration is emerging as a controversial method for resolving disputes between employers and employees not represented by a union.

***

Employment arbitration holds great promise as a dispute resolution process for employees who otherwise would never have a hearing on their claims against an employer. The procedural justice literature strongly suggests that the mere fact of a hearing before an apparently impartial decision-maker (rather than a settlement between lawyers with no arbitration hearing) will enhance employees' satisfaction with the outcome, whether they win or lose. In other words, some hearing is better than no hearing at all.... Moreover, employers likely will benefit from the elimination of the outlier jury award, concerns over which have motivated substantial changes in personnel practices, at some significant cost.

However, critics argue that mandatory arbitration is a new corporate tool used to advantage by large companies against consumers, employees, and other "little guys." Commentators in the press have reported claims that employment arbitration will disadvantage women, because the panels are predominantly comprised of male arbitrators. In particular, critics caution that in the absence of a union, the process is skewed against the employee, particularly the unrepresented employee. Some have expressed concern that, as institutional repeat players who will use the arbitration process for multiple cases, employers have an advantage over employees, who are unlikely to use it more than once or twice in their lifetimes....

The purpose of this article is to determine whether there is a measurable repeat player effect, to examine possible explanations for its existence, and to identify policy issues for employment arbitration that are raised by the effect.

***

* Editors' Note: Lisa B. Bingham, the author of this article, is now known as Lisa Blomgren Amsler.

Lisa B. Bingham [Lisa Blomgren Amsler], *Employment Arbitration: The Repeat Player Effect* In: *Discussions in Dispute Resolution*. Edited by: Art Hinshaw, Andrea Kupfer Schneider, and Sarah Rudolph Cole, Oxford University Press (2021). © Oxford University Press. DOI: 10.1093/oso/9780197513248.003.0056

Professor Marc Galanter gives us a framework for [repeat player] analysis in his classic article on the limits of legal change.

***

[Galanter] suggests that built in advantages in the legal system can best be identified and understood through an analysis of elements including the rules, the institutional facilities, lawyers, and parties. His typology of parties divides actors into the categories of repeat players and one-shotters. Repeat players have frequent recourse to the courts or institutional facilities, while one-shotters will have few such occasions. He identifies a collection of advantages repeat players will generally enjoy over one-shotters, including: (1) experience leading to changes in how the repeat player structures the next similar transaction; (2) expertise, economies of scale, and access to specialist advocates; (3) informal continuing relationships with institutional incumbents; (4) bargaining reputation and credibility; (5) long-term strategies facilitating risk-taking in appropriate cases; (6) influencing rules through lobbying and other use of resources; (7) playing for precedent and favorable future rules; (8) distinguishing between symbolic and actual defeats; and (9) investing resources in getting rules favorable to them implemented. One-shotters, on the other hand: (1) have more at stake in a given case; (2) are more risk averse; (3) are more interested in immediate over long-term gain; (4) are less interested in precedent and favorable rules; (5) are not able to form continuing relationships with courts or institutional representatives; (6) cannot use the experience to structure future similar transactions; and (7) have limited access to specialist advocates. Galanter observes that most litigation is brought by repeat player plaintiffs against one-shotter defendants (landlord-tenant, creditor-debtor, prosecutor-accused criminal, and IRS-taxpayer being salient examples). The one-shotter plaintiff against the repeat player defendant is comparatively infrequent (and includes personal injury, for example).

... It is not surprising then, given Galanter's analysis, that employers as repeat players might use this experience to structure their relationships and transactions with employees to better advantage.

***

III. Empirical Evidence of the Repeat Player Effect

The instant study examines a larger, two-year sample of employment arbitration awards. The above discussion leads to the following hypotheses:

H(1): Employees will win less frequently and/or will recover a lower proportion of their claims (have lower Outcome) in cases involving repeat player employers.

H(2): White collar workers will win more frequently and recover a greater proportion of their claims (have higher Outcome) than blue or pink collar workers in employment arbitration.

A. Method

***

This study examines a 270-case sample consisting of arbitration awards decided in 1993 under the AAA Commercial Arbitration Rules (n =186), and arbitration awards decided in 1993 and 1994 under the AAA Employment Dispute Resolution Rules (n=84). ***

Table 1. Distribution of Employees and Claims in Repeat Player and Non-repeat Player Employment Arbitration Cases

	Repeat Player (N=35)		Non-Repeat Player (N=235)	
Commercial or Employment Rules				
Commercial	9	(26%)	177	(75%)
Employment	26	(74%)	58	(25%)
Employee Collar Color				
White	10	(29%)	170	(72%)
Blue	15	(43%)	17	(7%)
Pink	9	(26%)	16	(7%)
Unknown	1	(2%)	32	(14%)
Employee Gender				
Male	30	(86%)	189	(80%)
Female	5	(14%)	40	(17%)
Unknown	0		6	(3%)
Arbitrator Gender				
Male	29	(83%)	191	(81%)
Female	6	(17%)	36	(15%)
Unknown	0		8	(4%)

Independent variables include whether the case is an employer or an employee claim, and whether the case involves a Repeat Player employer, defined as an employer who uses arbitration more than once in the sample (coded 1 for yes and 0 for no). In addition, independent variables include job category of the employee, specifically whether the case involves a White, Blue or Pink collar employee....

Dependent variables include the dollar amount of damages, if any, awarded by the arbitrator (Damages Amount), and the percentage of claim recovered (a ratio of Damages Amount divided by Demand, or amount of money the claimant indicated was at stake). This ratio was used to create a variable named Outcome.

***

Employees were generally claimants in disputes concerning the termination of their employment, terminal compensation including stock options, and other compensation disputes.

Table 3, Damages by Repeat Player, indicates the lower frequency with which arbitrators award damages in any amount in repeat player cases involving employee claims.

Table 3 shows that employees lose significantly more frequently in cases involving Repeat Player employers, Pearson Chi Square = 34.39, DF 1, P<.001.

Table 3. Contingency Table Showing Damages (rows) by Repeat and Non-repeat Player Employer (columns), Employee Claims Only

	Repeat Player		Non-Repeat Player		Total	
Damages	5	(2%)	142	(61%)	147	(63%)
No Damages	26	(11%)	59	(26%)	85	(37%)
Totals	31	(13%)	201	(87%)	232	(100%)

Employees also have significantly lower Outcomes in cases involving Repeat Player employers. A one-way analysis of variance using Repeat Player as the independent variable and Outcome (the proportion of their original Demand that employees are awarded as damages), was significant, F=6.53 (DF 1, 213), P<.01. Table 2 [deleted] shows that in repeat player cases, employees recover only 11% of what they demand, on average, while in cases involving non-repeat player employers, employees recover an average of 48%; the analysis of variance shows that this difference is statistically significant.

***

Conflict resolution scholars have suggested that dispute resolution procedures should be evaluated from not only a microjustice perspective (i.e., how satisfied the participant is in a particular case), but also from a macrojustice perspective, that is, in terms of the patterns in the aggregate distribution of outcomes. In labor arbitration cases, grievants win something in 52% of all cases. In employment arbitration, using the sample in this study, employees won something in 63% of the total employee claims sample (n=232), including repeat and non-repeat player employers (Table 3). However, looking at the subsample of repeat player cases (n=31), employees won something only 16% of the time. Employees dealing with non-repeat player employers recovered on average 48% of what they demanded, while employees dealing with repeat player employers recovered only 11% of what they demanded ... These differences in employee success are statistically significant. For lack of better terminology, let us call this the repeat player effect.

There are several possible explanations for the repeat player effect, and research is ongoing.... One possible explanation is unequal information in arbitrator selection. Another possible explanation is unequal representation in the hearing itself.

Researchers have found that a party does better in labor arbitration when it has legal counsel and the other party does not. There may, of course, be systematic differences in the merits of these cases, in that employees in repeat player cases may have weaker legal claims [than] employees in the non-repeat player cases .... The preliminary evidence is that repeat player cases tend to involve personnel manuals, while non-repeat player cases involve express written individual contracts. Personnel manuals are more likely to be the product of a repeat player employer unilaterally structuring the employment relationship and dismissal transaction to its best advantage.

This in turn might reflect unequal bargaining power. Professor Marc Galanter noted that litigation requires information and skills, and that complaints come disproportionately from better educated, better informed, and more politically active households. The fact that white collar employees have systematically superior outcomes to blue or pink collar employees is consistent with this theory.... They win significantly more frequently than blue or pink collar workers, and they recover a larger percentage of what they demand.

The decision standard for the arbitrator may vary. Employers may get better at screening cases with repeat experience in the process, and learn to settle the cases they otherwise would lose. One theory is that arbitrators respond to the economic incentive of repeat business, but that incentive might be present with the first case an arbitrator hears for an employer. It has been suggested that arbitrators become more familiar with repeat players and/or their lawyers, and develop a relationship of trust. Where the evidence is equally balanced, this may make a difference in the outcome. All of these hypotheses warrant investigation.

***

The repeat player effect creates the perception of an uneven playing field. In dispute resolution, the perception of a fair process can be as important as the reality of impartiality. The procedural justice literature tells us that satisfaction with the fairness of the process is strongly correlated with satisfaction with the outcome of that process. This is why it is not too early to address possible causes through appropriate reasonable changes in arbitration rules.... What protections that directly address the repeat player effect should providers consider and parties look for in employment arbitration? What reforms might address the imbalance of information about arbitrators in the selection process? The labor and employment law community should explore alternatives to address both the perception of an unequal playing field, and any underlying reality. A few issues to begin examining are disclosure rules, random assignment to lists, and substitute repeat players.

***

Employment arbitration is still in its infancy, but it has begun to walk. It is becoming more widespread, and the question is how the labor and employment relations community can influence its structure. The process has the potential to provide a meaningful opportunity to be heard by employees who otherwise may have no voice in their dismissal. However, there are emerging patterns of repeat player use and significantly different outcomes based on whether an employer is a repeat player in cases decided before the Due Process Protocol and the most recent AAA Rules for employment disputes. These patterns suggest that it was appropriate for the dispute resolution user and provider community to be proactive in developing the structures and institutions that will foster employment arbitration's growth, such as the Protocol. The Protocol is a major step forward in self-regulation, but not all providers have adopted the Protocol, and not all employers adopt plans that comport with basic notions of due process, such as the right to a jointly selected arbitrator. Moreover, it remains to be seen how effectively signatories can enforce its terms. It is necessary to assess the employment arbitration process and its outcomes as we continue to move incrementally forward with reform.

Comments

The River's Source: Empirical Research and Lisa Blomgren Amsler's *Employment Arbitration: The Repeat Player Effect*

Alexander J.S. Colvin

Lisa Blomgren Amsler's classic article was a groundbreaking piece of work in the genuine sense that it broke new ground on an important issue and laid the path for subsequent work in the area. As I will describe in this commentary, my own research, along with that of others in this field, was deeply influenced by the crucial initial steps that Amsler took.

By the late 1990s mandatory employment arbitration had become a topic of increasing academic and public policy debate. Public policy concerns had led to the creation of the Due Process Protocol. Important legal scholarship on the topic by scholars such as Katherine Stone and Richard Bales had already been published. What Amsler's article brought to the issue, however, was a new focus on empirical analysis of what was happening in employment arbitration and a new set of issues to examine.

Amsler's article is most known for raising and examining the question of whether there was a repeat player effect in employment arbitration. Repeat player effects had been famously identified in the litigation arena long before by Marc Galanter, analyzed elsewhere in this volume. But Amsler was the first to identify and systematically analyze repeat player effects in employment arbitration. Her article was built on the crucial insight that the ability of the parties to select the decision maker in an arbitration procedure increased the potential for a repeat player effect favoring employers.

My own engagement with this line of research was inspired in part by some of the responses that Amsler's article received. Advocates and critics of mandatory arbitration alike quickly recognized that the existence of repeat player effects favoring employers would undermine arguments for the fairness of arbitration and bring into question whether it was really just a substitution of forum with no effect on substantive outcomes. Advocates for mandatory arbitration, like David Sherwyn and Samuel Estreicher, critiqued specific features of Amsler's research methods.

These critiques raised some reasonable methodological issues with Amsler's original study. However limitations in an empirical study does not mean one should throw out the baby with the bath water. Social science research generally builds insights through multiple studies on a topic over a period of time with research methods being gradually advanced and refined so that conclusions become stronger with confirmation in subsequent studies. For me, an exciting feature of Amsler's article was that it raised a signpost for future research directions, with opportunities for subsequent

Alexander J.S. Colvin, *The River's Source: Empirical Research and Lisa Blomgren Amsler's* Employment Arbitration: The Repeat Player Effect In: *Discussions in Dispute Resolution.* Edited by: Art Hinshaw, Andrea Kupfer Schneider, and Sarah Rudolph Cole, Oxford University Press (2021). © Oxford University Press. DOI: 10.1093/oso/9780197513248.003.0057

researchers to gather additional data and further develop the research methodologies in this area.

Amsler herself took some initial steps in further developing this research stream. She collected additional data on employment arbitration cases administered by the American Arbitration Association (AAA) and refined her analysis in a couple of important ways (Bingham [Amsler] & Sarraf). One was to begin separating out from the effect of being a repeat employer the impact of having the same arbitrator hear multiple cases involving the same employer. The second advance was to begin separating out employment arbitration cases involving individually negotiated agreements (mostly part of executive employee contracts) from true mandatory arbitration cases based on employer promulgated procedures. Most of the early 1990s cases administered by the AAA were actually individually negotiated arbitration cases, limiting their utility for making inferences about what was going on in mandatory arbitration.

Amsler stopped doing research on employment arbitration in the early 2000s and moved on to new research areas, notably her outstanding multiyear research project on employment mediation at the US Postal Service. My understanding from personal conversations with Amsler is that a factor in this shift is that the AAA stopped providing access to the case data that she had used for her earlier research. The AAA is a private organization and entitled to do this. Relative to other service providers it has often been more open and willing to provide access to researchers, myself included. However, it does point to a problematic feature of the privatization of justice in mandatory arbitration in that a private organization is able to control access to information about how our major public statutory employment rights are being enforced.

My own research in the late 1990s and early 2000s had been focused on exploring the corporate adoption of nonunion grievance procedures. Perhaps to the surprise of legal scholars who mostly know my subsequent work showing limitations of mandatory arbitration, much of this research published in industrial relations journals was showing the relatively widespread adoption of conflict resolution procedures in nonunion workplaces and identifying types of procedures that are relatively effective in resolving workplace conflict. This had led me to an interest in mandatory arbitration as I looked at many companies that had introduced arbitration as the final step in multistep internal grievance procedures. However, in this research I was looking at what organizations were doing rather than at the type of arbitration cases Amsler had examined.

This changed around 2004–05 when I became aware of a new rule that had been added to the California Code of Civil Procedure. It required that any arbitration service provider doing business in the state of California had to provide specified public disclosures on any cases it administered involving consumers or employees. Crucially, this rule required disclosure of all cases that the service provider had administered anywhere in the country, not just in California. My understanding is that the adoption of this rule was inspired in part by the recognition of the insights from Amsler's article and the hope that it would allow identification of potential repeat player problems.

From my perspective as an empirical researcher, these disclosures were a potential goldmine of data that I could use to explore what was going on in mandatory arbitration. It overcame two major limitations of Amsler's data. One is that it only consisted of mandatory arbitration cases, since the service providers were not required to disclose information about individually negotiated agreement cases. The second is that it provided a much larger set of cases, which would provide greater statistical power and permit further analysis of issues like the repeat player effect.

Fortunately, the consumer and employment arbitration disclosures were provided on the web, and the AAA in particular had done a good job of providing relatively thorough and complete disclosure.

My initial publication from this research stream was an article that analyzed data on all the mandatory arbitration cases the AAA had administered over a four-year period (2003–07) (Colvin, pp. 405–47). The results confirmed the key insight of Amsler's 1998 article, showing a repeat employer advantage in the outcomes of cases, and then extended it by showing a statistically significant effect for employers who had multiple cases before the same arbitrator, over and above the effect of being a repeat employer. This result indicated that while there were limitations in Amsler's original empirical evidence, her basic insight was correct: there was a repeat player effect in mandatory arbitration that favored employers.

As with Amsler's research, my own initial efforts had their limitations. In subsequent years, I was able to collect additional data, increasing the statistical power available. I was also able to conduct more sophisticated statistical analyses, constructing multivariate analyses that controlled for multiple factors affecting outcomes of arbitration. This led to a 2011 article, where I was able to present a more complete and robust empirical set of results on various aspects of mandatory arbitration, now drawing on seven years' worth of case data (Colvin, *Empirical Study*, pp. 1–23). In this subsequent analysis, however, the same core result held, that I found statistically significant advantages accruing to repeat employers and additionally to those employers with multiple cases before the same arbitrator.

Most recently, in a 2015 article with Mark Gough, using eleven years of case data and some 2,802 decisions, we were able to employ more advanced statistical estimation models and an estimation approach that captured the effects of increasing numbers of repeat employer and repeat employer-arbitrator interactions (Colvin & Gough, pp. 1019–42). This article represents the largest data set and most empirically sophisticated analysis that I have been able to do looking at mandatory arbitration case outcomes. Yet the line connecting it and Amsler's original 1998 article is clear, as is Amsler's basic insight that it confirms, that employers are achieving systematic repeat player advantages in mandatory arbitration.

Reflecting on the contribution of Amsler's 1998 article to the field, it is clear that it offered both important theoretical and empirical insights and addressed a problem of practical significance. Subsequent research owes a great debt to it. However, in the policy debates around mandatory arbitration, at times the repeat player problem has been too exclusive a focus. Looking at the empirical research findings on mandatory arbitration, in my own view a greater problem is the general tendency of arbitrators to find less often for employees and make much smaller damage awards than is the case in litigation in the courts.

One reason it took longer to recognize the problem of poorer employee outcomes in mandatory arbitration is that the initial studies of employment arbitration outcomes in the 1990s used smaller data sets with many more negotiated arbitration cases than mandatory arbitration cases. Involving executive-level employees and contractual claims, these cases produced much higher employee win rates and larger damage amounts. Amsler's later work was some of the first to identify that outcomes looked different and much less favorable to employees in mandatory arbitration. Hill and Eisenberg made similar findings, though overreached their interpretation by trying to argue that the appropriate comparison to litigation was negotiated arbitration cases involving executives rather than mandatory arbitration involving regular employees (Eisenberg & Hill, pp. 44–55). More recent research, including my own described previously, has shown that mandatory arbitration outcomes are much less favorable for employees than those in litigation. This finding is troubling from a policy perspective and suggests the importance of future research investigating further the factors driving these differential outcomes.

For a long period, mandatory employment arbitration was a topic of passionate debate among academic and practitioner experts in the field, but not an issue that ignited the interest of the broader public policy community, much less the general public. This has begun to change. A prominent series of investigative reporting articles on mandatory arbitration published by the *New York Times* in October–November 2015 gave a wider audience to the issues in this area. The recent Supreme Court decision in *Epic Systems v. Lewis* 584 U.S. (2018) affirming the use of mandatory arbitration clauses to curtail class action claims brought new attention to the impact of mandatory arbitration agreements. And the recent explosion of attention to issues of sexual harassment in the workplace for plaintiffs like Gretchen Carlson has brought attention to the use of mandatory arbitration clause in these cases. A recent survey I conducted found that over half of the nonunion, private sector workforce is now covered by mandatory employment arbitration. With mandatory arbitration having its needed day in the sun of broader scrutiny, it is important to recognize the crucial early work that Amsler did in bringing to bear the tools of empirical legal research on this important topic.

References

Lisa B. Bingham [Lisa Blomgren Amsler] & Shimon Sarraf, "Employment Arbitrations Before and After the Due Process Protocol for Mediation and Arbitration of Statutory Disputes Arising Out of Employment: Preliminary Evidence that Self-Regulation Makes a Difference," Ch. 13 *in* ALTERNATIVE DISPUTE RESOLUTION IN THE EMPLOYMENT ARENA, PROCEEDINGS OF NEW YORK UNIVERSITY 53RD ANNUAL CONFERENCE ON LABOR, KLUWER LAW INTERNATIONAL (Samuel Estreicher & David Sherwyn eds., 2004).

Alexander J.S. Colvin, *Empirical Research on Employment Arbitration: Clarity amidst the Sound and Fury?*, 11 EMPLOYEE RTS. & EMP. POL'Y J. 405–47 (2007).

Alexander J.S. Colvin, *An Empirical Study of Employment Arbitration: Case Outcomes and Processes*, 8 J. EMPIRICAL LEGAL STUD. 1–23 (2011).

Alexander J.S. Colvin & Mark Gough, *Individual Employment Rights Arbitration in the United States: Actors and Outcomes*, 68 ILR REV. 1019–42 (2015).

Theodore Eisenberg & Elizabeth Hill, *Arbitration and Litigation of Employment Claims: An Empirical Comparison*, 58 DISP. RESOL. J. 44–55 (2004).

Arbitration's Catalyst for Empirical Studies

Martin H. Malin

In a 1979 article in the *Yale Law Journal*, more than a decade before *Gilmer v. Interstate/Johnson Lane Corp.*, 500 U.S. 20 (1991), where the Supreme Court started giving employers the green light to mandate as a condition of employment that their employees arbitrate their statutory claims, Julius Getman cautioned against the wholesale importation of arbitration under collective bargaining agreements to other types of disputes (Getman 1979). Responding to the criticism of Judge Paul Hayes (Hayes 1966), who regarded labor arbitration as corrupted by the arbitrators' financial dependence on repeatedly being selected by the parties, Getman argued that arbitrators' need for acceptability by the parties actually furthered the process as part of the parties' overall system of collective bargaining. Furthermore, "[t]he desire to maintain acceptability makes it important for arbitrators not to project either a pro- or anti-union bias. As a result, this desire serves to insulate the process from personal political attitudes . . ." He concluded, "The selection process thus helps arbitration to achieve neutrality and, together with the collective agreement, fosters fairness and promotes conflict reduction."

In contrast to labor arbitration where union and employer are both repeat players, Getman cautioned that in employment arbitration where there would be only one repeat player, "private selection [of the arbitrator] would be disadvantageous to employees, since an arbitrator could improve his chances of future selection by deciding favorably to institutional defendants: as a group, they are more likely to have knowledge about past decisions and more likely to be regularly involved in the selection process."

In the years following *Gilmer*, scholars, practitioners, and judges debated the significance of the employer being the only repeat player in the system endorsed by the Supreme Court. Would arbitrators' ethics and professionalism or arbitrators' concern for their reputation for integrity mitigate against overt or implicit pro-employer bias? Would the organized plaintiffs' bar play a role comparable to the role played by unions in balancing the advantage of employers in the arbitrator selection process?

Amsler's article was pathbreaking as it was the first systematic empirical examination of one of the most troubling issues in employment arbitration.

Amsler's study focused on a two-year sample of cases administered by the American Arbitration Association (AAA). She found that employers who were repeat players in arbitration during the study were significantly more likely to win and received significantly better outcomes than employers who appeared only once. Her study suffered from a small sample size, from a large number of cases involving individually negotiated contracts rather than the arbitration mandates imposed en masse by employers on their workforces, and her time frame predated AAA's overhaul of its employment

Martin H. Malin, *Arbitration's Catalyst for Empirical Studies* In: *Discussions in Dispute Resolution.* Edited by: Art Hinshaw, Andrea Kupfer Schneider, and Sarah Rudolph Cole, Oxford University Press (2021). © Oxford University Press.
DOI: 10.1093/oso/9780197513248.003.0058

arbitration rules and the adoption of the *Due Process Protocol for Mediation and Arbitration of Statutory Disputes Arising out of the Employment Relationship*. But her study led to further empirical studies that vindicated her findings.

Chief among the further empirical studies that Amsler's work inspired were those of Alexander J.S. Colvin, J. Ryan Lamare, and David B. Lipsky. Colvin discusses his work in his contribution to this volume. I shall focus on Lamare and Lipsky.

Lamare and Lipsky advanced Amsler's work in several respects. Significantly, unlike Colvin who, like Amsler, analyzed only AAA cases, Lamare and Lipsky expanded the analysis to arbitration under the auspices of the Financial Industry Regulatory Authority (FINRA) (Lamare & Lipsky 2014).

Lamare and Lipsky analyzed all cases since FINRA began its arbitration system through 2006. They confirmed the existence of a repeat player effect. They found that for each additional case an employer had in the system, the outcome was significantly more favorable to the employer whether measured by absolute employee recovery or by employee recovery of a percentage of the amount claimed. They also found that the more cases an arbitrator had, the more likely a negative outcome for the employee as measured by percentage of the amount claimed.

Significantly, Lamare and Lipsky found no repeat player effects for employer or employee counsel. Increase in the number of FINRA cases handled by attorneys for either side had no effects on the award. This finding casts considerable doubt on the suggestion that the organized plaintiffs' bar may play a role similar to unions in offsetting the influence of employers in the arbitration process.

One significant difference between Lamare and Lipsky's findings and Colvin's concerns the impact of repeat employer-arbitrator pairings. Colvin found that employers appearing before the same arbitrator multiple times received significantly more favorable outcomes than employers appearing before the arbitrator for the first time. This could reflect increased employer ability to select pro-employer arbitrators or to cater their case to a particular arbitrator's proclivities, but it could also reflect arbitrator bias in seeking future business. Lamare and Lipsky found no significant repeat employer-arbitrator effects in their FINRA database. They suggested that this may be due to procedural safeguards FINRA had to guard against arbitral bias, such as "disclosure statements, sworn oaths and a variety of other methods to preserve impartiality."

The specific procedural safeguards that Lamare and Lipsky cited, however, expansive arbitral disclosures and sworn oaths, were also present in the AAA system that Colvin studied. Lamare and Lipsky did not consider another possible explanation—the financial incentive for arbitral bias. FINRA sets the arbitrator's fee, whereas in the AAA system arbitrators set their own fees. During the period studied by Lamare and Lipsky, FINRA paid arbitrators $200 per day, and the chair of a three-arbitrator panel received an additional $75. Currently, according to its website, FINRA pays $600 per day and an additional $175 to the chair. AAA arbitrators' fees, in contrast, tend to run in the hundreds of dollars per hour and thousands of dollars per day. Moreover, in AAA cases, the arbitrator bills not only for the hearing days but also for prehearing work such as case management conferences, resolving discovery disputes, ruling on motions, and preparation for the hearing; and for posthearing work including study and writing time producing the award. In AAA cases that go all the way to a written award, the arbitrator's fee can easily be *forty* times the daily fee that FINRA pays for the hearing.

Looking to repeat employer–repeat arbitrator effects as a sign of potential arbitral bias misses a key point made by Getman. In labor arbitration, the arbitrator's need to maintain acceptability to both players (employer and union) to secure future work ensures arbitral neutrality. In employment arbitration, however, the only source of future work is the employer, and this imbalance may lead to arbitral bias even in the first case an arbitrator has with a particular employer. Recent studies by Pat Chew and by Martin Malin and Jon Werner may evidence this concern.

Chew examined sex discrimination claims in AAA employment arbitrations conducted between 2010 and 2014 (Chew 2017). She found no significant differences in outcomes between cases handled by male arbitrators and female arbitrators. Lamare and Lipsky similarly found no significant differences in FINRA case outcomes based on the gender of the arbitrator. Whereas Lamare and Lipsky hailed their finding as showing the absence of gender bias in FINRA arbitration, Chew found her finding disconcerting.

Chew compared her finding of the lack of effect of arbitrator gender on outcomes in sex discrimination cases to studies that have consistently found significant effects of judges' gender on case outcomes in sex discrimination litigation. Sex discrimination plaintiffs were significantly more likely to win at the trial level when the judge is a woman, and in sex discrimination cases on appeal, plaintiffs are significantly more likely to win when there is at least one woman on the appellate panel. The effects of adjudicator gender on case outcomes have been attributed to the different life experiences of women and men. Even when there is only one woman on a three-judge appellate panel, she is often able to educate her male colleagues about her perspective and influence their votes.

Chew suggested that the need for arbitrators to maintain acceptability with employer repeat players may explain the difference. This concern may be amplified by the fact that the overwhelming majority of arbitrators are male. Female arbitrators who are selected by employers may be those who have shown themselves to be pro-management, or they may suppress their life experiences in an effort to decide the case in a way that fosters their acceptability.

Additional evidence of the effects of arbitrator needs to maintain acceptability comes from Canada. In Canada, labor arbitrators are not only authorized to adjudicate statutory claims, they are obligated to do so. Statutory claims that are not arbitrated are adjudicated before administrative tribunals rather than litigated in court, and most employment law is provincial rather than federal. Malin and Werner studied the arbitration of discrimination claims, called human rights claims in Canada, in Ontario (Malin & Werner 2017). They compared the adjudication of human rights claims in labor arbitration in Ontario to their adjudication before the Human Rights Tribunal of Ontario (HRTO).

They found considerable differences in the remedies awarded. Most striking were the differences in ordering the development or modification of an employer's human rights policy, mandating human rights training for an employer's management or workforce, and requiring periodic reporting of human rights compliance, collectively called public interest remedies. Among potential remedies, these are the ones employers find most intrusive. Malin & Werner found that although the HRTO awarded public interest remedies in a significant minority of cases, arbitrators almost never did. After ruling out several alternative explanations, Malin & Werner suggested that the difference may be explained by arbitrators' need to maintain acceptability.

Thus we are seeing significant evidence that in the arbitration of statutory claims, the arbitrator's interest in developing or maintaining acceptability with the one repeat player in the process, that is, the employer, may be affecting the outcome of the arbitration. As researchers continue to run with the baton passed to them by Amsler, they should focus on this concern, and if the evidence continues to mount, scholars and providers of arbitration services should turn their attention to how to mitigate these effects. Amsler's legacy is the continued empirical research and the use of that research to further refine employment arbitration systems to make them fairer to all parties.

References

Pat K. Chew, *Comparing the Effects of Judges' Gender and Arbitrators' Gender in Sex Discrimination Cases and Why It Matters*, 32 Ohio St. J. on Disp. Resol. 195 (2017).

Julius G. Getman, *Labor Arbitration and Dispute Resolution*, 88 Yale L.J. 916 (1979).

Paul Hayes, Labor Arbitration: A Dissenting View (1966).

J. Ryan Lamare & David B. Lipsky, *Employment Arbitration in the Securities Industry: Lessons Drawn from Recent Empirical Research*, 35 Berkeley J. Lab. & Emp. L. 113 (2014).

Martin H. Malin & Jon M. Werner, Penn Plaza LLC v. Pyett: *Oppression or Opportunity for U.S. Workers; Learning from Canada*, 14 U. Chi. Legal Forum 347 (2017).

The Historical Context of Lisa Blomgren Amsler's Empirical Work on Employment Arbitration

Richard Bales

Appreciating the critical importance of Lisa Blomgren Amsler's contribution to the scholarly literature on arbitration requires understanding the context in which she began her scholarship. Supreme Court jurisprudence on the topic was inconsistent—the Court had recently transitioned from a love-hate relationship with arbitration to a besotted lovefest.

Scholarly reaction to this abrupt transition, particularly regarding employment arbitration, was normative and often anecdotal. Lisa Amsler was the first scholar to investigate empirically whether, under what circumstances, and how employment arbitration might systematically advantage one particular class of parties (typically employers) over another class of parties (typically employees). Professor Amsler's legacy is both her long-term study of how employment arbitration works *in practice* (as opposed to normative theory) and on inspiring scholars like Alex Colvin and Mark Gough to continue expanding on her empirical work. This comment locates Professor Amsler's groundbreaking scholarship within the historical framework of the Supreme Court's jurisprudence on labor and employment arbitration

Starting at the beginning, under common law, an arbitration agreement was revocable by either party any time before the arbitrator issued an award. However, the 1925 Federal Arbitration Act (FAA) required courts to enforce arbitration agreements related to commerce and maritime transactions. Nonetheless, in the 1953 decision of *Wilko v. Swan*, the Supreme Court refused to enforce an arbitration clause in a dispute involving securities law. Lower federal courts routinely interpreted *Wilko* to mean arbitration agreements involving statutory claims were unenforceable.

A different rule, however, applied to arbitration agreements in collective bargaining agreements. Four years after *Wilko*, the Supreme Court in *Textile Workers Union v. Lincoln Mills* held that federal courts could enforce such arbitration clauses, though the Court relied on Section 301 of the Labor-Management Relations Act of 1947 (LMRA), not the FAA, for this holding. In the 1960 *Steelworkers* Trilogy, the Court strongly endorsed arbitration for resolving collective bargaining disputes, again relying on the LMRA and distinguishing *Wilko* because of the unique context of labor relations. Whereas *Wilko* assumed the inadequacy of arbitrators and arbitral procedures for resolving statutory claims, the *Steelworkers* Court found labor arbitrators were more experienced and competent on labor issues than "the ablest judge."

Richard Bales, *The Historical Context of Lisa Blomgren Amsler's Empirical Work on Employment Arbitration* In: *Discussions in Dispute Resolution*. Edited by: Art Hinshaw, Andrea Kupfer Schneider, and Sarah Rudolph Cole, Oxford University Press (2021).
 DOI: 10.1093/oso/9780197513248.003.0059

In 1964, Congress enacted Title VII, which prohibited employment discrimination based on race, color, religion, sex, and national origin; subsequent federal and state statutes extended legal protection to, among other classifications, age, pregnancy, disability, sexual orientation, and gender identity. This expansion in employment rights was accompanied by a dramatic increase in litigated employment claims (Summers 1988), and an issue soon arose over whether these new rights were arbitrable labor claims or nonarbitrable statutory claims. The Supreme Court initially leaned toward the latter, when it ruled in the 1974 case of *Alexander v. Gardner-Denver Co.* that an employee's arbitration of a just-cause claim under a labor agreement did not foreclose subsequent litigation of a statutory discrimination claim based on the same facts. The Court denigrated arbitration as a forum for resolving statutory employment claims.

However, in the 1985–89 *Mitsubishi* Trilogy, the Court overruled *Wilko* and enforced arbitration agreements covering antitrust, securities, and racketeering laws. In these cases, the Court interpreted the FAA as creating a presumption that statutory claims are arbitrable, and made this presumption rebuttable only upon a showing by the party opposing arbitration that Congress specifically intended otherwise. This was the start of a long series of Supreme Court cases strongly favoring arbitration, not only for commercial claims but also for employment and consumer claims. One of the more important of these cases was *Gilmer v. Interstate/Johnson Lane Corporation*, in which the Court held that the FAA permitted an employer to require a nonunion employee to arbitrate rather than litigate a federal age discrimination claim pursuant to a predispute arbitration agreement the employee had been required to sign as a condition of employment.

Early scholarly debate over employment arbitration was fiercely partisan. Proponents, such as Samuel Estreicher, argued that arbitration provided dispute resolution access to low- and middle-income employees who otherwise would not find legal representation and for whom judicial resolution therefore was unavailable (Estreicher, pp. 563–64). Critics, such as Katherine Van Wezel Stone, argued that arbitration was a form of second-class justice, the modern equivalent of the yellow-dog contract, particularly when employers foisted lopsided agreements upon employees whose only alternative was quitting (Van Wezel Stone 1017). Jean Sternlight, whose article is discussed in this volume, was one of the first to recognize that problems with employment arbitration were carrying over into consumer arbitration.

This early debate over employment arbitration occurred in a vacuum, with both proponents and critics making policy arguments devoid of empirical support. Professor Amsler's *Employment Arbitration: The Repeat Player Effect* was (and is) seminal not just because of what she found substantively but also because it was the first article to take a dataset of cases decided under the AAA Employment Dispute Resolution Rules and statistically analyze the outcomes. This research provided her and like-minded normative scholars with the tools they needed to show that the often pernicious effects of arbitration were not just theoretical and "in the air," but visited "on the ground" upon real people (such as employees and consumers) who often lacked the bargaining power to protect themselves from more powerful actors such as employers and companies.

Not only was Professor Amsler's article first, but more importantly, it inspired two generations (and counting) of scholars to follow in her footsteps, such as Theodore

Eisenberg and Elizabeth Hill, Michael H. LeRoy and Peter Feuille, Alexander Colvin, and Mark Gough. Professor Amsler herself continued to conduct empirical research on employment arbitration and mediation as part of a broader research agenda focusing on dispute-resolution design.

My own research remained steadfastly normative, but my normative analyses drew (and continue to draw) on the empirical work of Amsler and the empiricists she inspired. But perhaps the truest sign of Amsler's influence is that her work changed the discourse, in at least three different ways.

First, scholarship on the topic became more clearly focused. Some of the early arguments against arbitration—such as the theory that arbitrators would be unduly influenced by who paid them (as compared to who selected them)—receded as the arguments were found to lack empirical support. Scholars instead focused on issues like the disparity in damage awards in arbitration compared to litigation—issues that empirical research by Amsler and others demonstrated were more salient.

Second, Amsler's empirical findings prompted many normative scholars to rethink the positions for which they had previously advocated. The work of many early arbitration proponents—myself included—became less enthusiastic and more skeptical. The Supreme Court's averment that arbitration is simply an alternative forum fissured when Amsler showed that the change in forum had a real, measurable effect on case outcomes.

Third, the work of many normative scholars writing in this field (including my own) became far more specific and nuanced than it would have been absent Amsler's pioneering scholarship. Instead of relying, for example, on theoretical arguments for why an arbitrator might tend to favor the party (almost always the employer) who might hire him/her for the next case, scholars now were able to cite to real empirical evidence of a repeat-player effect. Instead of describing how structural bias might theoretically arise in arbitration, now we were able to describe how it had arisen and how the law might best respond. Amsler has realized every scholars' dream—she has had a lasting impact on the future scholarship of her research focus.

References

Richard A. Bales, *Contract Formation Issues in Employment Arbitration*, 44 Brandeis L.J. 415 (2006).

Richard A. Bales, *A Normative Consideration of Employment Arbitration at Gilmer's Quinceañera*, 81 Tulane L. Rev. 331 (2006).

Samuel Estreicher, *Saturns for Rickshaws: The Stakes in the Debate over Predispute Employment Arbitration Agreements*, 16 Ohio St. J. on Disp. Resol. 559 (2001).

Katherine Van Wezel Stone, *Mandatory Arbitration of Individual Employment Rights: The Yellow-Dog Contract of the 1990s*, 73 Denv. U. L. Rev. 1017 (1996).

Clyde W. Summers, *Labor Law as the Century Turns: A Changing of the Guard*, 67 Neb. L. Rev. 7 (1988).

Why the Haves Come Out Further and Further Ahead: The Repeat Player Effect, Control over Dispute System Design, and Justice

Lisa Blomgren Amsler

Let's start at the beginning of the yellow brick road that led to the *Repeat Player Effect* paper. I skipped my senior year of high school to attend a women's college (Smith) and double-majored in ancient Greek and philosophy, on account of which (cf. *Sleepless in Seattle* (Rosie O'Donnell as Becky relating how she ended up in a relationship with Rick "on account of the tree guy")) I fell in love with Hegel and Heraclitus. Hegel taught me about dynamic systems that functioned through thesis, antithesis, and synthesis, on account of which I fell in love with labor law. Heraclitus taught me you can never step in the same river twice as it is always changing, on account of which after ten years practicing labor law representing public sector management, I (eventually) became an academic in an interdisciplinary social science school. There, my research mentor for tenure said, "Study what you know," on account of which I studied arbitration. I thought I knew arbitration—a fair and balanced process produced by that wonderful Hegelian dialectic of workplace democracy. It was great to provide arbitration to nonunion employees, right?

In other words, when I started research on the repeat player effect, I was a former management labor lawyer and partner of Shipman & Goodwin (now the largest law firm in Connecticut), and a new arbitrator on both the American Arbitration Association (AAA) and Federal Mediation and Conciliation Service (FMCS) labor panels. I assumed my research would debunk criticisms of non-union employment arbitration.

Since other researchers on the repeat player effect have now pulled back the curtain revealing that little man pulling the fake wizard's strings, my thinking has evolved considerably. Initially, I identified the problem as differences in dispute system design (DSD). Who are the arbitrators? Experts in labor relations or management employment lawyers? Then it was who has *control* over DSD? Labor and management negotiating together, management acting unilaterally, or some third party? Were individual components of the DSD itself (like who pays filing and arbitrator fees, cost shifting of management attorney fees to employees, and limited discovery) the problems? Literature on DSD and Nobel Laureate and political economist Elinor Ostrom's (2005) work on institutional design help explain how these structural changes can act as independent variables affecting substantive outcomes. Ostrom identifies variables that characterize the action arena and relate to DSD, including participants, their

Lisa Blomgren Amsler, *Why the Haves Come Out Further and Further Ahead: The Repeat Player Effect, Control over Dispute System Design, and Justice* In: *Discussions in Dispute Resolution.* Edited by: Art Hinshaw, Andrea Kupfer Schneider, and Sarah Rudolph Cole, Oxford University Press (2021). © Oxford University Press. DOI: 10.1093/oso/9780197513248.003.0060

positions, potential outcomes, action-outcome linkages, the control that participants exercise, types of information generated; and the costs and benefits assigned to actions and outcomes (see discussion of Ostrom in Amsler, Martinez, & Smith 2020). These apply differently between mandatory arbitration and labor arbitration, especially as to the control that participants exercise.

However, while these structural features contribute to the pattern of employer victories, they do not tell the whole story. In her comments in this book, Professor Sternlight has documented how the pro-business majority of the US Supreme Court has reinterpreted the Federal Arbitration Act (FAA) to authorize mandatory arbitration to deprive workers of voice in the justice system, the right to engage in collective action, and economic power. The Court approved mandatory employment arbitration under the FAA as a tool for corporations to gut public law by minimizing enforcement to reduce costs on companies, just as the Social Darwinist Supreme Court used "freedom of contract" to strike down worker protection laws in the late nineteenth century.

After World War II, Milton Friedman led a wholesale strategy of political economy to undo the New Deal. Aided by the University of Chicago school of thought, this group successfully lobbied to change law and policy based on Friedman's arguments for: (1) an individual's freedom of choice to maximize utility; (2) a nation's measure of success as national wealth based on utility its individual members value; and (3) limited government to establish and protect free markets as the best means possible for rational, self-interested individuals to maximize aggregate wealth. (For a brief history, see President Larry Kramer's Memorandum to the William and Flora Hewlett Foundation Board of Directors, https://hewlett.org/wp-content/uploads/2018/04/Beyond-Neoliberalism-Public-Board-Memo.pdf.)

Nowhere in Friedman's frame are interests of society in the common or public good. In the 1970s, soon-to-be Supreme Court Associate Justice Lewis Powell led the US Chamber of Commerce to change from a bipartisan policy group to a right-wing lobbying entity working to change the laws and rules underpinning our democracy to favor corporate influence and power. It also actively and successfully sought Supreme Court appointees who would support this agenda. The success of this strategy has (re-)created the Gilded Age's extreme income inequality in the United States by allowing the top 10 percent to accumulate the great majority of the wealth generated through less regulated capitalism and demonizing government. It has systematically undermined enforcement of public law protecting people as employees or consumers. The Fair Labor Standards Act's (FLSA's) minimum wage protects almost all workers; Congress enacted it during the Great Depression. This was collective decision-making by citizens electing representatives in a democracy. Mandatory arbitration makes it hard to enforce the FLSA; it suppresses unknown numbers of claims by employees who have been misclassified as independent contractors or exempt employees who are denied overtime. Political scientists have recently proven that, at present, average US citizens have no impact on what Congress adopts as policy; elites and corporate interest groups have all the influence.

Here is an example of how they change the system with law: millennials now carry over $1.5 trillion dollars of student loan debt ("Student debt just hit $1.5 trillion," https://www.marketwatch.com/story/student-debt-just-hit-15-trillion-2018-05-08), often from fraudulent for-profit "educational" institutions, with mandatory arbitration clauses embedded in loan documents. On a Friedman analysis, eighteen-year-olds maximized their individual utility by using borrowed funds to attend college for an education that would allow them to earn more money. That high schoolers had no understanding of how the law or the debt system worked is irrelevant; the invisible hand of the minimally regulated free market would in theory sort things out. However, lenders got Congress to exclude student loans from bankruptcy. The Supreme Court allows lenders to use arbitration clauses under the FAA that forbid class actions.

Millennials with student loan debt now struggle for fewer well-paying jobs to pay back this debt, while corporations buy back stock and automate production, eliminating the middle class. Who has influence and power over making law and rules, the independent variables that shape how institutions work? Students, bound to arbitrate claims individually, cannot engage in class actions to challenge the terms of the debt or whether its interest rates are unreasonable in light a decade of low rates set by the Federal Reserve.

However, *it need not stay this way*. The FAA is legislation; it is not a provision of the US Constitution. While the members of the Supreme Court may be locked into a pro-corporate majority for the next generation, members of Congress are not. Just because Congress has failed to amend the FAA or pass the proposed Arbitration Fairness Act—*yet*—does not mean it is impossible.

Recent leading philosophers write and teach about the role of justice in shaping society. Amartya Sen argues for defining justice in terms of "the lives that people manage—or do not manage—to live," or "a realized actuality" (2009, p. 18). He rejects defining justice as the design of supposedly ideal social arrangements and institutions shaped by Friedman or other theories.

Michael Sandel describes three historic approaches to justice (paraphrased here): (1) maximizing utility or welfare (utilitarian, or the greatest happiness for the greatest number); (2) respecting freedom of choice, either libertarian (the actual choices people make in a free market) or liberal egalitarian (hypothetical choices people would make in an original position of equality); and (3) his view, which is "cultivating virtue and reasoning about the common good" (2009, p. 260). He concludes, "A just society can't be achieved simply by maximizing utility or by securing freedom of choice. To achieve a just society, we must reason together about the meaning of the good life, and to create a public culture hospitable to the disagreements that will inevitably arise" (p. 261).

Both scholars have conceptions of justice that incorporate people's voices, as in democracy. In other words, justice takes form in arbitration as a DSD when people—not just elites or corporate interest groups—cultivate virtue and reason together to shape it for the common good based on their lived reality.

Electing the right people to Congress and the presidency could fix this. Over 90 percent of the US voters agree on gun policies like more stringent universal background checks. What it takes to enact these is electing representatives who will vote for them and presidents who will sign the legislation. There are growing movements to strengthen democracy from the bottom up (Lappe & Eichen 2017). Arbitration is arcane to most Americans. Those of us who understand how this system works must pass on what we have learned; collectively, we can make rules and laws a political issue and structure our society to be fair and just.

Acknowledgments: I am deeply grateful for the important contributions to scholarship on arbitration made by commentators Professors Bales, Colvin, and Malin. Marty Malin had just founded a much-needed new law review (*Employee Rights and Employment Policy Journal*), unique in that it was refereed, when I submitted the *Repeat Player Effect* article to its first issue for publication. Alex Colvin's mentor, David Lipsky, also served informally as mine after I first presented early analyses at the Labor and Employment Relations Association (then IRRA) conference in 1997 and 1998. Rick Bales consistently provided me important arbitration law and practice context for employment arbitration. I would also like to thank former AAA Senior Vice President George Friedman, who later served as FINRA Dispute Resolution Director of Arbitration, for his support by providing access to data for the original employment arbitration research. I sent him drafts of the *Repeat Player Effect* paper for review before I presented or published it, and he approved ongoing access to data. The field has greatly benefited from the more rigorous empirical and quantitative research by Professors Colvin, Lamare, Lipsky, Malin, and others who confirmed the repeat player effect's existence, although theories about why vary.

References

Lisa Blomgren Amsler, Janet K. Martinez, & Stephanie E. Smith, Dispute System Design: Preventing, Managing, and Resolving Conflict (2020).

Marc Galanter, *Why the Haves Come Out Ahead: Speculations on the Limits of Legal Change*, 9 Law & Soc'y Rev. 95–160 (1974).

Frances Moore Lappe & Adam Eichen, Daring Democracy: Igniting Power, Meaning, and Connection for the America We Want (2017).

Michael J. Sandel, Justice: What's the Right Thing to Do (2009).

Amartya Sen, The Idea of Justice (2009).

PART 4

DISPUTE RESOLUTION PUBLIC POLICY

Article 4.1

Why the "Haves" Come Out Ahead: Speculations on the Limits of Legal Change

Marc Galanter

9 Law & Society Review 95 (1974)

* * *

I would like to try to put forward some conjectures about the way in which the basic architecture of the legal system creates and limits the possibilities of using the system as a means of redistributive (that is, systemically equalizing) change. Our question, specifically, is, under what conditions can litigation be redistributive, taking litigation in the broadest sense of the presentation of claims to be decided by courts . . .

* * *

I. A Typology of Parties

* * *

Because of differences in their size, differences in the state of the law, and differences in their resources, some of the actors [in society] have many occasions to utilize the courts . . . ; others do so only rarely. We might divide our actors into those claimants who have only occasional recourse to the courts (one-shotters or OS) and repeat players (RP) who are engaged in many similar litigations over time . . .

Let us refine our notion of the RP into an "ideal type" if you will, a unit which has had and anticipates repeated litigation, which has low stakes in the outcome of any one case, and which has the resources to pursue its long-run interests . . . An OS, on the other hand, is a unit whose claims are too large (relative to his size) or too small (relative to the cost of remedies) to be managed routinely and rationally.

We would expect an RP to play the litigation game differently from an OS. Let us consider some of his advantages:

(1) RPs, having done it before, have advance intelligence . . . It is the RP who writes the form contract, requires the security deposit, and the like.

Marc Galanter, *Why the "Haves" Come Out Ahead: Speculations on the Limits of Legal Change* In: *Discussions in Dispute Resolution*. Edited by: Art Hinshaw, Andrea Kupfer Schneider, and Sarah Rudolph Cole, Oxford University Press (2021).
 DOI: 10.1093/oso/9780197513248.003.0061

(2) RPs develop expertise and have ready access to specialists. They enjoy economies of scale and have low startup costs for any case.

* * *

(5) RPs can play the odds. The larger the matter at issue looms for OS, the more likely he is to adopt a minimax strategy (minimize the probability of maximum loss) … Assuming that the stakes are relatively smaller for RPs, they can adopt strategies calculated to maximize gain over a long series of cases …

(6) RPs can play for rules as well as immediate gains. First, it pays an RP to expend resources in influencing the making of the relevant rules by such methods as lobbying …

(7) RPs can also play for rules in litigation itself, whereas an OS is unlikely to … For the RP … anything that will favorably influence the outcomes of future cases is a worthwhile result …

… We would then expect RPs to "settle" cases where they expected unfavorable rule outcomes … RPs can select to adjudicate (or appeal) those cases which they regard as most likely to produce favorable rules …

* * *

… What this analysis does is to define a position of advantage in the configuration of contending parties … and to have their other advantages reinforced and augmented thereby. This position of advantage is one of the ways in which a legal system formally neutral as between "haves" and "have-nots" may perpetuate and augment the advantages of the former.

* * *

II. Lawyers

… Parties who have lawyers do better. Lawyers are themselves RPs … We might assume that RPs … who can buy legal services more steadily, in larger quantities, in bulk (by retainer) and at higher rates, would get services of better quality …

* * *

… Most specializations cater to the needs of particular kinds of RPs. Those specialists who service OSs have some distinctive features:

First, they tend to make up the "lower echelons" of the legal profession. Compared to the lawyers who provide services to RPs, lawyers in these specialties tend to be drawn from lower socio-economic origins, to have attended local, proprietary or part-time law schools, to practice alone rather than in large firms, and to possess low prestige within the profession …

* * *

Third, the episodic and isolated nature of the relationship with particular OS clients tends to elicit a stereotyped and uncreative brand of legal services . . .

* * *

Fourth, . . . these specialists have problems in developing optimizing strategies. What might be good strategy for an insurance company lawyer or prosecutor trading off some cases for gains on others—is branded as unethical when done by a criminal defense or personal injury plaintiff lawyer. It is not permissible for him to play his series of OSs as if they constituted a single RP.

* * *

The existence of a specialized bar on the OS side should overcome the gap in expertise, allow some economies of scale, provide for bargaining commitment and personal familiarity. But this is short of overcoming the fundamental strategic advantages of RPs--their capacity to structure the transaction, play the odds, and influence rule-development and enforcement policy.

* * *

III. Institutional Facilities

[RPs' strategic advantages] are related to the advantages conferred by the basic features of the institutional facilities for the handling of claims: passivity and overload.

These institutions are passive, . . . they must be mobilized by the claimant . . . Parties are treated as if they were equally endowed with economic resources, investigative opportunities and legal skills . . . [T]he broader the delegation to the parties, the greater the advantage conferred on the wealthier, more experienced and better organized. [These advantages] are accentuated by the chronic overload which typically characterizes these institutions . . . In several ways overload creates pressures on claimants to settle rather than to adjudicate:

(a) by causing delay (thereby discounting the value of recovery);
(b) by raising costs (of keeping the case alive);
(c) by inducing institutional incumbents to place a high value on clearing dockets, discouraging full-dress adjudication in favor of bargaining, stereotyping and routine processing;

* * *

Thus, overload increases the cost and risk of adjudicating and shields existing rules from challenge, diminishing opportunities for rule-change. This tends to favor the beneficiaries of existing rules.

* * *

V. Alternatives to the Official System

... Our analysis should consider the relationship of the characteristics of the total official litigation system to its use vis-a-vis the alternatives. [These include]:

* * *

(3) Resort to some unofficial control system ... in which disputes are handled outside the official litigation system. Here we should distinguish (a) those dispute-settlement systems which are normatively and institutionally appended to the official system ... from (b) those settlement systems which are relatively independent in norms and sanctions ...

What we might call the "appended" settlement systems merge imperceptibly into the official litigation system ... We find a continuum from situations where parties settle among themselves with an eye to the official rules and sanctions, through situations where official intervention is invoked, to those in which settlement is supervised and/or imposed by officials, to full-dress adjudication. All along this line the sanction is supplied by the official system ... and the norms or rules applied are a version of the official rules, although discounted for transaction costs and distorted by their selective use for the purposes of the parties.

* * *

VI. Strategies for Reform

Our categorization ... suggests a typology of strategies for "reform" (taken here to mean equalization-conferring relative advantage on those who did not enjoy it before.) ...

* * *

A. Rule-change

* * *

Litigation ... has a flavor of equality. The parties are "equal before the law" ... Thus, litigation is a particularly tempting arena for "have-nots," including those seeking rule change ...

* * *

Rule-change may make use of the courts more attractive to "have-nots." ... [I]t may stimulate organization, rally and encourage litigants. It may directly redistribute symbolic rewards to "havenots" (or their champions). But tangible rewards do not always follow symbolic ones . . .

* * *

D. Reorganization of Parties

The reform envisaged here is the organization of "have-not" parties . . . into coherent groups that have the ability to act in a coordinated fashion, play longrun strategies, benefit from high-grade legal services, and so forth.

One can imagine various ways in which OSs might be aggregated into RPs. They include (1) the membership association-bargaining agent [i.e., unions]; (2) the assignee-manager of fragmentary rights (performing rights associations like ASCAP); (3) the interest group-sponsor [i.e., NAACP or ACLU]. All of these forms involve upgrading capacities for managing claims by gathering and utilizing information, achieving continuity and persistence, employing expertise, exercising bargaining skill and so forth . . .

* * *

Reform and the Rest of the Iceberg

. . . How might [these suggested reforms] affect the rest of our legal iceberg?

We would expect more use of the official system. Those who opted for inaction because of information or cost barriers and those who "settled" at discount rates in one of the "appended" systems would in many instances find it to their advantage to use the official system. The appended systems, insofar as they are built on the costs of resort to the official system, would either be abandoned or the outcomes produced would move to approximate closely those produced by adjudication.

On the other hand, our reforms would, by organizing OSs, create many situations in which both parties were organized to pursue their long-run interest in the litigation arena . . .

Thus we would expect our reforms to produce a dual movement: the official and its appended systems would be "legalized" while the proliferation of private systems would "delegalize" many relationships . . .

* * *

Delegalization . . . would permit many relationships to be regulated by norms and understandings that departed from the official rules . . . On the other hand, the "legalization" of the official and appended systems would amount to the collapse of species of pluralism and decentralization that are endemic [in the legal system]. The current prevalence of appended and private remedy systems reflects the inefficiency, cumbersomeness and costliness of using the official system ...

* * *

Implications for Reform: The Role of Lawyers

* * *

... Litigation then is unlikely to shape decisively the distribution of power in society...

* * *

The thrust of our analysis is that changes at the level of parties are most likely to generate changes at other levels ... Rule changes which relate directly to the strategic position of the parties by facilitating organization, increasing the supply of legal services (where these in turn provide a focus for articulating and organizing common interests) and increasing the costs of opponents—for instance authorization of class action suits, award of attorneys fees and costs, award of provisional remedies—these are the most powerful fulcrum for change ...

The contribution of the lawyer to redistributive social change, then, depends upon the organization and culture of the legal profession ... The more that lawyers view themselves exclusively as courtroom advocates ... the less likely they are to serve as agents of redistributive change ...

Comments

For Pragmatic Romanticism in Law and Dispute Resolution: Reflections on Galanter's Remarkably Realistic Analysis of Why the Have-Nots Come Out Behind

John Lande

The 1960s was a time of great hope for many Americans seeking to redress historic injustices to make a better world. They were inspired by Warren Court decisions such as *Brown v. Board of Education*, President Lyndon B. Johnson's Great Society legislation, and public interest lawyers bringing impact litigation and representing disadvantaged populations. These developments inspired tremendous optimism that law and litigation would be vital instruments of social progress.

This was the context in which Marc Galanter wrote his classic article, *Why the "Haves" Come Out Ahead*. Based on a remarkably realistic review of mechanisms advantaging the "haves" in society, he provided a cautionary analysis of potential strategies that were more and less likely to help "have-nots." Inspirational images of advocates like Ralph Nader created unrealistic expectations of the potential for more law, courts, and lawyers to promote social progress. Galanter argued that while these factors could be useful in such efforts, organizing "one-shotters" (the "have-nots") into repeat-players (the "haves") was key. Without this transformation of the parties, repeat-players generally would be able to thwart one-shotters' legal strategies. Based on this analysis, he suggested plausible strategies for helping have-nots.

Galanter essentially cautioned against what Carrie Menkel-Meadow later called "litigation romanticism" (1995, p. 1172). Romantic views are idealistic, highlighting positive qualities of a subject, often ignoring its problems. Galanter critiqued the assumptions of proponents of public interest law who sought to help have-nots but did not recognize important realities of power relationships in society. Like Galanter, Menkel-Meadow favors romanticism about some things, including the legal system, and she argued that "to love an idea or institution realistically we need to see the object of our love as it really is."

This comment applies that perspective to alternative dispute resolution (ADR) romantics, calling on us to see our beloved ADR as it really is. So we absolutely should not abandon our idealistic hopes or efforts to realize them. Rather, we should be very pragmatic about understanding the real world and potential strategies to make it better.

John Lande, *For Pragmatic Romanticism in Law and Dispute Resolution: Reflections on Galanter's Remarkably Realistic Analysis of Why the Have-Nots Come Out Behind* In: *Discussions in Dispute Resolution*. Edited by: Art Hinshaw, Andrea Kupfer Schneider, and Sarah Rudolph Cole, Oxford University Press (2021).
DOI: 10.1093/oso/9780197513248.003.0062

I. Litigation Romanticism

Many of us in the legal and dispute resolution communities care deeply about the welfare of others, especially have-nots. Being passionate, it is easy to engage in unrealistic wishful thinking. Some litigation romanticists celebrate courts' implementation of the values of constitutional and statutory law by judges who can be held accountable through requirements to articulate their reasoning and appellate review. Romanticists praise adjudication for its procedural safeguards against prejudice including lifetime or lengthy appointment of neutral judges and the ethical codes that constrain their behavior. Due process protections require notice and opportunity to be heard. Parties are entitled to legal representation and their lawyers must sign papers filed in court certifying that they are not filed for improper purposes. Courts make orders establishing pretrial and trial procedures, and rules of evidence preclude or limit admission of prejudicial evidence. Procedural rules equalize access to information, which is presented publicly.

While these romanticists sometimes acknowledge flaws in the legal system, they have great faith that court adjudication is the best form of dispute resolution for maintaining social norms and protecting have-nots in society. These romanticists suggest that courts impartially dispense justice, largely immune from the power dynamics animating much litigation. They mostly ignore the reality that the legal system provides the "haves" have numerous mechanisms for taking advantage of "have-nots."

The legal system sometimes does live up to its ideals. But the systematic protections that romanticists trumpet often have proven ineffective to overcome powerful forces undermining those ideals, as Galanter's analysis demonstrates. These are not merely idiosyncratic failures—they are the result of systemic forces.

Jeffrey Seul (2004) provided a thorough rebuttal to litigation romanticists' arguments, showing that court adjudication often is a flawed mechanism for bringing legal values into reality while settlement sometimes does that better. Analyzing both the process of reaching court decisions as well as troubling court decisions themselves, Seul illustrated why we should be cautious about extolling categorical virtues of adjudication. Conversely, he demonstrated that negotiation sometimes advances litigation romanticists' ideals in ways that courts cannot, especially when the process involves true moral deliberation. This is not to suggest that negotiation is generally better than court adjudication as a process. Rather, the point is that we should be nuanced and realistic in our assessments of all dispute resolution processes rather than relying on overbroad generalizations based on our predispositions.

II. ADR Romanticism

Not surprisingly, the ADR movement has our own romantics. We want to promote ideals of self-determination, collaborative decision-making (rather than processes based on power or counterproductive legal processes), respectful interaction, efficiency, and outcomes tailored to parties' values and interests. We not only seek to improve the handling of individual cases, we also aspire to improve dispute resolution processes and outcomes at a societal level. Like litigation romanticists, we sometimes view our favored approaches through rose-colored glasses.

Some ADR proponents have had the more ambitious goal of creating a new and better system of justice. For example, the San Francisco Community Boards Program had the most idealistic ambitions, seeking to create an alternative to the government-run legal system. Community Boards created local forums providing informal, non-professional, and nonadversarial processes to make decisions based on community norms. These local boards were intended to promote social change, helping communities take control from the legal system. The new system would be of and by have-not groups in society. Although community mediation programs still handle disputes, programs like the San Francisco Community Board Program have not fulfilled their goals of creating truly autonomous community institutions displacing the legal system (Merry & Milner 1993).

In a more case-by-case framework, Frank Sander's (1976) multi-door courthouse reflects a more modest romantic ADR vision. It contemplated a technocratic process in which court clerks would analyze characteristics of each case at the outset of litigation (such as the nature of dispute, relationship between the parties, and amount in dispute) and direct litigants to the most appropriate dispute resolution process. This idea would take advantage of the growing array of dispute resolution processes and the ideal of "fitting the forum to the fuss." Yet, after initial experiments with multi-door courthouses, courts have not created the infrastructure for carefully analyzing cases nor is there an accepted methodology for directing cases to different processes. Instead, mediation has become the default alternative to litigation-as-usual. Indeed, mediation has become so routine that, in some courts, litigation has been transformed into what I have described elsewhere as a legalized "liti-mediation" process in which mediation is a standard step in litigation (Lande 1997, p. 841).

In the romantic vision of ADR, court-connected ADR has not been co-opted by the deeply engrained adversarial culture of the legal system. Such co-optation, however, runs throughout the history of ADR innovations, including commercial and labor arbitration, workers compensation, juvenile and family courts, small claims courts, court-connected arbitration and mediation, and collaborative law. When introduced, each of these innovations was seen as a challenge to the legal status quo. Over time, the legal system assimilated them, altering them in a process of "creeping legalism" so they became institutionalized as normal parts of the legal system. These innovations altered the legal system to some degree, though its fundamental character has endured.

Even if mediation could not transform society or litigation, some mediators and academics claimed that mediators could manage the process to "equalize" or "balance" the power between parties. This idea was so appealing that it was embodied in some statutes, but even on its face, it doesn't withstand cursory scrutiny. Consider the extreme example of a one-shotter with a modest claim against a Fortune 500 company. The company probably would not agree to mediate, and, if it did, there is little that a mediator could do to alter the fundamental power relationship. Even in disputes with apparently more balanced power relationships, power dynamics are so complex that it is not credible that mediators could fully understand the dynamics let alone equalize them as if on the iconic scales of justice. Galanter's "Haves" analysis applies to processes other than litigation and it provides a helpful explanation of the folly of this idea.

Some ADR romantics make broad empirical claims that are contradicted by the evidence. Perhaps most egregious is the confident assertion that mediation saves time and money as if this was a well-known scientific fact. The evidence, however, is quite mixed and does not support a general claim of time and cost savings (Wissler 2004). In general, parties who mediate probably do save time and money as compared to what would happen if they went to trial, but the vast majority of cases are resolved before trial. In some of the latter cases, using mediation actually can increase the time and expense, especially if it is conducted late in litigation.

Similarly, people sometimes make exaggerated claims about confidentiality in mediation. Mediators frequently promise that they won't disclose information to one side that they receive in a private meeting with the other side. While most mediators probably do not explicitly make unauthorized disclosures, their questions often give revealing hints about confidential information they committed to protect. So our claims of confidentiality can be very misleading.

III. Conclusion

Galanter's lesson in this article is not to abandon romanticism. Although his writing style is not romantic, his laudable goal is to help have-nots gain greater social influence and benefits by making them more like the "haves." This might be called "pragmatic romanticism." While some romantics might aim to achieve complete equality, pragmatic romantics, recognizing the inevitability of some inequality, strategize to achieve the best realistically achievable advantages for have-nots. Galanter's article illustrates a clear-eyed view of the world, unbiased (as much as possible) by romantic aspirations. This is important so that idealists can develop realistic expectations, make real progress, and persist in long-term efforts to improve our communities.

For ADR romantics to apply this approach, we must see ADR as it really is. In the legal-oriented ADR context, this involves a careful analysis of the interests of the repeat-players in the legal system including, but not limited to, judges and lawyers. For them, a particularly important interest may be to act consistent with their desired individual and institutional identities. For ADR romantics to achieve our goals, we must understand situations as accurately as possible so that we can help devise strategies to minimize the problematic effects of creeping legalism on ADR processes. This same analytical stance should be applied in efforts to improve other institutions, such as businesses. We should not surrender our ideals or ideas to improve society. Rather, we should be realistic and pragmatic in our efforts to promote them.

This is much harder than it sounds. Understandably, people are strongly attached to their favored visions. Our brains often trick us into seeing what we want to see rather than what is in front of us. As Galanter would tell us, we need to let go of some cherished theories that don't fit the real world very well so that we can advance our deepest ideals with more realistic theories.

References

John Lande, *How Will Lawyering and Mediation Practices Transform Each Other?*, 24 FLA. ST. U. L. REV. 839–901 (1997).

Carrie Menkel-Meadow, *Ethics and the Settlements of Mass Torts: When the Rules Meet the Road*, 80 CORNELL L. REV. 1159–221 (1995).

SALLY ENGLE MERRY & NEAL MILNER, THE POSSIBILITY OF POPULAR JUSTICE: A CASE STUDY OF COMMUNITY MEDIATION IN THE UNITED STATES (1993).

Frank E.A. Sander, *Varieties of Dispute Processing*, 70 F.R.D. 111–34 (1976).

Jeffrey R. Seul, *Settling Significant Cases*, 79 WASH. L. REV. 881–968 (2004).

Roselle Wissler, *The Effectiveness of Court-Connected Dispute Resolution in Civil Cases*, 22 CONFLICT RESOL. Q. 55–88 (2004).

A Prescient Warning of the Vulnerabilities in ADR

Dwight Golann

In a sense Marc Galanter's article, *Why the "Haves" Come Out Ahead*, is not about alternative dispute resolution (ADR) at all, in that it applies concepts and advocates goals and tactics unrelated, and even opposed to, modern concepts of dispute resolution. The article is seminal, however, because it identifies important vulnerabilities in ADR processes and offers prescient warnings about how they can be manipulated to the detriment of less advantaged members of American society.

Professor Galanter's article is "non-ADR," first, in its goals. Galanter is clear that his purpose is to develop strategies that disadvantaged persons can use to fight the legal advantages accrued by more powerful actors (p. 95). He divides American society into two groups, those who use the legal system repeatedly and are able to influence laws and court processes, particularly large corporations ("repeat players"), and those who interact with legal institutions only occasionally and have little power to affect them ("one-shot players") (p. 97). Galanter then provides a pathbreaking analysis of how repeat players use their resources and interactions with the courts and the political system to manipulate rules, processes, and policies to the disadvantage of weaker one-shot players. Galanter goes on to suggest strategies that one-shot players can use to counteract their adversaries' efforts and gain power for themselves.

The ADR movement has very different goals. Writers and teachers typically describe the core values of dispute resolution as to facilitate participants' ability to exercise self-determination and help them realize personal interests and preferences. ADR is not generally thought of as a method to help some gain power versus others or change the social order.

Galanter also differs from ADR scholars over tactics. Most forms of negotiation and mediation have as their object a consensual agreement. Galanter, however, suggests that settlements of legal disputes are often undesirable, because they can be manipulated by repeat players to maintain their social power (p. 101–2). In devaluing settlement Galanter also appears to reject other concepts emphasized in ADR, such as reconciliation and peace.

In place of settlement, Galanter advocates adjudication as the best vehicle for one-shot players to achieve social change: "Our question, specifically, is under what conditions can litigation be redistributive . . ." (p. 95). ADR processes have little place in such a campaign: although negotiation and mediation can be used to change the status quo, for instance, through "reg-neg" administrative rulemaking, they do not involve adjudication at all. Arbitration does, but it is poorly designed to achieve social change because repeat players cannot be compelled to enter the process and arbitral decisions generally do not apply to anyone other than the immediate parties.

Dwight Golann, *A Prescient Warning of the Vulnerabilities in ADR* In: *Discussions in Dispute Resolution.* Edited by: Art Hinshaw, Andrea Kupfer Schneider, and Sarah Rudolph Cole, Oxford University Press (2021).
DOI: 10.1093/oso/9780197513248.003.0063

Why the "Haves" Come Out Ahead also clashes with modern ADR teaching in the meaning it gives to key terms. Galanter recognizes, for instance, that repeat and one-shot players have interests, but he sees them as opposed rather than complementary (p. 96). Galanter characterizes repeat/one-shot interactions as zero-sum contests, which, he argues convincingly, are usually won by the strong. He recognizes that players of similar status, such as neighborhood residents and interdependent companies, may, although he does not say so explicitly, accommodate each other in ways that resemble interest-based bargaining (p. 130). But the idea that an employee might negotiate cooperatively with an employer to design creative terms of separation, or that a business would voluntarily create a balanced complaint-resolution process for its customers, is foreign to his argument.

Galanter would also not agree with the concept that parties should seek to negotiate according to objective standards (Fisher, Ury, & Patton, pp. 85–87). He instead treats rules merely as tools which repeat players manipulate—"play"—to exploit one-shot players—and that one-shotters would presumably use against repeaters if they could (p. 100). Finally, while ADR teaching emphasizes emotions and cognitive forces as key explanators of disputants' behavior, Galanter treats players as entirely rational actors, discussing irrationality only as a tactic which a player might use to unsettle an opponent (p. 99 n.10).

It's not surprising, then, that Galanter's ideas for reform do not include the use of ADR. To change the distribution of power in a society, he argues, one-shot players should organize into large units, for example, unions, which can accumulate knowledge and power and thus manipulate legal rules against repeaters. Alternatively, he says, they might obtain, through the mechanism of class actions, lawyers with the resources needed to litigate effectively on their behalf (pp. 141–43).

Although *Why the "Haves" Come Out Ahead* does not endorse ADR goals or apply its concepts, the article does offer prescient warnings about how repeat-player "haves" can influence (or distort) processes of dispute resolution, as they do litigation, to gain advantages over "have-nots." Arbitrators who look for "objective" standards to guide their decisions, for example, are likely to apply laws and court decisions that have been influenced by or are the result of repeat players' use of the litigation system. And when parties in litigation follow the advice to weigh settlement offers against their litigation alternative (Fisher, Ury, & Patton, p. 104), the effect is to try to mirror the very system that Galanter decries.

His concern about the tendency of settlement to reinforce the status quo has also resonated in ADR scholarship. Professor Richard Delgado, for example, wrote, "The movement toward alternative dispute resolution … is an excellent way of seeming to be doing something about intractable social problems while actually doing relatively little … [P]roblems are not faced, responsibility is diffused, grievants are cooled out, while everyone leaves thinking something positive has been done" (Delgado, p. 151).

Galanter also warns about the effect of devolving responsibility for process to the disputants, a key value of ADR: "[T]he broader the delegation to the parties, the greater the advantage conferred on the wealthier, more experienced and better organized party" (pp. 120–21). *Why the "Haves" Come Out Ahead* does not discuss race or culture as factors in the struggle between one-shot and repeat players, for example, whether individual African Americans or Hispanics might have more difficulty than whites in dealing with repeat players. Nor does Galanter probe whether disputants from minority cultures might be more willing to accept unequal outcomes or a neutral's directiveness.

Others, however, have extended Galanter's concerns to these areas: "The formalities of a court trial are calculated to check prejudice.... [They] also encourage minority-race persons to press their claims more forthrightly.... [ADR's] structureless setting and absence of formal rules increase the likelihood of an outcome colored by prejudice, with the result that the haves once again come out ahead ..." (Delgado, p. 154). Empirical studies of ADR have not confirmed, however, whether or not such bias exists in practice (Bachar & Hensler 2017).

Galanter's analysis of how repeat players may "play" adjudicative processes also has parallels in ADR. Corporations and large law firms, for example, can use information gathered over multiple cases to select mediators and arbitrators sympathetic to their arguments, and can offer the prospect of future work to neutrals hungry for cases. One-shotters can sometimes gain access to repeat users through contingent fee arrangements (p. 118). Plaintiff tort attorneys and lawyers who practice before the Financial Industry Regulatory Authority, for instance, acquire knowledge and power as repeat users of neutral services. As Galanter notes, however, in the great bulk of litigation one-shotters appear as defendants rather than plaintiffs (p. 108)—for example businesses' use of small claims courts for debt collection—and such defendants typically lack legal representation either in court or ADR.

Galanter would also predict that repeat players would seek to distort or misuse ADR processes to their advantage. Indeed, after a decades-long campaign waged in the courts and Congress, financial institutions and employers have largely succeeded in using arbitration clauses to cut off consumer and employee access to the courts. See *AT&T Mobility v. Concepcion*, 563 U.S. 333 (2011). Nor would Galanter be surprised that repeat players have used obscure contract clauses to frustrate one of his most important recommendations, that one-shot players accumulate power through class actions (pp. 143, 150). Professor Galanter's discussion of the role of lawyers also helps to explain the evolution of arbitration from a process that emphasized equity and procedural simplicity to one that now resembles the traditional court system (Stipanowich).

Why the "Haves" Come Out Ahead advanced ADR theory in other ways as well. The first was by presenting a more sophisticated definition of the concept of "best alternative to a negotiated agreement." Fisher et al. discuss the concept as if it were a concrete option, for instance a competing offer to buy or sell a car (pp. 103–4). Galanter, by contrast, recognizes that in litigation a party's "alternative" consists a range of possible outcomes, each with a different cost and likelihood of success. The literal meaning of "best" alternative in litigation—winning decisively— is therefore misleading, and should be replaced with "most likely" or "a weighted range" of outcomes.

Another important aspect of the article is its presentation of the concept of how grievances become disputes. Other scholars had noted that potential legal claims often fail to enter the legal system or disappear before adjudication, but Galanter uses the metaphor of an "iceberg" to convey the concept that very few disputes ever attain the visibility of a court case or persist in the formal judicial system (p. 134), and goes on to describe the wide variety of ways in which one-shot players, in particular, are induced to abandon, compromise, or drop their claims. In doing so, Galanter provides a pioneering vision of what we now call the dispute pyramid (Felstiner, Abel, & Sarat, p. 544), as well as a comprehensive explanation of why the pyramid narrows so dramatically at the top.

Although *Why the "Haves" Come Out Ahead* does not embrace key concepts and values of the modern ADR movement, it offers an insightful and prescient explanation of why ADR has not achieved some of the most important dreams of its pioneers.

References

Gilat Bachar & Deborah Hensler, *Does Alternative Dispute Resolution Facilitate Prejudice and Bias? We Still Don't Know*, 70 SMU L. Rev. 817 (2017).

Richard Delgado, *ADR and the Dispossessed: Recent Books About the Deformalization Movement*, 13 Law & Soc. Inquiry 145 (1988).

William L.F. Felstiner, Richard L. Abel, & Austin Sarat, *The Emergence and Transformation of Disputes: Naming, Blaming, and Claiming . . . ,"* 15 Law & Soc'y Rev. 631 (1981).

Roger Fisher, William Ury, & Bruce Patton, Getting to Yes (1991).

Thomas Stipanowich, *Arbitration: The "New Litigation,"* 2010 U. Ill. L. Rev. 1 (2010).

Galanter's Analysis of the "Limits of Legal Change" as Applied to Criminal Cases and Reform

Cynthia Alkon

Marc Galanter's *Why the "Haves" Come Out Ahead: Speculations on the Limits of Legal Change* was not intended to be an in-depth analysis of the criminal legal system. Instead, it asks the reader to look broadly at the legal system to examine what might help decrease inequalities for the have-nots in our society. I will focus on a few of these limitations and the impact (or lack thereof) on criminal legal reform.

I. Some Historical Context

The US criminal legal system in the early 1970s was, in some ways, a more hopeful time for those concerned about defendants' rights. In the previous fifteen years, the Supreme Court had decided a series of landmark criminal procedure cases, including *Gideon v. Wainright* and *Miranda v. Arizona*, which expanded criminal defendants' right to counsel and improved protections surrounding confessions. However, it was also a time of increasing public fear about violent crime and rising crime rates. Crime became a political issue and politicians passed "tough on crime" laws. Despite crime's politicization, many assumed that the courts would continue to improve protections for criminal defendants as the Warren Court had done. Galanter disagreed, instead presenting a complex analysis focusing on the parties themselves and whether they are "haves" or "have-nots" and the impact of being a one-shot player versus a repeat player. As the last four decades have shown, this view is accurate in the criminal context. Courts refused to protect criminal defendants from legislative changes that gave prosecutors more power through increased criminalization, mandatory minimum sentences, and longer terms of imprisonment—policies that resulted in mass incarceration.

II. Criminal Defendants as Have-Nots

Galanter discusses "have-nots" as one-shot players in the system, and no group falls more firmly in the "have-not" category than most criminal defendants.

For Galanter, one distinguishing feature of the one-shotter is the primary desire to take care of an individual case, not to make law. This is an accurate assessment.

Cynthia Alkon, *Galanter's Analysis of the "Limits of Legal Change" as Applied to Criminal Cases and Reform* In: *Discussions in Dispute Resolution*. Edited by: Art Hinshaw, Andrea Kupfer Schneider, and Sarah Rudolph Cole, Oxford University Press (2021).
 DOI: 10.1093/oso/9780197513248.003.0064

Galanter recognizes this as a structural problem, as the one-shotter has nothing to gain by trying to "make law" when what is needed is an immediate resolution of their problem.

Galanter recognizes that many criminal defendants are repeat players but did not focus on the serious disadvantage repeat player status can have for a criminal defendant. Repeat offender laws (and enhanced penalties) existed in the 1970s. However, those penalties have substantially increased over time, giving prosecutors increased leverage in plea bargaining. It is therefore understandable that Galanter did not focus on the serious disadvantages for repeat player criminal defendants nor did he discuss the fact that one-shot criminal defendants tend to get the best deals precisely because they are one-shotters and have no prior criminal record.

Furthermore, Galanter did not recognize that repeat player criminal defendants are much less likely to use their case to make law because the potential consequences are much greater as they are often facing increased penalties due to prior convictions. A repeat player criminal defendant rarely enjoys the advantage that Galanter seemed to assume in other types of cases. The current structures of criminal codes, with potentially longer sentences puts pressure (and often extreme pressure) on both one-shotter and repeat player defendants to plead guilty and not challenge their cases. When both one-shotters and repeat player defendants focus on their individual case, and not on the bigger picture, it can perpetuate serious violations that ultimately protect the "haves," which can sometimes include abusive police officers and unethical prosecutors.

III. Prosecutors and Defense Lawyers as Repeat Players

Galanter characterizes repeat players as parties who tend to have more power. An interesting question Galanter examines is whether a skilled and specialized criminal defense lawyer can offset the advantage a repeat player prosecutor has against a one-shotter criminal defendant. This is where the article's age shows as Galanter's assumptions about defense lawyers no longer holds true due to the growth of public defender services. However, Galanter's basic analysis still holds true as the rate of plea bargaining, regardless of how the individual lawyers are paid (by the case or through a salary), encourages the kind of mass processing that Galanter feared. Furthermore, Galanter's discussion of the permanent client being the forum is still a concern, particularly with private appointed counsel systems where lawyers are paid by the case to represent indigent defendants and where their livelihood depends on continuing appointments. In these circumstances, Galanter correctly identified that the "source of business generally counts for more than the client" causing the mass processing of cases rather than careful individual attention, as lawyers plead out cases as quickly as possible to position themselves for future appointments.

Galanter assumed criminal defense lawyers were not the equals of prosecutors, characterizing them as the "lower echelons" of the legal profession with lower socioeconomic origins and degrees from lower ranked law schools. Perhaps due to this assumption, Galanter did not discuss whether equally qualified criminal defense lawyers could level the playing field with prosecutors. Does equal stature and experience of lawyers minimize other differences and work to equalize power imbalances? The number of public defender offices grew dramatically in the 1970s, which has also leveled the playing field in terms of the quality of training and experience. Today, it is as competitive to get a job as a public defender as it is to get a job as a prosecutor. However, the increased numbers of good defense lawyers with strong experience and training were unable to counter the system's structural problems, resulting in mass incarceration.

IV. Plea Bargaining

Galanter recognized the importance of plea bargaining, but he calls it "court supervised/imposed settlement" rather than "routine processing." Plea bargaining could and still can be viewed as "court supervised" because judges must approve a plea deal and accept the defendant's change of plea. Some jurisdictions prohibit judges from getting involved in the actual plea discussions or negotiations. However, if not prohibited, judges can be involved in supervising, encouraging, or helping the parties negotiate a settlement. But judicial involvement is less in cases with "standard deals." And less serious cases tend to have "standard deals," although the sentence may vary, depending on where the case is prosecuted. In standard cases, judicial involvement is often limited to reciting the standard plea colloquy, asking standard questions, and accepting the plea deal.

Plea bargaining is more accurately viewed as routine processing, a category of claims that Galanter describes as "mass processing with little of the individual attention of full-dress adjudication" (p. 109). A recurring concern in plea bargaining is that there is little negotiation and that defense lawyers are not providing adequate assistance of counsel in the plea negotiation process. However, the courts have had a narrower area of concern, for example, in *Padilla v. Kentucky*, *Lafler v. Cooper*, and *Missouri v. Frye*, the Supreme Court has focused on the client-counseling phase of plea bargaining rather than the negotiation process itself. The "state of law" is of great interest to both prosecutors and defense lawyers, but less so to the individual defendant. It was only in 2012 when the US Supreme Court recognized in *Lafler* that "the criminal justice system today is for the most part a system of pleas, not a system of trials."

When considering meaningful reform, it matters whether plea bargaining is routine processing or fits more into the court supervised/imposed settlement category. Court supervised/imposed settlement is, arguably, easier to reform as reformers can focus on just one part of the legal system: the judges. But "routine processes" are so deeply embedded into the legal system, and the system is so reliant on them, that they become resistant to change. Judges, prosecutors, and defense lawyers all rely on plea bargaining to manage their workloads. Reforming plea bargaining requires the buy-in from those three categories of professionals and perhaps from the general public and law enforcement. In the context of plea bargaining, routine processing helps the haves resist change that may help the have-nots.

V. Reform

Galanter gives four basic "strategies for reform," all of which remain highly relevant in any discussion of meaningful criminal legal reform. He recommends "rule change," both through the courts and through legislation. Meaningful criminal legal reform, particularly reform aimed at decreasing mass incarceration, depends on changing the underlying law. Until that happens, process protections could be helpful. One such suggestion I've made is to decrease the amount of prosecutorial discretion available to file a number of charges with a variety of possible penalties for the same basic acts (Alkon 2015, pp. 203–204). As Galanter recognizes, litigation is an unreliable strategy for reform, and it is unlikely that the US Supreme Court will place any meaningful limits on prosecutorial behavior in plea bargaining.

The "improvement in institutional facilities" which means "timely full-dress adjudication of every claim put forward" is Galanter's second reform strategy. If prosecutors had to prove every case to a jury, it would dramatically change which cases are prosecuted. But as enticing a thought as this is, it remains unrealistic to expect this to happen without serious rule changes and a dramatic change in political culture as the numbers of criminal cases prosecuted would plummet.

Increasing legal services, Galanter's third reform strategy, remains a key and crucial area to help the "have-not" criminal defendant. Even with the increased professionalism of indigent defense services, it remains hit and miss what kind of legal services an indigent defendant will receive. Absent change in the underlying law, however, it is unlikely that simply having good defense lawyers would have the far-reaching impact that Galanter seems to assume. The underlying laws also need to change.

Galanter's final strategy, reorganizing parties "into coherent groups that have the ability to act in a coordinated fashion," is limited in the criminal context. Criminal cases cannot be handled as a group in a way that is consistent with a defense lawyer's ethical duty of zealous representation to each client. However, it is possible to focus on some categories of civil cases that attack violations of rights for a group, such as prisoners' rights, which could lead to structural reforms. One example of such a victory was *Brown v. Plata*, the case against California for failure to provide adequate healthcare to prisoners due to prison overcrowding. The Court mandated reductions in prison populations, which also led to legislative change to reduce prison sentences. But this strategy has its limits and on its own is unlikely to lead to far-reaching reform that will make a meaningful difference for have-not criminal defendants.

VI. Conclusion

Galanter's broad look at how to help the "have-nots" in our society is still highly relevant. Although not focused on criminal justice issues, Galanter's recommendations, and his caution about the limits of litigation and process to make meaningful change, is an important contribution to discussions about criminal legal reform.

References

Cynthia Alkon, *An Overlooked Key to Reversing Mass Incarceration: Reforming the Law to Reduce Prosecutorial Power in Plea Bargaining*, 15 Md. L.J. Race, Religion, Gender & Class, 191 (Fall 2015).

Cynthia Alkon, *What's Law Got to Do With It? Plea Bargaining Reform after Lafler and Frye*, 7 Y.B. on Arb. & Mediation (Penn State University School of Law) 1 (2015).

Stefanos Bibas, *Plea Bargaining Outside the Shadow of Trial*, 117 Harv. L. Rev. 2464 (2004).

Nancy J. King & Ronald Wright, *The Invisible Revolution in Plea Bargaining: Managerial Judging and Judicial Participation in Negotiations*, 95 Tex. L. Rev. 325 (2016).

John F. Pfaff, Locked In: The True Causes of Mass Incarceration and How to Achieve Real Reform (2017).

Reflections on *Why the "Haves" Come Out Ahead*

Marc Galanter

That *Why the "Haves" Come Out Ahead* retains substantial relevance after half a century is surprising and of course gratifying. The preceding comments helpfully note some of its omissions and anachronisms. What endures is the perspective that law is, among other things, both an arena and an instrument in the struggle for human felicity and fairness. Although law is not the master orderer of human societies—a realization that remains hard to digest for many who practice, produce, and chronicle it—it is a powerful instrument of social control and social change.

The *Haves* article was written in a different age—before the ascent of law and economics, before the emergence of Critical Legal Studies and its progeny, before the intensified exposure of the legal world by journalism, scholarship, and the internet, and before the beatification of alternative dispute resolution (ADR). Its core was composed—unanticipated and unplanned—in the fall of 1970 amid the turmoil and hopeful ferment of movements for civil rights, the arrival of public interest law, the emergence of assertive legal services on behalf of the poor, and many initiatives in access to justice. It was a heady time for those who imagined that law might be transformed from a buttress of the status quo and instrument of oppression into a tool of liberation.

My response to this enlivening time was deeply affected by my experience of India. In 1957, a year after graduating from law school, I sailed to India as a Fulbright scholar, my first journey outside the United States. Enthralled by the post–*Brown v. Board of Education* turmoil, and attracted by the emergence of a vast and heterogeneous new democracy, I set off to study the abolition of untouchability (i.e., the domination and oppression of the lowest castes). When I wrote the *Haves* I had been working primarily on Indian law for more than ten years. My passage to India was also a passage beyond the perspectives and assumptions of my American legal training. Although India is hardly mentioned, the *Haves* embodies a view of the legal process shaped by my encounter with Indian law. I can't repeat too often my homage to the purifying fire of immersion in another legal system.

Writing the *Haves* was the return voyage from this "Journey to the East," a return greatly facilitated by the arrival in the 1960s of a pioneering empirical "law and society" literature critically observing American legal institutions—a literature in which I found my India-inspired intuitions mirrored, enlarged, and refined.

As the *Haves* paper evolved, I realized that the repeat players in contemporary American society are increasingly not persons (as English speakers ordinarily use the term) at all but corporate entities. The extent to which this is so differs from one

Marc Galanter, *Reflections on* Why the "Haves" Come Out Ahead In: *Discussions in Dispute Resolution*. Edited by: Art Hinshaw, Andrea Kupfer Schneider, and Sarah Rudolph Cole, Oxford University Press (2021). © Oxford University Press. DOI: 10.1093/oso/9780197513248.003.0065

setting to another—the relation is contingent not inherent. As I summarized in the Afterword:

> Basically this repeat player–one-shotter distinction is between the casual participant for whom the game is an emergency and the party who is equipped to do it as part of his routine activity. The sailor overboard and the shark are both swimmers, but only one is in the swimming business, . . . It is generally organizations that can be repeat players—because law in America is a complex and expensive activity requiring employment of full-time specialists. Organizations can use the law routinely because, compared to the cost of remedies, organizations are the right size and almost all individuals are too poor to play. (Afterword, p. 363)

Decades later in the *Planet of the APs*, I attempted to explicate in more detail the enhanced competence and litigative prowess of organizations in contemporary American society.

The *Haves* paper was a challenge to the judicial triumphalism that was the received wisdom of the progressive wing of the American legal academy (which may account for the great difficulty in getting it published). In effect, it attempted to show that, examined from the bottom up, the American legal setting displayed features that frequently vitiated the impact of top-down reforms. In the Indian setting, these obstacles were glaringly evident to an outsider with the benefit of no allegiance to the prevailing myths.

Since I embarked on the *Haves* almost half a century ago, there have been many significant changes in the legal landscape. Confining myself to the American setting, we can observe:

- a striking increase in the number of lawyers, who are more intensely stratified;
- much larger firms that are more hierarchical and in which tenure is less secure;
- judges, surrounded by more auxiliaries, are more engaged in case management, and conduct fewer trials;
- while trials are increasingly rare in the ceremonially enhanced "regular" courts, there is a proliferation of trial-like proceedings at legal locations with less visibility, less prestige, and less elaborated proceedings;
- this shift in the ecology of trials occurs amid a general legalization throughout society, with more rules and more forums;
- at the same time we see in the surrounding society an intense proliferation of new information and communication technologies, some of which can be applied to providing legal services in untraditional formats; and
- all of this is taking place as the income compression of the mid-twentieth century gives way to growing inequality.

In the 1970s, a robust discourse presented ADR as offering a new and superior mode of addressing disputes. In arguing the virtues of ADR, this discourse frequently proceeded as if adjudication in court were the principle and prototypical dispute institution in contemporary society and as if trials were what typically transpired in courts. Actually, neither of these depictions was descriptive even forty years ago when

ADR was entering the main tent. For a long time most cases had been settling or otherwise leaving courts short of adjudication at trial. Trials have now shrunk to a tiny fraction of what civil courts do—and a larger but also shrinking fraction of what criminal courts do.

The post–World War II decades saw an increase of what we might call "litigation up"—that is, claims by actual persons (injury-victims, consumers, etc.) against various sorts of APs. Increased judicial responsiveness to such claims gave rise to mounting dismay about litigation in business circles and in some sections of the judiciary and the legal establishment. Chief Justice Warren Burger deplored the turn to litigation and proposed to devise a "Better Way" to resolve disputes. Campaigns against litigation—especially decrying the ravages of tort litigation—flourished; anti-litigation polemicists (e.g., Peter Huber, Philip Howard, Walter Olson) commanded attention. The campaign to make ADR an independent process separate from litigation attracted major foundation support.

In practice, ADR, like other nostrums, falls short of its ideals. Just as litigation can be idealized as decisive impartial disinterested adjudication, so ADR is idealized as an insightful, inventive, and endlessly patient third party producing a win/win outcome (without the expense of trial)—an even more demanding role than the rule-following, occasionally rule-creative judge.

When ADR and the campaign to displace litigation arrived on the scene in the 1970s, the trial was already in decline—at least in the most visible and emblematic locations. In the federal courts, trials have fallen from 12 percent of civil dispositions in the early 1960s to a bit more than 1 percent in recent years. What has replaced the trial is not the much touted and promoted ADR, except in instances where it is imposed by contract or court fiat. What typically transpires in civil cases is an elaborated version of settlement negotiations that we might call "litigotiation," coupled with an enlarged mix of judicial determinations of the insufficiency of claims. Full-blown litigation is very much alive—indeed growing—not in the most visible and prestigious courts, but displaced to less visible and celebrated agency proceedings, whose volume of caseload is far greater than that of all the courts and ADR institutions combined. The civil trial has migrated to less exalted and less visible precincts. At the same time the criminal trial has been largely replaced by prosecution-dominated bargaining.

Just what is going to happen to trial and settlement? We should not assume that the trends of the past half-century will proceed relentlessly until the trial is virtually extinguished. Half a century ago no one envisioned that we would be where we are now — with few trials in the regular courts, massive numbers of (mostly less elaborated) trial proceedings in other (mostly administrative) forums, further large numbers of claims blockaded by routinized deployment of arbitration clauses, managerial judging, and the increasing expense of litigation, declining trial experience for lawyers, and outsourcing of claims to ADR. All of this is taking place amid significant change in the technology of legal work and important additions to our knowledge of the dynamics of institutions like courts and juries. Whether these new technologies and new knowledge will be deployed in a way that revivifies the trial as an institution remains to be seen. Similarly, we may wonder whether the advantages of the corporate "haves" will be diminished in that unknown future.

References

Marc Galanter, *Afterword: Explaining Litigation*, 9 LAW & SOC'Y REV. 346 (1975).

Marc Galanter, "Haves Ascendant," *in* GALANTER, WHY THE HAVES COME OUT AHEAD: THE CLASSIC ESSAY AND NEW OBSERVATIONS (2014).

Marc Galanter, *Planet of the APs: Reflections on the Scale of Law and Its Users*, 53 BUFF. L. REV. 1369 (2006).

Marc Galanter, *Why the "Haves" Come Out Ahead: Speculations on the Limits of Legal Change*, 9 LAW & SOC'Y REV. 95 (1974), reprinted with commentary in WHY THE HAVES COME OUT AHEAD: THE CLASSIC ESSAY AND NEW OBSERVATIONS (2014).

Article 4.2

Varieties of Dispute Processing

Frank E.A. Sander

70 Federal Rules Decisions 111 (1976)

Last year ... Professor John Barton pointed out that if federal appellate cases continued to grow for the next 40 years at the same rate at [as they are now], ... by the year 2010 we can expect to have well over one million federal appellate cases each year, requiring five thousand federal appellate judges to decide them and one thousand new volumes of the Federal Reporter each year to report the decisions. Since the number of cases initiated in the federal system each year is approximately ten times the number of decided appeals, one can readily extrapolate Professor Barton's projections to the trial level....

* * *

... [H]ow we might escape from [this problem?] ... First, we can try to prevent disputes from arising ... through appropriate changes in the substantive law....

* * *

A second way of reducing the judicial caseload is to explore alternative ways of resolving disputes outside the courts....

Let me turn now to [two issues]:

* * *

2) How can [various dispute resolution mechanisms] be utilized so that.... we can.... develop some rational criteria for allocating various types of disputes to different dispute resolution processes?

* * *

Criteria

* * *

Frank E.A. Sander, *Varieties of Dispute Processing* In: *Discussions in Dispute Resolution*. Edited by: Art Hinshaw, Andrea Kupfer Schneider, and Sarah Rudolph Cole, Oxford University Press (2021). © Oxford University Press.
DOI: 10.1093/oso/9780197513248.003.0066

1. Nature of Dispute

* * *

... [T]here is a need for developing a flexible mechanism that.... sort[s] out the large general question from the repetitive application of settled principle. I do not believe that a court is the most effective way to perform this kind of sifting task....

... I am not persuaded that the courts have sufficient competence, resources or remedial power to run mental hospitals, schools or welfare departments. Yet where serious constitutional denials are at issue, they can hardly decline jurisdiction. This seems to me an area where one can make no headway without talking about very specific cases and exploring in detail alternative dispute resolution mechanisms....

2. Relationship Between Disputants

A different situation is presented when disputes arise between individuals.... in a long-term relationship [with] an isolated dispute.... [T]here is more potential for having the parties, at least initially, seek to work out their own solution, for such a solution is likely to be far more acceptable (and hence durable). Thus negotiation, or if necessary, mediation, appears to be a preferable approach in the first instance....

* * *

Fortunately [several] courts around the country, ha[ve] a program under which, ... case[s] can be referred to a panel of three trained mediators drawn from the local community. The panel will attempt to let each of the disputants fully state her side of the story, and then, through skillful probing, will seek to elicit points of tension in the underlying relationship....

Of course, it might be suggested that a court could also induce.... a settlement.... [T]here is a world of difference between a coerced or semi-coerced settlement of the kind that so often results in court and a voluntary agreement arrived at by the parties.

* * *

Another long-term ... relationship that may be amenable to this type of dispute resolution mechanism is the family....

... [I]n a sense we have developed a mediative solution for most family conflict-social work and family therapy. Still where there is a breakdown of the family as a result of death or divorce, the courts have customarily become involved and it is here that alternative dispute resolution devices-particularly mediation-need to be further explored.

* * *

3. Amount in Dispute

... [A]mount in controversy has been an item consistently looked to determine the amount of process that is "due". The Small Claims Court movement has taken as its premise that small cases are simple cases and that therefore a pared-down judicial procedure was what was called for.... [But] the Small Claims Court has failed its original purpose.... The need.... is for a preliminary investigative-conciliational stage ... with ultimate recourse to the court. This ... could readily screen out those cases which need not take a court's time ... and preserve the adjudicatory process for those cases where the issues have been properly joined and there is a genuine dispute of fact or law....

4. Cost

There is a dearth of reliable data comparing the costs of different dispute resolution processes.... [U]ntil better data become available one can probably proceed safely on the assumption that costs rise as procedural formalities increase.

The lack of adequate cost data is particularly unfortunate with respect to essentially comparable processes, such as litigation and arbitration. Assuming for the moment that arbitration would produce results as acceptable as litigation ... would cost considerations justify the transfer ... of entire categories of civil litigation to arbitration ... ?

5. Speed

The deficiency of sophisticated data concerning the costs of different dispute resolution processes also extends to the factor of speed. Although it is generally assumed—rightly, I believe—that arbitration is speedier than litigation....

Implications

1.... With the development of administrative law, the delegation of certain problems to specialized bodies for initial resolution has become a commonplace. Within the judicial sphere, too, we have developed specialized courts to handle family problems and tax problems, among others.

... Perhaps the time is now ripe for greater resort to an alternate primary *process*.... [S]uch a step would be particularly appropriate in situations involving disputing individuals who are engaged in a long-term relationship. The process ought to consist initially of a mediational phase, and then, if necessary, of an adjudicative one. Problems that would appear to be particularly amenable to such a two-stage process are disputes between neighbors, family members, supplier and distributor, landlord and tenant....

Receptivity to such an alternate primary process imposes special obligations on the Bar.... [I]t is possible that there will be a lesser role for lawyers in this new world....

[which] poses a test to the Bar of its capacity to support innovative experimentation despite a temporary adverse economic impact for the profession.

... [W]e should give strong consideration to greater use of arbitration, particularly where we are dealing with specialized issues or issues whose confines have been fairly well chartered out by a contract between the parties, by governing legislation, or by prior court decision.

2.... I am impressed by the experimental work that has been undertaken ... to divert certain types of minor criminal offenses ... to a mediational proceeding.... [which] can also be seen in the larger context of a movement towards a community "moot", offering informal and supportive services to community members....

3. While the mediation-arbitration model earlier referred to is [useful], another device that bears further utilization is ... the screening-adjudication model....

* * *

4. What I am thus advocating is a flexible and diverse panoply of dispute resolution processes, with particular types of cases being assigned to differing processes (or combinations of processes), according to some of the criteria.... [O]ne might envision by the year 2000 not simply a court house but a Dispute Resolution Center, where the grievant would first be channelled through a screening clerk who would then direct him to the process (or sequence of processes) most appropriate to his type of case....

... [A] court might decide of its own to refer a certain type of problem to a more suitable tribunal. Or a legislature might ... build in an appropriate dispute resolution process. Institutions such as prisons, schools, or mental hospitals also could ... establish[] indigenous dispute resolution processes.... Finally, once these patterns begin to take hold, the law schools ... should shift from their preoccupation with the judicial process and begin to expose students to the broad range of dispute resolution processes.

5. I [need to address] some of the substantial impediments to reform.... First, particularly in the criminal field, cries of "denial of due process" will undoubtedly be heard if an informal mediational process is sought to be substituted for the strict protections of the adversary process. In response to this objection it must be asserted candidly that ... we may have over-judicialized the system, with concomitant adverse effects on its efficiency as well as its accessibility to powerless litigants....

A related concern is ... the need to retain the courts as the ultimate agency capable of effectively protecting the rights of the disadvantaged. This is a legitimate concern ... consistent with the goals I have advocated. I am not maintaining that ... novel constitutional claims ought to be diverted to mediation or arbitration. On the contrary, the goal is to reserve the courts for those activities for which they are best suited and to avoid [clogging] them with cases that do not require their unique capabilities.

Finally, we are robbed of much-needed flexibility by the constitutional requirement of jury trial.... But one is bound to wonder whether ... the requirement of jury trial still makes sense in the run-of-the-mill civil case....

Conclusion

It seems appropriate to end ... on a modest note. There are no panaceas; only promising avenues to explore. And there is so much we do not know. Among other things, we need far better data than are presently available ... on what is in fact going on in the courts [in order to] develop some sophisticated notion of where the main trouble spots are and what types of cases are prime candidates for alternative resolution. We need more evaluation of the comparative efficacy and cost of different dispute resolution mechanisms. And we need more data on the role played by some of the key individuals in the process (e.g., lawyers)....

Above all, however, we need to accumulate and disseminate the presently available learning concerning promising alternative resolution mechanisms, and encourage continued experimentation and research....

... [A]t the conclusion of this meeting the organizers of this conference might designate a small group of dedicated individuals who would take it upon themselves to monitor the progress of some of the promising ideas that will be cast adrift here.... In this way we may all be able to continue to contribute to the solutions of the many grave problems that presently beset the courts and that presumably brought us here.

Comments

How Useful Is Court ADR If Litigants (Still) Don't Know about It?

Donna Shestowsky

In his landmark paper, *Varieties of Dispute Processing*, Frank Sander articulated the need to develop mechanisms to reduce the nation's judicial caseload. Decades after delivering his essay at the 1976 Pound Conference, Sander's ideas remain at the core of the dialogue about court-sponsored alternative dispute resolution (ADR). Sander asserted that, unless the courts developed additional procedures for resolving disputes, the continued growth of litigation could ultimately undermine the US judicial system's ability to help constituents resolve conflicts in a timely and equitable fashion. Accordingly, he prescribed his now-famous framework for modern-day ADR within the court system—later coined the "multi-door courthouse"—which fueled the idea that courts should offer a range of options for addressing disputes.

Sander helped to shift the discourse about the appropriate use of courts to achieve litigant satisfaction from a focus on securing purely law-based "wins" for disputants to an emphasis on obtaining resolutions that better reflected the diverse, complex needs of disputing parties. He maintained that resolving certain subsets of cases outside the courtroom would provide disputants with extra time and personalized attention, and ultimately increase their satisfaction with the legal system. Further, he posited that this increased participation in, and satisfaction with, the dispute resolution experience would improve voluntary compliance with case outcomes. At their core, Sander's ideas sparked our imagination by suggesting that courts could offer their constituents psychological satisfaction by guiding them to procedures that might deliver greater benefits than trials. Subsequent empirical research ultimately supported Sander's views regarding disputant satisfaction and outcome durability.

I. The Legacy of Sander's Multi-Door Courthouse: Current Research

While extremely influential, Sander's vision did not come to fruition exactly as outlined at the Pound Conference. While numerous jurisdictions experimented with his multi-door model, only a few established successful, long-running programs that paid homage to his framework. Other court-sponsored programs that were at least partly inspired by his ideas were relatively short-lived. The economic crisis of 2007–09, which forced forty-three states to make substantial cuts to their judicial budgets,

Donna Shestowsky, *How Useful Is Court ADR If Litigants (Still) Don't Know about It?* In: *Discussions in Dispute Resolution*. Edited by: Art Hinshaw, Andrea Kupfer Schneider, and Sarah Rudolph Cole, Oxford University Press (2021).
DOI: 10.1093/oso/9780197513248.003.0067

had particularly negative consequences for ADR offerings. In the aftermath, the wait time for civil trials grew considerably. Sander's prediction became a reality: the nation's overburdened court system made it increasingly challenging for many to obtain civil justice.

While an increase in wait times for civil trials—measured using available data—is one meaningful indication of an overburdened system, it is important to track other potential indicia that might be harder to assess. Sander lamented the dearth of data that might help scholars understand and improve the legal system, and, although there has been some progress through empirical studies, his observation still rings true today. Continued reliable, useful research is needed to optimize existing ADR programs and guide the development of new ones. For example, recent research has helped us to understand that even in courts that offer a menu of options, barriers to the use of ADR remain. My empirical work, for example, suggests that litigants are often unaware of the alternatives to trial. When my research team surveyed litigants who were eligible for both court-sponsored mediation and arbitration, we discovered that only about one-quarter knew their court offered a mediation program, only 27 percent knew their court offered arbitration, and only 15 percent were aware that it offered both procedures (Shestowsky, *Ignorance Is Not Bliss*, p. 212).

These results are disheartening to scholars and practitioners who, like Sander, believe that litigants should have a say in how their cases are resolved. Insofar as ADR procedures might be more effective than trial in terms of helping certain litigants meet their needs and achieve their goals, only these litigants can fully understand their needs and goals and how they prioritize them. For example, if the parties want to actively shape the outcome of their case and believe that outcome compliance will be enhanced by this type of active participation, ADR procedures such as mediation might be preferable to trial. In addition, parties who want industry norms or financial considerations to shape the outcome of their dispute, in addition to, or instead of, the law, might also benefit more from ADR than trial. Moreover, as Sander suggested, depending on the degree of conflict between the parties, ADR might better facilitate the preservation of their relationship.

In courts that offer voluntary ADR, as well as ones with programs that allow disputants to opt out of their "mandatory" procedure in favor of another option that they find mutually attractive, litigants can play a meaningful and informed role in deciding how to resolve their dispute. To achieve this goal, however, litigants must be aware of all their options, both court-connected and private (Shestowsky, pp. 196–200). Education, followed by informed consent, is critical.

II. The Importance of Litigant Education

There are several methods for ensuring litigants know about their ADR options. The first is through their lawyers, which would require that lawyers themselves be knowledgeable about available ADR alternatives. The second is through courts independently providing this information to litigants.

Lawyers who receive appropriate training can play a crucial role in helping litigants to evaluate their priorities and identify the best procedural course for their disputes. In an ABA-published debate on the role attorneys should play in educating litigants regarding procedure choice, Sander argued that just as doctors are required to obtain informed consent for medical procedures by letting patients know about treatment options, lawyers should be required to inform clients about alternatives to trial. Over time, changes in state law, court policy, and rules of professional responsibility have reinforced the notion that attorneys should counsel clients about ADR options, especially when litigation is likely or already pending. But the data on whether lawyers can be counted on to effectively counsel their clients about ADR paints a bleak picture. Survey research conducted by Roselle Wissler (2004) found that attorneys failed to discuss the use of voluntary ADR in about one-quarter of their filed cases. Research by McAdoo and Hinshaw (2002), which explored how frequently attorneys discuss ADR with clients in contexts where rules were changed to require such conversations, found that 20 percent of litigators reported "hardly ever" informing clients about ADR or waiting until "right before trial" to do so. My own study of state court litigants revealed that those who were represented were no more likely to be able to correctly identify their court-sponsored ADR options than their unrepresented counterparts. Together, these findings raise questions about whether attorneys are effectively meeting Sander's call to educate their clients.

Empirical work suggests that lawyers are less prone to explore ADR with their clients when they have less knowledge about ADR procedures (Wissler 2004). Thus, it is important that attorneys be adequately educated in the area of ADR education. Sander highlighted this need when he called for "more diverse training in law schools" (p. 127) and argued that "law schools ... should shift from their preoccupation with the judicial process and begin to expose students to the broad range of dispute resolution processes" (pp. 132–33). Sander's assertion remains particularly relevant today. Given the important role that ADR can play in providing litigants with access to justice, and promoting the legitimacy of the legal system, such education should be mandatory at some point in the law school curriculum and should not be relegated, as it is at so many schools, to small seminars that can accommodate a limited segment of the student population. The widespread implementation of effective ADR education can cultivate a new generation of lawyers who are more willing and able to educate clients about alternatives to trial in the court context and beyond. Disputants should, consequently, become better equipped to make informed decisions about how to handle their cases.

As Sander might have predicted, litigant knowledge of ADR options has important consequences. Notably, litigants have significantly more favorable views of their court when they know it sponsors mediation, and less favorable views when they believe it does not (Shestowsky, pp. 213–14). Moreover, when litigants know that their court offers arbitration, they are significantly more likely to consider using it for their case (Shestowsky, pp. 213–14). Although courts may not be able to offer an array of procedures in the way Sander envisioned, by informing litigants about ADR, they can increase the possibility that cases are matched with the best available procedure and, in some instances, elevate litigant perceptions of the court's institutional legitimacy.

Courts can also take several steps to better educate litigants. First, courts should not assume that lawyers will adequately educate their clients about ADR despite the fact that relaying some level of information is an ethical obligation in many jurisdictions. Rather courts should take a proactive role in litigant education, especially with respect to their own programs. While some courts already require lawyers to attest to the fact that they have informed their clients about alternatives to trial, courts should do more. The US District Court of Northern California is a promising example: the court requires lawyers and their clients to sign a form declaring that they have read the handbook describing the court's ADR procedures, have discussed both court-sponsored and private options, and have considered whether their case might benefit from ADR. Courts might also consider penalizing attorneys who do not comply with such rules. In addition, courts should create help desks staffed by court personnel or neutrals from their roster who can answer litigants' questions about ADR procedures, much like Sander's idea of a screening clerk. Finally, courts could hold ADR information sessions on a periodic basis and encourage, or even require, parties to attend.

In addition to improving litigant education, courts should consider revamping how they evaluate their ADR programs. Some courts already use exit surveys to assess litigants' satisfaction with their court-sponsored ADR programs, but they should also survey litigants who did not utilize their programs to determine why they did not do so. To the extent that litigants were aware of court offerings but did not use them, courts should explore what could be done to make them more attractive from the litigant's perspective and dismantle any access barriers litigants face when trying to use them. If exit surveys reveal that that many litigants are unaware of their ADR programs, courts should investigate ways to better advertise them. Over time, courts could use the accumulated feedback to design ADR options that more effectively meet the needs of litigants and improve access to justice.

III. Conclusion

Sander's call to action, in which he urged practitioners, researchers, and legislators to "forge links" (p. 133) to build a judicial system that is economical, efficient, and fair, should continue to shape our attempts to improve the civil justice system. Most notably, law schools should ensure that their students graduate with the knowledge they need to adequately counsel clients about their procedural options. As Sander first argued more than forty years ago, when litigants are adequately informed about their procedural options and can influence the trajectory of their dispute's resolution in a meaningful way, we can expect court efficiency to improve and access to civil justice to more readily prevail.

References

Bobbi McAdoo & Art Hinshaw, *The Challenge of Institutionalizing Alternative Dispute Resolution: Attorney Perspectives on the Effect of Rule 17 on Civil Litigation Practice in Missouri*, 67 Mo. L. Rev. 473 (2002).

Frank E.A. Sander & Michael L. Prigoff, *Professional Responsibility: Should There Be a Duty to Advise of ADR Options?*, 50 A.B.A. Journal 76 (1990).

Donna Shestowsky, *When Ignorance Is Not Bliss: An Empirical Study of Litigants' Awareness of Court-Sponsored Alternative Dispute Resolution Programs*, 23 Harv. Negot. L. Rev. 196 (2017).

Tom R. Tyler, Why People Obey the Law (2006).

Roselle L. Wissler, *Barriers to Attorneys' Discussion and Use of ADR*, 19 Ohio St. J. on Disp. Resol. 463 (2004).

Dispute Processing beyond the Courts: New Complexity, Old Problems

Lydia Nussbaum

I. Introduction

Nearly four decades after Frank E.A. Sander addressed the Pound Conference, his conception of the role alternative dispute resolution (ADR) can and should play in the American legal system remains profoundly influential. Sander's remarks focused on alleviating overburdened courts and questioning the fundamental assumption that judges hold a monopoly on resolving disputes. He developed a matrix that crossed dispute characteristics—the nature of a dispute, the relationship between disputants, the amount in dispute, litigation costs, and need for speedy resolution—with different methods of dispute resolution, ranging from courtroom litigation to less formal alternatives such as mediation and negotiation. Sander envisioned a court of the future that considered carefully the interplay of dispute characteristics in order to match dispute types with methods of dispute resolution. By "fitting the forum to the fuss," courts could lighten judges' dockets, better serve disputants, and improve the delivery of justice. This idea, that courts could facilitate dispute resolution without judges, was revolutionary.

One of the most prescient observations Sander made in *Varieties of Dispute Processing* involves the important dynamic between changes to substantive law and the utility of ADR, particularly mediation. When Sander was a young law professor at Harvard, he began teaching and writing about family law just as California enacted the first no-fault divorce statute, sparking the "no-fault revolution" in family law. With the question of fault off the table, husbands and wives no longer had to convince a judge of one another's adultery, cruelty, or abandonment to win release from their marriages. This change profoundly impacted the mechanism of dispute resolution. Once the question of fault was no longer relevant, disputants could focus their energy on how to remediate their situation. Parties did not (necessarily) need a judge to determine those remedies but instead could sit down and determine them together, through direct negotiation or with the assistance of a third-party mediator.

From an ADR policy standpoint, Sander's important contribution is: the substantive law underlying a dispute informs procedure and courts should therefore curate a selection of dispute resolution processes accordingly. What Sander may not have anticipated, however, was that ADR's institutionalization would spread far beyond the judiciary and the added complexity this expansion would bring to the substance-procedure dynamic. When Sander presented *Varieties of Dispute Processing*, he was largely thinking about courts as the institutions that would match parties to the

Lydia Nussbaum, *Dispute Processing beyond the Courts: New Complexity, Old Problems* In: *Discussions in Dispute Resolution*. Edited by: Art Hinshaw, Andrea Kupfer Schneider, and Sarah Rudolph Cole, Oxford University Press (2021). © Oxford University Press. DOI: 10.1093/oso/9780197513248.003.0068

appropriate dispute resolution method. Today, legislatures have also taken on this role. However, legislatures use ADR as a policy tool, directing parties toward a particular ADR process to advance concrete public policy goals. They do not always take into careful consideration all the dispute characteristics that Sander proposed with his matrix. As the remainder of this commentary discusses, Sander's foundational insight continues to be a central component of ADR policy; but, so does the challenge of sorting disputes and matching them to appropriate ADR processes.

II. Legislative Uses of ADR to Advance Public Policy Outcomes

While Sander's foundational insight into the substance-procedure relationship still holds, ADR has shifted from his original vision of an alternative forum where parties bargain in the shadow of the law into a regulatory instrument that policymakers use to achieve substantive policy outcomes. Legislatures do this in a wide variety of contexts (Nussbaum, *Mediation as Regulation*, pp. 381–84). Sometimes legislative mandates tap a court, administrative agency, or other public entity to develop and oversee the ADR process, and other times the mandate regulates private parties before they come into contact with the state. Despite these variations, a common theme is legislatures utilize ADR as a procedural intervention to address a perceived societal problem.

For example, as the 2008 foreclosure crisis unfolded, it became apparent that automated loan servicing practices were contributing to snowballing foreclosure rates and a cratering securities market. To interrupt these procedures, policymakers in several states required lender representatives and homeowners to sit down in mediation to explore alternatives to foreclosure that would benefit them both. The mediation intervention offered no guarantee of ending the foreclosure crisis, but, if enough foreclosures could be avoided in the aggregate, then the devastating impact of foreclosure might be reduced (Nussbaum, *ADR's Place in Foreclosure*, pp. 1909–15).

In addition to imposing ADR requirements on private parties, policymakers also use ADR to change public entities' behavior. For example, to help dismantle the school-to-prison pipeline, some lawmakers required schools to replace zero-tolerance discipline, which diverts children from school and into the criminal justice system, with ADR processes based on restorative justice principles. Before schools suspend or expel a child, or make referrals to law enforcement, they must first utilize ADR processes to address the root causes of student misbehavior and its impact on others in the community (Nussbaum, *Realizing Restorative Justice*).

Sometimes the procedural intervention changes as legislatures' understanding of the policy problem evolves. For example, during the last quarter of the twentieth century, a series of contractions in the medical malpractice insurance market sparked fears that physicians might shutter their practices. Policymakers first assumed the culprit was unmeritorious patient litigation and unreasonably high jury awards. As a consequence, states passed tort reform legislation that included mandatory ADR procedures such as expert medical screening panels and arbitration. The intent behind this legislation was to make it harder for patients to get into court and to prevail once they got there. However, in the late 1990s, new data about patient litigation rates and revelations about the prevalence of medical errors in the healthcare system reoriented the reform agenda. Instead of hampering patient claims, legislatures sought to help *more* injured patients obtain redress through ADR legislation promoting informal processes such as mediation and "early discussion and resolution" to assist communication and to improve patient safety (Nussbaum, *Trial and Error*).

III. New Complexity in the Substance-Procedure Dynamic

Legislatures' use of ADR as a policy instrument adds new dimensions to the substance-procedure dynamic that Sander identified in *Varieties of Dispute Processing*. What we have now is even more complex: to advance a public policy agenda, legislatures (1) require parties to engage ADR processes to assert their substantive rights; (2) regulate parties' behavior inside these ADR processes; and (3) sometimes introduce relaxed substantive legal standards for particular statutory ADR processes.

To begin, by embedding specialized ADR requirements into substantive law, disputants must first engage in a prescribed ADR process in order to assert or defend their legal rights (Nussbaum, *Mediation as Regulation*, pp. 380–84). We saw this in the foreclosure crisis, when loan servicers had to engage in mediation before they could initiate a foreclosure. Even though the homeowner's breach of the mortgage contract was never in question, lenders still had to take this additional procedural step before they could lawfully proceed. In the medical malpractice context, this phenomenon appears in statutes requiring patients to submit their claims to a medical screening panel or to attend arbitration. This procedural "interference" has been found unconstitutional in some jurisdictions for violating individuals' right to access the courts (Nussbaum, *Trial and Error*, pp. 267–77).

Second, some legislative mandates do more than simply require an ADR procedural step and in fact regulate parties' behavior inside these ADR processes. Sometimes these regulations are intended to correct informational asymmetries and ensure informed negotiations, such as child support mediation statutes requiring pre-mediation exchange of affidavits and financial documentation. Regulations can also be aimed at assisting a less empowered party; for example, California bars legal counsel from insurance mediations when the insured party is unrepresented, and a Vermont mediation statute requires certain landlords to provide tenants with justification for rent increases. In contrast, legislation can also serve to protect defendants. Before someone can file a lawsuit against a nursing home in Florida, she must first notify the home of the incident and furnish a certificate of merit from a licensed attorney before attending a mandatory mediation. Sometimes a statute creates economic risk for a complainant who refuses to settle within the confines of a mandated ADR settlement process; for example, Michigan requires a patient who pursues litigation after a negative screening panel decision to post a $5,000 bond for each named defendant (Nussbaum, *Mediation as Regulation*, pp. 384–95).

And, finally, legislatures can also construct different substantive legal standards for extrajudicial ADR processes. For example, in Oregon, patients pursuing medical malpractice claims against their healthcare providers can use an "Early Discussion and Resolution" process that utilizes a different legal standard than court adjudication. This alternative standard operates like *res ipsa loquitur* in that patients do not have to establish causality to support their injury claim. Only in this specialized ADR process can parties apply this more patient-friendly standard for determining liability, thereby helping patients, who are already disadvantaged in claims against providers, obtain redress for injuries sustained from their medical treatment (Nussbaum, *Trial and Error*, pp. 285–92).

Taken together, the current role ADR plays in the public policy sphere adds new dimensions to the interaction between substantive and procedural law that Sander identified in *Varieties of Dispute Processing*. By mandating ADR processes for particular kinds of disputes and, in some instances, guiding parties' behavior inside these processes, legislatures impact parties' substantive rights, sometimes for better and sometimes for worse.

IV. Back to the Future . . . and the Old Sorting Problem

The proliferation of ADR processes embedded in legislative regimes and used as instruments to affect policy change underscores the continued challenge for ADR policy: *How to match disputants with an appropriate process?* The continuing challenge is that legislators do not always engage in the kind of carefully considered sorting process that Sander proposed. Sander attempted to resolve this challenge with his matrix of dispute characteristics and the idea that someone in the court would, much like Dumbledore's magical Sorting Hat, direct disputants to the appropriate ADR process. Given the expanded institutionalization of ADR, Sander's original idea for a sorting mechanism is ready for some updating.

First, the matrix needs new categories for dispute and disputant characteristics. Factors like parties' unequal legal sophistication, financial vulnerability, and previous ADR experience can be exploited in a dispute resolution process lacking institutional oversight or with procedural rules of engagement that unfairly favor one party over another. Thus, in addition to the original characteristics Sander identified, these features should be considered when requiring parties to participate in ADR processes.

Second, the entity responsible for sorting remains a puzzle. With legislatures imposing ADR requirements on parties before they even reach the courthouse steps, the idea that a court would provide the only sorting mechanism is outdated. Yet, as both Donna Shestowsky and Deborah Eisenberg's commentaries observe, the sorting process Sander envisioned never worked that well to begin with. If courts cannot manage the job of sorting cases, it seems highly unlikely that legislatures will, particularly since they lack deep substantive and procedural knowledge. A few states, like New Mexico, have experimented with a centralized administrative bureau tasked with providing mediation services, offering training, as well as consulting on ADR program design and policy development for a variety of public sector mediation programs.

While gathering ADR expertise under one roof might be an improvement over the alternative—dispersed and nonstandard practices—the agency may have limited discretion and would likely be subject to the whims of the legislature's mandate. And, such an agency would have to promulgate its own sorting protocols, which might not fare better than the courts'.

Either way, it falls to us in the ADR policy field to continue educating policymakers about the potential uses and abuses of ADR, the burdens and benefits each process offers its participants, and to urge careful consideration when contemplating procedural interventions.

References

Lydia Nussbaum, *ADR's Place in Foreclosure: Remedying the Flaws of a Securitized Housing Market*, 34 CARDOZO L.J. 1889 (2013).

Lydia Nussbaum, *Mediation as Regulation: Expanding State Governance over Private Disputes*, 2016 UTAH L. REV. 361 (2016).

Lydia Nussbaum, *Realizing Restorative Justice: Legal Rules and Standards for School Discipline Reform*, 69 HASTINGS L.J. 583 (2018).

Lydia Nussbaum, *Trial and Error: Legislating ADR for Medical Malpractice Reform*, 76 MD. L. REV. 247 (2017).

Frank Sander: Father of Court-based Dispute Resolution

Deborah Thompson Eisenberg

Someone once told me the story of a boy who said to his father, "Dad, I have a great idea!" When asked to elaborate, the boy said, "A cure for cancer!" The father pushed for details, and the son replied, "No, *that's* the good idea—a cure for cancer! I don't know how to do it yet."

Like the boy with the good idea of a cure for cancer, Frank E.A. Sander's *Varieties of Dispute Processing* speech at the 1976 Pound Conference gave birth to the idea of a "cure" for overloaded court dockets. Sander challenged us to think beyond litigation as a way to resolve all of society's conflicts and advocated for "flexible and diverse panoply of dispute resolution processes, with particular types of cases being assigned to differing processes" (pp. 130–31). He criticized the single-minded assumption of lawyers and law teachers that "courts are the natural and obvious dispute resolvers" (p. 112). Sander's remarks have been dubbed a "big bang" moment for alternative dispute resolution (ADR) in the legal arena, encouraging us to think about "what" processes we should use to resolve legal disputes, "how" we should implement those processes, and "why" we need conflict resolution options other than litigation.

I. What?

Sander offered thoughtful proposals about the contours of potential remedies for a society overly reliant on the judiciary to resolve every conflict. A family law and tax scholar, Sander embarked on a "crash course" prior to the Pound Conference to learn about the ADR landscape. Based on his own experience with the limitations of litigation, he proposed transforming the courthouse into a "comprehensive justice center" that offered a variety of processes in different rooms. In his vision, a screening clerk would review disputes brought to the court and direct the parties to the most appropriate process based on a variety of criteria, such as the parties' relationship, complexity of the issue, cost, and speed.

Although Sander did not mention the terms specifically, his remarks gave birth to the concept of the "multi-door courthouse." Sander clarified that he was not seeking to replace the courts, but to prevent them from being overloaded with cases for which a judicial solution may not be the best approach. In his view, "the goal is to reserve the courts for those activities for which they are best suited and to avoid swamping and paralyzing them with cases that do not require their unique capabilities"

Deborah Thompson Eisenberg, *Frank Sander: Father of Court-based Dispute Resolution* In: *Discussions in Dispute Resolution*. Edited by: Art Hinshaw, Andrea Kupfer Schneider, and Sarah Rudolph Cole, Oxford University Press (2021). © Oxford University Press. DOI: 10.1093/oso/9780197513248.003.0069

(p. 132). In other words, Sander urged courts to "fit the forum to the fuss" (Sander & Goldberg 1994).

Many aspects of Sander's vision came true. For example, a "follow up" Pound Conference task force recommended the development of Neighborhood Justice Centers (Levin & Wheeler 1979, p. 301). The US Department of Justice provided funding for three such centers and others blossomed around the nation. Today, such centers continue to offer free or low-cost conflict resolution services to the public and receive case referrals from the courts.

Courts also began to integrate ADR into civil and, over time, criminal dockets. The dominant mode of judicial dispute resolution has completely flip-flopped since 1976. Trials are nearly extinct, with more than 95 percent of cases resolved through some process other than trial. The Alternative Dispute Resolution Act of 1998, 28 U.S.C. § 651 (2012), prompted every federal court to offer some type of ADR, including mediation, settlement conferences, neutral case evaluation, and summary jury trials. Many state judiciaries have well-developed ADR programs for civil cases. Some states also use diversionary processes, such as restorative conferencing, victim-offender mediation, and problem-solving courts, for criminal and juvenile justice matters. Indeed, ADR options have become so well integrated into the practice of law that we now speak of "appropriate" rather than "alternative" dispute resolution.

Legal education slowly evolved in the face of these changes. When Sander spoke in 1976, few law schools offered ADR courses. Today, the American Bar Association's law school accreditation standards recognize negotiation and conflict resolution as core learning competencies for lawyers. Many law schools offer specialized ADR tracks and a varied menu of ADR courses.

Sander was not the first person to propose the use and study of ADR, but his speech marked a "tipping point." His stature as a Harvard Law School professor and his thoughtful remarks about the potential benefits of ADR—combined with the purpose of and influential audience at the Pound Conference—kicked off an explosion of ADR experimentation.

II. How?

And yet, "the more things change, the more they stay the same." ADR remains a relatively nascent field and has much learning and growing ahead. Sander noted the "recurring nature of many of the issues" discussed at the Pound Conference (p. 134). Some courts have cut ADR programs in the face of budget constraints. Even though most law practice involves negotiation and processes other than trials, law schools remain overly focused on the trial model. Some law schools have retreated, eliminating ADR programs or faculty lines. The ADR field continues to grapple with the core questions Sander raised, especially concerning the implementation of ADR. These foundational issues include:

Who decides? Sander proposed that the court (through a screening clerk) would suggest or mandate a particular dispute resolution process based on certain criteria: the parties' relationship, the type of case, the cost of litigation, the time involved, and the amount in dispute. The criteria delineated by Sander continue to factor into the evaluation of dispute resolution options, but debate continues about who—the parties or the court—should decide whether ADR is appropriate. Some courts mandate mediation, especially in child custody cases. Others offer a voluntary menu of ADR options, honoring the fundamental tenet of party self-determination. Some state ethical codes require that attorneys advise clients about dispute resolution options other than litigation.

Quality of the process. ADR may offer significant benefits in the right contexts and cases, yet "more" ADR may be counterproductive in the absence of quality processes. The field remains divided about the characteristics of a fair and effective ADR process. We continue to grapple with whether and how the rights of the disadvantaged and less powerful can be protected in informal processes like mediation. We have not resolved whether mediators and other neutrals should be governed by licensing standards and what the contours of such a system should be. The very definition of "mediation" continues to spark lively debate. For example, should mediators be "evaluative" or "directive" to help the parties settle the case, or be more "facilitative," helping the parties have a conversation and devise their own self-determined solutions to their conflict?

Need for rigorous data. As we continue to refine dispute processing, Sander's piece offers some wise guidance. To start, Sander called for better data about what exists and for evaluations of the efficacy and costs of different dispute resolution mechanisms. There has been significant progress in this regard over the past four decades, but questions remain. For example, studies have found that mediation outperforms litigation on several measures, including party satisfaction with process and outcome (Wissler 2002). Studies have also found compliance rates for mediation agreements to be higher than court-imposed orders. A study comparing the experience of small claims litigants who used day-of-trial ADR to those who used trial found that ADR improved party attitudes toward and relationships with each other, gave parties a greater sense of empowerment and voice, increased their taking responsibility for the dispute, and increased their overall satisfaction with the judiciary (Charkoudian et al. 2017).

Researchers also are delving more rigorously into questions of the specific program characteristics and techniques that promote positive outcomes in ADR. In the first generation of ADR research, most evaluations focused on settlement rates and party satisfaction. The ADR field now seeks to put a finer empirical point on "what works" in ADR (ABA 2017). Although such studies are difficult to do, research is emerging about the impact of specific interventions or strategies used by the mediator in various types of cases.

III. Why?

In addition to developing the "what" and "how" of ADR, we continue to examine the "why" of ADR. What "problem" is ADR trying to solve? Sander grabbed our attention with the specter of litigation rates spiraling out of control. He worried that courts lacked "sufficient competence, resources or remedial power" to address the myriad social problems presented to them (p. 120). Sander's core concern resided in efficiency concerns, especially the prevention and avoidance of litigation.

A closer reading of Sander's speech reveals another underlying theme: the need for community-based conflict resolution. Sander worried that we were turning to the courts to resolve issues that previously had been handled by other institutions of society—families, churches, and communities (p. 114). Had we as a society lost our sense of self-efficacy—the ability to work through our conflicts and resolve them without legal intervention? While expressing concern about the collapse of certain societal institutions, Sander's primary focus was the impact on the legal system. His proposed solutions were likewise law-centric: what courts, lawyers, and lawmakers can do to turn off the spigot of lawsuits.

While Sander's proposals focused on legal settlements, his concern about our inability as a populace to resolve conflicts peacefully strikes an especially relevant chord today. In an era of extreme political polarization, the ADR field is starting to explore the role that conflict resolution theory and practice play not only in the context of legal disputes but in our democracy more generally.

Can ADR serve social justice or norm-creating purposes? Can ADR processes promote greater empathy and understanding, or at least facilitate our ability to talk to each other across polarized divides? Around the same time that Sander spoke at the Pound Conference, Norwegian criminologist Nils Christie argued that society did not have too many conflicts, but *too few*. He worried about the criminal justice system's impact on societal conflict resolution, positing that conflicts are property belonging to the people involved. He argued that conflicts are "social fuel" providing important opportunities for norm-clarification (Christie 1977). In Christie's view, lawyers and courts "steal" conflicts away from the individuals most affected, resulting in the stunted development of community norms.

Christie's piece provided the foundation for another type of ADR—restorative justice—which views conflicts not as legal disputes to avoid or "settle," but as harms that need to be repaired directly by the individuals involved. Legal scholars in a variety of fields are exploring the use of restorative justice to address a range of issues, including criminal justice reform, intimate partner violence, and the school-to-prison pipeline.

And so, we end back where Sander began. Sander did not provide all of the answers, but asked the right questions. He sparked our curiosity, nurtured our imagination, and set us on an adventure with the sage advice: "There are no panaceas; only promising avenues to explore" (p. 133). Sander's call for varieties of dispute processing, in our courts and in our society more generally, is more important and urgent than ever.

References

American Bar Association Section of Dispute Resolution, Report of the Task Force on Research on Mediator Techniques (June 12, 1977).

Lorig Charkoudian, Deborah T. Eisenberg, & Jamie Walter, *What Difference Does ADR Make: Comparison of ADR and Trial Outcomes in Small Claims Court*, 35 Conflict Resol. Q. 7–45 (2017).

Nils Christie, *Conflict as Property*, 17 BRIT. J. CRIMINOLOGY 1–15 (1977).
THE POUND CONFERENCE: PERSPECTIVES ON JUSTICE IN THE FUTURE (Leo A. Levin & Russell R. Wheeler eds., 1979).
Frank Sander & Stephen B. Goldberg, *Fitting the Forum to the Fuss: A User-Friendly Guide to Selecting an ADR Procedure*, 10 NEGOT. J. 49 (1994).
L.R. Wissler, *Court-Connected Mediation in General Civil Cases: What We Know from Empirical Research*, 17 OHIO ST. J. ON DISP. RESOL. 641–704 (2002).

Varieties of Dispute Processing: The Implications on Legal Education

Yael Efron

Sander's prophetic remarks in *Varieties of Dispute Processing*, along with the work of the other forefathers and foremothers of our field, have shaped dispute resolution reality worldwide on many levels: it has shaped policymaking in the sense that many dispute resolution mechanisms found their way into justice administration, civil and criminal, around the globe; it has brought to the attention of legal education institutions the need to enrich the legal curriculum with knowledge and skills required to function in the newly shaped administration of justice; it equipped the toolbox of legal professionals with much more diverse tools to assist clients; and it shifted the discourse in society about judicial satisfaction from "winning" to "getting what I needed."

Sander's advocacy for a flexible and diverse process for resolving disputes was illustrated by his vision of a Dispute Resolution Center, where the grievant would first be channeled through a screening clerk who would then direct him to the process (or sequence of processes) most appropriate to his type of case (p. 25). He also regarded the community as a resource for support in disputes, which would not only hold efficiency benefits but also societal advantages for healing and coming together (p. 22). This perception introduced a need for lawyers to collaborate with other professionals, such as community leaders, financial experts, therapists, policymakers and more.

I. A Worldwide Call for Change

Sander's seminal ideas of an interdisciplinary, client-focused, and interest-based approach to law, a novelty at the time, planted the seed for the contemporary legal curriculum all over the world. These concepts are illustrated throughout the recommendations of many investigatory reports—in the United States and abroad—to reform legal education. In the United States, the MacCrate Report and the Carnegie Report suggested shifting legal curricula to include many of Sander's ideas on expanding the goals of legal education beyond legal analysis alone. The competency of law graduates is often criticized outside the United States as well. In the United Kingdom, the courts scrutinized law schools after a group of law firms enacted their own private training programs to bridge the gap between the legal curriculum and the skills required for the profession. In Israel, the bar association often complains about the professional ethics and skills of law graduates, which it claims disservice clients, and currently leads an aggressive campaign against what it calls "the deterioration of the profession." The worldwide reported gap between what lawyers do and what

Yael Efron, Varieties of Dispute Processing*: The Implications on Legal Education* In: *Discussions in Dispute Resolution*. Edited by: Art Hinshaw, Andrea Kupfer Schneider, and Sarah Rudolph Cole, Oxford University Press (2021).
DOI: 10.1093/oso/9780197513248.003.0070

they learn made the legal community very receptive to Sander's call for a different approach to educating lawyers. Problem-solving and collaborative thinking, once foreign to a lawyer's skill set, are not only considered essential to the practice of the successful lawyering but teaching them is now considered best practices for legal education (Stuckey et al., pp. 11–21).

II. Sander-Inspired Curricular Reforms around the World

Although US law schools have been slow to shift their curricula to prepare students for effective and responsible practice, a growing number of legal educators understand the need to re-examine the goals and methods of legal education and include some of Sander's ideas to improve the preparation of their students for practice. These educators teach their students to:

> [D]iagnose and analyze problems, to talk to and listen to people, to facilitate conversations, to negotiate effectively, to resolve disputes, to understand and present complex material, to use ever-changing technologies, to plan, to evaluate both economic and emotional components and consequences of human decision-making, and to be creative—to use tried and true methods when they are appropriate, but not to fear new and category-smashing ideas or solutions. (Menkel-Meadow, p. 14)

Outside the United States, legal communities have adopted Sander's interdisciplinary, client-focused, and interest-based approach to law. The Law Society of England and Wales stated what it sees as the core characteristics and abilities that law graduates should possess. These include, among others, the capacity to communicate effectively with clients, colleagues, and members of other professions; to recognize clients' financial, commercial, and personal constraints and priorities; and to effectively approach problem-solving and use current technologies and strategies to store, retrieve, and analyze information (The Law Society, p. 6). These ideas, novice and bold at the time of Sander's address at the Pound Conference in 1976, are now commonplace and widely accepted around the Western legal world.

III. Further Need for Curricular Improvement

As profoundly as Sander's ideas affected legal systems, legal thought, and legal education, some problems identified in his 1976 address have not yet been solved. With regard to the unresolved idiosyncrasies still present in legal education, I see five areas where Sander's ideas are still poorly met in legal education: (1) the justice gap; (2) the aftermath of dispute resolution; (3) the effects of a technologically complex rich society; (4) interdisciplinary efforts; and (5) a lack of empirical data to inform theory.

While advocating for varieties of dispute processing, Sander notes the cost-benefit aspects of diverse dispute management systems, both for the parties as well as for the taxpayers in general (pp. 23–24). This socially conscious perception of Sander's is unfortunately less prevalent in legal education. One interjection between Sander's ideals with the reality of legal education is the corporate lawyering orientation of most legal curricula, often at the expense of cultivating public-cause and socially sensitive lawyering. A skewed view of legal education inhibits socially conscious graduates to pursue this line of practice, in the fear of the financial burdens that legal education might entail. Considering law schools' decline in enrollment due to poor job prospects and the justice-gap in legal services, a convergence of interests can be created. For those law schools that embrace access-to-justice goals, then alternative dispute resolution (ADR) classes, now present in most law schools, could be utilized as another aspect of access to justice. This could contribute both to graduates' job prospects as well as to societies in need that would regard ADR processes as their "court" experience.

Another predicament not yet fully resolved stems out of the question, "What happens after the ink is dry?" Education associated with alternative dispute processing is still mainly focused on reaching an agreement. We are still lacking theoretical and practical models for dealing with "the day after." Enforcement still requires turning to the judiciary, and many of its backloads have simply been shifted from lawsuits to other pleas before the courts. Legal education is largely missing post-agreement collaboration theories and practices. By broadening the scope and depth of ADR research and teaching in academe, novel theoretical models could be developed to inform practice: empirical data is needed to evaluate what are the fragile elements of negotiated agreements; attention to these pitfalls could be directed in teaching ADR; and mainstreaming ADR throughout the legal curriculum could contribute to the input of various legal experts, such as business law, contract law, and administrative law professors, to these questions.

A third aspect of a lack in education for lawyers is the effect technology has on the legal profession. The idea of a "technologically complex rich society" (p. 9) that allows for better conflict avoidance seemed appealing to Sander. Recent research suggests that although technology enables the capacity to avoid and resolve disputes—it has also contributed to the flourishing of others (from the ease of filing complaints at the push of a button to privacy issues, and more). Katsh and Rabinovich-Einy argue that increasingly sophisticated technology produces increasingly sophisticated conflicts (Katsh & Rabinovich-Einy, p. 3). For instance, technology creates risks to privacy, on one hand, and a veil for unfair compromise by disempowered parties, on the other. The technical literacy required also poses a risk of misusing legal tools and terminology that might determine a dispute. These risks, as well as others, of using technologies to resolve disputes without carefully educating lawyers of its hazards alongside its potential, could result not only in unsatisfied clients but also in worsening the burden on the judiciary.

Additionally, Sander briefly touches on the arm-wrestling game between the legal profession and other professions, concerning who's most qualified to solve a conflict (p. 22). Sander's variety of dispute processing introduced a need for skill sets wider and more diverse than the ones required for adjudication. To many lawyers' dismay, many other professionals master listening skills, empathy, and other constructive interpersonal communication skills far better than some lawyers and judges. The advantage for other professional in the dispute management arena caused a hurricane-alert among the legal bar and bench around the world. As a result, many states took firm actions against the "unauthorized practice of law," on the one hand, and, on the other, legal educators added several requirements geared toward adding "lawyering skills" to the curriculum. Teaching lawyers to humbly collaborate with other professionals is key for their professional development and success. Delicate buds, suggesting movement in this direction, can already be found in the growing "collaborative practice," found mainly in family disputes, and should be cultivated to encompass more fields of law.

In addition, shedding light on what is still missing from the legal curriculum and how gaps might be filled could drive the legal profession further toward fulfilling Sander's vision and legacy. Lande and Sternlight claim that law school curricula provide too little instruction in skills other than legal analysis and argument and call law schools to stress other relevant lawyering skills as well. These might include interviewing, counseling, process-selection advising, negotiation, advocacy, and transactional problem-solving (Lande & Sternlight, pp. 261–62). Providing law students with not only a wider skill set but also with a better understanding of its relevance could better realize Sander's prophecy.

Lastly, the overwhelming development of dispute processing mechanisms, research and theory evolution and educational reforms exposed the holes in the ever-growing net of knowledge surrounding legal conflicts. Yet the more we know, the more we are puzzled by disputes that don't conform to the theoretical models we've developed. A growing scope of conflicts seem intractable and satisfaction with the judicial process has not yet improved. As it was in 1976, more data is still required to improve the administration of justice. This is one place where legal educators can work with courts to participate in discovery and analysis. Too few academics do this kind of research, which is problematic as it may be among the most important work to be done in the legal field. Without it, how can dispute resolution systems, including trial and trial-related processing, improve?

IV. A Vision to Yet Be Fully Realized

We know today that Sander's address at the conference was his first cut at these ideas, simply reflecting his hopes and aspirations at the time. Based upon the foundation Sander laid, legal systems and legal thought have evolved to require a much richer portfolio of services which can be found all around the world—from prefiling protocols, through technology-administered disputes, to a wide (and yet widening) array of alternatives for dispute processing. Although law schools around the world are following these developments, many aspects of legal education are still dragging behind. Sander's forty-year-old ideas regarding the practice of law and its role in society are yet to be carried forward by the legal academy in full blast.

References

Ethan Katsh & Orna Rabinovich-Einy, Digital Justice: Technology and the Internet of Disputes (2017).

John Lande & Jean R. Sternlight, *The Potential Contribution of ADR to an Integrated Curriculum: Preparing Law Students for Real World Lawyering*, 25(1) OHIO ST. J. ON DISP. RESOL. 247 (2010).

THE LAW SOCIETY, QUALIFYING AS A SOLICITOR—A FRAMEWORK FOR THE FUTURE: A CONSULTATION PAPER (Mar. 2005).

Carrie Menkel-Meadow, *Taking Problem-Solving Pedagogy Seriously: A Response to the Attorney General*, 49 J. LEGAL EDUC. 14 (1999).

ROY STUCKEY ET AL., BEST PRACTICES FOR LEGAL EDUCATION: A VISION AND A ROAD MAP (2007).

Article 4.3

Against Settlement

Owen M. Fiss

93 Yale Law Journal 1073 (1984)

... I do not believe that settlement as a generic practice is preferable to judgment or should be institutionalized on a wholesale and indiscriminate basis. It should be treated instead as a highly problematic technique for streamlining dockets ... It is a capitulation to the conditions of mass society and should be neither encouraged nor praised.

The Imbalance of Power

... [T]he dispute resolution story that underlies ADR implicitly asks us to assume a rough equality between the contending parties. It treats settlement as the anticipation of the outcome of trial and assumes that the terms of settlement are simply a product of the parties' predictions of that outcome. In truth, however, settlement is also a function of the resources available to each party to finance the litigation, and those resources are frequently distributed unequally ...

The disparities in resources between the parties can influence the settlement in three ways. First, the poorer party may be less able to amass and analyze the information needed to predict the outcome of the litigation, and thus be disadvantaged in the bargaining process. Second, he may need the damages he seeks immediately and thus be induced to settle as a way of accelerating payment, even though he realizes he would get less now than he might if he awaited judgment. ... Third, the poorer party might be forced to settle because he does not have the resources to finance the litigation, to cover either his own projected expenses, such as his lawyer's time, or the expenses his opponent can impose through the manipulation of procedural mechanisms such as discovery. ...

* * *

We count, however, on the guiding presence of the judge, who can employ a number of measures to lessen the impact of distributional inequalities. ... Judgment aspires to an autonomy from distributional inequalities, and it gathers much of its appeal from this aspiration.

Owen M. Fiss, *Against Settlement* In: *Discussions in Dispute Resolution.* Edited by: Art Hinshaw, Andrea Kupfer Schneider, and Sarah Rudolph Cole, Oxford University Press (2021). © Oxford University Press. DOI: 10.1093/oso/9780197513248.003.0071

The Absence of Authoritative Consent

The argument for settlement presupposes that the contestants are individuals.... But ... the fact [is] that many parties are not individuals but rather organizations or groups. We do not know who is entitled to speak for these entities and to give the consent upon which so much of the appeal of settlement depends.

* * *

These problems become even more pronounced when we turn from organizations and consider the fact that much contemporary litigation involves even more nebulous social entities, namely, groups. Some of these groups, such as ethnic or racial minorities.... may have an identity or existence that transcends the lawsuit, but they do not have any formal organizational structure and therefore lack any procedures for generating authoritative consent....

The Federal Rules of Civil Procedure require that groups have a "representative"; this representative purports to speak on behalf of the group, but he receives his power by the most questionable of all elective procedures-self-appointment or, if we are dealing with a defendant class, appointment by an adversary. The rules contemplate notice to the members of the group about the pendency of the action and the claims of the representative, but it is difficult to believe that notice could reach all members of the group, or that it could cure the defects in the procedures by which the representative gets his power....

* * *

The Lack of a Foundation for Continuing Judicial Involvement

The dispute-resolution story trivializes the remedial dimensions of lawsuits and mistakenly assumes judgment to be the end of the process.... Often, however, judgment is not the end of a lawsuit but only the beginning.... In these cases, settlement cannot provide an adequate basis for that necessary continuing involvement, and thus is no substitute for judgment.

The parties may sometimes be locked in combat ... and view the lawsuit as only one phase in a long continuing struggle.... One of the parties will invariably return to the court and again ask for its assistance ... because the conditions that preceded the lawsuit have unfortunately not changed. This often occurs in domestic-relations cases, where the divorce decree represents only the opening salvo in an endless series of skirmishes over custody and support.

The structural reform cases that play such a prominent role on the federal docket provide another occasion for continuing judicial involvement. In these cases, courts seek to safeguard public values by restructuring large-scale bureaucratic organizations.... As a consequence, courts must oversee and manage the remedial process for a long time....

* * *

Settlement also impedes vigorous enforcement, which sometimes requires use of the contempt power. As a formal matter, contempt is available to punish violations of a consent decree. But courts hesitate to use that power to enforce decrees that rest solely on consent, especially when enforcement is aimed at high public officials....

Sometimes the agreement between the parties ... includes stipulated "findings of fact" and "conclusions of law".... Even assuming that the consent is freely given and authoritative, the bargain is at best contractual and does not contain the kind of enforcement commitment already embodied in a decree that is the product of a trial and the judgment of a court.

Justice Rather Than Peace

The dispute-resolution story makes settlement appear as a perfect substitute for judgment ... by reducing the social function of the lawsuit to one of resolving private disputes: In that story, settlement appears to achieve exactly the same purpose as judgment—peace between the parties—but at considerably less expense to society. The two quarreling neighbors turn to a court in order to resolve their dispute, and society makes courts available because it wants to aid in the achievement of their private ends or to secure the peace.

In my view, however, the purpose of adjudication should be understood [broadly]. Adjudication uses public resources, and employs ... public officials chosen by a process in which the public participates. These officials ... possess a power that has been defined and conferred by public law, not by private agreement. Their job is ... to explicate and give force to the values embodied in authoritative texts such as the Constitution and statutes: to interpret those values and to bring reality into accord with them. This duty is not discharged when the parties settle.

In our political system, courts are reactive institutions. They do not search out interpretive occasions, but instead wait for others to bring matters to their attention.... A settlement will thereby deprive a court of the occasion, and perhaps even the ability, to render an interpretation.... To be against settlement is not to urge that parties be "forced" to litigate, since that would interfere with their autonomy and distort the adjudicative process.... To be against settlement is only to suggest that when the parties settle, society gets less than what appears, and for a price it does not know it is paying. Parties might settle while leaving justice undone.... To settle for something means to accept less than some ideal.

* * *

... [S]ettlement is controlled by the litigants, and is subject to their private motivations and all the vagaries of the bargaining process....

The Real Divide

To all this, one can readily imagine a simple response by way of confession and avoidance: We are not talking about those lawsuits.... My response is twofold.

First, ... I doubt that the number of cases I am referring to is trivial.... [T]hey probably dominate the docket of a modern court system.

Second, it demands a certain kind of myopia to be concerned only with the number of cases.... All cases are not equal. The Los Angeles desegregation case, to take one example, is not equal to the allegedly more typical suit involving a property dispute or an automobile accident. The desegregation suit consumes more resources, affects more people, and provokes far greater challenges to the judicial power. The settlement movement.... must speak to these more "significant" cases, and demonstrate the propriety of settling them....

... The problems of settlement are not tied to the subject matter of the suit, but instead stem from factors that are harder to identify, such as the wealth of the parties, the likely post-judgment history of the suit, or the need for an authoritative interpretation of law.... Many of the factors that lead a society to bring social relationships that otherwise seem wholly private (e.g., marriage) within the jurisdiction of a court ... are also likely to make settlement problematic. Settlement is a poor substitute for judgement; it is an even poorer substitute for the withdrawal of jurisdiction.

... I suspect instead that what divides [me from ADR proponents] is much deeper and stems from our understanding of the purpose of the civil lawsuit and its place in society. It is a difference in outlook.

[They] see[] adjudication in essentially private terms: The purpose of lawsuits and the civil courts is to resolve disputes, and the amount of litigation we encounter is evidence of the needlessly combative and quarrelsome character of Americans.... I, on the other hand, see adjudication in more public terms: civil litigation is an institutional arrangement for using state power to bring a recalcitrant reality closer to our chosen ideals. We turn to the courts because we need to, not because of some quirk in our personalities. We train our students in the tougher arts so that they may help secure all that the law promises, not because we want them to become gladiators or because we take a special pleasure in combat.

To conceive of the civil lawsuit in public terms as America does might be unique. I am willing to assume that no other country ... has a case like Brown v. Board of Education in which the judicial power is used to eradicate the caste structure. .... Adjudication American-style is not a reflection of our combativeness but rather a tribute to our inventiveness and perhaps even more to our commitment.

Comments

ADR and Public Values Again

Amy J. Cohen

This comment revisits a long-standing debate about alternative dispute resolution (ADR) and public values. In *Against Settlement*, Fiss argued that ADR would undermine popular commitments to "public values" (1984). For Fiss, public values are moral truths about rights, justice, and social cohesion that all who comprise "the public" should want to uphold, and which the state is obligated to enforce. Fiss distinguished public values from subjective preference, or what any one individual actually desires. He submitted that by resolving disputes according to individual preference, ADR would replace public values with individual interests and replace state power with private social ordering. Hence, Fiss declared himself against settlement.

Against Settlement is reproduced in all major ADR casebooks, and many ADR proponents have marshaled a response. Some agree with Fiss that certain categories of cases are inappropriate for ADR. Others object that Fiss neglects the kinds of public values that ADR may promote. I argue that this standard engagement between Fiss and ADR overlooks the larger political and social implications of his ideas. Many ADR proponents assume that Fiss indicted ADR as intrinsically incapable of promoting public values. But rather than offering a structural critique of ADR as an institution, Fiss, I venture, assembled a political and provisional critique of settlement ideologies, which he predicted would erode popular commitments to the American welfare state. Fiss *did* divide dispute processing into two camps—but naming them adjudication and ADR misses the target of his ambitions. For him, the more salient distinction was between moral deliberation and interest satisfaction. Fiss defended adjudication *and* extrajudicial deliberative processes that aim to establish the truth of antecedent moral ideals through human reasoning. And he opposed extrajudicial processes that encourage bargained-for-exchange apart from concerns with moral truth. Let me elaborate these claims.

Before he published *Against Settlement*, Fiss warned that dispute resolution—with its emphasis on maximizing interests rather than adjudicating rights—would replace law with markets as a primary means of conflict resolution, and replace the state with individuals as the agents primarily responsible for social well-being. Adjudication, he insisted, is founded on principles of social justice—judges are constrained by norms and rules that "enable and perhaps even force the judge to be objective" and defend the public good (Fiss 1979). Dispute resolution, by contrast, reflects and reinforces a form of social and political organization where "there are no public values, only the private desires of individuals" (Fiss 1982a, pp. 122–23).

Amy J. Cohen, *ADR and Public Values Again* In: *Discussions in Dispute Resolution*. Edited by: Art Hinshaw, Andrea Kupfer Schneider, and Sarah Rudolph Cole, Oxford University Press (2021).
DOI: 10.1093/oso/9780197513248.003.0072

Numerous scholars have argued that Fiss overstates the coherence and rationality of the adjudicatory process. Others have submitted that privatization has come from within the courts themselves. I make a different point.

Fiss did not suggest that ordinary individuals could not or would never use extra-judicial processes to generate public values in the enlightened manner of the judge. It is just that individuals "need not" and hence, he inferred, they probably won't. Given "a social and political culture dominated by the privatization of all ends," Fiss predicted that American ADR would unfold as freedom-of-contract ideology (Fiss 1982b, p. 741). In the 1980s, he argued that state power was needed to stem regressive economic and social policies. Without the state—or rather without a public judiciary authorized to articulate values insulated from market forces—all we have are "politics dominated by the market," and we have ADR (Cohen 2009, p. 1157, quoting Fiss 1987).[1] Hence Fiss opposed American ADR because it was not required, and therefore it was unlikely, to engender or apply collective moral truths.

This argument is intelligible, and for some highly persuasive, from within the American context that Fiss was theorizing. But what would it mean to promote public values against markets in a different time and space: for example, in international contexts lacking supranational judicial bodies, or in developing states with weak courts? As Fiss was writing *Against Settlement*, the neoliberal ideologies he was challenging at home traveled abroad to developing economies, often through policies known as the Washington Consensus (e.g., trade liberalization, deregulation, and privatization), enforced by international financial institutions through conditions on loans.

In the early 2000s, when Fiss turned his attention to international development, he criticized the Washington Consensus for instrumentalizing law to serve market ends. He wanted law to embody public values—here defined as *human rights*—that could trump the exigencies of markets: "we can save law from the clutches of neoliberalism and the market," he argued, "only by affirming, as human rights advocates indeed do, the autonomy of law and its devotion to justice" (Cohen 2009, p. 1159, quoting Fiss 2001).

But even though Fiss argued that markets should yield to human rights, at times, he further insisted, human rights should yield to *democracy*. For example, Fiss did not categorically endorse the adjudication of human rights in international courts. In democratic states, he reasoned, citizens consent generally to the national system of which courts are a part; therefore, citizens needn't consent to specific judgments. But in countries transitioning to democratic rule this formula breaks down "in the case of human rights because, while human rights are of a global character, the processes of collective self-determination are essentially local in nature—they take place in the neighborhood, city, province, or nation-state" (Cohen 2009, p. 1159, quoting Fiss 2001). Fiss thus defined human rights as simultaneously universalizing and transcendent *and* of a democratic and dialogic character—their meaning, he argued, depends on the willingness of democratic publics to imagine the moral communities they wish to become. He, in turn, described a *conversational* search for justice and

[1] Editorial constraints prevent me from listing all of Fiss's articles I draw upon in this comment. Hence, some parentheticals reference the page numbers from Cohen 2009 where readers can find the full citations to Fiss's quoted work.

human rights that "contemplates a process of deliberation and discussion" (Cohen 2009, p. 1160, quoting Fiss 1999). Here, then, in diverse political contexts where public values may not emanate from a single center of national authority already legitimated through democratic processes, Fiss suggested that the promotion of public values—the kind of values he would set against market ideologies—can and should take place in popular domains outside of adjudication.

ADR scholars, familiar only with *Against Settlement*, may find Fiss's turn to popular deliberation surprising. But it is consistent with his larger body of work. In 1986, Fiss observed that "analytic arguments wholly internal to the law can take us only so far. There must be something more—a belief in public values and a willingness to act on them. Where will that belief come from?" (Fiss 1986, p. 14). In other words, Fiss himself described courts as contextual institutions—for him, it was not enough that courts perform state power by giving expression to moral values encoded in state law; they must also *receive* expressions of moral values, which are generated by cultivating popular commitments and belief. When courts are disconnected from robust democratic processes, popular deliberation is necessary to create the kinds of public moral commitments that Fiss would use to counteract neoliberalism.

Fiss never extended an olive branch to ADR—his writings endorse only deliberative democratic processes. Today, however, many scholars have proposed to redefine and reconstruct ADR processes as forms of democratic deliberation. Indeed, some have suggested that citizens in weak states can cultivate shared commitments to human rights and the rule of law by participating in newly created ADR systems. Given this convergence between Fiss's long-standing ideals and the emergent contemporary aspirations of ADR scholars, perhaps it is time for the field of ADR to espouse the promotion of public values: to embrace, not refute, Fiss's critiques, and embrace, not deflect, his social justice project. To conclude, I both advance and question this prescription.

Early proponents of ADR made significant concessions to Fiss. Even as they defended ADR, many endorsed adjudication for conflicts that they deemed involved the public's interest. Like Fiss, they distinguished between public value and subjective preference, and they agreed that *unlike* conflicts of moral value, conflicts of *interests* are properly subject to consensual bargaining and joint gains. At the same time, however, some ADR theorists and practitioners offered more radical criticisms of Fiss's normative commitments. They questioned the existence of the kinds of universalizing values that Fiss promoted, arguing that values and principles are invariably subjective, informed by prior experience, affect, perspective, and preference.

ADR's radicalism—its opposition to Fissian liberal legalism through its skepticism of universalizing values—was likely invisible to many legal scholars because, until recently, ADR did not claim to produce social norms or resolve large-scale social problems. Today, however, ADR proponents increasingly suggest that extrajudicial dispute resolution processes can promote good governance and human rights, facilitate reconciliation in the aftermath of war, and challenge oppressive cultural and social norms. Accompanying these shifts in ADR's social ambitions are new debates about morality and reason. Some theorists promote ADR as a better means to achieve the kinds of moral values Fiss envisions. Others argue that ADR should retain its traditional skepticism toward the emancipatory capacity of abstract moral reasoning.

These debates do not reference Fiss's work. Nonetheless they suggest that today we could read Fiss more as a mirror than as an adversary. We could ask how our endorsements of consensual dialogic processes reflect continuities, as well as breaks, with his liberal moral ideals. That is, we could ask how Fiss's arguments reveal central tensions *not* between adjudication and ADR but tensions *within* the discipline of ADR as it presently understands its own social and political commitments.

I suspect that many contemporary ADR scholars are likely to read *Against Settlement* more sympathetically than their predecessors: as a provocation to realign our problem-solving techniques with a mandate to produce public values and advance a social-moral good. But I end on a cautionary note. Even as I argued that Fiss's overarching allegiance is less to specific institutional forms than to universalizing moral ideals, I would resist any straightforward shift in focus from institutions to values. Fiss framed his moral claims from within and against particular social contexts. As such, I read his critique as deeply provisional and historical—as motivated by particular substantive commitments to the American welfare state. Recognizing the historically situated character of Fiss's arguments suggests that those of us who share Fiss's progressive aims should similarly continuously reevaluate the social contexts within which we labor.

In the 1980s, Fiss saw a clear line between the old state and the new market. And he proposed to deploy moral values embodied in law—sacred and noninstrumental—as a strategy to "strengthen our resolve to resist" the penetration of market rationalities into public governance and social life (Fiss 1986, p. 15). Today, however, analysts regularly observe that cultivating commitments to moral values—human rights, for example—can *advance* not simply constrain markets as a dominant form of social ordering. But the lesson I draw from left critics of "neoliberal human rights" is the same lesson I draw from Fiss: the necessity of relentlessly examining the social contexts within which we want institutions *and* values to accomplish particular work. So this comment reads *Against Settlement* not as institutional *or* moral prescription but as political critique. And as political critique, the irresolvable challenge that endures is not ADR versus adjudication, or, for that matter, interests versus values, but rather the recognition that our moral values, like our institutional tools, are shaped by the social conditions we would use them to transcend.

References

Amy J. Cohen, *Revisiting* Against Settlement: *Some Reflections on Dispute Resolution and Public Values*, 78 FORDHAM L. REV. 1143–170 (2009).

Owen M. Fiss, *The Forms of Justice*, 93 HARV. L. REV. 1 (1979).

Owen M. Fiss, *The Social and Political Foundations of Adjudication*, 6 LAW & HUM. BEHAV. 121–28 (1982a).

Owen M. Fiss, *Objectivity and Interpretation*, 34 STAN. L. REV. 739–63 (1982b).

Owen M. Fiss, *The Death of the Law?*, 72 CORNELL L. REV. 1–16 (1986).

What *Against Settlement* Got Right

Ellen Waldman

Professor Owen Fiss's article *Against Settlement* has, in the more than thirty-five years since its publication, become the essay alternative dispute resolution (ADR) enthusiasts love to hate. It boasts over twelve hundred citations, providing impeccably credentialed support for the proposition that nonadversarial dispute resolution erodes the proper role of the courts and sacrifices justice for an uneasy peace. The essay has had an enduring impact in part because of its poetic, sometimes quixotic, insistence on the public norm-enforcing function of the courts and its vision of litigation as a mechanism whereby state power is used "to bring a recalcitrant reality closer to our chosen ideals" (p. 1089).

The dichotomy Fiss constructed between an adversary system that generates and enforces public values and private interventions slavishly devoted to individual interest satisfaction has been much maligned. A rhetorical counterinsurgency has lobbed epithets of litigation romantic and settlement cynic in Fiss's direction. Mediation partisans note that most litigation does not reset society's ethical compass the way *Brown v. Board of Education* did, and not all settlement represents a coerced compromise whereby "society gets less than what appears.... for a price it does not know it is paying" (p. 1086). Still, just as one overdrawn character does not vitiate the power of a Shakespearean play, *Against Settlement* remains a classic, despite its sometimes histrionic tone and exaggeration. The text remains salient because it both foreshadowed ADR's bureaucratic appeal and potential misuse, while reminding us of the central role that justice—substantive, normative justice—must play in any dispute resolution system.

I. Efficiency, Not Philosophy Drives Alternative Dispute Resolution's Continued Growth

Fiss believed that the ADR movement gaining ground in 1984 was the product of accommodation, "a capitulation to the conditions of mass society" (p. 1075). Just as gas lines, electrical blackouts and water use restrictions are byproducts of scarcity, ADR represents a response to too many litigants forced to make do with too few judicial resources. But, triaging trial, Fiss argued, was hardly cause for celebration. ADR would grow, *Against Settlement* suggests, not because of its sound philosophical or political appeal; not because it offers a method of yoking the practice of deliberative democracy to the resolution of personal conflicts; not because it provides an opportunity for the expansion of empathy and empowerment; and not because Americans hunger for

Ellen Waldman, *What* Against Settlement *Got Right* In: *Discussions in Dispute Resolution*. Edited by: Art Hinshaw, Andrea Kupfer Schneider, and Sarah Rudolph Cole, Oxford University Press (2021). © Oxford University Press.
DOI: 10.1093/oso/9780197513248.003.0073

a kinder, gentler way of managing disputes. No, ADR would grow as a practical response to the increasing impracticality of trials.

And, to a large degree, Fiss was right. The explosive growth of ADR has been largely powered by state and federal courts and agencies anxious to cut costs, shorten time to disposition, and manage case backlogs. In the federal sector, the Civil Justice and Reform Act of 1990 (authorizing federal district courts to experiment with ADR processes), the Administrative Dispute Resolution Act of 1996 (replacing agency procedures with faster and less contentious processes), and the Alternative Dispute Resolution Act of 1998 (requiring every district court to offer ADR to parties in civil cases) all explicitly state they are based on policies of reducing litigation expenses and delays through the use of quicker and more efficient processes. At the state level, the impetus was similar.

At the same time that ADR was being promoted for its efficiency, the features that distinguish informal processes from adversarial procedures barely register in disputants' thinking. Recent multijurisdictional field research examining litigants' procedural preferences at the point of initiating litigation revealed that mediation received preference ratings similar to two vastly dissimilar processes: attorney negotiation with clients present and a trial to a judge. Examination of the procedural features litigants favored indicated a preference for vesting control in third parties (such as a judge, attorney advisor, or mediator) as opposed to retaining decisional control themselves. Assessing this finding, study author Professor Donna Shestowsky speculates that:

> litigants may have *perceived* these two procedures, [assisted negotiation with a mediator and unassisted negotiation with clients present] as offering some measure of third-party control.... Thus, the participation of the opposing party and his or her attorney ... or the involvement of a neutral third party (in the case of Mediation) appears to constitute third-party control in the minds of the litigants. (Shestowsky)

So, even when disputants reveal a preference for mediation, it is not for the qualities ADR is touted for, but rather a desire to be guided by a reputed expert toward resolution.

Recently collected data from six continents finds similar reasons for ADR's growth. As part of the Global Pound Conference Series (GPS)—a set of twenty-nine conferences held by the International Mediation Institute (IMI) in twenty-four different countries—732 ADR consumers, advisors, providers, and influencers/thought leaders were surveyed regarding mediation's development. When asked what disputants want when pursuing alternative dispute resolution processes in the commercial arena, the uniform answer was efficiency. In response to the question of what influences a disputant to pursue a particular dispute resolution process, the most frequently selected answer was "to obtain financial compensation"; the second most frequently selected answer was "prevent[ing] or require[ing] an action from one of the parties." Of course, money and injunctive relief are precisely the remedies courts are well situated to provide. ADR's unique capacity to transform relationships or foster procedural justice does not figure prominently in GPS respondents' choices. As Fiss predicted, the GPS respondents displayed only tepid interest in these benefits.

Against Settlement presaged the chasm separating mediation enthusiasts' grandiose claims from the crasser elements that would actually lead to ADR's institutionalization. Fiss himself reserved his own rhetorical arias for the rule of law, as elaborated by judges. Justice, in his view, could only be done through the adversary system, a process devoted to explicating and concretizing the nation's highest ideals.

II. Resources Matter, Not Just in the Courtroom, but in the Mediation Room

Fiss's second important point was that ADR would not insulate the poor from the consequences of their poverty. Being poor would be disadvantageous in the mediation setting, maybe even more so, than in the litigation process.

Fiss was among a pioneering group of ADR critics to sound the alarm regarding power imbalances in informal settings. Aligning with left-wing critics like Laura Nader, Jerome Auerbach, and Richard Delgado, Fiss worried about how traditionally marginalized parties would fare when negotiating against more powerful interests. In particular, he worried about the problem of disparate resources. Penury pushes people to agree to less money than they deserve because they cannot shoulder transaction costs or wait for a hard-fought payout. Additionally, if reaching settlement entails assessing offers on the table against possible judicial outcomes, Fiss frets that "the poorer party may be less able to amass and analyze the information needed to predict the outcome of the litigation . . ." (p. 1076).

Actually, the reality today is worse than what Fiss imagined. *Against Settlement* seems to assume that even the most poorly resourced individual would have access to a lawyer who could provide some summary of the legal landscape. Disputant poverty might curtail the sort of fact-finding needed for detailed, accurate predictions of judicial outcomes; consequently, impoverished disputants might be less adept than wealthier counterparts at bargaining in the shadow of the law. But, whereas Fiss imagined that less-resourced parties would suffer from not be able to "lawyer-up" as lavishly as a richer adversary, he did not contemplate how many of today's participants in mediation would be self-represented; that is, they would have *no access* to lawyers and consequently no knowledge of the legal norms that would be salient in a court of law. Nonetheless, courts and agencies shunt these self-represented parties into mediation programs where they are expected to advance their interests in a negotiation setting oriented more toward docket relief than their protection.

What do we know about the effects of entering into court mediation without legal representation or access to legal information? Parties at risk of foreclosure who worked with a housing counselor were three times more likely to obtain a loan modification and keep their homes than those without access to aid or advice (Temkin 2014). A similar dynamic exists in landlord-tenant disputes. Studies of housing courts reveal that represented tenants are three to nineteen times more likely to avoid eviction than are unrepresented tenants (Engler 2010). Statistics from the family arena tell a similar story. Analyses of outcomes in family court reveal that divorcing spouses who are represented are more likely to obtain their desired custody arrangements than those who proceed unrepresented. For example, sole custody was awarded to women in 54.8 percent of cases where only the mother had legal counsel, as opposed to in 13.4 percent of cases where only the father was represented. When fathers were the only party represented, they obtained sole custody in 16.2 percent of cases as opposed to 7.1 percent of cases when neither party was represented (The Women's Law Center of Maryland 2006). Studies of the effect of representation in family mediation reveal that mediators are less likely to screen for domestic violence when attorneys are not involved and that when attorneys thoroughly prepare their clients for mediation, disputants report feeling less pressure to settle and report higher levels of satisfaction with the mediation process (Wissler 2010).

Although data of this sort leads some ADR theorists to wincingly concede that unrepresented parties may not be well served in mediation, a common rejoinder is that litigation for the unrepresented is even worse. Fiss was well aware that asymmetries of knowledge, power, and money distort adversarial processes, making it more likely that rich, sophisticated parties will prevail over poorly resourced ones. But the difference, Fiss posited, lay in the ideals animating each process. Settlement, based on the parties' bargaining interaction "accepts inequalities of wealth as an integral and legitimate component of the process," whereas judicial judgment "knowingly struggles against those inequalities" (p. 1078). We fall short of our ideals, but that we have them in our mind's eye and work toward them, matters. For Fiss, the litigation prototype is always nobler and more heroic than its bargaining counterpart.

III. Conclusion

We need not agree with every assertion in *Against Settlement* to conclude it is a great piece. To be sure, the Manichean vision Fiss presents is exaggerated. Litigation does not always serve to hold a recalcitrant nation to its highest principles; it can be petty, ignoble, and sordid, just as settlement can be magnanimous, inventive, and balanced. But Fiss reminds us that an audience perhaps overly enamored with "peacemaking" must understand that party consent does not assure a just outcome. Instead, it may reflect one party's despairing, and perhaps erroneous, assessment of her options. More importantly, Fiss also reminds us that, with all its imperfections, the adversarial system represents our democracy's best attempt to give voice to its most sacred civilizing norms. Justice, as Fiss, reminds us, is an aspiration. The adversarial system may fall short, but this neither degrades nor delegitimizes the ideal. Keeping in mind Fiss's romantic vision of what justice requires can only improve our reform efforts as we strive toward the best balance of formal and informal dispute resolution processes.

References

Russell Engler, *Connecting Self-Representation to Civil Gideon: What Existing Data Reveal about When Counsel Is Most Needed*, 37 Fordham Urb. L.J. 38, 48–49 (2010).

Donna Shestowsky, *New Research Sheds Light on How Litigants Evaluate the Characteristics of Legal Procedures*, 34 Alternatives to High Cost Litig. 145, 153 (2016).

Kenneth M. Temkin et al., National Foreclosure Mitigation Counseling Program Evaluation, Final Reports 3 Through 5, 3, 57 (Urban Institute, 2014).

Roselle L. Wissler, *Representation in Mediation: What We Know from Empirical Research*, 37 Fordham Urb. L.J. 419, 433 (2010).

The Women's Law Ctr. of Md., Inc., *Families in Transition: A Follow-up Study Exploring Family Law Issues in Maryland* (2006), *available at* http:// www.wlcmd.org/pdf/FamiliesInTransition.pdf.

From Mass Adjudication to Settlement and Back

Adam S. Zimmerman

Owen Fiss's *Against Settlement* reflected his broader views about the role independent courts play in society. As Fiss explained elsewhere, courts "engage in a special dialogue" in a society (Fiss, *Bureaucratization of the Judiciary*, p. 1443). Unlike other branches of government, courts alone must "listen to all grievances, hear from all the interests affected, and give reasons for [their] decisions" (Fiss, *Forms of Justice*, p. 46).

So, at the time he wrote *Against Settlement*, Fiss worried about how courts were changing. Judges increasingly relied on clerical staff and other special administrative programs to resolve disputes (Fiss, *Bureaucratization of the Judiciary*, p. 1443). New changes to the Federal Rules of Civil Procedure were already beginning to encourage parties to settle at the earliest stages of litigation before magistrates, undermining judicial power to say what the law is. Fiss believed that courts existed precisely to resist bureaucratic thinking and lopsided bargaining that threatened important public values and rights (p. 1085); (Fiss, *Bureaucratization of the Judiciary*, p. 1443).

To appreciate Fiss's arguments in *Against Settlement* and elsewhere, one could contrast them with Robert Kagan's well-known global study of dispute resolution, *Adversarial Legalism*. According to Kagan, the tendency in the United States to resolve problems through court litigation generated more inconsistent results than bureaucratic planning. This kind of "adversarial legalism" was also more rigid, costly, and contentious than more flexible alternatives, like informal mediation or expert resolution. To be sure, courts contributed to new "justice claims and ideas" (Kagan, p. 23). But an overreliance on adjudication was a double-edged sword. It meant that important political decisions—ranging from environmental regulation to presidential elections—would be left to ad hoc, expensive, and sometimes even vexatious, legal challenges inside courts (Kagan, p. 32).

Although written a decade later, *Adversarial Legalism* was the mirror image of Fiss's work in the late 1970s and early 1980s. Unlike Kagan, Fiss was *against settlement* precisely because he was *for adjudication*. "To be against settlement is not to urge that parties be 'forced' to litigate," Fiss explained (p. 1085). To be "against settlement" instead was only to suggest that if "parties settle, society gets less than what appears, and for a price it does not know it is paying" (*Id.*). That price was the toll that routine settlements exacted on core features of the adjudication process to say what the law is. Direct participation and formality were features, not problems, in the American judicial system.

In mass adjudication, which makes up much of the American docket, it is hard to know whether Fiss or Kagan is right. Mass adjudication looks less like what Fiss

Adam S. Zimmerman, *From Mass Adjudication to Settlement and Back* In: *Discussions in Dispute Resolution*. Edited by: Art Hinshaw, Andrea Kupfer Schneider, and Sarah Rudolph Cole, Oxford University Press (2021).
DOI: 10.1093/oso/9780197513248.003.0074

embraced or the "adversarial legalism" Kagan criticized. For the hundreds of thousands of decisions rendered in multidistrict litigation and high-volume criminal courts, mass adjudication in the United States resembles the systems of expert judgment, bureaucracy, and mediated outcomes that Kagan extolled. Disputes are overwhelmingly resolved through settlement processes promoted by local rules, prosecutors' offices, steering committees, and administrative pilot programs. And yet, the norms and values of adjudication that Fiss described in *Against Settlement* persist in some unlikely places. Some have even migrated to special administrative programs designed to be alternatives to the courts themselves.

Section I of this essay discusses how Fiss correctly predicted the ways that new settlement procedures would transform courts, particularly in the area of mass adjudication. Beneath the surface, American courts now rely heavily on expert judgment, bureaucratic decisions, and mediated settlement schemes. Section II, however, suggests that the rise of alternative dispute resolution has been a two-way street. Even as some mass settlement schemes have supplanted adjudication, others have adopted procedures that engage in the same "special dialogue" that Fiss associated exclusively with courts. In the years ahead, a central challenge will be to identify how hybrid systems of dispute resolution can provide meaningful relief without sacrificing the values of public adjudication that Fiss championed.

I. Administrative Settlement in the Adjudication

Today, mass adjudication dominates federal courts and beyond. Almost 40 percent of pending civil cases on the federal docket are managed according to the streamlined processes of multidistrict litigation (MDL). And the overwhelming majority of individual cases in MDLs (89 percent) reside in twenty-one mass tort MDLs that have over one thousand cases each. According to a 2016 report to the Judicial Panel of Multidistrict Litigation, in most of these cases, judges managed "settlements . . . involving a majority or a substantial number of cases" using a wide variety of case management techniques. This phenomenon is not limited to the federal courts. Almost half of the states also have complex litigation procedures that mirror the multidistrict litigation rules in federal district courts.

The growth of more structured settlement approaches in federal MDLs was a response to Supreme Court decisions in the late 1990s that scaled back the use of class actions. Parties accordingly turned to MDLs to settle massive disputes. Over the next two decades, the Judicial Panel on Multidistrict Litigation (JPML) consolidated more and more cases, on average between 70 percent and 80 percent of those filed with the JPML, with limited argument and subject to informal arrangements that quickly dispatched cases to judges with experience managing big cases.

Once consolidated before a federal judge, the Federal Judicial Center's Manual for Complex Litigation recommends that judges resolve cases using many tools that Fiss criticized in *Against Settlement*. Judges appoint special masters and steering committees of lawyers, sometimes without clients, to develop facts, science, and damage models to facilitate settlement. Experienced judges recommend appointing liaison counsel who "play well with others." Some judges have explicitly warned against trials, which may produce outlier or clustering verdicts that are difficult to average and threaten the chances of global settlement. In the area of mass litigation, courts have become large bureaucratic organizations designed to facilitate settlement resolution.

In some cases, the managerial approach to dispute resolution in court is an extension of another level of administrative policymaking inside federal agencies. The National Highway Safety and Transportation Administration and the Consumer Product Safety Commission have issued guidance for courts that issue "umbrella discovery orders" in mass litigation—agreed procedures for the quiet exchange of information. In criminal law, the Bureau of Justice Assistance funds and helps spread mass alternative dispute resolution programs inside state criminal courts, promoting the Justice Department's goals in fighting opioid addiction, combating domestic violence, and responding to the special needs of veterans.

The push to resolve cases through informal, expert, and bureaucratic procedures reflects the perceived benefits of administrative programs seeking to resolve disputes without adversarial hearings. In *Walters v. Radiation Survivors*, for example, the Supreme Court touted the benefits of such programs when it rejected a Due Process challenge to the Veterans Administration (VA) benefit program that functionally barred the use of attorneys. From 1865 through the late 1980s, VA rules prevented lawyers from charging more than $10 for representing veterans in disability hearings. The Supreme Court held that Congress had good reason to create a large adjudication systems without lawyers. Pointing to school disciplinary proceedings, parole hearings, and other mass adjudication systems, the Court said that lawyers and formal hearings would just gum up the works:

> Lawyers, by training and disposition, are advocates, and bound by professional duty to present all available evidence and arguments in support of their clients' positions and to contest with vigor all adverse evidence and views. The role of the hearing body itself... may become more akin to that of a judge at a trial.

According to the Court, full-blown adversarial adjudication was the problem: "The decision-making process will be prolonged, and the financial cost to the State—for appointed counsel ... will not be insubstantial." Mass adjudication in federal courts, state courts, and administrative programs frequently pursue the same end: bureaucratic programs with informal procedures designed to reduce haggling over who deserves what.

But, as Fiss and Kagan both observed, independent courts offer an important failsafe to protect the procedural, substantive, and rule-of-law values threatened by bureaucracies and mass settlement (p. 1085); (Kagan, p. 23). Judicial oversight can combat groupthink, correct systematic error and bias, or require hierarchical organizations to adapt to new developments. Because of weak judicial review in the VA, for example, veterans and commentators complained that disability determinations were subject to systemic errors and average wait times that exceeded six years.

Some courts have attempted to police the integrity of judicial proceedings with "information-forcing" approaches—setting ground rules for the exchange of information and requiring parties to justify difficult trade-offs in mass adjudication. But, overall, American courts rely heavily on expert judgment, bureaucratic decisions, and mediated settlement schemes to resolve mass disputes.

II. Adjudication in Administrative Settlement

But there's another trend not addressed in *Against Settlement* or *Adversarial Legalism*—the extent to which features of public adjudication have worked their way into mass dispute resolution out of court.

Many out-of-court programs have adopted norms from adjudication—vesting neutral decision makers with new tools to collectively hear claims, uncover problems, articulate rights, and improve future decisions. A recent study found that twenty-six federal agencies gave parties express private rights of action in alternative forms of adjudication to supplement administrative enforcement (Sant'Ambrogio, pp. 24–25). Although the specific procedural rights of parties vary by administrative scheme, they include "the ability to submit briefs and evidence, call and examine witnesses, participate in oral arguments, appeal administrative decisions to a higher authority in the agency, and ultimately seek judicial review" (*Id.*). Some of these cases have had significant impact. For example, the Equal Employment Opportunity Commission's (EEOC's) pathbreaking decision in *Baldwin v. Foxx*, interpreting US Supreme Court precedent to bar discrimination against gay and lesbian employees, grew out of an alternative EEOC dispute resolution program for federal employees.

The September 11th Victim Compensation Fund, an alternative dispute resolution program for families impacted by the September 11, 2001, terrorist attacks, adopted a "test case" procedure. Representative claimants presented evidence of their distinct injuries to administrators to establish clearer rules for similar future cases, while resolving difficult questions of distributive justice (Sant'Ambrogio & Zimmerman, p. 2032). Some cases exposed how the Fund would make awards for high-wage earners, like stockbrokers, who died in the attack; others helped settle the question of how the Fund would handle claims brought by low-wage earners, orphans, or family members who provided unpaid but invaluable services, like taking care of a sick relative or doing household chores. Since that time, similar programs have used test cases to resolve difficult issues, like determining compensation through the BP Oil Spill Fund, evaluating whether vaccine preservatives caused autism in children, and resolving difficult scientific causation questions raised by first responders to the September 11 attacks (*Id.* at p. 2033).

Even the VA itself, where the Supreme Court once warned about the dangers of lawyer-driven litigation, has begun to adopt tools designed to promote fact-finding and the adjudication of public rights. For the first time, the Federal Circuit held that a specialized court could hear class actions challenging systemwide problems at the VA. The Federal Circuit reasoned that permitting the Veterans Court to hear class actions would allow it "to serve as lawgiver and error corrector simultaneously." Already a number of service organizations and legal clinics have filed class actions to challenge unlawful rating decisions, mass delays, and regulations denying groups of veterans benefits for radiation exposure.

III. Conclusion

These examples highlight how no single approach to dispute resolution needs to dominate. As courts rely on bureaucratic decision-making and settlement facilitation, our large public and private bureaucracies have adopted tools from adjudication to articulate new rights and reform public programs. If we accept these hybrid models of decision-making, the question becomes one of institutional design: What combination of tools will make a dispute resolution system respond best to the needs of its citizens? Fiss's *Against Settlement* reminds us that, whatever the solution, governments should make room for an independent person in power to listen to people's legal claims, explain their decisions, and "explicate and give force to" shared public values (p. 1085).

References

Owen Fiss, *The Bureaucratization of the Judiciary*, 92 YALE L.J. 1442 (1983).
Owen Fiss, *The Forms of Justice*, 93 HARV. L. REV. 1 (1978).
ROBERT KAGAN, ADVERSARIAL LEGALISM (2001).
Michael Sant'Ambrogio, *Private Enforcement in Administrative Courts*, 72 VAND. L. REV. 425 (2019).
Michael Sant'Ambrogio & Adam S. Zimmerman, *The Agency Class Action*, 112 COLUM. L. REV. 1992 (2012).

The Haunting Specter of Fiss's *Against Settlement*

Marjorie Corman Aaron

Why is Professor Owen Fiss's *Against Settlement* a "foundational piece" in the field? Or is it? By what measure? In which field?

A website dedicated to "Evaluating Research & Publications in Educational Research" addresses the question, of what makes a piece foundational or seminal, with these two excerpted responses:

- Some papers are of central importance to a research topic, often because they report a major breakthrough, insight, or a new and generative synthesis of ideas . . . [and] may describe a study that changes our understanding of a topic. . . .
- The model begins with a new theory. . . . If the scholarly community comes to accept the validity of the new theory this paper is considered a seminal paper. . . . [It] influences the scholarly community's thinking and ultimately, the body of knowledge . . . [and] stimulates the writing of other scholarly papers. . . . [N]ovel thinking, expressed in the seminal paper and subsequent scholarly papers, is organized into new patterns of thinking . . . (About Research & Assessment: Seminal Work, What is a seminal work?, http://libraryresearch.weebly.com/seminal-works).

Well then, should *Against Settlement* be considered "foundational"? Many trees were sacrificed on its altar, but mostly in opposition and rejection. Fiss's central critiques of settlement in alternative dispute resolution (ADR) never gained acceptance as valid or led to new patterns of thinking. To me, most of Fiss's "insights" reflected little awareness of the way litigation, ADR, and settlement work, naïve views on the relationship between courts, truth, and justice, and, in some instances, glib failure to address inconvenient counter-realities and arguments.

So why has *Against Settlement* stuck in the academic ADR field's collective consciousness for so long? Did any of Fiss's troubling visions impact ADR's practice evolution? *Against Settlement* seems a haunting, hovering presence, not often apparent in earthly form but not yet extinguished by time or critique.

I. Why Against Settlement Remains Present in ADR's Academic Field

When ADR was coming of age, folks teaching and writing in this new field were idealistic, optimistic, and intent on doing good. Many were applying theory to practice

Marjorie Corman Aaron, *The Haunting Specter of Fiss's* Against Settlement In: *Discussions in Dispute Resolution*. Edited by: Art Hinshaw, Andrea Kupfer Schneider, and Sarah Rudolph Cole, Oxford University Press (2021).
DOI: 10.1093/oso/9780197513248.003.0075

as creators of court, community, and corporate ADR programs, as mediators, arbitrators, facilitators, and consensus builders, and as teachers and trainers. They had witnessed the impact of our court systems' delays and costs. They were dismayed by the way litigation squandered parties' financial resources and disrupted personal, professional, and corporate fates. They met parties lacking agency and alienated from their own disputes. They recognized litigation's frequent failure to solve underlying problems and its inadequate instruments for redress. ADR—"alternative" or "appropriate" dispute resolution—offered such promise. With pure hearts, ADR pioneers advocated and taught various flavors of mediation, thoughtful design for court-connected and organizationally based programs, and sound approaches to consequential public disputes. They resolved class action and multidistrict civil rights and environmental litigation. ADR found success in parties happy to feel agency and self-determination and to escape litigation's costly grind; in resolutions that optimized mutual benefits; and in creation of earlier docket space for cases requiring public trial.

When Owen Fiss, respected law professor at Yale, accused ADR of undermining the justice system, as if depriving it of caseload calcium needed for healthy bones: that was a slap. His claim that ADR reified and worsened power imbalances delivered another jolt. While ADR proponents might not agree on whether a mediator should tackle power imbalances, I dare say most were horrified by the idea of making them worse.

Imagine ADR in 1984 as a thirty-something, highly educated character who had learned from substantial professional experience and, drawing from it, sought to launch a new venture. Our protagonist's motivations were good. He had done research, consulted expertise, and crafted a plan. Just about everyone wished him well and predicted success. Then, unexpectedly, his generally smart and sympatico uncle raised a slew of arguments, objections, and predictions of perverse consequences. If raised by anyone else, the protagonist would have rejected them forthwith. But, because it was *that* uncle, the protagonist fully considered each of his points before concluding that most were poorly premised, badly reasoned, or factually incorrect, reflecting lack of on-the-ground experience in the field. Our protagonist moved ahead, and the venture succeeded by any measure. That his uncle's words may haunt him still is all to the good, as it motivates greater vigilance against harm to people, institutions, and cherished principles.

I posit that Fiss's paper impacted the academic ADR cohort much as the uncle's words impacted our fictional protagonist. After respectful and reasoned consideration, they mostly rejected its central critiques of settlement. Still, *Against Settlement* leveled a few charges against ADR practice that have borne some truth and require continued vigilance.

II. *Against Settlement* as Not So "Seminal" for ADR's Practice Playing Field

My unscientific survey of ADR practitioners who are not steeped in the academy indicates that most were either unruffled by or completely unaware of *Against Settlement*. I first encountered Professor Fiss's piece and another roughly contemporaneous law review article or two critiquing mediated settlements in 1990-ish, after having mediated for some time at Endispute and through the Middlesex Multi-Door Courthouse program inspired by another famous law professor, Frank Sander. I was not then in academe; Professor Fiss was not my academic uncle. Without angst, and lacking patience for esoterica, I dismissed Fiss's and other similar law review articles as naïve, uninformed, and unuseful. I didn't then and still don't see much value in theory untethered to reality.

Litigation does not deliver Fiss's idealized notions of justice. Thus, opting to settle doesn't sacrifice them. Given litigation's realities, ADR's encouragement of and assistance toward settlement creates great value. Telltale signs of Fiss's predicted harms are absent: legislation for the public good (or not) seems unconnected to ADR; class action settlements are enforceable and constructive. While many settlements are private, court filings are not. Grievances of public concern now more easily find their way into multiplying media news sources. Increased corporate power and wealth disparities may mean greater power imbalances, but responsibility for this truth cannot be laid at ADR's door.

Since 1984, ADR programs and providers have achieved much good by encouraging and assisting settlements. Unarmed with specific statistics, yet generally aware of studies and feedback on court programs and provider organizations, it seems fair to say that parties and lawyers are mostly well served by ADR's promotion and encouragement of settlement.

III. Selected Prescience as Seminal: Which Visions Have Haunted Us, or Should Have?

Having reread *Against Settlement*, and put aside its dominant flaws, I believe we should acknowledge three potential harms in promoting settlement that Fiss identified and too often ring true. With these, perhaps *Against Settlement* may lay claim to having seminally haunted its readers or nonreaders with similar experience, concerns, and conscience.

IV. About Coercion

When *Against Settlement* complains of coercion in ADR, most of the coercive forces it describes arise from realities of law, legal process, and external imbalances of power and resources, and have similar impacts on negotiated settlements. They do not arise from ADR programs or settlement itself.

And yet, I confess to having heard far too many anecdotes about claimants or defendants who felt pressured to settle by the mediator and/or their lawyer in mediation. Some describe feeling "ganged up on." I've heard of mediators saying: "Nope, you're not leaving here until this settles." In caucus, mediators have witnessed lawyers piling on pressure, overselling risks, or implicitly or explicitly threatening abandonment if the lawyers' settlement advice is rejected. We all know of parties who seek to undo a settlement the next day. Sometimes it's about buyer's remorse, or recrimination from someone who wasn't at the table. But sometimes the desire to undo reflects settlement experienced as coercion, not by motivated choice.

Fiss sounded a discerning warning to vigilantly guard against coercion within mediation. While we cannot expiate financial, legal, or other pressures, there is no excuse for failure to honor a party's desire to eschew settlement in favor of the law's process.

V. Power Imbalance Due to Uneven Access to Legal Knowledge

Against Settlement's exhortation against mediation where parties have unequal access to information or lack awareness of their legal rights also rings true.

Our field tends to conflate neutrality with "non-directive" or "non-evaluative"—what I'll call "non-generative" or "non-activist" behavior. Many training programs teach mediators not to raise arguments or highlight facts that participants themselves have not. (See Rule 2.4 of the ABA Model Rules of Professional Conduct (2013), ABA-SDR Resolution on Mediation and the Unauthorized Practice of Law (2002).) Even with unrepresented parties, mediators are often cautioned that providing legal information or evaluating legal issues comes too close to legal advice.

While mediators cannot provide legal advice, much less settlement advice, I read *Against Settlement* as suggesting a sea change: mediators proactively seeking to create a level playing field as to information and legal awareness.

Consider a case where the plaintiff lacks access to (discoverable) company files: the mediator might request bringing relevant information to the table. What if one party tries to pull the wool over the other using disingenuous damage claims, questionable case references, and irrelevant statistics, and the other party is unrepresented or their lawyer is too uninterested or incompetent to notice? Shouldn't the mediator (likely in caucus) ask whether legal and factual issues matter to the parties? If so, couldn't the mediator raise questions about the damages spreadsheet, discuss the holdings in the referenced cases, and question the statistics? Yes, tactfully, and with attention to neutral phrasing. In my view, information about and critical discussion of law and facts are not inherently partisan or non-neutral. Neutrality is violated if, and only if, the mediator steers settlement toward terms favoring one side.

Our field would do well to heed *Against Settlement* on this point: self-determination in settlement requires information about legal process, law, and facts. Mediators can be neutral and proactive. Mediator practice should reflect settlements by parties informed of legal and factual realities, if these matter to them.

VI. Public Danger of Private Settlements and Arbitrations

Fiss sounded prescient warnings about public dangers of private settlements and private arbitration. *Against Settlement* emphasizes benefits of a lawsuit's public airing of claimed malfeasance and defenses through evidence and testimony. Trials about race discrimination, dangerous products, and fraud are what make media take notice, consumers aware, regulators enforce, and legislators legislate.

Recent revelations of private settlements between celebrities and women they sexually assaulted or harassed, or between the president and various sex partners, make the point. The Me Too movement demonstrates that bought silence enables bad actors to prey again. We also see the public consequences of private settlements in product liability, environmental, and other cases, although some federal agencies require reporting for certain claims. Another child is injured, another father burned, another family suffers toxic exposure. When the public learns of nondisclosure agreements and settlements in such cases, they see malfeasance.

Unfortunately, *Against Settlement* offers no remedy. An ADR "cease and desist" would not avoid secret settlements. Incentives to bury evidence of wrongdoing are overwhelming when settlement offers confidentiality. Many settle before suit, others postfiling but without ADR involvement—outside the arena Fiss sought to influence.

Fiss's concerns about the public consequences of private arbitration may soon be realized. Under the Supreme Court's recent rulings, we may be forced to arbitrate disputes from cradle to grave. Our claims and their outcomes will be hidden, power imbalances increased, and light turned away from widespread or serial wrongs.

VII. Against Settlement as Foundational

Against Settlement did not shape the ADR field. ADR scholars mostly dissected and rejected it; most ADR leaders and providers missed, ignored, or dismissed it. That is fortunate, given ADR's benefits for so many.

So, Fiss was mostly wrong. Still, back when ADR was a shiny new venture, he offered a few seminal points for today's realities. Perhaps we are wise not to give up *Against Settlement*'s ghost, but to heed only the words that should haunt us, while being unapologetically for settlement.

References

American Bar Association, *Model Rules of Professional Conduct*, Rule 2.4 (2013).

American Bar Association—Section on Dispute Resolution's Resolution, *Mediation and the Unauthorized Practice of Law* (2002).

Eleanor Smith, http://libraryresearch.weebly.com/seminal-works.html. The website piece cites its source for the second description as Lussky, J.P. (2004), "Bibliometric Patterns in an Historical Medical Index: Using the Newly Digitized Index Catalogue of the Library of the Surgeon General's Office, United States Army." Thesis, College of Information Science and Technology, Drexel University, pp. 4–15. Full text available at http://dspace.library.drexel.edu//retrieve/3815/Lussky_Joan.pdf.

Article 4.4

Pursuing Settlement in an Adversary Culture: A Tale of Innovation Co-Opted or "The Law of ADR"

Carrie Menkel-Meadow

19 Florida State Law Review 1 (1991)

I. Introduction

... A field that was developed, in part, to release us from some-if not all-of the limitations and rigidities of law and formal legal institutions has now developed a law of its own ... [I]issues about alternative dispute resolution (ADR) increasingly have been "taken to court." As a result, we are beginning to see the development of case and statutory law and, dare I say, a "common law" or "jurisprudence" of ADR.

* * *

II. Why Pursue Settlement?

... [W]e see two basically different justifications for processes that resolve cases short of trial ... quantitative-efficiency claims versus qualitative-justice claims. These different conceptions of the purposes of ADR represent vastly different ideologies and perspectives on how disputes should be resolved in our society... [A] model of community empowerment, party participation, and access to justice was championed by those concerned with substantive justice and democratic process ...

Others ... have argued that [ADR] ... could lead to outcomes that were efficient ... making both parties better off without worsening the position of the other. In addition, the processes themselves would be better because they would provide a greater opportunity for party participation and recognition of party goals ...

In the mid-to-late 1970s ... judicial administrators began to ... lament the litigation explosion. They began to advocate the use of [ADR] ... [to] reduc[e] caseloads and process[] cases more quickly.

* * *

Carrie Menkel-Meadow, *Pursuing Settlement in an Adversary Culture: A Tale of Innovation Co-Opted or "The Law of ADR"*
In: *Discussions in Dispute Resolution.* Edited by: Art Hinshaw, Andrea Kupfer Schneider, and Sarah Rudolph Cole, Oxford University Press (2021). DOI: 10.1093/oso/9780197513248.003.0076

From yet [another] perspective, law and economics scholars study the efficiency of settlement... from the perspective of the parties to determine when settlement is "rational" and "efficient." ...

The crucial point here is that different constituencies have pursued settlement or ADR for vastly different reasons ... [These] purposes behind [ADR have] led to important policy decisions and legal rulings which have given expression to different values underlying particular forms of ADR.

* * *

... [T]he key to answering the question "why pursue settlement?" is to know what the alternatives are and to determine by what standards both settlement and the alternatives will be measured. This implicates two of the major theoretical and philosophical questions confronting the innovations of ADR: (1) are there principled reasons for preferring one process or result over another? and (2) by what standards of appropriateness for dispute resolution should such decisions be measured?

* * *

III. The Institutionalization and Legalization of ADR

* * *

... [C]ourts have used the primary forms of dispute resolution by encouraging negotiation and settlement, by increasing the use of mandatory settlement conferences, and by instituting both mandatory and more consensual forms of arbitration and mediation...

* * *

... [It soon] became clear that [for some] ADR was just another stop in the "litigotiation" game [to manipulate] rules, time, information, and ultimately, money.

* * *

A. Contradictions in "Mandatory" ADR

Much of what motivates the "quality" proponents of ADR is the notion that the parties [must] want to resolve their disputes in a different way ... [I]n its purest form, the key to effective dispute resolution is found in voluntary participation by the parties and commitment to the [mediation process].

* * *

... Many of the alternative settlement practices were designed to decrease the time that corporate executives and other busy litigants were to spend in litigation ... [It] may be prescient in seeing the mandatory settlement conference ... causing more time to be expended in litigation, rather than less... If party attendance at settlement proceedings becomes the norm rather than the "exception," litigation costs in money and time may in fact increase ...

* * *

... [W]hile many commentators argue that settlement processes should proceed only consensually in the courts, ... the line should be drawn between abusive uses of mandatory processes and those used within the bounds of fairness and our existing rules ... Some good mandatory practices offer the possibility of subjecting all cases to similar treatment ... to allow some adversarial testing ... of the quality and justice of these procedural innovations ...

B. Public Access to Settlements

From another quarter ... one of the major critiques of the development of ADR techniques has been that ADR privatizes disputing ... Some critics charge that with so much private settlement there will not be enough ... cases going through the traditional adversary system, to produce good law.

* * *

... [O]ne of the primary values of ADR—confidentiality—is clearly implicated when ADR techniques are used in public spaces ... Our legal system encourages private settlements. With a party-initiated adversary system, the parties can choose to take the case out of the system at any time ...

* * *

... To suggest that all settlement functions should be conducted in public is likely to greatly diminish the use of techniques and devices that often promote settlement.

* * *

C. The Constitutionality of ADR

* * *

... As ADR proceeds in its various forms through the courts, advocates have raised issues about violations of the right to jury trial, due process, equal protection, and separation of powers. Most of these claims have failed, and ... with certain protections like nonbinding results, rights to de novo hearings, and limited penalties, ADR can constitutionally be conducted in the courts ...

* * *

As advocates have grabbed hold of ADR, they have transformed it into another arena of battle. The interesting question is what are the implications of this "capture" of ADR by the courts and its advocates?

IV. The Implications of the Legalization and Institutionalization of ADR

* * *

The use of settlement activity in the courts should be understood as the clash of two cultures. To the extent that settlement activity seeks to promote consensual agreement through the analysis of the point of view of the other side, it requires some different skills and a very different mindset from what litigators usually employ. Thus, the issue is whether judges and lawyers in the courts can learn to reorient their cultures and behaviors when trying to settle cases or whether those seeking settlement continue to do so from an adversarial perspective ... If one of the purposes of the legal system is to specify legal entitlements from which settlements may be measured, or from which the parties may depart if they so choose, then having adjudicators engage in too much mediative conduct may compromise the ability of judges to engage in both fact-finding and rulemaking. If courts fail to provide sufficient baselines in their judgments, we will have difficulties determining if particular settlements are wise or truly consensual ...

* * *

A. The "Colonization" of Alternatives by Conventional Advocates

... [T]here is an unspoken resistance to [ADR] that derives in part from the tendency instilled by our adversarial training to distrust alternative forms of consciousness, such as a focus on solving the problem rather than winning the case ... But as these cases travel through the courts, ... lawyers are approaching settlement adversarily. They are ready to raise legal, technical, and procedural claims about how cases are being processed, and they are questioning whether settlement comes at the expense of other legal entitlements.

* * *

... For lawyers and judges who have been taught to argue, criticize, and persuade, rather than to listen, synthesize, and empathize, some changes in behavior will be necessary. Adversarial practices may be problematic in settlement not only because of the obvious risk of stalemate and hostility, but also because extreme positions most often produce unprincipled compromise even if a settlement agreement is reached ... Good settlement practice may be difficult to adapt to traditional adversarial forms.

* * *

C. Issues, Proposals, and Reforms for Innovation and Evaluation of ADR in the Courts

... If ADR is to meet the basic levels of fairness, then the following questions must be addressed, and the following data must be collected to prevent ADR from becoming totally swallowed by the adversarial system:

1. To what extent will courts lose their legitimacy as courts if too many other forms of case-processing are performed within their walls? ...
2. Should some case types be excluded from alternative treatment?
3. What are the purposes for using particular forms of alternative dispute resolution? Caseload management and docket reduction may suggest entirely different processes than a search for a better-quality solution which might be quite costly and time-consuming ...
4. What forms of ADR should be institutionalized? ... How much regulation of each process should there be? How clear should the rules be before parties can elect different processes or before they can be "ordered" to attend? ... By what standards should practices under these rules be evaluated?
5. What are the politics of ADR? Does ADR serve the interests of particular groups? ... Will "free market" forces decide the fate of ADR? Who will control decision-making about ADR-judges, lawyers, clients, or legislators? ...
6. What are the cultural forces producing these legal changes at these particular times? ...
7. How are different forms of ADR actually functioning? ... We need to know more about how these processes actually work in terms of processes used and outcomes achieved, as well as ... party satisfaction.

... [ADR] and the pursuit of settlement in the courts will, and should, continue ... In order for ADR to develop in a way that enhances our trust in the American legal system, several important reforms should accompany our experimentation.

First, some forms of ADR should remain mandatory, but not binding ... I have seen many good settlements emerge through the skilled intervention ... [of] negotiators or third parties, even in cases where settlement seemed impossible ...

Second, if some settlement processes are ... mandatory, certain essential legal protections may have to flow from those processes. If they do not, then processes may have to be chosen consensually or voluntarily ...

Third, if settlement processes are to be conducted within the courts, they should be facilitated by those who will not be the ultimate triers of fact ... [G]ood settlement practice frequently depends on the revelation of facts that would be inadmissible in court ...

* * *

Fifth, we must provide the evidence for systematic evaluation of alternative dispute resolution devices ... [I]t should be possible to create data sets of case treatments that would permit the kind of systematic analysis necessary to compare outcomes and processes of greater variety and in greater depth ...

* * *

V. Conclusion: Whither Goest ADR?

Obviously, I am not happy with all of the developments and turns that ADR has taken ... [M]y fear is that we may be pouring old wine... into new jugs ...

... I still seek dispute resolution processes that are designed to solve problems, not make them worse ... [H]owever, ... we must understand that our innovations do not occur in a vacuum—they are enfolded into an already existing legal culture.... The key is not to compromise, but to work toward a principled and fair resolution of the issues.

Comments

Dimensions of Quality of Justice

Ellen E. Deason

In her 1991 article, *Pursuing Settlement in an Adversary Culture: A Tale of Innovation Co-opted or "The Law of ADR,"* Professor Carrie Menkel-Meadow identified the dynamics of change in the legal landscape as courts embraced dispute resolution. She asked if alternative dispute resolution (ADR) would transform the courts as they became sponsors of these programs, or if the adversarial system would co-opt dispute resolution innovations. Menkel-Meadow identified ways in which both institutions could alter the other, but her answer to this question centered on the deleterious effects of court institutionalization on dispute resolution. Just as important as her answer, however, is that she asked and explored the questions, identifying important tensions in the values underlying court adjudication and private settlement. Those tensions persist and continue to influence what has become today, in many ways, a single system combining litigation and dispute resolution.

I. A Matter of Values

One of the article's strengths is its focus on the forces shaping ADR. In her analysis of how dispute resolution was transformed through its adoption by the courts, Menkel-Meadow conceptualized issues that continue to resonate today. A major portion of the article traces the early development of law to address issues generated by ADR's use in the courts—law on mandatory participation, public access to settlement processes, and constitutional questions. This treatment of the growth of law governing ADR is not, however, the source of the most enduring interest in the article today. Instead, its lasting contribution is Menkel-Meadow's analysis of a clash of cultures—and their underlying values—which articulated fundamental issues and themes that scholars still explore.

The important questions Menkel-Meadow asked are best expressed as follows:

> As ADR becomes institutionalized within the court system, one can ask whether advocacy is one of many tools of dispute resolution, or whether forms of dispute resolution will be captured by the dominant culture of adversarial advocacy. If the processes of adversarial adjudication and "facilitated" settlement are joined in the same institutions, what are the implications for each process? More importantly, what are the implications for justice? (p. 13)

Ellen E. Deason, *Dimensions of Quality of Justice* In: *Discussions in Dispute Resolution.* Edited by: Art Hinshaw, Andrea Kupfer Schneider, and Sarah Rudolph Cole, Oxford University Press (2021).
DOI: 10.1093/oso/9780197513248.003.0077

In considering these questions, she contrasted two motivations for institutionalizing dispute resolution: efficiency and enhancing the quality of justice. Given courts' limited resources, a goal of caseload management and docket reduction can predominate over approaches to ADR that emphasize aspirations to find better quality solutions, which can be costly and time consuming. In the years since Menkel-Meadow wrote her article, scholars have recognized that design choices express the underlying values of court ADR programs, and argued for structures and priorities that preserve the core values of mediation (such as self-determination of the parties) and enhance the quality of the services mediators deliver.

Menkel-Meadow also emphasized that institutionalization means ADR must co-exist with the adversarial nature of litigation. Institutionalization enhanced the influence of lawyers, who brought their adversarial assumptions both to representing clients in court-sponsored ADR and to serving as neutrals. Indeed, this culture clash persists. Dispute resolution scholars today complain about legal practitioners who, while they may have embraced mediation, often insist on avoiding joint sessions, reflexively select evaluative mediators, and de-emphasize their client's participation in the process.

II. Questions of Justice

The article is particularly noteworthy for a subsidiary, but parallel, theme. In articulating the tension between emphasizing settlement as an efficiency measure and seeing it as an opportunity to achieve a quality resolution to a problem, Menkel-Meadow is solidly in favor of a vision of ADR that prioritizes "pursuit of 'quality' solutions" (p. 3). For her, quality includes an *outcome* that is Pareto-optimal in that it makes both parties better off and a *process* that provides opportunities for party participation and takes account of party goals (pp. 7–8). But she acknowledges that the values defining "quality" are unsettled, both in terms of process and substantive justice. She describes the field of dispute resolution as having developed, at least in part, to "release us" from "the limitations and rigidities of law and formal legal institutions" (p. 1). She points out that, nonetheless, many still tend to measure justice against court outcomes: "A number of writers on the settlement process find something philosophically wrong with results that do not track our legal rules" (p. 7 n.25). And she concludes that there is little agreement on the fundamental values that determine what we regard as fair and just (p. 34 n.172). This is a particularly prescient aspect of her article, for that disagreement persists today.

If one rereads Professor Len Riskin's article that coined the phrase "lawyers' standard philosophical map" (Riskin, pp. 43–44), one will remember that this phrase refers to more than lawyers' adversarial mindsets. Lawyers are characterized by rule orientation—an assumption that disputes can best be "resolved through application, by a third party, of some general rule of law" (Riskin, p. 44). As Riskin observed, "[l]awyers are trained to put people and events into categories that are legally meaningful, to think in terms of rights and duties established by rules" (Riskin, p. 45). The idea that the law is "the exclusive measure of fairness and equity" is imbued in the first-year law curriculum and is very difficult to counteract, even with programming designed for that purpose (Coben, p. 737). Rule orientation emphasizes cognitive and analytical skills, often to the neglect of emotions, which can be important to the parties. It reduces the richness of individuals' concerns to legal definitions and binary win-lose results with monetary remedies based on general principles, not the particular situation.

In contrast, the settlement activity Menkel-Meadow endorses—which "seeks to promote consensual agreement through the analysis of the point of view of the other side"—requires different skills than litigation (p. 32). Some of the skills—such as information-sharing—are at odds with an adversarial mindset. Many others—such as considering solutions beyond what a court could order, taking the future into account as well as the past, and recognizing the social, psychological, political, and moral dimensions of issues rather than only the legal aspects—are at odds with a predominant emphasis on legal outcomes (p. 32, n.166).

III. Departing from Adherence to Legal Standards

Judging the quality of a settlement outcome can, certainly, require reckoning with the standards imposed by legal rules, for parties often "bargain in the shadow of the law" (Mnookin & Kornhauser, p. 968). But the famous article that coined this term recognized that a legal shadow is not the only factor that affects settlement outcomes, ranking it with other influences: parties' preferences, uncertainty about legal outcomes, transaction costs along with parties' abilities to bear them, and strategic behaviors. Adhering to legal rules can, however, provide a safeguard against the tendency of some of the other influential factors to impair the justice of a settlement. Moreover, one way to encourage settlements can be through merits-based assessments. Surely no one doubts there is a role in settlement for considering legal rules.

What is objectionable is the narrow focus of the tendency that Menkel-Meadow observed—to measure justice primarily through comparison to court outcomes. This approach elevates legal entitlements over the legitimacy of any other factor. Professor Maria Glover, for example, advances the premise that it is crucial to ensure that "settlement outcomes reflect the merits" (Glover, p. 1716). She proposes nothing less than a full-scale redesign of the Federal Rules of Civil Procedure to provide information on the merits in order to influence settlement outcomes. She even asserts that "the fundamental goal of our litigation system"—including settlement—is "to align case outcomes with the dictates of substantive law" (Glover, p. 1776).

This attitude that legal rules should be the absolute touchstone for settlement prompts two questions. First, can the freedom to depart from legal rules—both procedural and substantive—*enhance* the quality of settlements? One answer is that settlement's potential for value creation can improve the quality of justice and that honoring parties' preferences can make them better off than the remedies available in court. Consensual outcomes can be more responsive to individual needs and party preferences than general legal rules, so they can yield a more particularized form of justice. As Menkel-Meadow subsequently stated in expanding upon the theme of quality in settlement:

> Settlement (and its sometime rejection of law) [can] be seen as a democratic expression of individual justice where rules made for the aggregate would either be unjust, or simply irrelevant to the achievement of justice in individual cases. (Menkel-Meadow 1995, p. 2676)

And, as she also observed, at a societal level such settlements can identify the limits of law and point the way for law reform (Menkel-Meadow 1995, p. 2676).

Another potential benefit of departing from a strictly merits-based framework is an increased flexibility in defining issues. Rather than shoehorning their concerns into legal categories, parties can address nonfinancial and nonlegal aspects of a dispute, and even their emotional needs. However, the universe of just and principled outcomes can be broadened beyond legally cognizable interests only if settlements are not judged solely by their fidelity to likely court results.

But it is important to recognize that not all departures from rule-based outcomes provide advantages in settlement. Some of the factors on Mnookin and Kornhauser's list that exert influences unrelated to the legal merits may pose dangers to a settlement's fairness. This prompts a second question: Can we lessen the pressure of factors that *reduce* justice in settlement? This essay cannot be long enough to give this question the attention it deserves, but Menkel-Meadow points us in two important directions. Noting that the law is "a constant baseline of choice and comparison" for settlement, she stresses that this "assumes that the parties know what the 'legal' results would be and have the resources to effectuate them if they so choose" (Menkel-Meadow 1995, p. 2678 n.72).

Moving these two assumptions toward reality would be an important improvement. Lack of resources threatens justice in both litigation and dispute resolution processes. This is especially true when there are differences in resources, such as unequal abilities to bear transaction costs. This puts a priority on containing costs and on enhancing the participation of those with fewer resources.

Understanding potential legal results is another prime area for reform. Many self-represented parties lack a basic awareness of legal entitlements and rules, knowledge necessary to exercise informed self-determination and give meaningful consent in settlement. They need to know the rule-based standards before they can intelligently decide to depart from them. This is difficult to achieve without attorneys, and putting a burden to deliver basic legal information on mediators would threaten to compromise ethical rules that emphasize neutrality. We may need to develop a more complex view of appropriate ethical rules, or cultivate alternative sources of legal information, perhaps through court programs.

In more complex cases, uncertainty about legal outcomes is a significant barrier to settlement. Litigants need confidence that they can credibly evaluate the range of potential court outcomes as a starting point for settlement. Thus, lawyers may believe they need significant amounts of discovery or decisions on particular motions, thereby delaying settlement efforts and increasing the resources spent on litigation.

Here, proposals on pleading practices, discovery, motion timing, and preliminary assessments deserve serious consideration.

Following Menkel-Meadow's example can strengthen these reform proposals. The goal in litigation should be developing the aspects of cases that are crucial for settlement, rather than merely producing settlements that better replicate court outcomes. Menkel-Meadow prefers to see neither black nor white, but rather grey, purple, and red. In her words, these colors represent the "complexity of human issues that appear before the law for resolution" (Menkel-Meadow 1995, p. 2663). An array of colors can also represent a worldview that avoids one-sided answers and oversimplified analyses. We would do well to emulate Menkel-Meadow's comprehensive approach and acknowledge complexity as we consider what quality of justice means in the evolving relationship between the institutions and the cultures of litigation and settlement.

References

James R. Coben, *Summer Musings on Curricular Innovations to Change the Lawyer's Standard Philosophical Map*, 50 U. Fla. L. Rev. 735–51 (Sept. 1998).

J. Maria Glover, *The Federal Rules of Civil Settlement*, 87 N.Y.U. L. Rev. 1713–78 (Dec. 2012).

Carrie Menkel-Meadow, *Whose Dispute Is It Anyway?: A Philosophical and Democratic Defense of Settlement (In Some Cases)*, 83 Geo. L.J. 2663–96 (Sept. 1995).

Robert H. Mnookin & Lewis Kornhauser, *Bargaining the Shadow of the Law: The Case of Divorce*, 88 Yale L.J. 950–97 (Apr. 1979).

Leonard L. Riskin, *Mediation and Lawyers*, 43 Ohio St. L.J. 29–60 (1982).

ADR's Place at the Justice Table

Elayne E. Greenberg

I. Introduction

As alternative dispute resolution (ADR) innovations become institutionalized into the court system, ADR's promise to humanize and personalize justice too often becomes co-opted by the more dominant values of the traditional legal system. Professor Menkel-Meadow refers to this co-opting as a "clash of two cultures." This "clash" is actually the legal system's ongoing acculturation of ADR, focusing on efficiency and settlement often at the expense of preserving the distinct qualitative benefits such innovations offer the justice system. Why does this co-opting happen? From a sociological perspective, it can also be understood to be an extension of the ongoing feminist struggle to gain voice and legitimacy within the legal system and within broader society. This comment invites the reader to re-examine the institutionalization of ADR innovations through this acculturation lens. Although the focus will be on the institutionalization of court annexed mediation programs, these lessons have broad applicability to many court annexed ADR innovations.

II. The ADR Movement Is an Extension of the Feminist Movement

For many, the 1976 Pound Conference marks the beginning of the ADR movement. At that meeting, Frank Sander introduced an improved vision of the justice system that included a menu of appropriate dispute resolution procedures, not just litigation. This vision held out the promise that by including appropriate dispute resolution options in the existing adversarial system, the legal system would be better able to respond to nuanced, human problems. This approach would result in a more encompassing and strengthened justice system.

The dispute resolution revolution took root against the backdrop of the feminist movement, a movement spearheaded by committed women and empathetic men. Since the 1960s, the feminist movement had been sounding the clarion call for women's equality, asserting the importance of dignifying women's values, and appreciating women's contributions in their families, the workforce, the legal system, and society. The movement has had uneven gains, however, and fifty years later, it is still striving to achieve equality for women and end discrimination in its many forms.

From this sociological perspective, the ADR movement can be understood to be a movement that, fueled by the ardor of the feminist movement, had embraced

Elayne E. Greenberg, *ADR's Place at the Justice Table* In: *Discussions in Dispute Resolution.* Edited by: Art Hinshaw, Andrea Kupfer Schneider, and Sarah Rudolph Cole, Oxford University Press (2021).
DOI: 10.1093/oso/9780197513248.003.0078

previously devalued "feminine values" such as the importance of human connectedness and the value of emotions in resolving disputes. These "feminine values" recognize that when people are in conflict, listening and empathizing may ultimately help develop more effective resolutions than arguing, attacking, and persuading the other side that one side is right. The ADR movement, thus, can be understood as the "feminization" of the justice system, dedicated to improving the quality of justice processes and resulting resolutions, beyond the adjudication of legal rights. ADR's ongoing struggle to gain institutional legitimacy mirrors the ongoing feminist struggle to claim women's legitimacy. Sadly, many ADR innovations are frequently misunderstood, consistently undervalued for their justice contributions, and continue to be coopted by an adversarial legal system that is undergirded by male values.

III. The Culture Clash Begins at the Design Innovation Phase

The culture clash between ADR and traditional legal cultures often begins when courts first develop a court-annexed mediation program. More specifically, that would be when *conceptualizers*, a term used to describe those academics and judicial activists who spearhead court innovations, first meet with the courts, the *implementers* of the mediation program. Courts and conceptualizers often have different motivations, understandings, and visions about the proposed program. These differences are reflected in three process-defining ways: how success is measured, which cases are selected, and who the mediators are.

The conceptualizers may envision a mediation process that allows participants to discuss what is important to them and consider nuanced resolutions in addition to those provided by the law. According to the conceptualizers, mediation success is not measured by a resolution of all the legal issues, but by each party's personalized assessment of whether they received justice. As with the feminist movement, conceptualizers believe that ADR is about resolving human issues.

Courts, however, may come to the mediation innovation stage with a very different viewpoint. From this dominant culture's perspective, mediation is all about cost-effective and efficient resolution of legal issues. Courts may see mediation, instead, as an innovation that helps manage overflowing dockets given their limited economic and personnel resources. Success is measured by the efficient resolution of the legal issues.

Even though conceptualizers recognize that courts and conceptualizers fundamentally have different understandings about the value of mediation, conceptualizers often choose to ignore these differences. Instead, buoyed by an optimistic overconfidence and magical thinking, they prefer to hold on to the belief that courts will grow to appreciate the true value of mediation once the program is implemented and satisfied mediation participants sing mediation's praises. Experience has shown, however, that courts may never have such an epiphany. Rather, as the dominant legal culture, courts continue to evaluate the effectiveness of mediation through their lens of the cost-effect and efficient resolution of legal issues.

Such cultural clashes are ubiquitous throughout the innovation stage. Although each design choice is an opportunity to reconsider whether the dominant values of the traditional legal culture will be preserved or whether mediation's more expansive human values will be embraced in the proposed program, the values of the dominant legal culture often prevail. These value-laden decisions are evident in which type of cases will go to mediation; who will be the mediators; what, if any, training will mediators receive; what topics will be included in the training; will mediators be compensated, and how much time is allocated for mediation

For example, too often, the values of the traditional legal system dominate and shape the selection of mediators for the proposed program. From the court's perspective, court personnel, lawyers with subject matter expertise, and former judges may be preferred as potential mediators because they know how to settle legal cases efficiently After all, mediation is just about settlement. According to many court administrators overseeing ADR programs, training should focus on the presenting legal issues in the cases the mediation program will handle. However, if the mediator pool consists only of those who are knowledgeable about the law and skilled in settlement, they may be lacking the human understanding and mediation skills that support mediation participants in their personal decision-making process.

Another example of value co-opting, is the decision about which cases are referred to mediation. Blanket rules referring all cases to mediation or referring just one in five cases to mediation programs are lost opportunities to determine which are the appropriate cases that might benefit from mediation. Moreover, such rules diminish the likelihood that the mediation referral will be a meaningful one. Even if the courts are taking the time to refer appropriate cases to mediation, attorneys and judges may not understand the value of making appropriate referrals. I have seen judges refuse to refer emotional cases to mediation, believing emotion has nothing to do with mediation. Without a true appreciation of what mediation offers, conceptualizers fear that the traditional legal system will continue to misuse mediation and risk losing mediation's value

IV. The Culture Clash Continues during the Implementation Phase

The adversarial culture continues to co-opt the mediation culture during the mediation program's implementation phase. Such co-opting is evident in how lawyers advocate in the mediation, how mediators conduct the mediation, and how the program is evaluated. Too many lawyers represent their clients in mediation with the same adversarial advocacy style they learned in law school and rely upon in court. When advocating in mediation, attorneys may even bring the same nomenclature they use in court proceedings into the mediation. Thus, attorneys may refer to the mediation parties as plaintiff and defendant rather adopt the more informal practice of using participants' names. Unfortunately, the failure of attorneys to alter their advocacy style results in lost opportunities to address the human dimensions of their client's problem.

The adversarial approach also influences how some mediators may conduct their mediations. Even those mediators who are well grounded in the distinct values of mediation may feel the pressure to abandon these values and conform to the market demands of the dominant culture if they want lawyers and judges to select them as mediators. Thus, increasing numbers of mediators conduct mediations without the use of joint sessions because adversarial lawyers mistakenly believe that joint meetings are too emotional and a waste of time. In another illustration of mediators being co-opted by the dominant culture, mediators are providing mediation evaluations rather than supporting mediation parties to conduct their own evaluations within the mediation process. The dominant culture believes that mediation is just about efficient settlement and mediator evaluations will help mediation parties get there faster.

V. The Culture Clash Continues in the Evaluation Phase

Another example of value co-opting, the sustainability of court-connected mediation is determined by how efficiently these programs resolve the presenting legal problem that brought them to court. Many mediators can glowingly recount mediations in which mediation participants were able to have difficult conversations that they couldn't have anywhere else but in mediation. These participants then became empowered to develop resolutions that responded to their concerns. However, when programs are ultimately evaluated solely by the efficiency in resolving cases, the human gains mediation participants experience are marginalized.

VI. Going Forward, There Are More Effect Ways to Manage These Cultural Clashes

The continuing culture clash and acculturation of ADR innovations that Professor Menkel-Meadow had observed in 1991 is still evident today. ADR's role in the legal system will remain co-opted and stagnant unless we take a different approach. Two ideas to consider are how we might ally with law schools to elevate ADR values in legal education; and how our profession might recalibrate to gain greater legitimacy and more successful engagement within the traditional legal culture

Of course, we can always hope that the feminist movement will continue to help women gain greater societal legitimacy. The hope is that as women's perspectives and contributions become more legitimized and accorded greater value, there will be a commensurate recognition of the value of ADR. In this more vibrant world, emotions and feelings will no longer be marginalized to those lower valued, female-dominated, "pink professions." Then the legal system will accord greater value to dignifying litigants' humanity and valuing the human quality of dispute resolution processes. Are we willing to wait?

In the meantime, we must look at how law schools can become ADR's allies. Law schools, the primary educators of legal values, marginalize ADR. Even though increasing numbers of law schools offer clinics, courses, and centers that teach law students the fundamentals of ADR, the legal system's adversarial values dominate legal education. Reinforcing the message that the legal system trumps ADR, many law schools marginalize ADR educators by giving them lower status and less pay. This must change.

The ADR community, too, must re-examine what we might do better to legitimize our profession. Professor Menkel-Meadow raised the need for quality empirical research about ADR to legitimize the values and practices the field promotes. Since 1991, quality empirical research about ADR practices has increased; more is needed. The ADR community can do its part by incentivizing this challenging and necessary work with greater pay and recognition.

The field must also acknowledge that there is no consensus about how to proceed. Our colleagues differ on how they view these culture clashes and the steps to be taken. Some believe ADR already has a respected place at the table and that these problems are just part of acculturation. Others, believing that these issues delegitimize ADR's contributions, call for a more respected place at the table. Still others want the table reset with ADR securely placed at the head of the table.

For many in the ADR profession, our glass-half-full optimism motivates us to view conflict as an opportunity for improvement. Thus, this culture clash is an opportunity for the ADR profession to rethink our efforts. We can work to secure ADR's respected place at the table, and building on our successes, we can even hope to reset the table.

Foundational Because Prescient (and Unfortunately, Cassandra-like Prescience)

James Coben

I. Introduction

As a law professor who teaches civil procedure and mediation, *Pursuing Settlement* reads like a history. Menkel-Meadow's uncanny accuracy in predicting the future, her prescient fears for where institutionalization of alternative dispute resolution (ADR) might take us, and the remarkable continued relevance of her suggested reforms and accompanying experimentation combine to make an easy case for declaring her work foundational.

She challenged us to consider "whether new forms of dispute resolution will transform the courts or whether, in a more likely scenario, the power of our adversarial system will co-opt and transform the innovations designed to redress some, if not all, of our legal ills" (p. 5). And she offered a qualified "no" to the query whether the growth and expansion of ADR within institutions has changed the consciousness of those who solve legal problems.

II. What We Now Know

With the benefit of almost 30 years of pursuing settlement in the shadow of litigation, what do we now know? Turns out, very little beyond what Menkel-Meadow presaged for us. Without question, I could now teach my entire procedure course using only case law decisions about disputed mediation issues (Coben 2015). Exactly as Menkel-Meadow predicted, lawyers now routinely "use" mediation as the all-purpose excuse for all sorts of failures and omissions ranging from incomplete discovery and failing to designate trial experts to late-filed motions and untimely requests to amend pleadings (Cole et al. 2019, ch. 5).

Lawyers (and clients) fail to realize the numerous ways mediation participation (or nonparticipation) influences litigation decisions quite distinct from the mediation itself. Courts have, among other things, treated the failure to participate in mediation as a factor in justifying: the prejudgment attachment of property in aid of security, awards of prejudgment interest, and denials of continuance requests. Mediation behavior also is commonly invoked to support or deny awards of attorney's fees.

Moreover, "traps for the unwary" abound (Coben 2013). Parties have been deemed to have waived objections to venue and personal jurisdiction based on mediation participation. Requesting time to mediate has been deemed evidence of the lack of

James Coben, *Foundational Because Prescient (and Unfortunately, Cassandra-like Prescience)* In: *Discussions in Dispute Resolution*. Edited by: Art Hinshaw, Andrea Kupfer Schneider, and Sarah Rudolph Cole, Oxford University Press (2021).
 DOI: 10.1093/oso/9780197513248.003.0079

imminent harm to justify granting of a temporary restraining order. Information exchanged in mediation has been relied upon to establish or negate the amount in controversy necessary to justify federal court diversity jurisdiction and removal. State court mediation efforts have been cited as a reason for federal courts to decline supplemental jurisdiction over state law claims. In my home state of Minnesota, a settlement reached in mediation is evaluated under the law of contracts, except that a mediated settlement must include the parties' affirmance that they intend the agreement to be binding upon them for the agreement actually to become binding—an affirmance that most first-year law students learn very early in their studies is akin to the "wax seal" or "ribbon" triviality no longer necessary to create a binding contract.

Courts routinely find information disclosed in mediation sufficient to constitute notice of claims or defenses, and then go on to dismiss claims as untimely as a result. Moreover, judges frequently, and often in unexpected ways, invoke mediation participation (or nonparticipation) to help justify their decision on substantive merits. Imagine being the parent subject to an adverse custody decision based on your refusal to mediate visitation issues. Or, imagine a Fair Labor Standards Act claim for overtime compensation being denied because you had represented your employer in mediations and therefore must be an exempt employee not entitled to overtime compensation. Live and learn.

And, sadly, mediation itself is now often a trigger for entirely new litigation (Coben 2006). Parties battle over mediation costs and attorney's fees, sometimes offering Aquinas-like ruminations on the number of lawyers who may seek compensation for representing someone at a mediation (short answer in most cases: not more than two). Cross-motions for sanctions for alleged bad behavior in mediation often draw a "pox on both our houses" response from the courts, though not frequently enough to chill such motions outright. In employment disputes, parties frequently cite mediation behavior to support or reject allegations of post-mediation retaliatory discrimination. The acts or omissions of insurers during mediation is a treasure trove for failure to defend and bad faith failure to insure claims. The response of many state legislatures to create mandatory mediation schemes when confronting disasters (natural and man-made) leads to endless court disputes about triggering events and fulfillment of mediation duties (Cole et al. 2019, ch. 6). Lawyer malpractice claims stemming from mediation abound, ranging from alleged failures to conduct sufficient pre-settlement discovery to failures to adequately disclose the benefits and risks of a mediated settlement, to entering into final agreements without client consent.

And, of course, all of this omits the largest category of litigation about mediation—disputes about enforcement of settlements, which based on my own research over the last two decades is approximately 40 percent of all reported mediation case law decisions in US state and federal courts (Coben 2006). What did Menkel-Meadow have to say about settlement enforcement? With uncanny accuracy, she advised us to watch out for the "security" of settlements reached through ADR, speculating that "post hoc attacks and appeals on their 'coerciveness'" might increase "in a civil analogue to efforts to undo a guilty plea in the criminal context" (p. 24). Well put. Today, mediation settlement enforcement litigation runs the full gamut of contract defenses, with colorful allegations of duress, fraud, mistake, and lack of capacity, not to mention the vexing challenge of unenforceable agreements to agree, disputes about the lack of material terms, or the parties' inability to successfully negotiate the terms of the standard release language agreed to at mediation but deferred for later drafting.

III. A Clash of Cultures

Just like Cassandra predicting the destruction of Troy (and in particular the warning about the Greeks hiding inside the Trojan Horse), Menkel-Meadow foresaw all too accurately the potential hazards of ADR institutionalization and legalization. The clash of cultures she described has indeed played out with coercive impact—both undermining the hoped for transformative power of mediation and compromising the quality of justice delivered by judges within the legal system. Two examples make the point.

In many jurisdictions, joint session has been abandoned altogether. Keeping parties separated hardly serves mediation's transformative potential—the desired innovation for which Menkel-Meadow and other founders of the field eloquently advocated. Alas, it would appear that the "limited remedial imagination" of the courts has taken over; mediation is more often than not an evaluative settlement conference, where respected current or former litigators are hired by the parties to value the various claims in the case and use that valuation in private session discussions to frighten clients (and lawyers) about the costs and risks of the litigation process. As it turned out, our collective pursuit of settlement in an adversary culture has simply resulted in a switch in centralized decision-making: with judicial decision making being traded for a mediator's proposal.

And how has litigation faired in this combination? It hasn't escaped unscathed. Judges have, in some contexts such as class action litigation, offered far too much deference to the recommendations and decisions of private mediators—a select and elite group that judges themselves often choose to join when they leave the bench (Coben 2013). Mediators, not judges, have become the first-line deciders on the quality of bargaining and even the substantive merits of settlements. These mediators testify to help enforce the settlements they broker, and often do so precisely when those settlements are being challenged by absent class members who lack the ability to even learn about what transpired in the mediation. No matter how "virtuous" these highly skilled mediators are, the judicial system has undermined its own accountability and transparency by treating them as if they were Special Masters and abdicating its duties to them.

Menkel-Meadow did not precisely foresee this particular development of ADR institutionalization; however, she forcefully recommended that "if settlement processes are to be conducted within the courts, they should be facilitated by those who will not be the ultimate triers of fact" (p. 43). Unfortunately, that recommendation remains an unfulfilled aspiration in many jurisdictions. In fact, the prevailing wisdom as attested to in numerous court decisions: judges who preside over settlement negotiations (inside mediation and out) are perfectly well qualified to handle motions (nondispositive and dispositive) and even final trial. Despite studies that show otherwise (see, e.g., Wistrich, Guthrie, & Rachlinski 2005), judicial officers believe they can compartmentalize the information they receive and only rely upon admissible evidence relevant for a particular decision.

And what about justice? Menkel-Meadow succinctly summarized the risks of informal disputing and privatization. She acknowledged her own "awkward" position—"considered by some to be an unmitigated apologist for ADR, and by others to be downright hostile to ADR" (p. 45). Ultimately, she threaded the needle by suggesting the pursuit of settlement, even with obvious risk, might be worth it given the holy grail of ADR aspirations: the notion that ADR-brokered agreements "have the potential of realizing an outcome that is fairer, more sensitive to the complex needs of the parties, and more likely to be followed" (p. 12). She also cautioned us that this lofty aspiration should not compel use of ADR "when a moral principle must be enunciated, or a legal precedent is necessary, or the parties are not equally empowered with respect to their dispute" (p. 12). And she advocated forcefully for "systematic evaluation of alternative dispute resolution devices" (p. 43). Alas, such systematic research has been lacking, so much so that even a critical question like whether ADR facilitates prejudice and bias remains unanswered despite voluminous academic speculation on the topic.

IV. Going Forward

So what is to be done now? Despite my gloomy report, we should "play the long game." The core idea of ADR's potential to better serve parties remains intact, albeit compromised (at least for now) by institutionalization. Let's continue to be inspired by Menkel-Meadow herself, who seeing the seeds of innovation co-opted almost 30 years ago nonetheless believed that "social innovation and transformation are possible" and with a mediator's optimism challenged us all to keep a sharp eye on the innovations and their effects. Menkel-Meadow's concluding recommendations for reforms to accompany our future experimentation still ring true today: continue to experiment but with a stronger commitment to systematic evaluation; remain skeptical of ADR mandates and continue to insist on the separation of judicial responsibility for adjudication and settlement; ensure that legal frameworks (in particular confidentiality) permit challenges to fundamentally unfair ADR processes; and insist on training for settlement facilitators. Not a bad recipe for the next generation of ADR leaders to follow.

References

James R. Coben, *Barnacles, Aristocracy and Truth Denial: Three Not So Beautiful Aspects of Contemporary Mediation*, 16 Cardozo J. Conflict Resol. 779–805 (2015).

James R. Coben, *Creating a 21st Century Oligarchy: Judicial Abdication to Class Action Mediators*, 5 Penn. St. Y.B. Arb. & Mediation 162–93 (2013).

James Coben & Peter N. Thompson, *Disputing Irony: A Systematic Look at Litigation about Mediation*, 11 Harv. Negot. L. Rev. 43–145 (2006).

Sarah R. Cole et al., Mediation: Law Policy & Practice (2019).

Andrew J. Wistrich, Chris Guthrie, & Jeffrey J. Rachlinski, *Can Judges Ignore Inadmissible Information? The Difficulty of Deliberately Disregarding*,"' 153 U. Pa. L. Rev. 1251–345 (2005).

Institutionalizing ADR: Clashing Values

Carrie Menkel-Meadow

I appreciate the thoughtful reflections of Jim Coben, Ellen Deason, and Elayne Greenberg on the teachings and legacies of my 1991 article, which attempted to capture the beginning of several types of institutionalization and co-optation of some of the key ideas of the "ADR movement." Sadly, much of what I commented on then has, in my view, only gotten worse as the adversary model is gaining, not losing, ascendancy (Menkel-Meadow 2019a).

Instead of a "clash of cultures" as I framed it, I will take up Ellen Deason's focus that the clash is more intense and basic—a clash of *values*. From the beginning, some of the promoters of various forms of ADR were focused on what I called the "quantitative" argument for ADR—efficiency and quicker, or cheaper forms of case processing. I focused on the "qualitative" arguments for ADR—better, more tailored, Pareto-optimal, creative solutions to legal problems, and more party participation in the solution-devising processes. I hoped, with other founders of the field, to empower parties to create wise solutions that worked for them rather than the brittle "win/lose" binary solutions most courts provided and to encourage a different form of legal thinking—problem-solving, not "defeat the other side" as a means to some other end.

In this short essay I will report on what has actually become worse with more institutionalization and cultural co-optation. I will also point to a few things that have become better in the last three decades and offer us some hope that pursuing settlement (of some, not all) cases with a different mindset, might still have some influence on our legal and problem-solving culture.

I. What's Worse?

Though many see the institutionalization of ADR as mostly a court/litigation process, in recent decades the institutionalization of ADR has taken many other forms, including mandatory, nonconsensual assignment to arbitration in many contracts (consumer, employment, commercial, health, securities, etc.), assignment to mandated grievance procedures in the workplace, prisons, hospitals, and schools (including now much contested mandatory processes for sexual assault on campuses), and strongly incentivized or even coerced choices of dispute resolution in more modern forms of online dispute resolution and customer service.

The key for me in these forms is what is missing—*informed consent* or *voluntariness* in engaging in a particular process and the possibilities of choice, or as I prefer to call it, "process pluralism." Just as brittle litigation outcomes don't serve everyone the same way, in dispute resolution "one size does not fit all." So some forms of

Carrie Menkel-Meadow, *Institutionalizing ADR: Clashing Values* In: *Discussions in Dispute Resolution*. Edited by: Art Hinshaw, Andrea Kupfer Schneider, and Sarah Rudolph Cole, Oxford University Press (2021). © Oxford University Press.
DOI: 10.1093/oso/9780197513248.003.0080

institutionalization of ADR occur in the public sphere (e.g., courts) and others in the private sphere (contract). And with "automatic" referral or assignment to some processes, neither lawyers nor clients fully understand the impact that process choices can have on substantive justice and outcomes.

The policies behind institutionalization or "streamlined" dispute processes have been mostly efficiency, economics, and "co-optation" or even elimination of legal claims and rights through forced assignment to particular processes. Since I wrote *Pursuing Settlement*, the Supreme Court has sustained mandatory arbitration and narrowed use of class actions to, in effect, limit the possibilities of choice for a variety of legal claims, leading some to conclude that some uses of "ADR" in fact have "erased" access to substantive legal justice (Resnik 2015). To paraphrase Malcom Feeley's trope of sociolegal studies in criminal law, "the process is the punishment"; in this case, the process may eliminate the legal merits entirely. So the relationship of the role of the "rule of law" remains understudied and theorized as legal cases and disputes outside of the legal system are assigned to some forms of "alternative" and not, in my view, "appropriate" dispute resolution.

While many of us in the early days of ADR conceptualization and implementation sought indicators and factors for "fitting the forum to the fuss," including court "menus" of choices for different types of cases, and even the exclusion of some case types (constitutional cases, prisoner's rights, Social Security), none of the categories actually worked empirically—the appropriateness of a particular process (negotiation, mediation, settlement conference, arbitration, fact-finding, ombuds, or other hybrids) too often depended on the parties and personalities, organizational structural factors, idiosyncratic and complex facts, and varying desires to "adjudicate the past" or "solve the problem for the future" (Menkel-Meadow 2010). Efforts to institutionalize by "scientific" assignment of cases simply does not work, though now many jurisdictions outside of the United States are trying to do this. In fact, many users complain that courts' mandatory assignments to various forms of ADR have added more cost and time by adding another layer of process into litigation.

Instead of the value of "efficiency" alone (and I do value efficiency), other values were the primary motivators in the early days of the ADR movement. Whether called *party participation*, *self-empowerment*, or *deprofessionalization*, one key founding principle was *party, not professional, choice* about both processes to be used and the outcomes to be achieved. The consumer movement, as well as the feminist movement as described by Elayne Greenberg here, were focused on more direct forms of redress, where courts were part of, but not the only forum for achieving justice. "Being heard," or "voice," was (and still is) a rallying cry for those who criticized the arcane rules of procedure, long waits for trials, or dependence on lawyers or others to frame and argue legal and other social claims. Early ADR conceptualizers pointed to other values in dispute resolution—catharsis, narration, understanding, recognition, and the ability to "tell one's own story" in addition to achieving a particular outcome. As an experienced trial lawyer I was always skeptical about whether formal rules and evidence allowed enough expression of the real "truth" in the simplification of reality that occurs in courts.

The early days of mediation were critical in suggesting that good solutions for the "future" were just as important as "adjudicating" the facts of the past. For me, the hope of early ADR was that different mindsets or orientations to problem-solving would focus on more "creative," tailored solutions to disputes and conflicts, exactly the opposite of "off the shelf" boilerplate clauses in contracts or routinized settlement ranges in litigated cases. Thus, "institutionalization" of "mediation-lite" or "fast-track arbitration" was, as a matter of dispute system design, counterproductive to the kinds of values I hoped our ADR movement would infuse into the legal system and to the culture at large. As James Coben describes here, moving mediation (a consensual, often time-consuming and intense emotional process) into the court setting has often led to a distorted form of process, with neither the benefits of intense privately worked out solutions or rigorously presented public presentations and is now often challenged after the fact in post-agreement litigation. In virtually every jurisdiction I have worked in recently, the model of the joint session to encourage communication, understanding, and joint problem-solving (especially for continuing relations cases) has been replaced by the caucus, shuttle diplomacy model in which third parties control all the information between the parties, often leaving parties with less information about their matters than they would have had in a public court hearing. I still see training programs for lawyers for "Winning at Mediation" (see Menkel-Meadow, *Pursuing Settlement*, p. 35), demonstrating the conflation of goals and purposes of different processes. The "solution" to so-called litigation overload has become part of the "problem." The distortions of mediation and problem-solving negotiation (now challenged by Trumpian "win at all costs" methods) in modern practice threaten all of the fundamental values of original ADR conceptions.

II. What's Problematic?

Use of the variety of ADR processes has certainly led to "morphing" of "pure" mediation (evaluative mediation, med-arb, arb-med) and other forms of dispute resolution (baseball and final offer arbitration, ombuds, conciliation) into more complex hybrids, located both in public and private spheres. As I have written in many other places, Lon Fuller decried the blending of processes (mixtures of public and private, or mixing of mediation and arbitration) when each process has its own particular ethics, integrity, goals, and contexts (Fuller 2001). The pressure to "settle" and reduce caseloads or conflicts has increased the use of a variety of these processes in many settings. The World Bank, for example, provides an "integrated dispute resolution system," which includes five possibilities: mediation, ombuds, whistle-blowing (ethics), peer (staff association), and "administrative" (litigation within the organization) processes for dealing with a variety of disputes and conflicts within an organization which is not answerable to any legal sovereign authority (see World Bank, *Conflict Resolution System*, resolution@worldbank.org).

The adaptation of pure forms of dispute resolution to more hybridized processes is, in fact, very complex and involves a variety of important issues: transparency, accountability, party choice and voice, costs, access, representation, precedent or not, flexibility versus routinized outcomes, not to mention substantive and "perceived" justice (Menkel-Meadow 2019b). The development of these hybrid uses of "ADR" in a variety of different contexts, both domestic and international is for me a "mixed blessing." I applaud the development of tailored processes to different contexts (workplaces, universities, government agencies, manufacturers and service providers, and yes, some courts), but each of these processes promises different things (awards, solutions, suggestions, rulings, etc.), and it is very important that users of these systems understand what they do and do not promise. Enforcement of outcomes, for example, is highly variable, both legally and practically (consider international cross-border mediations). The proliferation of these hybrid processes illustrates the growing sophistication of process variations, but dangerously also allows some dispute system designers to develop processes to benefit themselves (e.g., major corporations and employers that "internalize" justice systems).

III. What's Better?

Despite my concerns about the distortions of the original conceptions of ADR, I do see some positive developments in ADR's institutionalization. Recently a state court trial judge said to me, "mediation is firmly in our legal culture now—everyone knows that they have to try it, so they are looking for the best ways to do it." This makes me somewhat hopeful, that even in some distorted forms, lawyers are learning to engage in some problem-solving and information exchanges to look for better (and their own) solutions before heading into costly litigation with, perhaps, brittle results. Virtually every law school (and business school) in the United States now teaches negotiation (whether creative problem-solving or adversarial individual maximization models are taught is a different matter), and many have mediation instruction, including mediation clinics, so students can see there is a different way to resolve legal disputes. There are disputes and challenges within the constituent professions about ethical standards and zealous advocacy "vs." collaborative lawyering. There are judges and dispute system designers who debate whether to require what antecedents to litigation (mediation, settlement conferences, arbitration). Most importantly for me, since writing *Pursuing Settlement*, I have now taught and trained lawyers, diplomats, judges, government officials, and dispute designers in over twenty-six countries. The movement to teach students many forms of legal process and decision-making and to restructure legal systems is clearly moving around the world and institutionalization is taking many forms, including mandatory mediation or negotiation training in a few places.

So, as an ADR scholar and practitioner, as well as a sociolegal empiricist, I am hopeful that as ADR travels to different legal cultures, we will be able to study and assess where and how legal cultures and dispute resolution cultures use, adapt, and express different values. I am still hoping for the cultural meme of "problem-solving" through "appropriate dispute resolution" to spread around the world.

References

Lon L. Fuller, The Principles of Social Order: Selected Essays of Lon Fuller (Kenneth Winston ed., rev. ed. 2001).

Carrie Menkel-Meadow, *The Culture of Negotiation: Trumpian Imprints on the Future?*, 35 Negot. J. (Special Issue: Negotiation and Conflict Resolution in the Age of Trump) (Jan. 2019a).
Carrie Menkel-Meadow, "Hybrid and Mixed Dispute Resolution Processes: Integrities of Process Pluralism," *in* Comparative Dispute Resolution Handbook (M. Palmer, M. Roberts, & M. Moscati eds., 2019b).
Carrie Menkel-Meadow, "Dispute Resolution," *in* Oxford Handbook of Empirical Legal Research (P. Cane & H. Kritzer eds., 2010).
Judith Resnik, *Diffusing Disputes: The Public in the Private of Arbitration: The Private in the Courts and the Erasure of Rights*, 124 Yale L.J. 2804–939 (2015).

Commenter Biographies

Marjorie Corman Aaron is a Professor of Practice and Director of the Center for Practice at the University of Cincinnati College of Law, teaching client counseling, negotiation, mediation, trial practice, and decision analysis. She was formerly Executive Director of the Program on Negotiation at Harvard and a Vice President at Endispute. Since 1988, Professor Aaron has practiced as a mediator and arbitrator and taught workshops for law firms, corporations, and other organizations. Professor Aaron is the author of *Risk and Rigor: A Lawyer's Guide to Decision Trees for Assessing Cases and Advising Clients* (DRI Press 2019) and *Client Science: Advice for Lawyers on Counseling Clients Through Bad News and Other Legal Realities* (Oxford University Press 2012) and many articles, chapters, simulations, and videos. A graduate of Princeton University and Harvard Law School, she initially practiced litigation at Goodwin Procter and as a prosecutor in Massachusetts.

James J. Alfini is Dean and Professor Emeritus at South Texas College of Law Houston. He is also Professor Emeritus at Northern Illinois University College of Law, where he was Dean from 1991 to 1997, and previously was a member of the law faculty at Florida State University, where he also served as Director of Education and Research for the Florida Dispute Resolution Center. He has served as Chair of the American Bar Association Dispute Resolution Section and Chair of the Association of American Law Schools Alternative Dispute Resolution Section. His publications in the ADR field include the co-authored *Mediation Theory and Practice*, a law school textbook published by Lexis Law Publishing. He serves as a delegate from the Dispute Resolution Section to the House of Delegates of the American Bar Association. He received his undergraduate degree from Columbia University and his J.D. from Northwestern University.

Cynthia Alkon is a Professor of Law and Director of the Criminal Law, Justice, & Policy Program at Texas A&M University School of Law. Professor Alkon teaches criminal law, advanced criminal procedure, and negotiation. Prior to joining academia, Professor Alkon was a Deputy Public Defender with the Los Angeles County Public Defender's Office. Professor Alkon also spent over seven years working in Eastern Europe and the former Soviet Union providing rule of law development assistance, primarily for criminal justice reform. Professor Alkon's scholarship focuses on dispute resolution in the criminal context, including plea bargaining.

Lisa Blomgren Amsler (formerly Lisa B. Bingham) is Distinguished Professor, Keller-Runden Professor of Public Service, Indiana University O'Neill School of Public and Environmental Affairs, and Saltman Senior Scholar, Boyd School of Law, University of Nevada, Las Vegas. A graduate of Smith College (A.B. 1976, magna cum laude, high honors in ancient Greek) and University of Connecticut School of law (J.D. 1979, high honors), her research addresses dispute resolution and dispute system design. Amsler directed the U.S.P.S. REDRESS National Evaluation Project on mediating employment discrimination complaints (1994–2006). A National Academy of Public Administration Fellow, Amsler received awards for outstanding research from the American Bar Association Section of Dispute Resolution, International Association for Conflict Management, and American Society for Public Administration. She has co-edited three books (with Rosemary O'Leary), has published over 120 articles and book chapters, and her book *Dispute System Design: Preventing, Managing, and Resolving Conflict* (with Janet Martinez and Stephanie Smith), was published by Stanford University Press in 2020.

Hiro N. Aragaki is a Professor of Law at Loyola Law School, Los Angeles, and a Professorial Research Associate at SOAS Law School, University of London. He teaches and writes in the areas of arbitration, mediation, negotiation, contracts, and civil procedure. His scholarship on arbitration law has appeared in top law reviews and formed the basis of several amicus curiae briefs, including one he filed in the groundbreaking case of *AT&T Mobility v. Concepcion*, 131 S. Ct. 1740 (2011). In addition to his research and teaching, Professor Aragaki sits as an arbitrator and mediator, and has trained judges and lawyers and provided dispute systems design and ADR reform advice throughout Asia and Africa. He holds degrees from Yale, Stanford, and Cambridge, and is dual qualified in the United States and in the United Kingdom.

Erin R. Archerd was introduced to dispute resolution during her days as a research assistant to Deborah Hensler and Donna Shestowsky at Stanford University. She continued her education at Harvard Law School, where she was Advanced Training Director for the Harvard Mediation Program. After a few years negotiating technology transactions in the Bay Area at Covington & Burling LLP, she moved to the Midwest and ran the Mediation Clinic at the Ohio State University Moritz College of Law as the Langdon Fellow in Dispute Resolution. She now teaches Commercial Law and ADR as an Associate Professor of Law at the University of Detroit Mercy School of Law. Erin is on the Executive Committee of the State Bar of Michigan Dispute Resolution Section, serves as Co-Chair of the American Bar Association Dispute Resolution Ethics Committee, and spends her free time with her spouse running after their twins.

Richard Bales is a faculty member at Ohio Northern University Law (visiting at Akron Law 2018–20). He teaches a wide variety of ADR and labor/employment courses, torts, and civil procedure. He has published more than eighty scholarly articles and authored or co-authored eight books on a variety of topics related to labor/employment/ADR. His most recent book, *The Cambridge Handbook of U.S. Labor Law for the Twenty-First Century* (co-edited with Charlotte Garden), was published in December 2019. In addition to teaching and writing, Rick is a part-time labor arbitrator. He is a member of the National Academy of Arbitrators and serves on FMCS and AAA panels.

Rishi Batra, Professor, is a nationally recognized speaker and scholar in the field of alternative dispute resolution. He is currently a Professor of Law and the Director of the Leadership and Appropriate Dispute Resolution program for the US Air Force Academy. Professor Batra was previously a professor at Texas Tech University School of Law. Professor Batra's scholarship focuses on alternative dispute resolution, and in particular applying dispute resolution perspectives to diverse fields such as criminal procedure and election law. Professor Batra earned his J.D. (cum laude) from Harvard Law School, where he served as Training Director for the Harvard Mediation Program and as a teaching assistant in Harvard's Program on Negotiation. Professor Batra did his undergraduate work at the University of California, Berkeley, where he received a B.S. (honors) degree in Electrical Engineering Computer Science and a B.A. (high honors) degree in Cognitive Science.

Kristen Blankley is a Professor of Law at the University of Nebraska College of Law and Director of the Robert J. Kutak Center for the Teaching and Study of Applied Ethics. Professor Blankley teaches in the areas of arbitration, mediation, facilitation, and legal ethics. Professor Blankley's scholarship focuses on areas of arbitration law, as well as the intersection of dispute resolution and ethics. In addition to her teaching and writing, Professor Blankley is an active mediator, facilitator, and arbitrator.

Robert C. Bordone is an expert, author, speaker, and teacher in negotiation, conflict resolution, mediation, and facilitation. A Senior Fellow at Harvard Law School, Bordone served on the full-time faculty at Harvard Law School for two decades as the Thaddeus R. Beal Clinical Professor of Law, Director, and Founder of the Harvard Negotiation & Mediation Clinical Program before launching his consulting, advisory, speaking, and training practice. He is the co-author of two books: *Designing Systems and Processes for Managing Disputes*, 2nd edition (Wolters-Kluwer 2019), and *The Handbook of Dispute Resolution* (Jossey-Bass 2005). He has also published articles in leading dispute resolution journals. His writing and commentary have appeared in various print and broadcast media outlets, including *NBC News*, the *Boston Globe*, the *Washington Post*, the *Los Angeles Times*, and the *Chicago Tribune*. Bordone earned his J.D. from Harvard Law School, and his A.B. from Dartmouth College.

Kelly Browe Olson is an Associate Professor and the Mediation Clinic Director at the UA Little Rock Bowen School of Law. She teaches family law, ADR, domestic violence, and mediation seminars. She mediates in family and dependency/neglect cases and oversees a statewide Special Education mediation project. She is a national speaker on family conflict resolution, communication, mediation, and children's legal issues. Professor Browe Olson serves on the Arkansas Parent Counsel Commission, the Arkansas Access to Justice Commission, the Association of Family and Conciliation Courts Board of Directors, and the Family Court Review editorial board. She has worked with the Arkansas ADR Commission and the Arkansas Coalition Against Domestic Violence. She helped create the UA Little Rock Graduate Certificate Program in Conflict Mediation. She won the Bowen Faculty Excellence Public Service

Award in 2004 and 2013. She has a University of Michigan J.D. and a Loyola Chicago LL.M. in Child Law.

Alyson Carrel is a clinical associate professor at Northwestern Pritzker School of Law, is Assistant Director of their nationally ranked Center on Negotiation and Mediation, and was their first appointed Assistant Dean of Law & Technology from 2017 to 2019. In these roles she received a grant to purchase wearable cameras for negotiation simulation courses and a fellowship to integrate the A2J Author platform in her mediation advocacy clinic, and launched Teach LAW, a demonstration series for instructional technology. Today, as part of a small working group, she is developing a new client-driven lawyering model for the twenty-first century, called the Delta Model, which recognizes the importance of technology fluency and emotional intelligence in the delivery of legal services.

James Coben is a Professor at Mitchell Hamline School of Law and a Senior Fellow in the law school's Dispute Resolution Institute, which he directed from 2000 to 2009. He teaches civil procedure and a wide variety of ADR courses. He is a co-author of the Thomson Reuters trial practice series treatise *Mediation: Law, Policy & Practice* (2018–2019), a co-editor of the four-volume *Rethinking Negotiation Teaching Series* (DRI Press 2009–2013), and a former editorial board member of the American Bar Association's *Dispute Resolution Magazine*, for which he co-writes a "Research Insights" featured column.

Amy J. Cohen is the John C. Elam/Vorys Sater Professor of Law, Ohio State University Moritz College of Law, where she researches and teaches in the areas of alternative dispute resolution and law and economic development. She has held visiting professorships at Harvard Law School, Osgoode Hall Law School, the University of Turin Faculty of Law, UNSW Sydney, and the West Bengal National University of Juridical Sciences. Her research has been funded by the Radcliffe Institute for Advanced Study at Harvard University, the American Institute of Indian Studies at the University of Chicago, the Collegio Carlo Alberto, and multiple grants from the Fulbright Program.

Michael T. Colatrella Jr. is Professor of Law at University of the Pacific, McGeorge School of Law, where he teaches mediation, negotiation, Section 1983 Prisoner Civil Rights Mediation Clinic, civil procedure, professional responsibility, and The Legal Profession. He is co-author of the interdisciplinary text *Mediation—Skills & Techniques* (Lexis/Nexis 2008) that is widely used in law schools, graduate schools, and schools of diplomacy. His primary areas of research is on mediation, ethics, and legal education, and his articles have appeared in the *Ohio State Journal of Dispute Resolution*, the *Review of Litigation*, the *Cardozo Journal of Conflict Resolution*, and elsewhere. Prior to joining the faculty at McGeorge, he served as Director and Senior Lecturer at Southern Methodist University's Center for Dispute Resolution & Conflict Management in Plano, Texas, a program offering a Master's of Arts in Conflict Management.

Sarah R. Cole is the Michael E. Moritz Chair in Alternative Dispute Resolution, Moritz College of Law, Ohio State University; B.A., University of Puget Sound (cum laude); J.D., University of Chicago Law School (cum laude). Professor Cole clerked on the Ninth Circuit for Eugene A. Wright. She practiced labor and employment law and was on the faculty at Creighton University School of Law before joining the Moritz faculty in 1998. She is co-author, with Nancy Rogers, James Coben, Peter Thompson, and Craig McEwen, of *Mediation: Law, Policy and Practice* and of *Dispute Resolution: Negotiation, Mediation and Other Processes*, with Nancy Rogers, Stephen Goldberg, and Frank Sander. She is the Director of the Program on Dispute Resolution at Moritz. In 2013, Ohio State awarded her the Alumni Award for Distinguished Teaching. She serves on arbitration and mediation panels for AAA and the State of Ohio and visited at Harvard Law School in fall 2019.

Alexander J.S. Colvin is the Kenneth F. Kahn '69 Dean and the Martin F. Scheinman '75 MS '76 Professor of Conflict Resolution at the ILR School, Cornell University. His research and teaching focuses on employment dispute resolution, with a particular emphasis on procedures in nonunion workplaces and the impact of the legal environment on organizations. His research projects include empirical investigations of employment arbitration and cross-national studies of workplace dispute resolution and labor law change. He is co-author of the books *An Introduction to Collective Bargaining and Industrial Relations, 5th edition* (with Harry C. Katz and Thomas A. Kochan), *Labor Relations in a Global World: An Introduction focusing on Developing Economies* (also with Harry C. Katz and Thomas A. Kochan), and *Arbitration Law, 3rd edition* (with Katherine Van Wezel Stone, and Richard Bales), and co-editor (with Bill Roche and Paul Teague) of the *Oxford Handbook of Conflict Management in Organizations*.

Carli N. Conklin is an Associate Professor at the University of Missouri School of Law and Associate Professor of Constitutional Democracy at the Kinder Institute on Constitutional Democracy. Her teaching and research interests are in the fields of dispute resolution and early American legal and intellectual history, including the history of arbitration in early America. Professor Conklin completed the dual-degree J.D./M.A. program in American legal history at the University of Virginia School of Law and Corcoran Department of History. She was awarded the School of Law's Madeleine and John Traynor Prize for her Master's thesis, which explored state court treatment of arbitration in early America. Professor Conklin returned to the University of Virginia to complete her Ph.D. in History. Her research has been published in the *American Journal of Legal History*, the Ohio State University *Journal on Dispute Resolution*, the University of Missouri *Journal of Dispute Resolution*, and *Washington University Jurisprudence Review*.

Ellen E. Deason is the Joanne Wharton Murphy/Classes of 1965 and 1973 Professor of Law at the Ohio State University Moritz College of Law. Deason's recent scholarship focuses on judicial mediation, combinations of mediation and arbitration, and enforcement of mediated settlement agreements. She has also written extensively on the topic of confidentiality in mediation. Her honors include selection for an Ohio

State University Alumni Award for Distinguished Teaching and as College of Law Professor of the Year. The Association of American Law Schools Section of Alternative Dispute Resolution recognized her article *Beyond "Managerial Judges": Appropriate Roles in Settlement* as the 2017 Article of the Year in the field of dispute resolution. She is the co-author of *Global Issues in Mediation* (with Jacqueline Nolan-Haley and Mariana H.C. Gonstead) and casebooks on Civil Procedure and Alternative Dispute Resolution. She teaches the Mediation Clinic, Dispute Resolution Processes, International Commercial Arbitration, and Civil Procedure.

Noam Ebner is a Professor of negotiation and conflict resolution in Creighton University's Department of Interdisciplinary Studies. Previously, he taught at a number of universities around the world while practicing as an attorney, negotiator, mediator, and mediator trainer. An early innovator in the online teaching of negotiation and conflict resolution, Ebner chaired Creighton's online graduate program on Negotiation and Conflict Resolution for many years while spearheading the program's curricular and pedagogical development. He has consulted for online learning to programs, universities, and teachers, and taught a Massive Open Online Course (MOOC) on negotiation. Noam co-edited *The Palgrave Handbook of Cross-Cultural Business Negotiation* (2019) and *Assessing Our Students, Assessing Ourselves; Vol.3 in The Rethinking Negotiation Teaching Project* (2012). His writing focuses on negotiation, online dispute resolution, and the future of the negotiation, mediation, and legal fields. Currently, he is co-editing a book on *Star Wars and Conflict Resolution*.

Yael Efron is an LL.D. graduate from the Faculty of Law at the Hebrew University, Jerusalem, and the Vice Dean at Zefat Academic College School of Law in Israel. Dr. Efron teaches civil procedure, alternative dispute resolution, and family law. She also heads the legal clinics and directs the Legal-Aid Clinic for the Underprivileged at ZAC. Dr. Efron is a visiting scholar at Masaryk University Law Faculty in the Czech Republic under the auspices of the Theodore Herzl Distinguished Chair and a visiting instructor at the Osgoode Professional Development program at York University, Canada. Dr. Efron is the recipient of the Halbert Centre for Canadian Studies Post-Doctoral Fellowship and of the Theodore Herzl Distinguished Chair Award. She has published widely on legal education, pedagogy and curriculum design, negotiation, dispute resolution, and other subjects. Some of her publications can be accessed through http://ssrn.com/author=1146543.

Deborah Thompson Eisenberg is a Professor of Law and Faculty Director of the Center for Dispute Resolution at the University of Maryland Francis King Carey School of Law. She studies and teaches in the areas of dispute resolution, civil procedure, and employment law, and directs the Mediation Clinic. Professor Eisenberg has testified as an expert about equal pay and employment discrimination before the US Senate and Equal Employment Opportunity Commission. Her recent scholarship focuses on the impact of mediator strategies and the application of dispute resolution strategies to accomplish social change. Professor Eisenberg serves on the Executive Committee of the American Association of Law Schools Dispute Resolution Section and Co-Chairs the AALS Clinical Law Section ADR Committee. She brings to her teaching and scholarship a perspective grounded in fifteen years of complex civil rights and employment litigation experience. She received her J.D. from Yale Law School in 1994.

Donna Erez-Navot is the Assistant Director of the Kukin Program for Conflict Resolution at Cardoza Law School and Director of the Cardoza Mediation Clinic. Prior to joining the faculty at Cardoza Law School, she was the founding Director of the Mediation Clinic at University of Wisconsin Law School. In conjunction with her work at the UW Law School Mediation Clinic, she partnered with local counties to establish several mediation programs, including two small claims mediation programs and two child protection mediation programs. Before moving to Wisconsin, she was employed as a mediator in the Child Permanency Meditation Program in the NYC Family Court, where she mediated issues surrounding placement of children in foster care, custody/visitation/guardianship petitions, conditional surrenders, and other issues. Donna is a graduate of Cardoza Law School in New York. After attaining her undergraduate degree at Emory University, Donna studied Social Work at Tel Aviv University.

Douglas N. Frenkel, the Morris Shuster Practice Professor of Law at the University of Pennsylvania Law School, was the architect and director of Penn's renowned clinical program for twenty-eight years. In the early 1980s, he chaired a national initiative on conflict resolution teaching and research that spawned many of today's classroom approaches. Frenkel founded and has led Penn's Mediation Clinic for over three decades and frequently serves as a mediator in a broad range of matters. Frenkel is the co-author (with James Stark) of *The Practice of Mediation: A Video-Integrated Text*, a book that has been adopted for classroom use at over seventy law schools in the United States and other nations and has served as the basis for many professional mediator training programs. His articles on persuasion effectiveness in mediation and on the potential for mediation training/experience to de-bias lawyers' judgment, co-authored with Stark, have won critical acclaim.

Marc Galanter, John and Rylla Bosshard Professor Emeritus of Law and South Asian Studies at the University of Wisconsin-Madison and formerly LSE Centennial Professor at the London School of Economics, studies litigation, lawyers, and legal culture, mainly in the United States and in India. He has been editor of the *Law & Society Review*, President of the Law and Society Association, Chair of the International Commission on Folk Law and Legal Pluralism, a Guggenheim Fellow, and a Fellow of the Center for Advanced Study in the Behavioral Sciences. His works include *"Why the 'Haves' Come Out Ahead"* (1974, 2014); *Competing Equalities: Law and the Backward Classes in India* (1984, 1991); *Law and Society in Modern India* (1989, 1992); *Tournament of Lawyers: The Transformation of the Big Law Firm* (1991); *Lowering the Bar: Lawyer Jokes and Legal Culture* (2005); and *Jews and the Law* (co-editor, 2014).

Dwight Golann, Professor of Law at Suffolk University, has been teacher of dispute resolution and mediator for more than twenty-five years. He is the author of a leading book on commercial mediation techniques, *Mediating Legal Disputes*, a text on advocacy; *Sharing a Mediator's Powers*; and three textbooks as well as articles. Professor Golann has led trainings for federal and state courts, the European Union, and ADR organizations around the world. Professor Golann was formerly a litigator in private practice and served as Chief of the Trial Division of the Massachusetts Attorney General's Office, where he tried and argued cases at every level of the American court system. He is the recipient of the Lifetime Achievement Award of the American College of Civil Mediators and is currently a Scholar-in-Residence for the International Academy of Mediators.

Michael Z. Green has served as a Full Professor at Texas A&M University School of Law since its beginning in August 2013 and as the Director of its Workplace Law Program since 2015. He has published several law review articles and book chapters in support of his scholarly agenda focused on workplace law issues and their intersection with dispute resolution and race. He has also discussed his scholarly endeavors at many national and international venues. As a member of the Labor Law Group, a collection of scholars engaged in producing quality casebooks for instruction in labor and employment law, he co-authored the fourth edition of *ADR in the Workplace* by West, published in 2020. In September 2019, he was selected as a member of the National Academy of Arbitrators in recognition of his scholarly achievements and service as a labor arbitrator. More biographical information is available at http://law.tamu.edu/faculty-staff/find-people/faculty-profiles/Michael-z-green.

Elayne E. Greenberg is Assistant Dean for Dispute Resolution, Professor of Legal Practice and Faculty Director of the Hugh L. Carey Center for Dispute Resolution at St. John's Law School. She is a mediator and dispute system designer who has developed programs, and educated, trained, and written on dispute resolution. Her interdisciplinary scholarship has focused on how the inclusion of alternative dispute resolution values and skills could strengthen court justice outcomes. The ideas she has expressed in this book are informed, in large part, by the domestic and international court-connected dispute resolution programs she has helped develop and implement.

Jill I. Gross is Associate Dean for Academic Affairs and Professor of Law at the Elisabeth Haub School of Law at Pace University, teaching courses in ADR, securities law, and professional responsibility. She has held the Hopkins Chair, and directed the Legal Skills Program. She is co-author of the treatise *Broker-Dealer Law and Regulation*, has published dozens of book chapters and articles on the negotiation, mediation, and arbitration of securities disputes, and is a Senior Contributing Editor to the *Securities Online Litigation Alert*. She has chaired the AALS Section of Dispute Resolution, and is an arbitrator for the AAA and FINRA, a member of the Securities Experts Roundtable, and a former public member of FINRA's NAMC. She has testified as an expert in securities arbitration matters. She received an A.B. magna cum laude, Phi Beta Kappa, from Cornell University and a J.D. cum laude from Harvard Law School.

Art Hinshaw is the John J. Bouma Fellow in Alternative Dispute Resolution, the Founding Director of the Lodestar Dispute Resolution Center, and a Clinical Professor of Law at the Sandra Day O'Connor College of Law at Arizona State University. His research bridges dispute resolution theory and practice, and he is a co-author on the acclaimed textbook *Dispute Resolution and Lawyers: A Contemporary Approach* (6th ed.). Currently he serves on the ABA's Standing Committee on Mediator Ethical Guidance and is a regular contributor to *Indisputably* the ADR law professor blog.

Rebecca Hollander-Blumoff is Professor of Law at Washington University, where her work focuses on law and psychology in the context of dispute resolution. Professor Hollander-Blumoff received undergraduate and law degrees from Harvard University, as well as a Ph.D. in social psychology from New York University. Professor Hollander-Blumoff is the past Chair of the Executive Committee of the Association of American Law Schools Section on Civil Procedure and the past Chair of the Faculty Senate Council at Washington University. Before becoming a law professor, she clerked for the Hon. Kimba M. Wood of the U.S. District Court for the Southern District of New York, and practiced law at Lankler Siffert & Wohl LLP, a litigation firm in New York City specializing in white collar criminal defense. Professor Hollander-Blumoff has been a Visiting Professor of Law at Notre Dame Law School and at Harvard Law School.

David Horton is a Professor of Law at UC Davis. He teaches and writes in the areas of wills and trusts, arbitration law, and contracts. He has won the Association of American Law Schools' Scholarly Paper Competition, the Mangano Dispute Resolution Achievement Award, and the Distinguished Teaching Award. Horton's work has appeared in the *Yale Law Journal*, *Stanford Law Review*, *N.Y.U. Law Review*, *University of Pennsylvania Law Review*, *California Law Review*, *Northwestern University Law Review*, *Georgetown Law Journal*, *UCLA Law Review*, and *Vanderbilt Law Review*, among many other journals. Horton received his B.A. cum laude from Carleton College in 1997 and his J.D. from UCLA School of Law in 2004. At UCLA, he was elected to the Order of the Coif and served as Chief Articles Editor of the *UCLA Law Review*.

Becky L. Jacobs is the Waller Lansden Professor of Law at the University of Tennessee College of Law. She directs its Civil and Family Mediation Clinics, as well as teaches alternative dispute resolution, environmental law, and other courses. Becky joined UT's law faculty with more than a decade of international practice experience, including work as the Assistant General Counsel for Duke Energy International's Geração Paranapanema S.A. São Paulo, Brazil, subsidiary and as an in-house lawyer for Conoco and CNG Transmission. She also clerked for the Honorable Pasco M. Bowman on the 8th Circuit U.S. Court of Appeals and practiced with the law firms of Gibson, Dunn and Crutcher and Shook, Hardy & Bacon, spending time in the London offices of both firms. Becky was the top graduate in her law class at the University of Georgia School of Law and was named to the Order of the Coif.

Russell Korobkin is the Richard C. Maxwell Distinguished Professor of Law at the UCLA School of Law. He is the author of *Negotiation Theory and Strategy* (3rd ed., 2014), *K: A Common Law Approach to Contracts* (2nd ed., 2015), and more than fifty journal articles on the subjects of negotiation, contracts, and other areas of law, business, and human behavior. A former San Francisco management consultant and Washington, D.C., lawyer, Professor Korobkin earned his undergraduate and law degrees from Stanford University. In addition to UCLA, he has taught full time at the University of Illinois, University of Texas, and Harvard University Law Schools, and he has taught intensive negotiation courses to undergraduates, MBA students, and law students at ten universities on four continents. He also provides negotiation training for professional groups, negotiation consulting, and mediation services.

Kimberlee Kovach has been a leader and visionary in the modern mediation and alternative dispute resolution movement for over forty years. She was a founding officer and Chair of the ABA Section of Dispute Resolution, and also served as Chair of the ADR Sections of both the Texas and Houston Bar Associations. Kovach created and conducted the first mediation training in the state of Texas in 1980 and has taught a variety of ADR courses in legal education for over twenty-five years. She has published numerous articles and book chapters on a variety of ADR related topics and was instrumental in the early creation of law school mediation clinics. Kovach was honored with the prestigious Lifetime Achievement Award by the International Academy of Mediators in recognition of her extensive work in mediation, and currently serves as an arbitrator, mediator, and trainer, and is a member of several national neutral panels.

John Lande is the Isidor Loeb Professor Emeritus at the University of Missouri School of Law and former director of its LL.M. Program in Dispute Resolution. He has received numerous awards for his work. He earned his J.D. from Hastings College of Law and Ph.D. in sociology from the University of Wisconsin-Madison. He began practicing law and mediation in California in 1980, and he directed a child protection mediation clinic in the 1990s. The American Bar Association published his books, *Lawyering with Planned Early Negotiation: How You Can Get Good Results for Clients and Make Money and Litigation Interest* and *Risk Assessment: Help Your Clients Make Good Litigation Decisions* (co-authored with Michaela Keet and Heather Heavin). You can download his publications at his website, https://www.law.missouri.edu/lande.

Lela Porter Love is a Professor of Law and Director of the Kukin Program for Conflict Resolution at Benjamin N. Cardozo School of Law (NYC), which has been ranked by *U.S. News and World Report* among the top ten law school programs in dispute resolution since 2000. She has served as a mediator in a wide range of cases and conducts domestic and international mediation training programs and courses. A past Chair of the American Bar Association Section of Dispute Resolution, Professor Love received a Lifetime Achievement Award from the International Academy of Mediators in 2012 and from the American College of Civil Trial Mediators in 2010. She has written widely on the topic of dispute resolution, including *The Middle Voice* (with Joseph Stulberg), and two collections of stories about mediations—*Stories Mediators Tell* and *Stories Mediators Tell—World Edition*.

Martin H. Malin is Professor and Co-director of the Institute for Law and the Workplace, Chicago-Kent College of Law, Illinois Institute of Technology. He is also a practicing arbitrator and mediator, a former Vice President of the National Academy of Arbitrators (NAA) and a former member of the Board of Governors of the College of Labor and Employment Lawyers and of the Executive Committee of the Labor Law Group. He chaired one of two NAA committees that drafted the NAA's Guidelines for Standards of Professional Responsibility for Arbitrators in Mandatory Employment arbitration. He also served as Reporter for the Association of Labor Relations Agencies' Neutrality Project, which produced a Restatement-like mini-treatise on labor board and mediation agency impartiality. He has published more than eighty articles and seven books. He has a B.A. from Michigan State University and a J.D. from George Washington University.

Bobbi McAdoo, Professor Emerita at Mitchell-Hamline School of Law, was Professor of Law and Founding Director of the Dispute Resolution Institute at Hamline University School of Law. For three decades she taught negotiation and mediation theory and skills to law students, lawyers, judges, and other professionals in the United States and abroad. She was also the director of the Missouri LL.M. in Dispute Resolution program for two years. Professor McAdoo's empirical research and writing centered on the understanding and use of mediation by lawyers and judges in court-connected mediation programs. This work informed her service on statewide boards in both Missouri and Minnesota charged with implementing broad based ADR programs in the courts. Professor McAdoo initiated several law school courses centering on the concept that all lawyers need to be problem solvers, not just lawyers who are ADR professionals; and she pushed for more empirical work to be completed and utilized in the ADR field.

Carrie Menkel-Meadow, Professor, is Distinguished Professor of Law and Political Science at the University of California, Irvine, and A.B. Chettle Jr. Professor of Law Dispute Resolution and Civil Procedure, Emerita at Georgetown University Law Center. She is one of the founders of the modern ADR field, authoring early articles (some commented on in this volume) as part of more than the fifteen books and two hundred articles she has authored throughout her career. She has been honored with three honorary doctorates in the United States and in Europe, the first ABA Section of Dispute Resolution award for Outstanding Scholarly Work, and the American Bar Foundation Award for Outstanding Scholar. She has mediated, arbitrated, and litigated for over forty years and has been a conflict resolution/dispute system design consultant and evaluator for the World Bank, the United Nations, the International Red Cross, and the Federal Judicial Center, among many other institutions.

Robert H. Mnookin is the Samuel Williston Professor of Law at Harvard Law School, the Director of the Harvard Negotiation Research Project, and for twenty-five years chaired the Program on Negotiation at Harvard Law School. Professor Mnookin has applied his interdisciplinary approach to negotiation and conflict resolution to a remarkable range of public and private problems. He has written or edited ten books and numerous scholarly articles. In his most recent books are *Kissinger The Negotiator: Lessons from Deal making at the Highest Levels* (with J. Sebenius and R.N. Burns) and *The American Jewish Paradox: New Decisions for the "Chosen People."* An experienced mediator, Mnookin has served as a neutral in numerous high-stake commercial disputes and facilitated a number of "track-two" confidential meetings related to the Israeli-Palestinian conflict. A graduate of both Harvard College and Harvard Law School, Professor Mnookin clerked for Supreme Court Justice John Harlan.

Michael Moffitt is the Philip H. Knight Chair in Law at the University of Oregon School of Law, where he has been a professor since 2001 and served as Dean from 2011 through 2017. He was formerly the Roger D. Fisher Visiting Professor in Negotiation and Conflict Resolution at Harvard Law School, where he also served as the Clinical Supervisor of the Harvard Mediation Program. A graduate of Harvard Law School and Marietta College, he has worked in more than twenty countries on public-sector and private-sector negotiations.

Lauren A. Newell is a Professor of Law at the Ohio Northern University Pettit College of Law, where she teaches courses on negotiation, business organizations, and securities regulation. Professor Newell is also qualified as a nonpublic arbitrator of securities industry disputes through the Financial Industry Regulatory Authority. Her research focuses on the psychological aspects of negotiation and lawyering, including the emotional dimension of negotiation and the impact of new technology on negotiation and lawyering. Prior to joining the Ohio Northern faculty, Professor Newell practiced corporate law in New York City at the law firm of Boies Schiller Flexner LL.P. She received her J.D. from Harvard Law School and her B.A. in English from Georgetown University.

Lydia Nussbaum is a Professor of Law at the UNLV Boyd School of Law, where she also serves as the Director of the Saltman Center for Conflict Resolution. Before joining the faculty at Boyd, she taught at the University of Baltimore School of Law and also was a Fellow in the Leadership, Ethics, and Democracy Building Initiative at the University of Maryland Francis King Carey School of Law. She teaches courses on dispute resolution and family law and also directs the law school's Mediation Clinic. Professor Nussbaum's research explores questions of how and why states use ADR procedural interventions as instruments for shaping public policy and instituting societal reform. Professor Nussbaum earned her J.D. from the University of Maryland, and she received her B.A. for a double major in History and Italian, with distinction in all subjects, from Cornell University.

Brian A. Pappas, Ph.D., J.D., is Assistant Professor of Political Science and Assistant Vice President of Academic Affairs at Eastern Michigan University, where he oversees the Academic Human Resources office. Previously he directed the Conflict Management program at Boise State University as Assistant Professor of Public Policy and Administration. For ten years he worked as the Associate Director of the Alternative Dispute Resolution Program and as Clinical Professor of Law at Michigan State University's College of Law. Pappas has trained thousands of domestic relations and civil mediators, and his research explores the tensions between formal and informal dispute processes. Pappas also serves on the executive committee of the American Bar Association's Section of Dispute Resolution and on the board of the Mindfulness in Law Society.

Carol Pauli teaches legal writing and is part of the team teaching alternative dispute resolution to first-year students at Texas A&M University School of Law. She was a Westerfield Fellow at Loyola University New Orleans. She earned her J.D. with honors at the Benjamin N. Cardozo School of Law. Pauli's scholarship focuses on media, conflict, and conflict resolution, all related to her work at the *Associated Press* and *CBS News* in New York. Before teaching in a law school, she was an associate professor of journalism, mass communication law, and press history at Marist College in Poughkeepsie, New York, and an associate instructor at Columbia University's Graduate School of Journalism, where she had earned her Master's degree. She taught journalism as a Fulbright lecturer at the University of Botswana and later returned to Africa with the US Information Agency to lead workshops for reporters in Tanzania, Malawi, and Rwanda.

Sharon Press is Director of the Dispute Resolution Institute and Professor of Law at the Mitchell Hamline School of Law in St. Paul, Minnesota. In addition, Press coaches the Mediation Representation Team, and serves as the academic advisor to the students who are completing a Certificate in Conflict Resolution Theory and Practice. Press currently serves as Co-President of Community Mediation Minnesota, is treasurer for Community Mediation and Restorative Services, and serves on the board of the Institute for the Study of Conflict Transformation. She also mediates regularly in Conciliation, Housing, and Harassment Courts. Prior to joining Mitchell Hamline Law, Press served as director of the Florida Dispute Resolution Center, where she was responsible for the ADR programs for the Florida state court system. She received her B.A. from the George Washington University School of Public and International Affairs and her J.D. from the George Washington University National Law Center.

Peter R. Reilly is Professor of Law at Texas A&M University School of Law in Fort Worth, Texas. He is also adjunct professor within Georgetown University's Center for Public and Nonprofit Leadership, where he works with directors, board members, and other leaders of nonprofit and philanthropic organizations worldwide. Reilly's scholarship focuses on alternative dispute resolution, with a strong interest in corporate deferred prosecution, ethics, emotional intelligence, and theories of influence and persuasion in the negotiation context. Reilly earned a B.A. from Princeton University's Woodrow Wilson School of Public and international Affairs, a J.D. from Harvard Law School, and an LL.M. from Georgetown University Law Center, where

Reilly was a Hewlett Fellow in Conflict Resolution and Legal Problem-Solving. Reilly is past Chair of the Association of American Law Schools' Section on Alternative Dispute Resolution, and he is currently Chair of the American Bar Association's James B. Boskey Essay Contest on Dispute Resolution.

Jennifer Reynolds, Professor, teaches civil procedure, negotiation, conflict of laws, and dispute systems design. Her research interests include public disputes, cultural influences and implications of alternative processes, and plea bargaining. Reynolds has a J.D. from Harvard Law School, an M.A. from the University of Texas at Austin, and an A.B. from the University of Chicago. While at Harvard, Reynolds served as an editor of the *Harvard Law Review*; as a research assistant for Professor Arthur Miller on his treatise, *Federal Practice and Procedure*; and as a teaching assistant, researcher, and Harvard Negotiation Research Project Fellow for the Program on Negotiation. Before law school, Reynolds worked as a systems analyst and was an associate director for information technology at UT Austin. After law school, she was an associate at the Atlanta office of Dow Lohnes PLLC, working primarily on First Amendment and employment cases.

Amy J. Schmitz, Professor, is the Elwood L. Thomas Missouri Endowed Professor of Law at the University of Missouri. She teaches courses in contracts, lawyering, online dispute resolution, secured transactions, arbitration, international arbitration, and consumer law. She serves on the AALS Executive Committee on Commercial and Consumer Law, is a Fellow of the National Center for Technology and Dispute Resolution, is Co-Chair of the ABA Technology and Dispute Resolution Committee, and was an External Scientific Fellow of the Max Planck Institute Luxembourg. She also has taught in France, South Africa, and Oxford, England, and has been involved in the UN working group seeking to create a global online dispute resolution mechanism (UNCITRAL WG III). Professor Schmitz has published over fifty articles in law journals and books, and a book, *The New Handshake: Online Dispute Resolution and the Future of Consumer Protection*, with Colin Rule.

Andrea Kupfer Schneider is a Professor of Law and has taught dispute resolution, negotiation, ethics, and international conflict resolution for over twenty years. She is the inaugural director of the Institute for Women's Leadership at Marquette University and also the Director of the law school's nationally ranked dispute resolution program. She frequently publishes law review articles and book chapters on negotiation, gender, and international conflict and has co-authored several leading legal textbooks on ADR, negotiation, mediation and plea bargaining. Schneider is a founding editor of *Indisputably*, the blog for ADR law faculty and started the Dispute Resolution Works-in-Progress Annual Conference in 2007. She was named 2009 Woman of the Year by the *Wisconsin Law Journal* and, in 2016, gave her first TEDx talk entitled *Women Don't Negotiate and Other Similar Nonsense*. She was named the 2017 recipient of the ABA Section of Dispute Resolution Award for Outstanding Scholarly Work.

Donna Shestowsky is Professor of Law and Director of the Lawyering Skills Education Program at the University of California, Davis, and School of Law. She was awarded the 2016 Mangano Dispute Resolution Advancement Award and the Best Article of 2018 in the field of dispute resolution from the AALS Section on Alternative Dispute Resolution. She was the 2007 recipient of the Distinguished Teaching Award at the UC Davis School of Law. Dr. Shestowsky's commentary has appeared in national sources such as *CNN*, *NPR*, and the *New York Times*. Her research has been published in top journals in both psychology and law, including the *Stanford Law Review*, *Law and Human Behavior*, and the *Journal of Personality and Social Psychology*. Dr. Shestowsky was awarded a J.D. and Ph.D. in Psychology from Stanford University. From 2003 to 2004, she was a Visiting Assistant Professor at Northwestern University School of Law and the Kellogg School of Management.

Jean R. Sternlight is the Michael and Sonja Saltman Professor of Law and Founding Director of the Saltman Center for Conflict Resolution at the University of Nevada–Las Vegas Boyd School of Law. Frequently cited by courts and the media, Sternlight is co-author of *Psychology for Lawyers: Understanding the Human Factors in Negotiation, Litigation, and Decision* (ABA 2012), *Dispute Resolution: Beyond the Adversarial Model* 2nd edition (Aspen 2011), *Mediation Theory and Practice* 2nd edition (Lexis 2006), and *Arbitration Law in America: A Critical Assessment* (Cambridge University Press 2006). She has published articles on many aspects of dispute resolution in numerous well-respected journals and was named Outstanding Scholar by the ABA Section on Dispute Resolution in 2015. Sternlight received her B.A. (high honors) from Swarthmore College, and her J.D. (cum laude) from Harvard Law School.

Joseph B. ("Josh") Stulberg is the Emeritus Michael E. Moritz Chair in ADR at the Ohio State University College of Law. A former Vice President of the American Arbitration Association, he has mediated complex public policy disputes involving environmental controversies, Native American land claims, and state budget negotiations; facilitated planning processes among nongovernmental organizations, government leaders, and citizen groups in Central Europe; and regularly conducts mediation training programs domestically and internationally. Stulberg served as Reporter for the Model Standards of Conduct for Mediators (2005). He has published fifteen books and manuals and more than sixty-five articles on conflict resolution topics. He is the recipient of the American Bar Association/Section of Dispute Resolution Award for Outstanding Scholarly Work and the Lifetime Achievement Award of the American College of Civil Trial Mediators.

Imre S. Szalai serves as a commercial arbitrator, and he has written extensively about the history and development of the Federal Arbitration Act. Szalai is the Judge John D. Wessel Distinguished Professor of Social Justice at Loyola University New Orleans College of Law and a Senior Fellow at the University of Missouri's Center for the Study of Dispute Resolution. He is a graduate of Yale University, and he received his law degree from Columbia University, where he was named a Harlan Fiske Stone Scholar.

Elizabeth C. Tippett is an Associate Professor at the University of Oregon School of Law, and the Faculty Co-Director of its Master's Program in Conflict and Dispute

Resolution. Professor Tippett writes in the areas of employment law, business ethics, and dispute resolution. Professor Tippett is a co-author of the Fifth Edition of the West Academic textbook, *Employment Discrimination & Employment Law: The Field as Practiced*. Prior to joining the faculty, Professor Tippett represented technology companies in employment-related disputes. She also spent several years working at the Harvard Negotiation Project for the late Professor Roger Fisher, co author of *Getting to Yes*.

Karen Tokarz is the Charles Nagel Professor of Public Interest Law & Policy and Director of the Negotiation & Dispute Resolution Program at Washington University School of Law. An internationally recognized expert in dispute resolution, she has mediated over six hundred cases, primarily in the areas of civil rights, employment, and education. She has been named to Best Lawyers in America in Mediation every year since 2010 and is a Distinguished Fellow in the International Academy of Mediators. She has served as a Visiting Scholar at Harvard Law School, based in the Program on Negotiation, and as a Fulbright Senior Specialist at the University of Kwa Zulu-Natal in South Africa, consulted on international dispute resolution. Founder of the Washington University Global Public Interest Law Fellowship Program, she has coordinated placements for over two hundred law interns with conflict resolution offices, human rights organizations, and tribunals in Africa and around the world.

Ellen Waldman has been active in the fields of mediation and medical ethics for over two decades. Former Chair of the International Mediation Institute's ethics committee, and task-force member for the California judicial council's working group on training requirements for court-connected mediators, Waldman has been deeply involved in policy questions relating to the qualification and ethics training of mediators. A mediator for both community centers and superior courts in California and consultant for profit and nonprofit healthcare institutions, Waldman founded and directs the Thomas Jefferson School of Law Mediation Program, where she is also a full-time faculty member. She has published more than twenty-five articles on numerous dispute resolution topics and crafted the first book-length treatment of ethical dilemmas in mediation, entitled *Mediation Ethics: Cases and Commentaries*. She is currently a visiting professor and directing the mediation clinic at the Cardozo School of Law.

Stephen J. Ware is the Frank Edwards Tyler Distinguished Professor of Law at the University of Kansas, where he teaches alternative dispute resolution, bankruptcy, contracts, and Commercial Law: Secured Transactions. He is the author of three books—*Principles of Arbitration Law* (2017) (co-author), *Principles of Alternative Dispute Resolution* (3rd ed. 2016), *Arbitration Law in America: A Critical Assessment* (2006) (co-author)—and forty-two law review articles. His scholarship has been cited by the US Supreme Court and in at least thirty other federal and state cases. Professor Ware has testified on arbitration before both houses of Congress and in court as an expert witness. He is an arbitrator, elected member of the American Law Institute, and frequent speaker at professional and academic programs. He has been quoted in the

Wall Street Journal, the *New York Times*, the *Financial Times*, and many other publications, and has appeared on several television and radio stations.

W. Mark C. Weidemaier is the Ralph M. Stockton, Jr. Distinguished Professor of Law at the University of North Carolina at Chapel Hill.

Nancy A. Welsh is Professor of Law and Director of the Dispute Resolution Program of Texas A&M University School of Law. She was previously the William Trickett Faculty Scholar and Professor of Law at Penn State University, Dickinson School of Law. She has written more than sixty articles and chapters on dispute resolution and procedural law topics—including mediation, arbitration, judicial settlement conferences, and negotiation—and is co-author of a leading legal textbook, *Dispute Resolution and Lawyers* (6th ed.). She succeeded Harvard Law Professor Frank Sander as co-chair of the Editorial Board of the *Dispute Resolution Magazine*, conducted research as a Fulbright Scholar in the Netherlands, and served as Chair of both the ABA Section of Dispute Resolution and the AALS Alternative Dispute Resolution Section. Professor Welsh earned her B.A. magna cum laude from Allegheny College and her J.D. from Harvard Law School.

Gerald B. Wetlaufer is a Professor Emeritus at the University of Iowa College of Law. In addition to *The Limits of Integrative Bargaining*, 85 GEORGETOWN LAW JOURNAL 369–95 (1996) (here reprinted), he also authored a widely used article on *The Ethics of Lying in Negotiations*, 75 IOWA LAW REVIEW 1223–73 (1990), as well as *Rhetoric and Its Denial in Legal Discourse*, 76 VIRGINIA LAW REVIEW 1545–97 (1990), and *Systems of Belief in Modern American Law: A View from Century's End*, 49 AMERICAN UNIVERSITY LAW REVIEW 1–80 (1999). In addition to negotiations, he also taught a course on the differences between competing and incompatible legal theories and the possibilities of establishing dialogue between those theoretical positions. Prior to teaching, he graduated from Princeton and Yale Law School and practiced law for twelve years in Washington, D.C. He currently divides his time between Iowa City and London.

James J. White, the Robert A. Sullivan Professor of Law Emeritus, has written on many aspects of commercial law. His treatise, *Uniform Commercial Code* (with Summers and Hillman), is considered to be the most widely recognized treatise on the subject. In addition, he is the author of several casebooks on commercial, bankruptcy, and contracts law. Professor White has served as the reporter for the Revision of Article 5 of the Uniform Commercial Code and is a Commissioner on the Uniform Law Commission. He has also served on several American Law Institute committees dealing with the revision to the Uniform Commercial Code. He received the L. Hart Wright Award for Excellence in Teaching for 2001–02 and the Homer Kripke Achievement Award, given by the American College of Commercial Finance Lawyers. Professor White earned his J.D. from the University of Michigan Law School.

Adam S. Zimmerman is a Professor of Law and Gerald Rosen fellow at Loyola Law School, Los Angeles, where he specializes administrative law, complex civil procedure, and tort law. Professor Zimmerman's scholarship explores how overlapping accounts of public and private law—from mass torts and regulatory agencies to executive officers, corporations, and arbitration systems—provide justice for large groups of people. His recent articles have been published in the *Columbia Law Review*, *Duke Law Journal*, *New York University Law Review*, *University of Pennsylvania Law Review*, *Virginia Law Review*, and the *Yale Law Journal*. His recommendations about complex procedure have been formally adopted by federal agencies and appellate courts. He clerked for Judge Jack B. Weinstein in the Eastern District of New York and served as counsel to Special Master Kenneth R. Feinberg in the design and administration of the September 11th Victim Compensation Fund before entering private practice and the academy.